W. H. (William Henry) Goodyear

The Grammar of the Lotus, a new History of Classic Ornament

As a Development of Sun Worship

W. H. (William Henry) Goodyear

The Grammar of the Lotus, a new History of Classic Ornament
As a Development of Sun Worship

ISBN/EAN: 9783744746663

Printed in Europe, USA, Canada, Australia, Japan

Cover: Foto ©ninafisch / pixelio.de

More available books at **www.hansebooks.com**

THE GRAMMAR OF
THE LOTUS

A NEW HISTORY OF CLASSIC ORNAMENT

AS A

DEVELOPMENT OF SUN WORSHIP

With Observations on the "Bronze Culture" of Prehistoric Europe, as derived from Egypt; based on the Study of Patterns

BY

WM. H. GOODYEAR M.A. (YALE 1867)

Curator of the Department of Fine Arts in the Brooklyn Institute of Arts and Sciences;

MEMBER OF THE ARCHÆOLOGICAL INSTITUTE OF AMERICA; LECTURER ON THE HISTORY OF ART IN THE COOPER INSTITUTE, NEW YORK, BROOKLYN INSTITUTE, ETC., ETC.; FORMERLY CURATOR OF THE DEPARTMENT OF PAINTING IN THE METROPOLITAN MUSEUM OF ART, NEW YORK; AUTHOR OF "A HISTORY OF ART," "ANCIENT AND MODERN HISTORY," ETC., ETC.

WITH NUMEROUS ILLUSTRATIONS

LONDON
SAMPSON LOW, MARSTON & COMPANY
Limited
St. Dunstan's House
FETTER LANE, FLEET STREET, E.C.
1891
[*All rights reserved*]

To J. H., Esq.

"*I bring thee the flower which was in the Beginning, the glorious lily of the great Water.*"—TEXT FROM DENDERAH.

PREFACE.

I HAVE only been able to achieve the publication of this Work by an unspeakable kindness and generosity on the part of several people; among these must be mentioned—first, the gentleman whose initials follow my title-page.

To Miss Amelia B. Edwards I owe the first European recognition of my observation made in 1873 (through Cypriote vases), and published in 1888, that the Ionic Capital is derived from an actual natural appearance in the flower of the Egyptian water-lily. I owe her more than this—how much I will not say.

The first man of science who ever saw the original cartoons of the Plates which carry the argument of my Work, is the man of science who offered, of his own motion, to read and revise my proofs. There are some students who have written books, and some students who have not written books, who will understand what this gentleman has done for me after they have glanced through the volume; although he does not stand committed in any way to my views by this action. There must be something in the genial and kindly nature of this man of science which makes him a victim of "the Preface." I have observed that an enormous number of scientific works contain acknowledgments to Professor Reginald Stuart Poole. He shall not escape my Preface; there are none which owe him more. I have had from him the assistance of an Egyptologist and hieroglyphic scholar, of an Orientalist, and of a historian trained by the study of coins—the only study which suggests a knowledge of all art and of all history.

Finally, I owe to my American friends the gratitude which goes out to every warm heart and every helping hand. Among these are my own brother and a lady who shall be nameless.

I am under most peculiar obligations to Mr. John W. McKecknie (B.A. of Princeton), who prepared the designs for my Plates.

If my readers will pardon a suggestion made in their interest, I will say that the matter of every chapter presupposes a preliminary acquaintance with the Plates placed at its conclusion.

TABLE OF CONTENTS.

PART I.—EVOLUTIONS OF THE LOTUS MOTIVE.

	PAGE
The Lotus and Egyptian Gods	3—19
Plates i., ii.	21, 23
Lotus Forms mistaken for Nelumbiums	25—39
Plate iii.	41
Lotus Forms mistaken for Papyrus ...	43—61
Plates iv., v.	63, 65
Lotus Capitals of Egyptian Architecture	67—68
Plate vi.	69
Egyptian Lotus Ionic Forms	71—77
Plate vii.	79
The Problem of Concentric Rings ...	81—85
Plate viii.	87
Egyptian Introrse Scrolls	89
Plate ix.	91
Egyptian Meanders and Spiral Scrolls ... ...:	93—95
Plate x.	97
The Rosette	99—105
Plate xi.	107
The Egyptian Lotus Palmette	109—111
Plate xii.	113

	PAGE
Greek Ionic and Anthemion Forms ...	115—119
Plate xiii.	121
Greek Anthemions, Rope Patterns, and " Herzblatts "	123—131
Plate xiv.	133
Lotus Ionic Capitals and Details, showing the Sepal Volutes, with and without the Central Spike	135—137
Plate xv.	139
The Lotus Spiral on Cypriote, Rhodian, and Melian Vases	141—142
Plates xvi., xvii., xviii., xix.	145—147
The Rosette (continued from Plate xi.) ...	149—151
Plate xx.	153
The Egg-and-Dart Moulding	155—157
Plate xxi.	159
The so-called Ivy Leaf	161—163
Plate xxii.	165

PART II.—ASSOCIATIONS OF THE LOTUS MOTIVE.

	PAGE
Solar Symbolism in Ionic Forms ...	169—171
Plate xxiii.	173
The Lotus and the Sacred Tree ...	175—181
Plates xxiv., xxv.	183, 185
The Bull and the Lotus	187—191
Plate xxvi.	193
The Cow and the Lotus	195—196
Plate xxvii.	197
The Ram and the Lotus...	199—201
Plate xxviii.	203
The Lion and the Lotus	205—207
Plates xxix., xxx.	209, 211
The Sphinx and the Lotus	213—219
Plates xxxi., xxxii., xxxiii., xxxiv. ...	221—227

	PAGE
The Deer, Gazelle, Oryx, Ibex, Wild Goat, and Lotus	229—243
Plates xxxv., xxxvi., xxxvii., xxxviii., xxxix.	245—253
The Lion, Bull, and Lotus	255—257
Plate xl.	259
The Chimæra and the Lotus ...	255—257
Plate xl.	259
The Phenician Palmette	261
Plate xli.	263
The Fish and the Lotus	265—266
Plate xlii.	267
The Bird and the Lotus	269—281
Plates xliii., xliv., xlv., xlvi. ...	283—289

PART III.—PREHISTORIC DIFFUSION OF THE LOTUS MOTIVE.

	PAGE		PAGE
Geometric Lotuses of Cyprus	... 293—301	The Swastika	... 347—356
Plates xlvii., xlviii., xlix., l. ...	... 303—309	Plate lx.	... 359
Lotus Motives of the "Mycenæ Culture"	... 311—317	The Horse and the Lotus ...	... 361—363
Plates li., lii., liii., liv., lv.	... 319—327	Plate lxi.	365
The Greek Geometric Style and Prehistoric		The Lotus Patterns of Ancient America	... 367—374
		Plates lxii., lxiii.	... 377, 379
European Ornament	... 329—337	Modern Kabyle and Ancient Cypriote Pottery...	381—383
Plates lvi., lvii., lviii., lix.	... 339—345	Plate lxiv.	385

PART IV.—MISCELLANIES.

	PAGE		PAGE
The Ankh and the Lotus	... 389, 391	The Phœnician "Sacred Triangle"	... 395, 396
Plate lxv. ...	393	Plates lxvi., lxvii.	... 399, 401

LIST OF TEXT ILLUSTRATIONS.

	PAGE
1. Detail from the Myth of Osiris, as represented at Philœ	19
2. Egyptian Blue Lotus. From Nature	26
3. Egyptian Blue Lotus. From Nature. Showing three sepal spikes	27
4. Egyptian Blue Lotus. From Nature. Showing sepals curled over	27
5. Ovary Stigma, White Lotus	28
6. Ovary Stigma, Blue Lotus	28
7. Ovary Bulb of the Lotus, gone to seed	28
8. Dried Ovary Stigma of the Lotus, after seeding. From Nature	29
9. Typical Three-spiked Lotus, from the Monuments, with a palmate attachment on the central spike	29
9A. Typical Three-spiked Lotus, from the Monuments	29
10. *Nelumbium Speciosum* (" Rose Lotus "), showing Flower, Seed-pod, Bud, and Leaf	30
11. Unknown Plant, supposed to be a *Nelumbium Speciosum* by the original publication	39
12. Conventional Outline Lotus	43
12A. Lotus with Conventional Outline at the Top	43
13. Papyrus. From Nature	44
14, 15. Supposed Papyrus. Beni Hasan	48
16. God Horus on the Lotus Column	48
17. Wooden Toilet Tray. Lotus supporting a Leaf	50
18. Lotus supporting a Leaf	50
19. Detail from the Temple-portico, Denderah. Isis-Hathor bearing Lotus Stems with attached Buds. Sketch from Photograph	51
20. Campaniform Lotus Capital. (Karnak)	51
21. Lotus-sceptre, held by Isis-Hathor, Denderah. From Author's sketch	52
22. From Turin Papyrus No. 10. So-called papyrus form specified as lotus by the leaf. From Author's sketch	52
23. From Turin Papyrus No. 10. Bell Capital, specified as a lotus by Fig. 22. From Author's sketch	53
24. From Turin Papyrus No. 10. Colonnette Amulet (so-called papyrus), specified as a lotus by Fig. 22, same Papyrus. From Author's sketch	53
25. From Turin Papyrus No. 10. Head of the Sacred Bark, so-called papyrus form, specified as a lotus by Fig. 22, same Papyrus. From Author's sketch	53
26. Hieroglyphic in Ra-hotep's Tomb, Maydoum. From Author's sketch. So-called papyrus, specified as lotus by Fig. 24	54
27. Hieroglyphic, Tombs of the Kings. From Author's sketch. So-called papyrus, specified as a lotus by Fig. 24	54
28. From Turin Papyrus No. 51. Lotus Capital, coloured green, with red top. From Author's sketch	54
29. From Turin Papyrus No. 7. Lotus Capital, coloured green, with red top and yellow petal sheath. From Author's sketch	55
30. Lotuses from Tombs of the Kings, Thebes, supporting leaves and with leaves attached to the stem. From Photograph for the Author	55
31. From Author's Sketch in Tomb No. 125, Abd-el-Kourneh	56
32. From Author's Sketch in Tomb No. 125, Abd-el-Kourneh	57
33. Asp with Crown for "the North," resting on a lotus as sign for "the North," Denderah. From Author's sketch	57
34. From Author's Sketch in Tomb of Ra-hotep at Maydoum. Growing plant, coloured green, outline black, detail red	58
35. Sebak holding the true Cyperus Papyrus, before an altar crowned by the Lotus. From Author's sketch of a picture in the Turin Papyrus No. 10.	60
36. Photograph from an Altar of Offerings at Dehr-el-Bahri, with a conventional papyrus plume laid on the altar, and another erect beside it	60
37. Picture in LEPSIUS, Denkmäler (Ab. II. 12), supposed by Wilkinson to represent making a boat of papyrus	66
38. Demonstration for the hieroglyph called Papyrus as being a Lotus, by association with the leaf	66
39. So-called Papyrus supporting a Lotus Bud inverted	66

LIST OF TEXT ILLUSTRATIONS.

	PAGE
39A. Lotuses of the IVth Dynasty	66
39B. Conventional Outlines of the XVIIIth Dynasty .	66
41. Greek Ionic Capital...	71
42. Cypriote Ionic Capital	71
43. Cypriote Tombstone (Golgoi)	71
44. Cypriote Ionic Capital	71
45. Egyptian Ionic Lotus supporting an Inverted Bud	73
46. Cypriote Vase, N.Y. Museum	74
47. Cypriote Pottery Lotus	74
48. Cypriote Pottery Lotus	74
49. Cypriote Pottery Lotus with pendant Sepals ...	76
50. Capitals in Relief on Pillar at Karnak	78
51. Formation of the Spiral Scroll from Lotus with one Volute	82
52. Lotuses and Spiral Scroll. Scarab in Leyden ...	83
53. Rudimentary Lotuses with Spiral Scrolls. Scarab in Leyden	83
54. Ankhs with Solar Hieroglyphics. Scarab... ...	83
55. Evolution of the Spiral Scroll	94
56. Orchomenus Lotus Spirals with Rosettes (Schliemann). "Mycenæ" Culture	95
57. Gold Ceremonial Vase with stems supporting Rosettes in symbolizing fashion	104
58. Egyptian Lotus Palmette	109
59. Egyptian Lotus Palmette	109
60. Assyrian Palmette with Lotus Bulb. From fresco, British Museum	110
61. Assyrian Palmette with Lotus Bud. From fresco, British Museum	110
62. Assyrian Palmette. Textile Ornament, on Stone Relief	111
63. Greek Necking Ornament on a Column found at Naukratis	115
64. Type of the Anthemion considered to be "lotus and papyrus" by Mr. John Pennethorne ...	119
65. Type of the "lotus and papyrus" considered to be the origin of the Anthemion by Mr. John Pennethorne	119
66. Greek Terra-cotta Anthemion	123
67. Anthemion of the Parthenon	124
68. Anthemion from an Athenian Tombstone... ...	124
69. Anthemion from an Athenian Tombstone... ...	124
70. Late Anthemion, Macedonia	124
71. Rhodian Vase	125
72. Egypto-Phenician Detail on Bronze. From the Regulini-Galassi Tomb	125
73. Egypto-Phenician Ivory Detail from Nineveh ...	126
74. Greek Etruscan Detail. Bronze *Repoussé* ...	126
75. Greek Pottery Anthemion	126
76. Greek Architectural Detail in colour	126
77. Greek Pottery Details	126

	PAGE
78. Saracenic Algerian Detail	127
79. Evolution of the Guilloche	127
80. Greek Anthemion, Macedonia	128
81. Assyrian Lotus Detail	128
82. Assyrian Lotus Detail	128
83. Greek Pottery Detail	128
84. Sindh Pottery Detail	128
85. Sindh Tile Detail	128
86. Greek Pottery Detail	128
87. Renaissance Carving	128
88. Lotus Buds and Anthemions, Asia Minor. From Perrot	129
89. Greek Anthemion, Sicily	130
90. Greco-Scythian Gold Helmet from Kertch. St. Petersburg...	131
91. Assyrian Ionic. Relief, Khorsabad	137
92. Syrian Ionic Capital	137
94. Cypriote Lotus	151
95. Ionic Capital with Rosette	151
96. Lotus Border with Bunches of Grapes	155
97. Cypriote Lotus	156
98. Erechtheium "Egg and Dart" Moulding	156
99. Doric Capital (original surface design in colour) ...	157
100. Bronze Detail, Olympia	157
101. Assyrian Base	157
102. Assyrian Capital	157
103. Detail from a Stone Relief. Museum of Bologna. Lotus with so-called ivy leaves. From Author's sketch	161
104. Stone Relief Detail. Museum of Bologna. So-called "ivy leaf" with spiral. From Author's sketch	163
105. Lotus Details, from Nature	163
106. Relief Capitals at Karnak	169
107. Capital in wood, or wood and metal	169
108. Egyptian Mirror Handle	169
109. Capital in wood, or wood and metal	169
110. Ionic Lotus supporting Sun and Moon. From an Assyrian Cylinder...	170
111. Ionic Lotus associated with symbols of the Sun and Moon. Cypriote Capital	170
112. Ionic Lotus associated with the symbols of Sun and Moon. Cypriote Tombstone	170
113. Lotus supporting the Head of Hathor. Cypriote Tombstone	170
114. Ionic Lotus supporting the Sun. Detail from the Sippara Tablet	171
115. Ionic Lotuses supporting the winged solar disk. From Hittite Relief	171
116. The Sun, the Worshipper, and the Lotus Flower. Assyrian Seal	171

LIST OF TEXT ILLUSTRATIONS.

	PAGE
117. The Moon-god, the Worshipper, and the Lotus Flower with Buds. Assyrian Seal	171
118. Ionic Capital of the Erechtheium	171
119. Stone Cone, a common terminal ornament of Cypriote Tombstones	177
120. Cypriote Tomb Stelè, showing an abbreviated Cone	177
121. Assyrian "Sacred Tree"	180
122. Horus, with Lotuses	180
123. Lotus Bulb Tile Ornament	181
124. Lotus Bulb Tile Ornament	181
125. Lotus Bulb with Buds and Flowers. Detail from a statue of the Nile-god in the British Museum...	181
126. Lotus Bulbs with Anthemion. From Author's sketch	181
127. Hathor with Cow-ears and Lotuses	195
128. Detail of a Tomb-relief in the Bologna Museum. Demonstration for the so-called "ivy leaf" as a Lotus leaf. From Author's sketch	206
129. "The Sphinx and the Lotus." Demonstration for the so-called "ivy leaf" as a Lotus leaf. From a Tomb-relief in Bologna. From Author's sketch	214
130. Greek Vase in the Louvre	218
131. Detail on Bronze. From the Regulini-Galassi Tomb	218
132. The Sphinx and the Lotus. Persepolis. ...	219
133. Deity with Ceremonial Branch and Ibex, facing a Sacred Tree of Lotus Buds	232
134. The Gazelle and the Lotus. From a panel in the Temple-portico at Denderah. Photographed for the Author	236
135. The Ibex and the Lotus. From an Egyptian fresco fragment in Turin. From Author's sketch	236
136. "Le Dieu Cornu." Detail from a Gallo-Roman Tombstone	238
137. The Ibex and the Lotus. Detail of a Phenician bronze *patera* from Nineveh	240
138. The Tam with Antelope Head. Detail of a Stone Tablet in the British Museum. From Author's sketch	242
139. Tam in Bruce's Tomb at Thebes. (Gazelle Head.) From Author's sketch	242
139A. Deity bearing the Tam	243
140. The Gazelle, the Goose, and the Lotus. From a panel in the Temple-portico at Denderah. Sketch from a photograph made for the Author ...	250
141. Lion devouring Deer. Detail, Greek Vase ...	256
142. Chimæra with Gazelle horn. Engraved gem. Owens College, Manchester	257
143. Gryphons (with "Phenician Palmette"). Detail, Curium *patera*	261

	PAGE
144. Seal, Naukratis. (Fish and Lotus.)	265
145. The Goose and the Lotus. Detail, Rhodian Vase	271
146. The Bird and the Spiral. Dahomey	274
147. Detail of Birds and Winged Lotus Tree. Portal of San Giovanni Evangelista, Ravenna	275
148. Isis-Hathor, the Cow, the Goose, and the Gazelle. Detail of a panel in the Temple-portico at Denderah. Photographed for the Author.	277
149. The Goose (Swan) and the Lotus. Detail of a panel in the Temple-portico at Denderah. Photographed for the Author	278
150. Lotus Buds and Ionic forms of Swans' Heads, supporting demi-rosettes	280
151. Cypriote Vase, Lawrence-Cesnola Collection. Showing an inverted Lotus triangle with "bosses," supported by a panel band with "bosses" ...	297
152. Cypriote Vase. Lawrence-Cesnola Collection. Showing an inverted Lotus triangle with "bosses"	298
153. Detail of a Cypriote Vase, New York. Panel band with bosses and pendant geometric buds ...	298
154. Vase from Cyprus. "Mycenæ" or Archipelago style (New York). Showing an outline ornament derived from the elongated Cypriote Boss ...	299
155. Cypriote Pottery Motive of Elongated Bosses. Vase in New York	299
156. Evolution of the Cypriote "Boss" in vases of the Archipelago and "Mycenæ" style	300
157. Typical Necking Ornament of Cypriote Amphoras	300
158. Cypriote Vase, New York. Showing the typical Neck-border of Cypriote Amphoras	300
159. Diagram showing the origin of the Necking Ornament	301
160. Rhodian Vase. Showing Lotuses with Pendant Sepals	313
161. Detail of Fig. 160	314
162. Cypriote Lotuses, Pendant Sepals. New York ...	314
163. Byzantine or Saracenic Motive. Algeria	316
164. Mycenæ Gold Amulet. Cats (?) (Goddess Bast) on the Lotus	317
165. "Mycenæ" Leaf Motive in wood-carving. Lake Dwellers of Scotland. From Robert Munro ...	317
166. Gold Ornament of a Series from a Tomb at Spata, in Athens. From Author's sketch	324
167. Chevron Ornament, Lotuses inverted. Detail of a Mummy-case in the Turin Museum. From Author's sketch	334
167A. Chevron Ornament. Lotuses inverted. Detail of a Mummy-case in the Gizeh Museum. From Author's sketch	334
168. Swedish Bronze Axe, with Spiral Scrolls	337
169. Modern Egyptian Water Jar. From Author's sketch	346

LIST OF TEXT ILLUSTRATIONS.

	PAGE
170. Meander Detail with Solar Geese. Greek "Geometric" Vase in the Louvre. From Author's sketch	353
171. Meander Detail with Solar Geese. Greek "Geometric" Vase in the Cabinet des Médailles. From Author's sketch	353
172. Meander Detail with Solar Geese. Greek "Geometric" Vase in the British Museum. From Author's sketch	353
173. Swastika with Solar Geese. Greek "Geometric" Vase in the British Museum. From Author's sketch	353
174. Meander with Swastika. Detail of a Vase in the Polytechnic, Athens. From Author's sketch	354
175. Swastika Diagrams	355
176. Swastika Diagrams	355
177. Swastika Diagrams	355
178. Coptic Lotus Crosses. Relief at Medinet Habou. Specially photographed for the Author	356
179. Cross of Lotuses. Turin Scarab. From Author's sketch	356
180. Birds with a Horse's Mane. (Hallstatt bronze *repoussé*.)	362
181. Horses and Birds with a Horse's Mane. (Hallstatt bronze *repoussé*.)	363
182. The Bird and the Lotus. From a Zuni Vase in the National Museum at Washington. From Author's sketch	367
183. The Bird and the Lotus triangle (?). From a Zuni Vase	367
184. The Deer (Elk) and the Lotus. From a Zuni Vase in the National Museum at Washington. From Author's sketch	368
185. Sun-Disk surrounded by Lotuses and Lotus Buds. Detail of a Pompeiian fresco. From Author's sketch	369
186. Carian Inscription. From Grave Creek, West Virginia. Discovered in 1838. Announced as Carian by the Author, 1890.	370
187. Mexican Terra-cotta Sphinx. New York Museum	371
188. Dyak Lotus Spiral, Borneo. Carving on Wooden Scabbard, British Museum	372
189. Helmeted Head. Ancient Mexican Relief.	374
190, 191, 192, 193. Lotus Leaves as Hieroglyphics	389
194. Superimposed Lotuses. From a Stelè in Florence. (To explain the origin of the Tat.)	390
195. Blue Enamel Tat in the Louvre.	390
196. Nefer-Toum with Ankh. From a Royal Tomb, Thebes	391
197. Caduceus on an Italian Weight. To compare with Plate LXVII., for the origin of Mercury's staff	396
198. Bœotian Vase. Doubled Lotus	396
199. Greek Pottery Detail, Doubled Lotus	396
200. Gem. Winged Sun-Disk with attached Lotuses	397
201. Supposed Thunderbolt	397
202. Supposed Thunderbolt	397

PART I.

EVOLUTIONS OF THE LOTUS MOTIVE.

THE LOTUS AND EGYPTIAN GODS.

SOLAR, CREATIVE, AND MORTUARY SIGNIFICANCE.

(PLATES I., II., PAGES 21, 23.)

CURRENT popular references to the Egyptian lotus conceive it as a sort of national flower, comparable to the shamrock of Ireland or the thistle of Scotland. It is constantly mentioned in connection with the papyrus plant, which latter divides with it the honours, in popular estimation, of being a national Egyptian decorative symbol. This popular view of the kinship of lotus and papyrus is propagated and supported by a rendering of hieroglyphic symbols, which considers the hieroglyph for "the North" as a papyrus and the hieroglyph for "the South" as a lotus.[1] Hence, since a geographical division is supposed to be indicated by either plant, in certain hieroglyphic renderings, a tacit presumption of the use of both or either as national decorative emblems. In histories of art, and of decoration, the papyrus is invariably mentioned beside the lotus, and the distinctive forms of either plant are pointed out, with occasional hesitation for special cases.[2] Since the publication of the magnificent "Grammar of Ornament" by Owen Jones, in 1856, which has become a veritable bible of reference, at least to English and American decorators, the decorative artist, the cultivated amateur in æsthetic matters, and the professional architect, have all accepted his papyrus illustrations as authentic

---

[1] MASPERO, *Histoire Ancienne des Peuples de l'Orient*, p. 8. "Le papyrus se plaisait dans les eaux paresseux du Delta, le lotus au contraire fut choisie pour symbole de la Thébaide," a statement which comes very near to implying a geographical symbolism for the lotus.

[2] The hesitation habitually shows itself in a mention of both plants for an individual case, leaving the reader to make his own choice, as in the text of PRISSE D'AVENNES, where the expression "bouquet de lotus ou de papyrus" is very common. For instance, text, p. 387.

references for Egyptian Art. Wherever the influence of South Kensington has penetrated, it has carried with it the "Grammar of Ornament," and its views regarding the papyrus as a factor in Egyptian decoration, which are, moreover, those of Egyptologists in general. I shall be able to show, however, that the papyrus does not occur in Egyptian ornament at all.

The lotus was a fetich of immemorial antiquity, and has been worshipped in many countries reaching from Japan to the Straits of Gibraltar. None of the various water-lilies which are indicated by the word are confined to Egypt, and I am not acquainted with any facts which would show that the Egyptians regarded it as a national symbol, but it is quite clear that as long as the papyrus ranks with it as a factor in Egyptian ornament, so long it will be natural to suppose that a certain patriotic sentimentalism (rather than a deep rooted religious feeling) prompted the choice of the dominant Egyptian decorative patterns, in which the lotus, according to present views, would come in for only half share.

When we move back from popular or casual references to more exact accounts and statements, it appears that the lotus is a symbol of "life," of "immortality," of "renaissance" or of "resurrection."[3] Its mortuary significance and funereal uses are mentioned.[4] As a symbol of fecundity it is well known.[5] In this class of references there is a curious absence of parallel notices of the papyrus, which sinks out of sight, without apparent cause. It is not by any means an uncommon thing to find the lotus mentioned as a symbol of the sun,[6] but it is quite as common to find this reference wanting.

In Hindu mythology we find an exuberance of lotus symbolism, which may be reduced to solar relations by some attention to scattered facts, but these relations are not to be gathered from any systematic statements of authorities. The flower is an attribute of the distinctive Hindu Sun-god Surya, as noted by Sir William Jones in verses quoted by Moor's "Hindu Pantheon" (Ed. Wilson, p. 197): "Lord of the lotus, father, friend, and king."

3. PRISSE D'AVENNES, text. PIERRET, *Panthéon Égyptien*, p. 62. PIERRET, *Dictionnaire d'Archéologie Égyptienne*, under "Lotus." EBERS, *Egypt Descriptive, &c.*, I. p. 66.
4. OSBURN mentions the fact that bouquets of the lotus were presented to the guests at Egyptian funerals; *Monumental History of Egypt*, vol. i., p. 63.
5. WESTROPP, *Ancient Symbol Worship*, p. 77. INMAN, *Ancient Pagan and Modern Christian Symbolism*; many references. KING, *Gnostics and their remains*, p. 174, on the lotus of Isis and the Lily of the Virgin. As an emblem of fecundity the lotus is well known to the Brahmans, Buddhists, and modern Theosophists.
6. In RAWLINSON's *Herodotus*, vol. ii., p. 149, where the authority of PROCLUS is quoted. COLONNA-CECCALDI, *Monuments antiques de Chypre*, p. 141, mentions this solar significance. So does EBERS, *Egypt Descriptive*, I. p. 66.

THE LOTUS AND EGYPTIAN GODS.

Of Brahma it is said: "Modern Brahmans consider the sun an emblem or image of their great deities jointly and individually; i.e. of Brahma, the Supreme One, who alone exists really and absolutely," and it is added that to the Brahmans, "the sun is the most glorious and active emblem of God" (Moor, p. 9). "Vishnu is a personification of the sun, or conversely, the sun is a personification of him" (Moor, p. 13). To which we will add the quotation that "Brahma having, by a generally received system, founded on the doctrines of the Vaishnavas, sprung on a lotus from the navel of Vishnu, to bid all worlds exist, has hence, and perhaps in all other points, relation to the lotus, but it is a more immediate attribute of Vishnu" (Moor, p. 8). Such a collation of facts relating to Brahma, Vishnu, the sun, and the lotus, must, however, be drawn from different pages of the given authority. The birth of Brahma from the lotus, frequently represented in Hindu art, has been also commemorated by the poems of Sir William Jones.

> "Above the warring waves it danced elate,
> Till from its bursting shell with lovely state,
> A form cerulean fluttered o'er the deep,
> Brightest of Beings, greatest of the Great:
> Who, not as mortals steep
> Their eyes in dewy sleep;
> But, heavenly pensive, on the lotus lay,
> That blossomed at his touch, and shed a golden ray.
> Hail, primal blossom ! hail, empyreal gem
> Kemel, or Pedma, or whate'er high name delight thee;
> Say, what four-formed God-head came,
> With graceful stole and beaming diadem,
> Forth from thy verdant stem !"

We may, however, read page after page, containing manifold references to the lotus, in works on Hindu art and mythology, without finding its solar relations stated either explicitly or by implication. A modern Japanese festival which associates the lotus with the sun will be mentioned later.

In reality, the solar significance of the lotus, which is also explicitly mentioned by ancient classical authority, is the elementary and most important one; not as overpowering or belittling the other relations to the tomb, the Resurrection, and the idea of "life" or creative power, but as explaining them and giving them full value. Hence, as there is no reference or monograph extant which unites and unifies the meanings of the lotus, and which considers the solar significance foremost, as explaining all the others, it will be well to establish this significance from Egyptian texts. For instance, a text at Denderah says: "The Sun, which was from the beginning, rises like a hawk from the midst of its lotus bud. When the doors of its leaves open in sapphire-coloured brilliancy, it has divided the night from the day."[7] Of the Sun-god, Horus, it is said: "He opens his eyes and illuminates the world. The Gods rise from his eyes and the men from his mouth, and all things are through him, when he rises, brilliant from the lotus."[8] At Denderah a king makes offering of the lotus to the Sun-god, Horus, with the words: "I offer thee the flower which was in the beginning, the glorious lily of the great Water."[9] A confessional chapter of the "Book of the Dead" closes with the words: "I am a pure lotus, issue of the field of the Sun" (p. 19). For these hieroglyphic texts we find parallel illustrations on Plate I., Nos. 1, 2, 3, 4, 5, 6, 8, 11. No. 2 shows the familiar instance of the youthful or infant Horus (the dawning sun and the sun by day [10]) rising from the flower. No. 5 shows the hawk (a form of Horus [11] and of all solar Gods [12]) supported by the flower.[13] No. 8 shows a hawk-headed Ra (the Sun), worshipped by the offering of the flower.[14] No. 6 shows Amon (Sun-god of Thebes [15]) worshipped in the same way. No. 4 shows Osiris (the sun at night [16]), father of Horus, in one of his habitual associations with the flower. No. 11 shows Nefer-Toum, or the good Toum (the setting sun, but also worshipped at Heliopolis as the sun in all other

---

7. BRUGSCH, *Religion und Mythologie der alten Aegypter*, vol. i., p. 103.

8. Ibid; vol. i., p. 104.

9. Ibid; vol. i., p. 121.

10. The all-prevalent and most universal form of Horus in Egyptian art is the winged solar disk (Plate xliii. 6) which is distinctive for him (BRUGSCH, *Mythologie*), whereas the hawk is not thus limited. The dawning sun is conceived as a child; hence the child rising from the flower. EMMANUEL DE ROUGÉ, *Notice Sommaire des Monuments Égyptiens exposés dans les Galeries du Musée du Louvre*, p. 142.

11. In speaking of four forms of Horus—the human, the hawk, the hawk-headed man, and the human-headed hawk; MASPERO says that "He is Horus under all four forms, and is not more himself under one of them than under another." *Histoire Ancienne des Peuples de l'Orient*, p. 47.

12. For the hawk, as common to all Egyptian solar gods, see PIERRET, *Panthéon Égyptien*, and MARIETTE, who says, "All gods with hawk-heads personify the sun": text for Pl. viii., *Album du Musée de Boulaq*. According to BIRCH, "Hawks were sacred to the sun from their brilliant eyes." *Egyptian Antiquities in the British Museum*, p. 36.

13. The hawk was a bird of Apollo (the sun), and of Mithra, LAJARD, *Culte de Mithra*, pp. 531, 532. For Mithra as the sun, see *Encycl pædia Britannica*, ninth edition, under "Zoroaster." According to EUSEBIUS, Ormuzd, Persian God of Light, was represented with the head of a hawk, LAJARD, *Culte de Mithra*, pp. 278 and 416.

HOMER compares Apollo to a hawk, *Iliad*, xv., 236-238. In the *Odyssey* he is the messenger of Apollo, xv., 525, 526.

14. The hawk was sacred to Ra (the Sun), "as the symbol of light and spirit, because of the quickness of its motion and its ascent to higher regions of the air," quoted from PORPHYRY in RAWLINSON's *History of Egypt*, i. p. 344.

For the hawk as a form of Osiris, see EMMANUEL DE ROUGÉ, *Notice Sommaire des Monuments Égyptiens exposés dans les Galeries du Musée du Louvre*, p. 137.

15. For Amon as the sun, see MASPERO, *Histoire Ancienne*, p. 31. Amon is a well-known "double" of Osiris.

16. The sun was conceived as passing around under the earth during the night in its return to sunrise, hence Osiris as the nightly sun became the God of the Lower World, the God of the Mummy, and the God of Resurrection.

THE LOTUS AND EGYPTIAN GODS. 7

phases[17]), with his customary lotus head-dress. For the Sun-hawk on the lotus, see also plate v. 5, 6, 7 [p. 65]; plate xliii. 3, 9 [p. 283].

Direct associations of the solar disk and lotus are common on the monuments (see page 24); less common in publication (i. 1, 3 [p. 21]). Direct associations of the winged solar disk with the lotus are instanced by several published Phenician and Assyrian seals (xxiv. 1, 2, 3, 7 [p. 183]; xxxii. 6, 11, 12 [p. 223]). The winged solar disk on such monuments is known to be of Egyptian origin.[18] The lotus in above-quoted instances has not been specified in the publications[19] from which they are taken, and it has been overlooked for Assyrian cylinders in all other publications known to me. Representations of the lotus are common in Phenician art, on votive tablets to solar and lunar gods (xxiii. 11 [p. 173]; lxvi. 4, 6, 12 [p. 399]; lxvii. 2, 4, 6, 10 [p. 401]); in related Syrian and Assyrian seals and cylinders with sun disk and lunar crescent or lunar crescent singly (xxiii. 9 [p. 173]; xxiv. 5, 12, 13, 14 [p. 183]); and in Cypriote Greek remains with sun and moon (xxiii. 10 [p. 173]). These instances are illustrations, in foreign adoption, of an Egyptian solar symbolism which finds equally palpable, though not equally visible evidence in the citations which follow.

The goose is commonly quoted as representing Seb (Solar god and father of Osiris), but represents also Osiris himself and Horus.[20] Hence the associations of the goose and the lotus (ii. 10 [p. 23]; xliii. 2, 4, 5, 8, 11 [p. 283]). Among these illustrations are offerings of geese and lotuses to Horus and to Ra. The hawk represents Horus, Ra, and belongs also to all solar gods.[21] Hence the associations of the hawk and the lotus, v. 5, 6, 7 [p. 65], and xliii. 3, 9 [p. 283]; xliv. 2, 6 [p. 285].

17. Toum, otherwise especially the declining and setting sun, was the local deity of Heliopolis, and there represented the sun at all points of hourly, daily, and monthly course. BRUGSCH, *Mythologie*, i. p. 279. The lotus borne on the head is confined to Toum as a type, but it can be cited for the Sun-lion (enamel amulet in the British Museum, Case 74, Third Egyptian Room), and also for the Sun-hawk; MARIETTE, *Fouilles d'Abydos*, i. 39 c.

18. MENANT, *Recherches sur la Glyptique Orientale*, PERROT ET CHIPIEZ, *Assyrie*, p. 87.

19. The cylinders and seals specified are originally from LAJARD's *Culte de Mithra*, the most extensive publication of such monuments. The publication of this work took place before cuneiform inscriptions were deciphered. The text appeared in 1847, lacking the parts left unfinished by the author's death. His projected section on plants was unwritten. The word lotus occurs only once in LAJARD's *Culte de Mithra*, and without significant matter (p. 546; referring to pl. xviii. 7, of his work).

20. An instance of the current quotations for Seb and the goose, in RAWLINSON's *History of Egypt*, i. p. 375.

For the goose as bird of Osiris and Horus, and also of Isis, see O. KELLER, *Thiere des Classischen Alterthums in Culturhistorischer Beziehung*, p. 286. At p. 454, Note 6, of the same work, reference to a silver statuette of Harpocrates and the Goose from the *Archæologische Zeitung*, xxvi., 71. There is an Egyptian text tablet mentioning the " Good goose of Osiris " in the Abbott Egyptian collection of the New York Historical Society, according to verbal communication of Mr. Charles Edwin Wilbour.

21. See Notes above, 12, 13, 14. Additional illustrations for the Sun-hawk and the lotus are, *Description de l'Égypte*, A. i. 96, 3—A. iii. 60; MARIETTE, *Dendérah*, i. 38 a, c— iv. 21; MARIETTE, *Fouilles d'Abydos*, i. 39, b, &c.

THE LOTUS AND EGYPTIAN GODS.

The Bull-god Apis is an incarnation of Osiris [22]; and an offspring of the Sun-god Ptah of Memphis.[23] The bull is otherwise known as a Solar god.[24] Hence the illustrations which relate to the bull and the lotus continue to emphasize its solar significance (ii. 1 [p. 23]; lxv. 5 [p. 393]; Bull Apis and the lotus, from a votive tablet of the Serapeum in the Louvre, xxvi. 1 [p. 193]). The asp, which is sometimes quoted as an emblem of royalty, belongs to the king as identified with the Solar god. It represents the seething and hissing heat of the sun.[25] Hence the lotus associations represented by plates ii. 2 [p. 23]; v. 2, 3 [p. 65]. The lion is a well-known solar animal and solar hieroglyphic. An Egyptian invocation to the sun is quoted by Brugsch: "Thou art the Sun, a powerful lion."[26] The lion was worshipped at Heliopolis and Sethroe.[27] He represents the splendour and raging violence of the sun, according to Birch,[28] and the sun is entitled by Egyptian texts, "the master of double strength," by a hieroglyphic picture of two lions.[29] Hence the associations of the lion and the lotus (ii. 4 [p. 23]; xxix. 1, 2, 6 [p. 209][30]; Phenician seal, winged lions with the lotus, xxxii. 9 [p. 223]; Assyrian cylinders, winged lions with lotus, and winged solar disk, xxxii. 12 [p. 223]). As lately shown by M. Le Page Renouf, the lions seated back to back (as at xxix. 5 [p. 209]) support the sun rising out of the Solar Mount, and represent "Yesterday" and "To-morrow," i.e. "Osiris is the sun which set yesterday and has risen again as Ra."[31] The Sphinx is a form of Horus,[32] i.e. a human-headed Sun-lion. (The Pharaoh was deified under this form, and the head of the Sphinx is that of the

---

22. For the Apis Bull, as incarnation of Osiris, see PIERRET, *Panthéon Égyptien*, p. 1.

23. Ptah, father of Apis, MARIETTE, *Album du Musée de Boulaq*, text for pl. iv. Ptah identified with the sun, MASPERO, *Histoire Ancienne des Peuples de l'Orient*, p. 31. Ptah as a local form of Osiris, BRUGSCH, *Mythologie* i. p. 84.

24. For Apis, a solar god, not exclusively son of Ptah, see PIERRET, *Panthéon Égyptien*, p. 1.

25. Les Uræus sévissent et brulent comme la lumière dont la déesse léontocephale personifie l'ardeur et la force," PIERRET, *Panthéon*, p. 30. " Die Schlange = verzehrende Gluth der Sommerhitze," BRUGSCH, *Mythologie*, ii.

26. BRUGSCH, *Mythologie*, i. p. 183.

27. Reference as above.

28. *Egyptian Antiquities in the British Museum*, p. 38.

29. "Les Égyptiens disaient que le soleil éclaire le monde de ses deux yeux, et ils voyaient dans sa lumière la force qui entretient la vie, et maintient l'ordre dans l'univers. Cette force resultant de ses deux yeux est dite *double*. L'astre dieu est appelé, 'le maitre de la double force,' et ce mot 'force' est écrit au duel avec l'hiéroglyphe du lion." PIERRET, *Panthéon*, p. 24.

30. For reference to an amulet of lion with lotus on the head, see Note 17 (identified with Nefer-Toum by the label). For an additional example of the lion crowned with the lotus at Edfou, see *Description de l'Égypte*, A. I., 64 A.

31. *Proceedings, Society of Biblical Archæology*, Dec., 1888, p. 26. An original papyrus picture exhibited in the British Museum with this explanation on the label.

32. Horus as Sphinx, BRUGSCH, *Reiseberichte aus Egypten*. "Hence Horus is represented as the Sphinx, whose face turned eastward is the radiant sun, and whose body in form of a lion is emblematic of his divine strength." The great Sphinx of Gizeh as representing Horus, PIERRET, *Panthéon*, p. 42.

reigning Pharaoh as identified with Horus.[33]) Hence the associations of the Sphinx and the lotus (ii. 5 [p. 23]; xxxi. 1, 2, 3, 4, 5 [p. 221]), and Assyrian examples with the lotus and winged solar disk (xxxii. 11, 12 [p. 223]). The Gryphon (ii. 8 [p. 23]) is a form of Horus.[34] Hence the Gryphon on the lotus (xxxi. 7 [p. 221]; and Phenician seal, xxxii. 4 [p.223]). The serpent is referred to in the address to Horus at Denderah, quoted at p. 5, which continues, "Thou risest like the sacred serpent, as living spirit . . in thy glorious form in the bark of the Sun-rise, &c."[35] Compare ii. 6. The ram was identified with the sun at Thebes, Latopolis (Esneh), and on the island of Elephantine.[36] Hence the association of the ram-headed God Khnoum (a form of Amon and Osiris)[37] on plate ii. 7 [p. 23], with lotus buds.

The matter in hand is to point out that the symbolism of the lotus—which is referred most frequently by modern writers to its phallic and generative, or to its funereal and mortuary bearings—is based upon a well-proven but not generally recognized solar significance. There is no easier way to show this than to appeal to the admitted fact that the Egyptian idea of the resurrection, and of a future life, was connected with a worship of the creative and reproductive forces of nature, which were conceived and worshipped as solar in character and origin. It is the supposed passage of the sun at night through a lower world, during its return to the dawn of a following day, which makes Osiris (the sun at night) the God of the Lower World, and of the dead [38]; hence himself represented as a mummy. As the God of the Resurrection, his special and emphatic character, he represents the creative energy of the Sun-god. Hence the lotus as attribute of Osiris (Plate i. 4, and Fig. 1, p. 19), is at once a symbol of the sun, of the resurrection, and of creative force

33. The great Sphinx has the head of Shafra, according to BRUGSCH, *Mythologie*, i. ; according to other authorities it may antedate the First Dynasty (SAYCE, *Ancient Empires of the East*). For the Sphinx as representing the reigning monarch, see BIRCH, *Egyptian Antiquities in the British Museum*, p. 60, and PIERRET, *Panthéon*, p. 42.

34. For the Gryphon as form of Horus, see ROSELLINI, Text M.d.C., p. 151, with his translation of the Egyptian text at Philae, relating to pl. ii., 8, of this work. For the Gryphon or hawk-headed lion, as combination of solar lion and solar hawk, see also PIERRET, *Panthéon*, p. 42.

35. BRUGSCH, *Religion und Mythologie*, i., p. 152. " Schlange = die verzehrende Gluth der Sommerhitze," BRUGSCH, ii. The serpent is quoted as a form of Ra and of Horus by BRUGSCH, i., p. 160. The human-headed serpent has been identified with Osiris by texts, and the God Toum has been identified with the serpent by texts (verbal communication of the hieroglyphic expert, Mr. Charles Edwin Wilbour). The serpent is also a form of Set, personification of the Typhonic and baleful aspect of the sun; and of Khnoum (CHAMPOLLION, *Panthéon*, pl. iii. bis).

36. BRUGSCH, *Mythologie*, i., p. 104.

37. Khnoum as a form of Amon, see EMMANUEL DE ROUGÉ, *Notice Sommaire*, &c., p. 123. Khnoum as a form of Osiris, see BRUGSCH, *Mythologie*, i., p. 160.

38. MARIETTE, *Notice des Monuments à Boulaq*, pp. 105, &c.

and power. These significations are all conceded to it by quoted authorities, and this threefold significance is to be considered in all cases and in all connections, but it is the solar significance which explains the others, and for the same reasons which have led the authorities to emphasize the solar character of the Egyptian gods as explaining their other attributes.

Since the doctrine of a future life, and the belief in a spirit world were ever present to the Egyptian mind, we cannot too strongly insist on the funereal symbolism of the lotus, after the origin of this meaning has been once established. Hence, for instance, its association with the Genii of Amenti (i.e. of the Lower World); the guardians of the viscera of the mummy, the Genii of the Dead and children of Horus and of Osiris.[39] The detail ii. 3, is taken from a picture of the Last Judgment, but the isolated representation is also a common one on sepulchral tablets (v. 1, 4 [p. 65]). Plates ii. 12 [p. 23], and iv. 14 [p. 63], illustrate the constant association of the lotus and the mummy. Bouquets of the lotus were given to the guests at Egyptian funerals,[40] and its significance on sepulchral tablets was familiar to classical antiquity in the Greco-Roman time.[41] Its use in Christian art must also be significant of immortality or resurrection, as on the Coptic shrine at Philae, figured in Miss Edwards' "A Thousand Miles up the Nile," p. 221.

As little can we overlook the phallic significance of the lotus, which is directly related to the idea of the Resurrection, according to Egyptian conceptions of creative and reproductive power, as apparent in the character of Osiris, and in texts which refer the lotus to him.[42] Publications of the ithyphallic Khem (the sun which conceives itself [43]), generally or constantly show him with the lotus. Plate i. 10 [p. 21] shows this god with the lotus leaf; at iv. 13, 16 [p. 63], are other instances; and his symbolic plant constantly appears surmounting the door of a shrine, as in these illustrations.[44] In India the phallic significance of the lotus is prominent in the Linga-Yoni worship,[45] and, by way of the Buddhists, it has been made known to the Theosophists of our own day, who are well acquainted

39. Genii of Amenti, as children of Horus—British Museum designations; as children of Osiris—DE ROUGÉ, *Notice Sommaire*, &c., p. 139.
40. See Note 4.
41. *Annali*, 1843, "Ornamenti Funebri."
42. According to verbal advice of the hieroglyphic expert, Mr. Charles Edwin Wilbour, which is based on Egyptian texts, the lotus represents the reproductive element in Osiris.

43. "Le soleil renaissant de lui-même que personifie Khem ithyphallique." PIERRET, *Panthéon*, p. 26.
44. References for Ithyphallic Khem or Amon with the lotus.—*Description de l'Égypte*, A., i., 89, 8 (Esneh) and A, iii., 15, 4. ROSELLINI, II., xli. CHAMPOLLION, IV., cccxlviii. DENON, 127, 10. PRISSE D'AVENNES, *Monuments*, xxi., &c., &c.
45. For this worship see MOOR's *Hindu Pantheon*;

with this meaning of the flower.[46] But in India the lotus is also an attribute of all the Brahmanic gods (through them, subsequently, of Buddha), and all these gods are related to the sun (p. 5), of which the lotus is also in India a special emblem.[47]

According to the obvious connection in the different characters of Osiris, as sun, mummy, and creator, we may understand the other Solar gods of the Egyptian Pantheon, and consequently the threefold meaning of the lotus as found connected with their various forms. To quote the words of Professor Maspero: " The assimilation and occasional complete identity of the Supreme God with the sun being once admitted, the assimilation and complete identity of the secondary divine beings with Ra (the sun) were a matter of course. Amon, Osiris, Horus, Ptah, were regarded sometimes as the living soul of Ra, sometimes as Ra himself."[48] The assimilation of the various local triads with that of Osiris, Isis, and Horus, in so far as it simplifies

---

INMAN, *Ancient Pagan and Modern Christian Symbolism*, and BIRDWOOD's *Industrial Arts of India* (Tantric worship), &c.

46. Verbal advice from a distinguished member of the sect. "*Le Lotus*" is the title of a French Theosophist journal.

47. The lotus pedestal, best known through statues of Buddha, is common to all Hindu gods.
For this and other lotus associations of the Hindu gods see the plates of MOOR's *Hindu Pantheon*, of INMAN's *Symbol Worship*, and of BIRDWOOD's *Industrial Arts of India* (South Kensington Museum Art Handbooks).
For mention of Surya, distinctive Sun-god, and the lotus, see BIRDWOOD, p. 67. The "holiest verse of the Vedas" is an invocation to the sun (BIRDWOOD, p. 5). "In the Vedic and Puranic Mythology everything seems directly or indirectly to merge in or radiate from the sun (Surya)." (BIRDWOOD, p. 51.)
For the lotus as a Hindu emblem of female beauty see MOOR, p. 19. Hence the name of Lakshmi, Consort of Vishnu (or Narayana), is "the lotus "— Padma or Pedmi and Kamala are the Hindu words. Thus the verse of Sir William Jones in MOOR, p. 76:—

" Shipped in a flower that balmy sweets exhaled,
O'er dulcet waves of cream Pad-mala sailed,—
So name the goddess from her lotus blue,
Or Kamala, if more auspicious deemed,—
With many-petaled wings the blossom flew."

Of the god Krishna, in love with a damsel whose relatives disturbed the peace of his visit to her, and made speech impossible, it is said (MOOR, p. 297):—

" He, with salute of deference due,
A lotus to his forehead prest,
She raised her mirror to his view,
And turned it inward to her breast."

The plant is used in coining poetical adjectives, such as the following:—
" When this dark lotus-leaf complexioned Hari is not present, there is no joy in the maternal dwelling" (MOOR, p. 127). Of Mahadeva (Siva) it is said, "His lotus-like feet blossom with the flowers of wisdom (MOOR, p. 101).

" In the Hindu cosmogony the world is likened to a lotus-flower floating in the centre of a shallow, circular vessel, which has for its stalk an elephant, and for its pedestal a tortoise. The seven petals of the lotus-flower represent the seven divisions of the world as known to the ancient Hindus, and the tabular torus [*Nelumbium speciosum*] which rises from their centre represents Mount Meru, the Hindu Olympus." (BIRDWOOD, p. 94.)

When Buddha was born, a lotus bloomed where he first touched the ground; he stepped seven steps northward, and a lotus marked each footfall (MOOR, p. 154).

The Buddhist prayer is often quoted, "Oh, God! the jewel in the lotus," or, " Holy jewel in the lotus, be it so."

48. *Histoire Ancienne des Peuples de l'Orient*, p. 31.

THE LOTUS AND EGYPTIAN GODS.

the confusion of names in the Egyptian Pantheon, also simplifies the comprehension of the symbolism of the lotus. Thus Amon, Maut, and Khons, at Thebes, repeat the above triad under these local names, this being an example chosen among many.[49] The illustration for the altar and the lotus (ii. 11 [p. 23]) is therefore chosen to indicate the universal presence of the lotus on the altars of all Egyptian gods, as shown by the monuments. The following combinations are also significant. The beetle (gods Ptah and Kheper) and the lotus [50]; the ibex (god Set [51]) and the lotus (xxxv. 11 [p. 245]); the antelope (god Set [52]) and the lotus (xxxv. 5 [p. 245]); the oryx (god Set [53]) and the lotus (xxxv. 1 [p. 245]). The association of the horse with the lotus (see Prisse d'Avennes' *Vases en Or*) is undoubtedly foreign, but it is also a solar association.[54] The ibis (god Thoth) with the lotus, can be quoted for unpublished monuments. The hippopotamus (goddess Thoueris and Hathor [55]) with the lotus, is illustrated by a rare and large enamel figure of the animal in the Louvre, of the Eleventh Dynasty, from a tomb at Drah-Abou-Neggah. The piece is covered with lotuses. There is a similar piece of inferior preservation, as regards the symbol, in the British Museum (other examples at Florence and in the Gizeh Museum). The god Bes (a form of Set or Typhon) stands on the lotus in amulets of the Leyden Museum,[56] and is connected with the solar winged disk by a Mesopotamian cylinder and by a Phenician seal.[57] For the lotus crowning offerings to the solar disk, see iv. 7. For the lotus combined with the *Ankh*, "symbol of life," see lxv. 1. The equivalent meanings of the *Ankh* and the lotus are shown by the contrast of lxv. 2, 5 [p. 393] with lxv. 3, 4.

As to the association of the lotus with various birds and animals, to be abundantly illustrated in later pages, and apparent on the plates especially in

---

49. BRUGSCH, *Mythologie*, vol. i.
50. Seal from Cyprus. KING, in CESNOLA'S *Cyprus*, p. 369, mistakes the plant on the gem for papyrus.
51. For the ibex as "devoted to Typhon," see ibex amulet so catalogued in British Museum, No. 1698A, Case 77, Third Egyptian Room.
52. "Der goldene Horus erscheint als ein Sperber auf dem kopfe einer weissen Antelope (Symbol des Set) in der Stadt Hierakonpolis." BRUGSCH, *Mythologie*, vol. ii., p. 664.
53. Description of a Leyden bronze Horus,—"Il foule sous ses pieds un Oryx, animal Typhonien." LEEMANS, in *Monumens Égyptiens du Musée d'Antiquités des Pays-Bas à Leyde*.

54. A reference for the horse as sacred to the Sun-god in Syria is furnished by ROBERTSON SMITH, *Religion of the Semites*, p. 275; quoting II. Kings, xxiii., 11, for the horse which the king of Judah had consecrated to this deity.
55. For Hathor as Hippopotamus, see the exhibited papyrus of Ani in the British Museum, with Hippopotamus Goddess thus designated and associated with lotuses.
56. LEEMANS, as above quoted, I., xv., 1190A, 1191; described at p. 13. "Typhon debout sur une colonne ornée d'un chapiteau à fleur de lotus."
57. LAJARD, *Culte de Mithra*, xxxii., 1. PERROT ET CHIPIEZ, *Phénicie*, fig. 296. The associations of Bes with the sun are implied by his identity with Set and Baal (British Museum designations).

THE LOTUS AND EGYPTIAN GODS.

question here, it is matter of commonplace information that such animal forms, either complete or associated with the human body, belong to a pictorial and hieroglyphic method of indicating the names, qualities, or existence of the Egyptian gods, and do not, in so far, reflect discredit on the purity or philosophic consistency of the religion which they represent. Most Egyptologists ascribe to the Egyptian religion a sublime recognition of divine power and unity, however disguised by severance of attributes under various polytheistic forms.[58] It is probable that all highly developed natural religions have moved from the fetich to the animal totem, and from the totem to the sun and other astral bodies, at first with, and then without, a distinct totem association. It is easy to admit that the Egyptians worshipped animals before they worshipped the sun, and necessary to admit that the worship of animals survived in the populace down to the latest days of Egyptian history, but in so far as Egyptian symbolism is concerned it is well to remember that its religious philosophy was a highly refined and intellectual system, and that it found expressions in the pictorial allegories supplied by reptile, beast, and bird, without detriment to this philosophic quality. Thus we understand the cow[59] and the fish[60] of the goddess Isis or Hathor[61] (i. 7 [p. 21], Isis-Hathor with cow's ears and lotuses; i. 12 [p. 21], Isis-Hathor as cow, with lotuses and Horus as calf;[62] and i. 9 [p. 21], Isis as fish with the lotus). A bronze in Liverpool shows Isis crowned with the fish (xlii. 7 [p. 267]). The famous spouse of Osiris and mother of Horus is conceived to represent the moon and the fertile earth.[63] As daughter of the sun,[64] mother of Horus and spouse of Osiris, the lotus would belong to her, but it is generally mentioned as her attribute in her character of Goddess of fecundity. Through her it has descended to later times, by a strange transposition of significance, as the Lily of the Virgin.[65] In Phenician (and Cypriote Greek) symbolism the lotus belongs equally to sun and moon (plate xxiii. 10, 11 [p. 173]; plates lxvi. 4, 6, 12 [p. 399]; lxvii. 2, 4, 6, 10 [p. 401.]).

58. EMMANUEL DE ROUGÉ, *Notice Sommaire, &c.*, p. 119.
59. For the cow as type of fecundity and of Isis, see BRUGSCH, *Mythologie*, vol. i., and PIERRET, *Panthéon*, p. 35.
60. For fish Oxyrynchus as Hathor, see *Revue Archéologique*, 1847, 2, p. 718, and BIRCH, *Eg. Antiq. in the British Museum*, p. 32. For Silurus fish and Hathor, same reference, p. 59.
61. For identity or assimilation of Isis and Hathor, see

BRUGSCH, *Mythologie*, vol. i., p. 84, and DE ROUGÉ, *Notice Sommaire*, p. 133.
62. Horus as calf, BRUGSCH, *Mythologie*, vol. i., p. 160.
63. For Isis as the Moon, see BRUGSCH, *Mythologie*, pp. 6, 12. For Isis as the fertile earth, and Osiris as the Nile, BRUGSCH.
64. Hathor, daughter of the Sun, DE ROUGÉ, *Notice Sommaire*, p. 133.
65. KING and WESTROPP, as quoted at Note 5.

THE LOTUS AND EGYPTIAN GODS.

On Assyrian and Syrian seals and cylinders the lotus also occurs with the lunar crescent alone (plate xxiv. 5, 6, 11, 12, 14 [p. 183]). In modern accounts of Egyptian mythology the references to the moon have been scanty, aside from the significance conceded to Isis, to Thoth, and to Khons, but Osiris is quoted for " the world of the moon " by both Birch and Brugsch, and in the recent second volume of Brugsch's *Mythologie* the moon is constantly mentioned as province of many Egyptian solar deities. Hence the constant union of sun and moon on Phenician symbols would not be at variance with Egyptian feeling. There is therefore no reason why the lotus should not belong to Isis in her character of Moon-goddess, for being once accepted as a divine symbol, it is by no means necessary to establish a solar origin or assimilation for every form or deity connected with it.

The frog (ii. 8) is interpreted as a symbol of the watery element and primitive slime, which was considered as the basis of created matter by Egyptian cosmogony.[66] " It was probably sacred to Noum, the deity of waters, and to Hapimou, the Nile, or to a female frog-headed deity called Hyk."[67] This goddess (Hyk, Hek, or Heka) belongs to a triad worshipped at Elephantine and Khnoumis. The hieroglyphs relating to the detail ii. 8, specify a goddess.[68]

The frog, as indicating the element in which the water-lily grows, brings us to the question why the lotus became sacred to the sun. Hindu explanations, which belong to a reflective and philosophizing period, cannot be considered conclusive for one of the most primitive and firmly rooted traditions of the Brahmanic and Egyptian Mythologies, and yet these explanations must be given their proper weight. They relate to the plant as type and growth of the watery element, made productive by heat or the element of fire.[69] Nor is it to be forgotten that Brahma springs from a lotus, which in its turn rises from the navel of Vishnu, or Narayana, the " Spirit moving on the Waters," who appears in Hindu representations of this birth of Brahma, as floating on the waters and supported by a lotus leaf. There is a coloured

---

66. LEEMANS, *Monumens*, &c., vol. i., p. 21; "La grenouille, emblême de la matière primitive et de la déesse Hak." BRUGSCH, *Mythologie*, " Der Froschkopf das Uranfängliche."

67. BIRCH, *Egyptian Antiquities in the British Museum*, p. 58. I have preserved the orthography of BIRCH, Noum = Chnoum or Khnoum.

68. ROSELLINI, Text, *Monumenti del Culto*, p. 151.

69. With the Hindus the lotus is the emblem of the productive power of nature, through the agency of fire and water. The lotus is the product of fire (heat) and water, hence the dual symbol of spirit and matter. There are passages in Plutarch which show that the Egyptians held similar theories and employed the same symbolism (see p. 16).

THE LOTUS AND EGYPTIAN GODS.

ivory model of this subject in the India Museum at South Kensington, and it is also figured in Moor's "Hindu Pantheon." The myth of Horus rising from the lotus, as found in the Egyptian hieroglyphic texts, is the exact counterpart of this idea, and as far as Brahmanism is concerned, is much the older. It is well known that the Brahman system and faith were not developed by the Hindus till they had conquered the Ganges country and Southern India, and there is no trace of this tradition or even of Brahma as a deity in the Vedas. In view of the possibility that this tradition and the entire Hindu symbolism of the lotus were borrowed (with other admitted influences) from the earlier conquered peoples of Hindustan, it may, or may not be, as primitive as the Egyptian myth. It is possible that the lotus symbolism of Egypt and of India dates from a race which divided into separate branches; also possible that Indian peoples experienced the influence, direct or indirect, of Egypt. The campaign of a conquering king would have no great significance in such connection, but the elephant hunts of Thothmes III. in Asia (about 1600 B.C.) have led Dr. Birch to believe that he reached India.[70] Such a fact might be at least significant of other international relations which are unknown to us, or insufficiently considered.

The known connections between India and Egypt are moreover not confined to the commercial intercourse by sea which is dated at least to 600 B.C. The Assyrian king Touklat-habal-assar made campaigns to the Indus in the eighth century B.C. (Maspero). The relations of Darius and Xerxes with India are well-known. Inscriptions showing Phenician characters are found in India of the third century B.C. At this time "the most intimate commercial intercourse was established with Syria and Egypt" (Birdwood). Our knowledge of Hindu art begins in the third century B.C., and none of the present popular forms of Hindu religion are presumed to be earlier than the ninth century A.D. (Moor, Ed. Wilson, p. 390). Later proofs for the dominance of lotus symbolism in Persia and in Assyria as early as the ninth century B.C. will therefore prove an unbroken land area for lotus symbolism comprehending both Egypt and the frontiers of India as early as the eighth century B.C. The Puranas display a wide knowledge of Egyptian geography, and a wide familiarity with Egypt, according to the essay of Lieut. Wilford in "Asiatic Researches" on "Egypt and the Nile."[71] This essay, written early in our century, is undoubtedly superseded in many ways by later study, but these essential facts

---

70. In *Proceedings, Society of Biblical Archaeology,* Nov., 1881.   71. Supplementary vol. ii

are undoubtedly proven by it. There is a curious reference by Sir William Jones to an Egyptian colony in India;[72] all the more curious by reason of his own conservative doubts in the matter. Among the points made by Wilford are references to Lucian's accounts of Hindu pilgrims to Hierapolis in Syria, and to the geographer Ptolemy's mention of the presence of Hindus in Alexandria. It is therefore possible that the Hindu tradition quoted, viz. that the lotus is a symbol of the productive union of solar heat and water, is related to the lotus solar-myth of Egypt. For in Egyptian cosmogony the watery element is the beginning of all things—"Das Urwasser," as it is termed by Brugsch—which was personified in the first instance by Noun, among whose forms was Noum or Khnoum (p. 12), whose symbol, the frog, has been above quoted. It is probable also that the lotus was connected with the symbolism of the inundation, because springing up and flowering in the pools which were made by it, as already mentioned by Herodotus.[73]

The above suggestions of Hindu tradition are so curiously substantiated by casual references of Plutarch, that we can scarcely doubt that at least one solution of lotus solar symbolism may be definitely postulated. Two passages of this author mention the Egyptian paintings of Horus rising from the lotus flower, as denoting the creation of the sun from the watery element. That this doctrine was held by the Egyptians appears from the accounts of Brugsch based on their original texts.[74] The often quoted theory of the philosopher Thales, that water was the basis of all things, was undoubtedly Egyptian, and this so-called Greek philosopher is said by Movers to have been a Phenician.[75] The passages of Plutarch are as follows:— "Nor can we suppose it the opinion that the sun, like a new-born infant, springs up every day afresh out of a lotus plant. It is true indeed they do characterize the rising sun in this manner, but the reason is that they may hereby signify to us that it is moisture to which we owe the first kindling of this luminary."[76] To this quotation we may add one from the same work, referring to the same theory of solar creation without mention of the lotus:—"They believe also that the sun and moon

---

72. *Asiatic Researches*, i. p. 174.
73. HERODOTUS, *Euterpe*, 92.
74. *Religion und Mythologie der alten Aegypter*, I. p. 129. "Vom Nun dem Vater gezeugt ging am Tage der Weltschöpfung das Sonnenkind aus dem Leibe der Nunnet hervor und der Himmelsozean wurde zu einer Göttin deren geläsende Kraft das Tägliche Licht der Welt schenkte."

75. *Geschichte der Phönizier*.
76. PLUTARCH, *De Iside et Osiride*, translated by Samuel Squire. See references to original at Note 81. The authorship by Plutarch has been called in question. The work is almost the only classical account of Egyptian religion which is cited with respect by Egyptologists.

do not go in chariots, but sail about the world perpetually in certain boats, hinting thereby at their feeding upon and springing first out of moisture."[77] The second passage of Plutarch which mentions the lotus is as follows:—" To this Serapio replied that sure the workmen thereby designed to show that the sun was nourished by moisture and exhalation, whether it was that he thought at that time of that verse in Homer,—

'The rising sun, then causing day to break,
Quits the cool pleasure of the oozy lake.'

or whether he had seen how the Egyptians, to represent sunrise, paint a little boy sitting on a lotus."[78] According to Brugsch, whose accounts are based on Egyptian texts—"On the day of creation the sun-child, created by Noun [the watery element], issued from the form of Nounnet [the female counterpart of Noun], and the sea of the sky became a goddess, whose maternal strength endowed the world with its daily light."[79]

It is known that in many senses Egyptian theories of natural phenomena go back to childish matter-of-fact perception—that, for instance, the sun was supposed to travel each night in reverse course under the earth, in order to return to the dawn of a following day. It may be that the philosophy of the priests as to the birth of the sun from moisture, was preceded by a matter-of-fact observation of a primitive race on the East African shore, and that the sun visibly rising from the sea was conceived actually to have such origin. To represent the sun as rising from a water-lily would have been in this case a pictorial and allegorical, rather than a philosophical or metaphysical, process. I have ventured this suggestion because it is difficult to believe that any metaphysical theory could have called forth such a universal, ancient, and manifestly popular pictorial symbolism as is attested by all classes of Egyptian monuments and relics, of whatever kind or period, for this especial plant. It is only students who have been in contact with Egyptian antiquities, or Egyptological publication, who can approximately realize the enormous amount of normal lotus ornament which has survived to our own day,

---

77. PLUTARCH, *De Iside et Osiride*, translated by WM. W. GOODWIN, *Plutarch's Morals.* IV. p. 94.

78. PLUTARCH's *Morals*, translated by William W. Goodwin, III. p 80. "*Why the Pythian Priestess ceases her Oracles in verse.*" The matter of the paragraph concerns a brazen palm-tree at Delphi, under which were represented frogs and aquatic animals—hence the dialogue as above. See reference at Note 81 to the original.

79. The original German at Note 74.

and which is once more an infinitesimal and absolutely insignificant fraction of that which once existed.

As a secondary explanation, which has possible value, must be quoted a reason for the solar significance of the lotus, suggested by Colonna-Ceccaldi,[80] that the moment of its opening corresponds with the dawn. It is of great interest to learn that the modern Japanese have a similar tradition and a festival based upon it.[81] There is, however, no present authority for dating the well-known lotus symbolism and lotus ornament of China and Japan before the Buddhist influence and missions. These are later than the Christian era in these countries. The entire lotus symbolism of the Buddhists is itself derivative, being borrowed from the earlier Hindu traditions, which we know as Brahmanic. The entire Buddhist ornamental system is borrowed from the West, or influenced by it, and not earlier than the third century B.C. as known to us. [82]

---

80. In *Monuments de Chypre*, p. 141; quoting the fact from PLINY's *Natural History*, lib. xiii., c. xvii.

81. A fact indirectly learned from Mr. Theodore Wores, an American artist, some time resident in Japan.

The following advices are from Mr. E. D. Sturtevant, who first naturalized *Nelumbium Speciosum* in the United States, and who owns water-lily gardens at Bordentown, New Jersey, and at Los Angeles, California. They are of great value as bearing on the tradition mentioned, and were furnished in response to questions put by me.

"*Nelumbium Speciosum* [the Rose Lotus] opens at dawn."

"It closes just past mid-day in fresh flowers, but those which are nearly ready to drop their petals (old flowers) remain open an hour or two longer."

"*Nymphæa Lotus* [the White Lotus], is night blooming, opening just after sunset, and closing the next morning about ten o'clock."

"*Nymphæa Cærulea* [the Blue Lotus], opens soon after sunrise, and closes an hour or two before sunset."

"I do not think that the promptness of these flowers in opening at dawn is more noticeable than in many other species."

It will appear in my next chapter that the *Nelumbium Speciosum* "Rose Lotus," is not found in typical Egyptian ornament. As this is the only water-lily quoted by Mr. Sturtevant for especially prompt opening at dawn, we cannot attach much importance to the suggestion of Colonna-Ceccaldi, as regards Egyptian art. It would appear quite as likely that the white lotus was a flower of Osiris, because blooming at night. It is probable that the original explanation regarding their solar significance is the same for all water-lilies. If this is so, the opening at dawn of *Nelumbium Speciosum* could not be the original explanation in the case of this plant.

VICTOR LORET furnishes a list of ancient classical references to the lotus in *Recueil de Travaux relatifs à la Philologie et à l'Archéologie Égyptiennes et Assyriennes*, i., p. 190. The list is copied herewith:—HEROD., *Hist.* ii., 92. THEOPHR., *Hist. plant.*, iv. 8, §§ 7—11, and *Caus. plant.*, ii., 19, § 1. STRAB., *Geogr.*, xvii, 1, § 15, p. 1151; DIOD. SIC., *Bibl. hist.*, i., 10, 1. DIOSCOR., *Mat. Medic.*, ii., 128 and iv., 112. PLIN., *Hist. nat.*, xiii., 32; xviii., 30; xxii., 28. ATHEN., *Deipn.*, iii., 1—3; xv., 21.

COLONNA-CECCALDI in *Monuments de Chypre*, p. 141, furnishes references to PLUT., *De Pyth. orac.*, c. xii., ed. Didot; *De Iside et Osiride*, c. xl, ed. Didot.

KING in *Gnostics*, p. 174, quotes from JAMBLICHUS metaphysical matter on lotus symbolism, viz. that the lotus was an emblem of perfection, because in leaf, flowers, and fruit it gave the figure of a circle—matter of no importance, except as showing the effort of a speculative age to explain a primitive tradition.

A reference to PROCLUS has been quoted by Note 6.

82. For the Greek character of early Buddhist decoration, see BIRDWOOD, *Industrial Arts of India* (South Kensington Museum Art Handbooks), p. 163; referring also to Dr. Leitner's Collection of Greco-Buddhist sculptures from the

THE LOTUS AND EGYPTIAN GODS.

From the point of view that Egyptian symbols are largely picture-writing based either upon correspondences of verbal sounds, or actual resemblances of some sort or other, I have thought that the brilliant yellow ovary stigma of the Egyptian water-lilies, with the rayed appearance common to the white and blue varieties, may have been considered as a picture and therefore as a type of the sun. As I shall prove the rosette to be an Egyptian lotus-motive (with concurrence of Mr. Percy E. Newberry), this suggestion is worth considering.

The illustration of plate ii. 9, is taken from the "Book of the Dead"—the lotus as one of the mystic habitations and migratory forms of the spirits of the Blest. There is no other plant which shares this mystic destiny—it is not assigned, for instance, to the papyrus. When found in the illustrated Papyri the design belongs to the confessional chapter lxxxi., "To make the transformation of the lotus," whose terms I translate roughly from the French version of Pierret.[83] "I am a pure lotus, issue of the beings of light. I guard the nostril of Ra, who guards the nostril of Hathor. I do the errands of Horus. I am a pure lotus, issue of the field of the sun."

Punjab. That Persian and Assyrian influences carried with them the Egyptian lotus forms has been already noted. *The Archæological Survey of Southern India*, by JAMES BURGESS, gives many illustrations of unnoticed purely Egyptian types; for instance, a normal Egyptian lotus border above the "Worship of a Sacred Tree by Spotted Deer," vol. I. p. 50. See also ALEXANDER CUNNINGHAM, *The Stupa of Bharhut* (third century B.C.). Normal Egyptian lotuses surrounding a rosette, Pl. xxi.; normal Egyptian lotuses, Pl. xl., &c., &c.

83. PIERRET, *Livre des Morts*, Chapitre LXXXI., Titre—De faire la transformation en lotus. Tableau—Une tête sortant de la fleur d'un lotus. " Je suis un lotus pur, sortant d'entre les lumineux. Je garde la narine de Ra, qui garde la narine de Hathor. Je fais les messages que poursuit Horus. Je suis un lotus pur, issu du champ du soleil."

1. DETAIL FROM THE MYTH OF OSIRIS, AS REPRESENTED AT PHILAE. From Champollion, I., xciii., 2.

PLATE I.

THE LOTUS AND EGYPTIAN GODS.

1. Solar disk supported by the flower. Detail from MARIETTE, *Dendérah*, II., 85, *a* 9.

2. Youthful Horus (the Dawning Sun) seated on the flower. Detail from the *Description de l'Égypte*, A. I., 78, 14.

3. Head-dress, with solar disk supported by the flower. From the series in ROSELLINI, M.R., XV. 64.

4. Osiris (the Sun in the Lower World) before an altar and offerings, crowned by the flower. Detail of a mummy case, from PRISSE D'AVENNES, *Histoire de l'Art Égyptien, Offrandes à Osiris*.

5. The Sun-hawk, supported by the flower. Detail from PRISSE D'AVENNES, *Monuments*, XXXI.

6. King Amenophis III. offering lotuses to the god Amon. Detail from Thebes. PRISSE D'AVENNES, *Pilastres Quadrilatérales.**

7. Isis (Hathor), crowned with lotuses. Detail from PRISSE D'AVENNES, *Piliers Isiaques* (xviii. Dyn.).

8. King Thothmes III. offering lotuses and geese to Ra (the Sun). Detail from Amada, ROSELLINI, III., ix. 4.

9. Fish (emblems of Isis), with flowers and leaves of the lotus. (Compare Isis crowned with the fish, xlii. 7.) Detail of a tray, from PRISSE D'AVENNES, *Ustensiles de Toilette*.

10. The God Khem, before a shrine supporting a leaf of the lotus. (Compare next chapter for the cleft leaf form.) From WILKINSON, *Manners and Customs of the Ancient Egyptians*, I., p. 405, 3rd Edition. Wilkinson mistakes this detail for a tree. In parallel designs at Thebes, the exterior plants do not appear to be lotus buds.

11. Nefer-Toum or Toum (the Setting Sun) crowned with the lotus. From RAWLINSON'S *History of Ancient Egypt*.

12. Isis or Hathor (as cow) in the lotus bower. Detail of a *patera* found at Cære ; in the Vatican. From PERROT ET CHIPIEZ, *Phénicie*, p. 790.

---

* References to PRISSE D'AVENNES indicate his *Histoire de l'Art Égyptien*, unless the *Monuments* are specified. References to Rosellini, Champollion, and Lepsius indicate their folio plate publications.

Pl. I., p. 21.

PLATE II.

THE LOTUS AND EGYPTIAN GODS.

1. Bull with lotus amulet pendant from the collar. Detail from a Theban tomb. ROSELLINI, M.C. XX., 8.

2. The Asp and the lotus. Detail from CHAMPOLLION, II., cix.

3. The "Genii of Amenti" (Guardians of the viscera of the mummy and Genii of the dead), on the lotus. Detail from a representation of the Last Judgment. *Description de l'Égypte*, A. II., 35 a.

4. The Sun-lions "To-morrow and Yesterday," otherwise Ra and Osiris; supporting solar disks in the lotus bower. From a Leyden papyrus published by LEEMANS.

5. Sphinxes and the lotus. Detail from PRISSE D'AVENNES, *Vases du règne de Thothmes III.*

6. The Serpent and the lotus in the solar bark. Detail from MARIETTE, *Dendérah*, II., 48.

7. The Ram (God Khnoum) and the lotus (buds). Detail from Esneh. *Description de l'Égypte*, A. I., 86.

8. The Frog (Goddess Hek, Hyk, or Heka, and God Khnoum) on the lotus, (with Osiris, and Lion-hawk or Gryphon form of Horus). Detail from Philae, ROSELLINI, M.d.C., xxii.

9. The lotus as mystic form or habitation of the departed spirit. From the related chapter (lxxxi.) of the "Book of the Dead." LENORMANT, *Histoire Ancienne de l'Orient*, III., p. 269.

10. The Goose (Seb, Osiris, Horus and Isis) and the lotus. Stone tablet in the Abbot Collection, New York Historical Society. From the original. Compare Seb, crowned with the goose (xliii. 7).

11. Altar with the lotus. Detail from Medinet-Habou. *Description de l'Égypte*, A. II., 16, 5.

12. The Mummy and the lotus, from the "Book of the Dead." LENORMANT, *Histoire Ancienne de l'Orient*, III., p. 271.

Pl. II., p. 23.

APPENDIX.

The following list notes some of the unpublished monuments which relate to deities or associations not mentioned in the foregoing chapter :—

Ibis (God Thoth), bearing a trefoil lotus on the head; large fresco from the temple of Isis at Pompeii, in the Naples Museum, No. 8562. Ibis on the lotus bouquet; fresco, Thebes, Tombs of the Kings. Tomb No. 6.

Cynocephalus (God Thoth), on the lotus stelè; bronze, *Salle des Ventes*, Gizeh Museum (1891.) Cynocephalus on the lotus stelè; relief, Hathor Temple, Denderah. Room V., Murray's plan.

God Anubis on the lotus bouquet, Denderah portico; relief, on the column bases.

Heron (Osiris, British Museum designations) on the lotus; relief, Hathor Temple, Denderah, lower passage. Heron on the lotus; fresco, Thebes, Tombs of the Kings. Tomb No. 16.

Vulture (Goddess Maut) on the lotus bouquet; Denderah portico, column bases. Head of the vulture wearing crown for the South, on the lotus; large bronze, Polytechnic, Athens.

Ichneumon (identified with God Toum by NAVILLE), large bronze of the animal seated erect on the lotus, with paws raised in adoration; Gizeh Museum, *Salle Religieuse*, Case A, No. 191. Three very large similar bronzes in the Polytechnic, Athens ; Nos. 271, 273, 274.

Cat (Goddess Bast) on the lotus stelè; large bronze in the Polytechnic, Athens, Case 4, No. 203.

Crocodile (God Sebek) on the lotus; large bronze, Gizeh Museum.

Human-headed Scorpion (Goddess Selk; the scorpion is also related to Isis) on the lotus; several bronzes in the Polytechnic, Athens; one in Bologna.

Hawk (Horus and Ra) on the lotus; two large bronzes in the Gizeh Museum. Hawk head on the lotus colonnette, very large porcelain; Polytechnic, Athens. A similar amulet has been published by LEEMANS, *Monumens*, etc.

Lotus supporting the "Sacred Eye ;" both in the solar disk supported by the solar bark; relief, lower passage of the Hathor Temple, Denderah.

Solar disk with human face, and surrounded by a circle of lotus buds and flowers; fresco from the Temple of Isis, Pompeii, in the Naples Museum, No. 9189. See Fig. 185, p. 369.

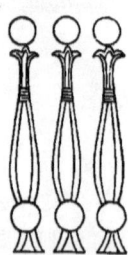

LOTUS COLONETTES SUPPORTING SOLAR DISKS.
Detail from the Bes Temple, Denderah, representing a pattern ornament of universal currency on Egyptian tombs and temples. From a photograph taken for the Author.

LOTUS FORMS MISTAKEN FOR NELUMBIUMS.

(PLATE III., PAGE 41.)

The various water-lilies which are indicated by the word lotus are divided into two groups—the *Nymphæas*, to which the word lotus properly belongs, and the *Nelumbiums*, to which the word lotus is also applied by general usage. The *Nelumbium Speciosum*, for instance, is habitually called the "rose lotus," and is generally supposed to have been the especially sacred lotus of the ancient Egyptians. The group of the *Nymphæas* is now represented in Egypt by white and blue varieties, which are practically identical in all respects but that of colour. The leaf is cleft nearly to its centre (Fig. 2), like the leaf of the common pond-lily. The bud has an envelope of only four calyx leaves or sepals (Fig. 2 and Fig. 3), which have a firm, coarse quality, and are distinctly dark green in colour throughout. These sepals entirely encase the bud (Fig. 2) till it begins to open. As it expands, the colour, coarseness, and large size of the sepals mark them distinctly in contrast to the delicate white or blue petals of the flower. As seen from any one of four special points of view, the opening flower exhibits therefore *three* dark-green spikes (Fig. 3), symmetrically divided, between which the numerous and delicate petals, white or blue, are very effectively relieved.

At various stages of expansion the sepals occasionally curl downward, thus leaving the flower quite distinct and separate, and presenting the appearance seen in Fig. 4. Figures 2 and 3, on the other hand, especially the latter, show the appearance of the spikes when erect. The distinction of colour, dark green against white or sapphire blue, makes this contrast still more obvious in nature than it is in the illustrations.

The ovary has a rayed saucer-shaped stigma of brilliant yellow (Figs. 5, 6), from which numerous brilliant yellow, petal-like stamens diverge. When the flower

2. EGYPTIAN BLUE LOTUS. From Nature.
From the *Description de l'Égypte, Histoire Naturelle.*

seeds, the ovary grows into a bulb (Fig. 7), which sinks down in the water, whereas the stem during the period of flower is erect and rises above the water, occasionally reaching an entire length of fully five feet.[1] The rayed ovary stigma continues to be apparent at the apex of the bulb after the flower has gone to seed. Fig. 8 represents a dried specimen of the ovary stigma taken from the bulb. The leaves, about a foot in diameter, each on a separate stem, float on the surface of the water.

The illustration of Webster's Dictionary for the *Nymphæa lotus* shows leaves

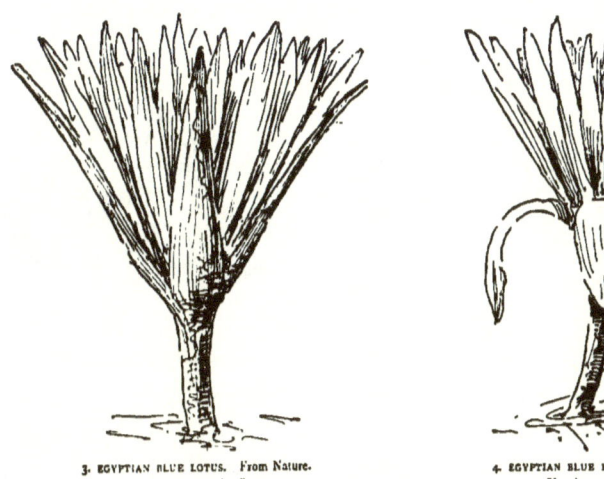

3. EGYPTIAN BLUE LOTUS. From Nature.
Showing three sepal spikes.

4. EGYPTIAN BLUE LOTUS. From Nature.
Showing sepals curled over.

rising above water; "New Edition of 1880," London, 1883. This illustration has been removed from the "Imperial Edition." The artist who made the sketch has been misled by a picture of the Nelumbium.

It is this white or blue variety of the Egyptian Nymphæa which is figured in the ornamental patterns of the monuments. The "Rose Lotus" may possibly be realistically represented in ancient Egyptian paintings, just as the palm and many other plants appear, but such cases must be extremely rare, as none can be found in the great folio publications of Egyptian antiquities, or in the typical

[1]. *Description de l'Égypte, Histoire Naturelle*, I. p. 303; where explicit, extended, and reliable accounts are given of the botanical forms.

ornaments exhibited by Egyptian museums. As far as the typical ornaments, or typical patterns, are concerned, the " Rose Lotus " is not to be found.[2]

The proof lies in the leaf and in the sepals. Whenever the leaf is represented it is cleft. Whenever the flower is represented it shows three spikes, excepting when the entire flower is shown by an outer conventional outline. As long as the flower is detailed, the three spikes appear (Figs. 9 and 9A). They are the last detail to disappear in the ornaments which tend to the conventional outline, generally specified as papyrus. Hence the illustrations of Plate iii. [p. 41]; and they will speak for themselves as regards these traits—the cleft leaf and the three-spiked

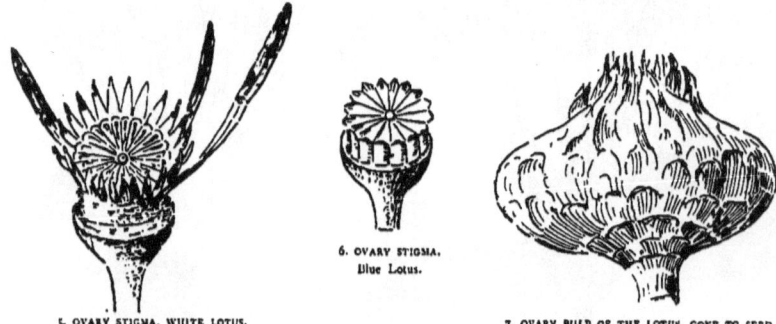

5. OVARY STIGMA, WHITE LOTUS.
Showing also a few stamens.

6. OVARY STIGMA,
Blue Lotus.

7. OVARY BULB OF THE LOTUS, GONE TO SEED.

Figs. 5, 6, and 7 are from the *Description de l'Égypte, Histoire Naturelle.*

form. Nos. 5, 6, 8, 9, 12 show numerous petals. Nos. 2, 3, 7, 11, 13 show a simplified form with two residuary petals, one on each side of the central spike. This central spike is the central sepal; conceiving the flower as viewed from one of the four sides of symmetrical appearance in which two of the sepal spikes form the boundary sides of outline. Nos. 1, 4, 10 show the spikes as residue of the detail. All these forms are typical, constant, and represented by thousands of examples in published monuments, and by countless examples in all Egyptian museums.

2. This fact antagonizes the current presumption of Egyptology, summed up by Perrot, *Égypte*, p. 578, in the words—" Le véritable lotus Égyptien c'est le lotus rose." Perrot's illustration from nature is borrowed from, and credited to, the *Histoire Naturelle* as above mentioned, but it is the "rose lotus" which he has chosen as type. In a recent publication (see reference No. 81, for plates i., ii.) on hieroglyphic renderings for different varieties of the lotus, Victor Loret follows the current assumption, which I have shared in an earlier publication on the " Egyptian Origin of the Ionic Capital and Anthemion," *American Journal of Archæology*, vol. iii. No. 4.

LOTUS FORMS MISTAKEN FOR NELUMBIUMS.

The second group of water-lilies, above specified, is the group of the Nelumbiums, and in this group we have to deal with only one variety, the *Nelumbium Speciosum*, or famous " Rose Lotus," so-called (Fig. 10). In botanical terminology

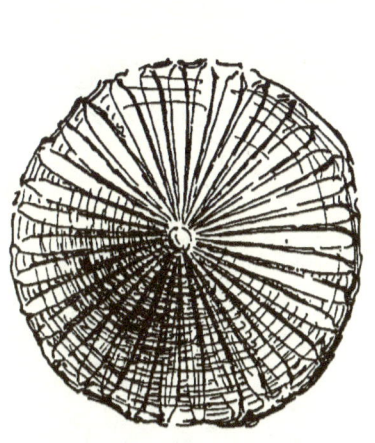

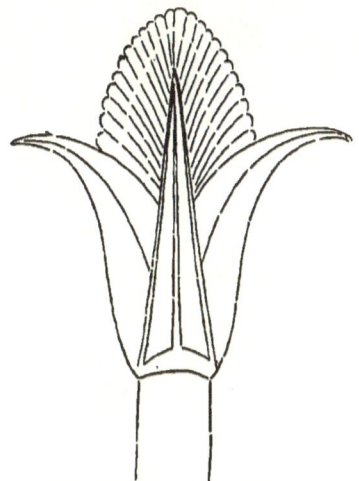

8. DRIED OVARY STIGMA OF THE LOTUS AFTER SEEDING.
From Nature.

9. TYPICAL THREE-SPIKED LOTUS, FROM THE MONUMENTS.
With a palmate attachment on the central spike.

this plant is not a lotus, which word is confined, botanically speaking, to the *Nymphæa Lotus* (white lotus), of which *Nymphæa Cærulea* (the Egyptian blue lotus) is a

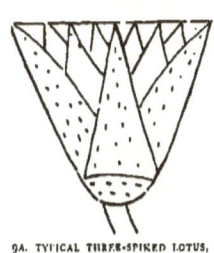

9A. TYPICAL THREE-SPIKED LOTUS,
FROM THE MONUMENTS.

colour variant. In popular use, however, the word "lotus" is generally supposed to designate especially the " Rose Lotus," undoubtedly because of its Oriental celebrity as an emblem and an ornament, and because modern Oriental art and symbolism have given the flower its vogue in æsthetic circles. An immediately obvious distinction is the leaf, which, unlike that of the *Nymphæa* water-lilies, rises on an erect stem to a height of several feet above the water. A minor number of leaves in a given plant may be found floating, the stems not having reached their full altitude, but the normal length of the stem from the root is specified as being four or five feet.

10. *Nelumbium Speciosum* ("ROSE LOTUS"), SHOWING FLOWER, SEED-POD, BUD, AND LEAF.
From the *Description de l'Égypte, Histoire Naturelle.*

Now, in all the great folio publications of Egyptian antiquities, of which the most important are those of Champollion, Rosellini, Lepsius, Prisse d'Avennes, and the *Description de l'Égypte*, there are many representations of lotuses and lotus buds growing in water and rising above it (unlike the two details of Plate iii., 2 and 3, where the plants are represented in water to indicate the water), but there are none in which the leaves are represented as growing on stems out of water. Such representation corresponds to the facts regarding *Nymphæa Lotus* and *Nymphæa Cærulea*, whose flower and bud stems rise out of water (see Note 1), and whose leaves do not rise out of water at all.

An equally important point is that the leaf of the "Rose Lotus" is bell-shaped (Fig. 10) and uncleft, with stem joining the leaf at the centre of the bell. Now in thousands of Egyptian representations of the lotus leaf there cannot be found a leaf which is not cleft. Hence, the illustrations of Plate iii., 2, 3, 5, 6, 8, 12, have been chosen to indicate this point. The cleft is indicated in a summary manner (compare Fig. 2, from nature), and the leaf has frequently a much more pointed form than in nature (see especially iii. 2, 5, 12 [p. 41]), but the relation to nature is obvious. This point is decisive for the absence of the "Rose Lotus" from Egyptian typical ornament.

A third point is equally conclusive. The bud of the "Rose Lotus" has a series of overlapping sepals, like scales, of varying sizes (Fig. 10). Consequently the flower in expansion does not exhibit the three-spiked appearance of the *Nymphæa Lotus* and *Nymphæa Cærulea*. The calyx leaves drop away or disappear from view by the expansion of the blossom, which is more irregular in form and more fully expanded than the more strictly bounded outline of the white and blue Egyptian lotus. The petals of the "Rose Lotus" are as broad individually as the calyx leaves, and the appearance in expansion is that of a full-blown tulip, whereas the fully expanded flower of the white and blue lotus does not generally pass the limit marked by the Figs. 2 and 3.

As we have seen that the Egyptian ornamental form continues to exhibit the three sepal spikes, distinct from petals, in all stages of summary indication, until the purely summary indication of a bounding outline is reached, it is clear that *Nelumbium Speciosum* is not represented in Egyptian pattern ornament.

For botanical distinction the seed-pods are also important. The seed-pod of the "Rose Lotus" is shaped like the spout of a watering-pot (Fig 10). Its seeds are of the size of filberts and are contained in cup-shaped cavities which are on the upper exterior surface (Fig. 10). The seeds of the white and blue lotus are small grains like poppy seeds, contained in the interior of their seed-pods, which have the circular and rayed ovary stigma as described (Figs. 5, 6, 8). The pod develops into a bulb (Fig. 7) which sinks into the water, while the spout-shaped ovary of the " Rose Lotus" remains standing on its erect stem until an advanced stage of decay. The illustration of Rawlinson's "History of Egypt" for the "Rose Lotus" is a curiously erroneous one. Each stem bearing a pod is represented as bearing a series of leaves, like rushes. No such leaves are found in the " Rose Lotus" or in the Nymphæas, and each leaf, pod, bud, or flower grows on a separate stem from the root of the plant. The projection of the seeds from the pod is also distorted in a remarkable way in the cut referred to (Fig. 11, to be compared with Fig. 10).

Since the days of Herodotus and his account of the "Rose Lotus" which he saw in Egypt,[3] or at least since the study of Herodotus in modern times, this plant has figured in popular accounts and in scientific works as the typically Egyptian and especially sacred Egyptian flower. Herodotus made no reference to the subject of Egyptian ornament, and yet he is indirectly responsible for one of the most curious scientific and popular mistakes of modern times. The human mind has joined two things together which had no actual connection. It has combined its knowledge of Egyptian ornament with its knowledge drawn from Herodotus that the "Rose Lotus" grew in Egypt, and with its knowledge of modern Oriental symbolism, on the plan of the gentleman who acquired his knowledge of " Chinese Metaphysics " by reading in the Encyclopædia under the words "China" and "Metaphysics" and combining his information. It is well known that the *Nelumbium Speciosum* is not now found in Egypt or in Africa, and that it is indigenous to India, but there are botanical and other writers well aware of this fact who still assert it to have been the typical Sacred Plant of Egypt.[4] It might appear a matter of

---

3. HERODOTUS, *Euterpe*, 92. " But to obtain food more easily, they have the following inventions: when the river is full, and has made the plains like a sea, great numbers of lilies, which the Egyptians call lotus, spring up in the water; these they gather and dry in the sun; then having pounded the middle of the lotus, which resembles a poppy, they make bread of it and bake it. The root also of this lotus is fit for food, and is tolerably sweet, and is round and of the size of an apple. There are also other lilies, like roses, that grow in the river, the fruit of which is contained in a separate pod that springs up from the root, in form very like a wasp's nest; in this there are many berries fit to be eaten, of the size of an olive stone, and they are eaten both fresh and dried." (Cary's Translation.)

4. *Garden and Forest*, April 10th, 1889, an American botanical journal. "But the true Egyptian lotus, the 'Sacred Lotus' of the whole East, is the plant with rosy flowers which Linnæus called *Nymphæa Nelumbo*, but

LOTUS FORMS MISTAKEN FOR NELUMBIUMS.

no great importance which form of lotus is the one copied by Egyptian ornament, and that even a universal scientific and popular mistake in such a matter is scarcely worth rectifying. To such possible suggestion it may be answered, first, that the "Rose Lotus" is not, botanically speaking, a lotus and that it is desirable to observe a certain amount of botanical accuracy in a work devoted to the subject; second, that important problems of early Hindu history may yet be determined by clear views on this question; third, that the influence of Egyptian art, and therefore of Egyptian civilization, on other countries and later times may be most clearly studied in the history of ornament, and that the peculiarities of this ornament, as above described, can only be comprehended by recourse to the natural forms which served as models. For instance, the ceiling motives of Orchomenos and Tiryns, which belong to the "Mycenæ" period and culture, and which have been made known by Dr. Schliemann (Fig. 56, and Plate li. 9 [p. 319]), can be specified by the central spike, and the publications of these patterns have designated them as "fan-shaped flowers"[5] and "large flowers"[6] because this detail has been overlooked. Attention to the form of the leaf enables us to recognize the lotus forms which have been mistaken for papyrus, which is a highly important correction for Egyptian archæology. The relations of the rosette to the lotus may be recognized through the ovary stigma of the white and blue lotus, but the ovary stigma of the "Rose Lotus" does not exhibit the rosette form. The sepals of the "Rose Lotus," though they are frequently pendant after expansion of the flower, do not curl over as they frequently do in the white and blue lotus (Fig. 4), and this peculiarity has a curious relation to the history of the Ionic form and of the Anthemion. Wilkinson is the solitary authority who states that the "Rose Lotus" does not occur in Egyptian ornament.[7] His brief reference to the subject has been disregarded by all later writers and authorities, and I have myself shared the prevalent error which uses the word "lotus" as indiscriminately indicating an Egyptian use of all three plants in ornament, in two separate publications which I have previously made on the subject.

which modern botanists have placed in another genus and called *Nelumbium Speciosum*. This no longer grows wild in the Nile, and perhaps was not a native of Egypt."

5. SCHLIEMANN'S *Tiryns*, in preface by F. Adler; otherwise justly emphasizing the Egyptian influences apparent in the "Mycenæ culture."

6. SCHLIEMANN'S *Tiryns*, p. 298.

7. WILKINSON, *Ancient Egyptians*, iii. p. 133; 3rd Edition. "It is never introduced into the sculptures as a sacred emblem, or indeed as a production of the country."

It may be then asked, "If Linnæus considered the 'Rose Lotus' a Nymphæa and named it 'Nymphæa Nelumbo,'[8] and if it has been reserved for the nineteenth century to change this classification, is it likely that the Egyptians were more pedantic in their choice of sacred water-lilies than the father of modern botany was in his science?" To this I answer—we have no grounds for asserting that the "Rose Lotus" was not a sacred water-lily in Egypt. A Roman mosaic (No. 9990) in the Naples Museum, showing the peculiar leaf and seed-pod, is from the Isis temple of Pompeii.[9] Since the "Rose Lotus" is not indigenous to Africa, and since both botanists[10] and Egyptologists[11] have explained its former presence there as due to foreign introduction or to the well-known proclivity of the Egyptians to introduce and cultivate foreign plants,[12] we have only to assume that the types of Egyptian ornament were fixed before the foreign plant was known, and that they had been fixed so long before, that the presence of a new sacred water-lily did not affect the ornamental methods of this extremely conservative nation.

The time of Herodotus was later than the close of Egyptian history as the history of an independent nation. Nine-tenths of the monuments belong to an earlier date, and it is uncertain how long before his time the Indian plant was grown in Egypt. The active commercial intercourse between Egypt and India is generally dated from the middle of the seventh century B.C., only two hundred years before Herodotus. The typical three-spiked form can be dated to the IVth Dynasty. The growth of the "Rose Lotus" in the United States is an indication of the rapidity with which this plant may make its way in a foreign country. It was introduced by Mr. E. D. Sturtevant at Bordentown, New Jersey, about 1876. After a year or two he tried the experiment of growing it in the open air. The experiment was made with one plant, which within eight years had spread over a water surface of three-quarters of an acre "in a solid mass of foliage and bloom." The boys of the neighbourhood discovered the edible properties of the filbert-like seed and made their nutting excursions to the new source of supplies, unconsciously imitating the ancient Egyptians, who drew a food supply from these seeds,[13] like the Hindus, and like the

8. See reference at Note 4.
9. WILKINSON, ii. p. 407, 3rd Edition, quotes the *Nelumbium Speciosum* for Roman Egyptian sculptures, the "Nile" of the Vatican, &c.
10. As implied in quotation, Note 4.
11. WILKINSON'S *Ancient Egyptians*, ii. p. 407, 3rd Edition. "The Nelumbium, common in India, grows no longer in Egypt, and the care taken in planting it formerly seems to show that it was not indigenous in Egypt."
12. As instanced by the botanical importations of Queen Hatasou, depicted at Thebes.
13. HERODOTUS, as quoted, Note 3.

LOTUS FORMS MISTAKEN FOR NELUMBIUMS.

American Indians who eat the seeds of *Nelumbium Luteum*.[14] It is probable that the "Rose Lotus" was introduced into Egypt as a food plant, and it is still cultivated in China for that use. Its rapid spread in the much less favourable climate of North America would enable us to understand that an abundant growth in the time of Herodotus might have resulted from an introduction made not many centuries before, and after the time when recorded commercial intercourse with India began. On the other hand, there are surviving forms of the lotus ornament in Egypt which date from the time of earliest known monuments, and not less than three thousand years before the recorded commercial intercourse with India.

It is my mission to state facts, not to explain them, but according to the records and known facts there is not the slightest difficulty in supposing that the "Rose Lotus" may have been as sacred a water-lily in Egypt, after it was known there, as it was in India, without in the slightest degree affecting the ruling types of Egyptian ornament. Mrs. Professor Huggins, wife and scientific assistant of the famous astronomer, has drawn my attention to a pilgrim bottle from Egypt (not in original, but shown by a drawing made by a conscientious and observing student many years ago) on which the rose lotus appears to be indicated. As compared with the present mass of publications and of monuments in the museums, the future discovery of a large number of such cases would amount to considerably less than a drop in the proverbial bucket as affecting our estimation of ornamental types; but additional cases of this class would be of great interest as rarities and thoroughly novel phenomena. There are points about the ware and shape of this pilgrim bottle which argue a foreign importation. The original is not accessible to inspection, and is known by drawing from a private catalogue.

A curious point is the hitherto unnoted fact that although both *Nelumbium Speciosum* and *Nymphæa Lotus* are quoted as sacred plants in India,[15] the lotus patterns of India are largely drawn from the Egyptian patterns based on the *Nymphæa*, and this in face of the fact that the "Rose Lotus" is by far the most quoted Hindu sacred flower. The explanation is simple; the history of Hindu patterns, as known to us, begins with the Buddhist time. Buddhist art, and con-

---

14. *Food and Fibre Plants of the American Indians*, by Dr. J. S. NEWBERRY, New York, D. Appleton, 1887.

15. BIRDWOOD, *Industrial Arts of India* (South Kensington Art Handbooks). List of sacred Hindu plants, p. 85.

LOTUS FORMS MISTAKEN FOR NELUMBIUMS.

temporary Hindu art, ornamental and otherwise, date from a time when Greek influences were dominant in the Punjab [16] and Indus country, and had spread thence to Southern India,[17] and these influences were preceded by Persian and Assyrian. If we examine, for example, the running lotus patterns of the Amaravati Tope of Southern India displayed in the main staircase of the British Museum, they will show the central spike of the Egyptian and Greco-Egyptian lotus, also present in the Egypto-Assyrian and Egypto-Persian lotus patterns, which must have had influence on India. Only the large rosettes of the Amaravati Tope (about three feet in diameter) appear to show the "Rose Lotus" spread out "in plan."[18] The marked indications of Assyrian influence in Hindustan have been pointed out by Fergusson and by Birdwood. An intercourse between Chaldea and India is proved by the discovery of teak wood in the ruins of Mugheir (Sayce, Hibbert Lectures, p. 137). At a later date Hindu art became saturated with Mahommedan lotus patterns. These were all originally borrowed in the countries conquered by the Mahommedan Arabs, during the seventh century A.D.—Syria, Egypt, North Africa, and Persia. The Arab art was therefore ornamentally based on the Sassanian Persian, and Byzantine, and these ornamental systems again drew their lotus patterns from Greco-Egyptian and Egypto-Persian sources. Hence the later Hindu ornament shows an immense amount of scroll-pattern, connecting phases of the type iii. 4, which is, as shown, a reminiscence of the three-spiked form of the blue and white lotus, and

16. The earliest dated examples of Hindu (Buddhist) gold and silver work are of absolutely Greek character, as shown by BIRDWOOD (p. 162). The same author gives full value to the evidences of Dr. Leitner's Collection of Greco-Buddhist sculptures, brought to Europe from the Punjab about 1870. The Greek characteristics are unmistakable in all Buddhist architectural carving. The Greek influences are dated from the Greek states in Bactria and on the Hindu frontier which followed Alexander's Indian campaign. The treaties with Greek sovereigns for the protection of the Buddhists are mentioned by Birdwood (p. 103) and by KING, *Gnostics and their Remains*, p. 14. "There is no known Hindu temple, Mr. Fergusson says, older than the sixth or fifth century of the Christian era, and all the earlier stone buildings in India are Buddhist" (Birdwood, p. 99). Hence, appeal to Buddhist art is decisive for the early Hindu art in general. Although the Greek influences conceded in this art are supposed to date from Alexander's campaigns, there is no doubt that the earlier Persian influence, in which Greek character is perceptible, in the fifth century B.C. must have reached India. This view is based on the lotus patterns in Buddhist stone carving. The earlier Assyrian patterns also had influence, and were also Egyptian in origin.

17. The Amaravati (Buddhist) Tope in Southern India was built in the fourth century A.D. The pattern system is foreign, showing mixed influences from the West, Greek included. The patterns are lotus motives, and the Egyptian three-spiked form is dominant. The Sanchi Tope at Bhopal (early first century A.D.) shows still more distinct classic influences in its lotus patterns and lotus spirals. Casts in the India Museum, South Kensington.

18. These rosettes show a central disk on which the cup-shaped cavities of the *Nelumbium* seed-pod are indicated, but the outer concentric circles appear to be composed of rows of the three-spiked lotus, in the style of the "Egg and Dart" Moulding (Pl. xxi.).

LOTUS FORMS MISTAKEN FOR NELUMBIUMS. 37

the origin of the "fleur-de-lys" (so-called).[19] (Compare the Saracenic trefoil lotus ornament from North Africa (Fig. 78) in its relation to earlier Byzantine and classic patterns.) The history of India thus explains why its apparently favourite water-lily has had so little influence on its ornamental patterns. The pedestals of statues and statuettes of the Hindu gods and of Buddha are almost universally lotus pedestals of the type familiar to Orientalists and lovers of Oriental art. In these pedestals only the projecting ends of rayed petals appear, and a decision based on floral resemblances, as between *Nelumbium* and *Nymphæa*, could not easily be reached. We may understand these pedestals as showing the outer circumference of a rosette which is supposed to show the flower, spread out "in plan." The rosettes of the Amaravati Tope indicate the seed-holes of the *Nelumbium* on a few of the central disks, which probably settles the question of the lotus pedestals.

Although naturalistic rendering of the "Rose Lotus" is found in ancient and modern Oriental art, it must be remembered that this has nothing to do with the dominance of a pattern, which is a matter of technical tradition; and technical traditions in the matter of ornament have been determined by the history of civilization. In so far as the civilization of India has experienced waves of foreign influence from the Assyrian campaigns of the eighth century on the Western frontier, which carried with them Egyptian lotus forms;[20] from the Persian conquests and contact, which did the same; from the Greek conquests and contact, which did the same; and from the Arab conquests and contact, which did the same, in so far is its ornamental art of foreign origin. And by reverse statement of the same fact it follows that the history of ornament is a very fair index of the amount of foreign influence which a nation has experienced. To sum up the results of these notes on Hindu art, it appears that the famous Indian water-lily exercised no visible influence on the art of Egypt, and that Egyptian patterns have invaded its own home by many paths, at many times, and borne by waves of historic influence which are admitted to have determined the character of Hindu art since the third century B.C., which is the first century in which this art is known to us.

There is but one more question to answer on the head of the "Rose Lotus."

---

19. This form is mistaken by INMAN, *Ancient Pagan and Modern Christian Symbolism*, for the *triad*; as explained by his work. His plate xlii. is full of unrecognized trefoil lotuses.

20. All the normal and recognized lotus patterns of Assyria are universally conceded to be Egyptian. See PERROT ET CHIPIEZ, *Assyrie*.

LOTUS FORMS MISTAKEN FOR NELUMBIUMS.

"Why is it, that since the days of the campaign of Bonaparte and the *Description de l'Égypte* (which was published as the result of this campaign) down to the most recent years—the colour of the " Rose Lotus" has been noticed by travellers on the Egyptian monuments, and quoted as especially representing this plant?"[21] The answer is—first, that although Egyptian design is remarkably faithful to natural fact (as long as it presents any detailed form) as regards outlines, and linear design, it is by no means equally attentive to the naturalism of colour. The realistic blue lotus is undoubtedly most frequent on the monuments which have preserved their colour. The realistic white lotus is much rarer, but fairly common. But if it should be argued that a red lotus which appears occasionally must be also realistic, we can appeal to the fact that green lotuses (detailed with sepals and petals) are very common on the papyri of the Turin Collection, and that many lotuses have red and white petals (same reference). Both latter cases are purely decorative and contrary to nature. The lotus is represented in Egypt in all the colours of the rainbow and from a decorative point of view. It is even represented with cross-bars of colour in some cases, to be quoted later. There is a more decisive answer. Admitting that the blue lotus and the white lotus are faithfully represented in colour on many occasions, we have to explain that a red colour may be equally faithful to a *Nymphæa* type, and without representing the much-quoted " Rose Lotus." There is a species of *Nymphæa* of small size, but answering all conditions of the Egyptian ornamental form, known as the *Nymphæa Zanzibarensis Rosea*. It is a colour variety of the *Nymphæa Zanzibarensis*, whose habitat is described by my authority[22] as "Africa," and presumably it is best known as from Zanzibar. It is uncertain if this flower has been seen in Egypt, but it would be hard to prove that it never grew there, for it is indigenous to Africa.[23] If the Egyptians ever gave a rose colour to the lotus for naturalistic reasons, the explanation must be sought here probably. " The flowers are of a deep rosy pink colour. The outside of the sepals [calyx leaves, four in number and three-spiked in side view] is of a lively green." The only alternative would be *Nymphæa Rubra*, a red Nymphæa which is indigenous to India, and which may have found its way to Egypt. It will appear in later pages that the recognition of the three-spiked form

LOTUS TREFOIL.
Repeated from
Plate iii., 4.

21. For instance by VICTOR LORET in matter quoted by Note 81, for Pls. i. and ii.
22. *Catalogue of Rare Water-Lilies*; E. D. STURTEVANT; Bordentown, New Jersey, U.S.A.
23. VILIERS STUART, *Funeral Tent of an Egyptian Queen*, p. 40, mentions a "pink lotus" as growing in Abyssinia.

LOTUS FORMS MISTAKEN FOR NELUMBIUMS.

as a typical lotus and conventional outcome of realistic rendering is one of vital importance throughout the subject treated. It is therefore most essential to show that the red lotus of the Egyptian monuments is not *the* "Rose Lotus," whose realistic rendering could not explain the details of the ultimate conventional types in question, including the Saracenic trefoil and Medieval "Fleur-de-Lys."

I have observed a few cases of five sepal spikes in Egypt, one in Lepsius' tomb, near the Great Pyramid (IVth Dyn.), where the flower is held by the owner of the tomb. There are also individual cases of five sepal spikes at Beni Hasan, among the growing plants; but I have never seen a flower in ornament which did not show the three-spiked form if detailed at all. The flowers in question were not red, and the sepals did not correspond to those of the *Nelumbium Speciosum*, which are of varying length and size.

11. UNKNOWN PLANT. Supposed to be a *Nelumbium Speciosum* by the original publication. (See p. 32.)
From Rawlinson's "History of Ancient Egypt," I. p. 58.

PLATE III.

LOTUS FORMS MISTAKEN FOR NELUMBIUMS.*

1. Egyptian type, showing the sepals of the *Nymphæa Lotus* or *Nymphæa Cærulea*. Detail from PRISSE D'AVENNES, *Monuments*, xviii.
2. Egyptian type, showing the sepals and leaf of the *Nymphæa Lotus* or *Nymphæa Cærulea*. Detail from representation of water in PRISSE D'AVENNES, *Chasse aux Marais*.
3. Egyptian type, showing the sepals and leaf of the *Nymphæa Lotus* or *Nymphæa Cærulea*. Detail from representation of water in PRISSE D'AVENNES, *Joute de Mariniers*.
4. Egyptian type, showing the sepals of *Nymphæa Lotus* or *Nymphæa Cærulea*. Detail from ROSELLINI, M.C. lxviii.
5. Egyptian type, showing the sepals, leaves, and buds of *Nymphæa Lotus* or *Nymphæa Cærulea*. Handle of a toilette tray in wood; detail from PRISSE D'AVENNES, *Boites et Ustensiles de Toilette*.
6. Egyptian type, showing the sepals, leaf, and bud of *Nymphæa Lotus* or *Nymphæa Cærulea*. Detail from PRISSE D'AVENNES, *Monuments*, xv.
7. Egyptian type, showing the sepals of *Nymphæa Lotus* or *Nymphæa Cærulea*. The flower is supported by a decorative reduplication (Egyptian lotus-Ionic form). Detail from LEPSIUS, *Denkmäler*, ix. 3.
8. Egyptian type, showing the sepals, leaf, and bud of the *Nymphæa Lotus* or *Nymphæa Cærulea*. Detail from PRISSE D'AVENNES, *Vases du règne de Thothmes III*.
9. Egyptian type, in decorative elongation, showing the sepals of *Nymphæa Lotus* or *Nymphæa Cærulea*. Detail from MARIETTE, *Fouilles d'Abydos*, I. 32.
10. Egyptian type, with decorative elongation of the central sepal, and palmette attachment, showing the sepals of *Nymphæa Lotus* or *Nymphæa Cærulea*. From PRISSE D'AVENNES.
11. Egyptian type, showing the sepals of *Nymphæa Lotus* or *Nymphæa Cærulea*. Detail of a spoon handle in wood, from CHAMPOLLION, II. clxix.
12. Egyptian type, showing the flower, partly opened flower, bud, and leaf of *Nymphæa Lotus* or *Nymphæa Cærulea*. Detail from PRISSE D'AVENNES, *Plantes et Fleurs*.
13. Egyptian type, flower with reduplicated form below, showing the sepals of *Nymphæa Lotus* or *Nymphæa Cærulea*. Detail from a tomb painting at Eileithyia of an edifice in wood; from CHAMPOLLION, II. cxliv.

* By the above heading it is not implied that the individual examples illustrated have been specially and individually mistaken for Nelumbiums, but rather that the mistake of assuming the Nelumbium to be a typical Egyptian form can be demonstrated by the traits which these individual examples show.

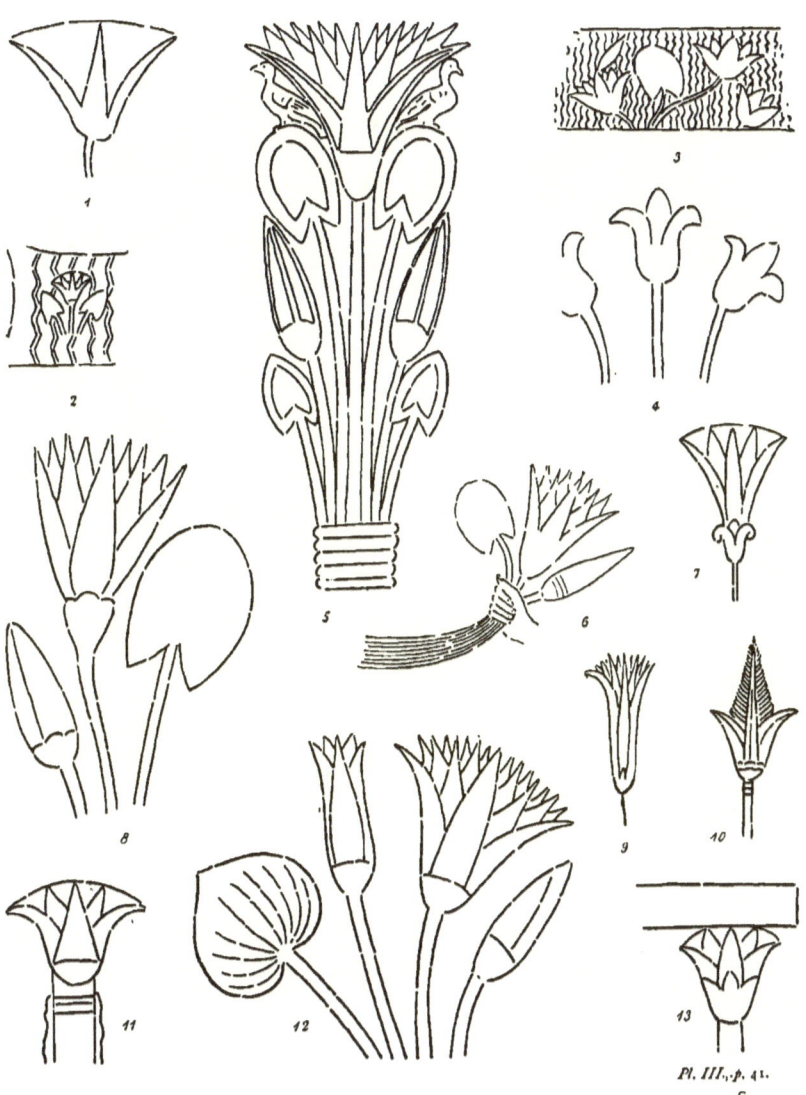

Pl. III., p. 41.

LOTUS FORMS MISTAKEN FOR PAPYRUS.

(PLATES IV., V., PAGES 63, 65.)

The presumption that a papyrus form exists in Egyptian ornament is as widespread as the knowledge of Egyptology, and as firmly rooted. This presumption has invaded the field of hieroglyphic renderings and has appropriated an emblem which belongs to the lotus in such manner that a lotus amulet can be cited as evidence of a papyrus symbolism.[1] Perhaps one-half of the lotus forms in Egyptian art are represented by the conventional outline of Fig. 12, and although the error of naming it a papyrus is by no means universal, as regards every individual case of the conventional outline, the balance of favourable exceptions is outweighed by a habit which the supposed frequency of a papyrus form has induced, of naming obvious and normal lotus patterns as papyrus, a mistake which Wilkinson and Maspero, for instance, have committed.[2] The doubts which a baseless supposition has naturally evoked in special cases, have crystallized into a habit of speaking of such and such a bouquet or motive as "lotus or papyrus,"[3] and the authors of the most valuable summary on Egyptian art have been driven by this dubious attitude of the specialists to the alternative of deciding the campaniform capital (Fig. 20, p. 51) to be neither.[4] Notwithstanding the fact that the given attitude would

12. CONVENTIONAL OUTLINE LOTUS.

12A. LOTUS WITH CONVENTIONAL OUTLINE AT THE TOP.

---

1. See BRUGSCH, *Mythologie* II. pp. 461-2. "Horus auf seinem Papyrusstengel" (Horus on his Papyrus) for type of V. 5.
2. WILKINSON, *Ancient Egyptians*, II., p. 14, 3rd Edition, mistakes normal three-spiked lotus with detailed petals for papyrus. MASPERO, *Archaeology*, translated by Miss Amelia B. Edwards, mistakes foot of a vase, a three-spiked lotus with detailed petals, for papyrus, p. 310, Fig. 279; and in referring to his Fig. 93, p. 87, uses the words "lotus or papyrus" for three-spiked forms with buds. PIERRET speaks of the detailed lotus bouquet of Kadesh (see cut facing) as papyrus,
Panthéon, p. 46. PERROT quotes Plate I. 12 [p. 21], as papyrus, converting the Hathor cow and Horus calf into a "scène de la vie rustique,"*Phénicie*, p. 790. BRUGSCH has mistaken representations of Isis and Horus in the lotus-bower (as in *Description de l'Égypte*, A. i. 63, 4) for Isis and Horus in the papyrus reeds; *Mythologie*, p. 330, *Zweite Ausgabe*. KING has mistaken lotus for papyrus in Cesnola's "*Cyprus*," p. 369. ULRICH KOEHLER has been misadvised as to the "papyrus" on the Mycenæ swords, *Mittheilungen aus Athen*, vol. vii. p. 241.
3. PRISSE D'AVENNES, Text for *Bordures et Soubassements*; Text for *Plantes et Fleurs*, &c., &c.
4. PERROT ET CHIPIEZ, *Égypte*, p. 580.

concede about half-share to the papyrus in the bulk of Egyptian ornament, there is no evidence of a corresponding prominence of the plant in symbolism.

Dr. Henry Brugsch has assumed symbolic meaning with justice for forms supposed to be papyrus which are really lotus (Note 2), and has also connected Horus as hawk with the papyrus (Note 1), when he really stands on a lotus colonette. Papyrus symbolism has not yet been demonstrated from the monuments.

The latter interpretation of Dr. Brugsch is determined by the rendering of a hieroglyphic sign supposed to be papyrus, and all citations by Egyptologists in favour of the papyrus which depend on this reading must be held subject to revision (pp. 53-61). I have no intention of denying that the papyrus was a "sacred plant," for there were many such. Pliny, for instance, cites the papyrus head as having no value unless to crown statues of the gods (Natural History, xiii. 32). But there are many "sacred plants" which have not originated ornamental patterns, and the papyrus is one of them. The Persea tree was sacred to Hathor, the Sycamore to Nut, and the Tamarisk to Osiris (Wilkinson, *Ancient Egyptians*, III., p. 349, 3rd Ed.), but there are no ornamental patterns derived from these plants in Egyptian art. [The "Persea leaf" of an enamel necklace in the British Museum, Fourth Egyptian Room, Case I, is proven a lotus leaf by association (Fig. 18, p. 50, and p. 106).]

13. PAPYRUS. From Nature.
From PERROT, *Egypte*.

The history of Egyptian ornament was undoubtedly ruled by symbolism, but according to decorative sense and decorative adaptabilities. What was more sacred than the form of the scarab, and where can we point to a pattern evolved from the scarab? It appears at best, in natural form, on a few tomb ceilings, &c. The evolution of a decorative pattern is dependent, among other things, on the adaptability of its original natural form to rapid decorative repetition in surface rendering. For, before the days of decorative art theories and South Kensington instruction, the evolution of conventional pattern was a natural and gradual one, and not the result of a theoretic canon. A glance at Fig. 13 of the papyrus will show that it is not an easy subject for repetition in pattern ornament.

In the case of the lotus we can point to myriad forms where the flower was carefully detailed, and to innumerable transitions to the more highly conventional forms, all descended from a time (for there was a first time) when the naturalistic pattern was the only one. If the cave-dwellers of the Stone Age began with realistic art,[5] we cannot doubt that the Egyptians did the same, and the history of their sculpture and of their painting, as far as we can trace it back, is proof that they did.

Let the advocate of papyrus ornament consider the startling fact that no one has pointed to a single realistically detailed picture of the papyrus in Egyptian art. By a realistically detailed picture we must understand one which represents the filaments of the head of the plant, separated one from the other and standing regularly or falling sideway, as the case may be (Fig. 13). To ask for such a picture is making no unreasonable demand of Egyptian art. The long spears of the Egyptian wheat are most carefully represented, individually and separately, in numerous Egyptian pictures, and their separation is not as obvious, and their size is not as great as is the case with the filaments of a head of the papyrus. I do not say that such pictures of the papyrus do not or did not exist but I say that no one has claimed them to exist—no one has published such a picture—and consequently no one has ever attempted to connect the supposed papyrus form of the monuments (Fig. 12) with such a picture.

There are only two even supposed cases of a picture specially devoted to the papyrus in the entire range of Egyptological publication.[6] These supposed cases show the plant in the supposed ultimate conventional stage of rendering (the outlined lotus form). In other words, the papyrus form must have begun at the conventional stage where the lotus ended, for no one has denied that the lotus is rendered by the conventional outline. This is a curious dilemma, considering that the lines of the papyrus head are much more complicated than those of the lotus flower. How does it happen that the lotus has many conventional forms and the papyrus only one? seeing that one-half the ornament in Egypt must be papyrus, if that one form be admitted. In other words, we can trace the evolution of the lotus patterns in

---

5. The frequently quoted prehistoric drawings on bone and ivory, of the mammoth, horse, and wild goat, in the British Museum and Museum of St. Germain, represent the first efforts of design, and are very successful pictures.

6. One is mentioned by PIERRET in his *Dictionnaire d'Archéologie Égyptienne*, under Papyrus, said picture being in ROSELLINI'S *Monumenti Civili*, xxxvi. 3. It is referred to by ROSELLINI (Text, p. 146) as the only picture which represents the harvesting or culture of papyrus, but no text is quoted. I have described this picture in matter which follows, p. 47. The cases where the papyrus is supposed to occur as a landscape accessory will be subsequently considered. The other picture, supposed to represent the manufacture of a papyrus boat, is mentioned at p. 66.

LOTUS FORMS MISTAKEN FOR PAPYRUS.

surviving traditional forms, which represent all stages of treatment, from the purely realistic to the purely conventional; and, in the case of the supposed papyrus patterns which constitute about one-half of Egyptian ornament, as known to us, we cannot point to one case of quoted realistic rendering.

Let us now move to the point that Egyptologists are not familiar with the actual *Cyperus Papyrus*, which is practically unknown, if not extinct, in Egypt. In the exhaustive botany of the "Description de l'Égypte," the author, Délile, was obliged to use a drawing from China for the "Rose Lotus," but he was unable to offer any illustration of the famous papyrus. It is now grown in the fountain basins of New York City, but it has been extremely difficult of access to students of Egyptology. It is mentioned by Pierret as found in Abyssinia; in the isolated region of Lake Menzaleh in the Delta;[7] and as occurring in one or two spots in Syria; and by Parrot as being grown in a few private gardens of Cairo.[8] The stream in which it grows near Syracuse is supposed to be the only well-known access for travellers to the papyrus in a state of nature, but it has been proven that even this access does not exist, and that the Cyperus of the Anapus is not the *Cyperus Papyrus*.[9] According to the usual view it is absolutely extinct in Egypt. Illustrations of it are rare in works on Egypt. The Encyclopædia Britannica and Webster Dictionary

---

7. PIERRET, *Dictionnaire*, &c. But this is doubted by Mr. PERCY E. NEWBERRY (verbal advice).

8. *Égypte*, in the matter on the campaniform capital.

9. "It now only grows in the Anapus near Syracuse, and it is said to have been found in a stream on the coast of Syria."—WILKINSON, *Ancient Egyptians*, II., p. 406, 3rd Ed. WILKINSON to the same effect in RAWLINSON'S *Herodotus*. But this is a mistake according to VICTOR HEHN, *Wanderings of Plants and Animals from their first home*; edited by JAMES STEVEN STALLYBRASS, 1888, p. 233. HEHN says that the Florentine Botanist, Parlatore, "first distinguished between two species of the plant—the old Egyptian papyrus . . . still living in Nubia and Abyssinia, which he calls *Cyperus Papyrus*, and the Sicilian papyrus, growing much taller, spreading at the top into a plume, and not into a cup [*sic*, see pp. 59-61], which was a native of Syria, and to which, therefore, he gives the name of *Cyperus Syriacus*." This plant was introduced at Palermo by the Arabs shortly before 900 A.D., and was not planted at Syracuse till after 1624. "All the specimens in European hot-houses seem to have been procured from Sicily." According to HEHN, the papyrus disappeared from Egypt because it was an exotic there, introduced from the Upper Nile, where it still grows rankly. According to Pliny, quoted by Wilkinson, *Ancient Egyptians*, II. p. 406, 3rd Ed., "the papyrus was not found about Alexandria, because it was not *cultivated* there." The italics are Wilkinson's, who adds that "the necessity of this is shown by Isaiah's mention of the paper reeds by the brooks . . . and everything *sown* by the brooks." In dwelling on the relative rarity of the papyrus, Wilkinson says, "It was particularly cultivated in the Sebennytic Nome (south central portion of the Delta). It is evident that other *Cyperi*, and particularly the *Cyperus Dives*, were sometimes confounded with the *papyrus* or *Byblus hieraticus* of Strabo, and when we read of its being used for mats, sails, baskets, sandals, and other common purposes, we may conclude that this was an inferior kind mentioned by Strabo, and sometimes a common Cyperus which grew wild, as many still do, was thus employed in its stead." WILKINSON also believes that the papyrus was not indigenous to Egypt, and that it was introduced from Nubia.

illustrations are borrowed from Bruce's "Travels" (18th century). Thus we understand that the incorrect specification of papyrus forms in Egyptian ornament is owing partly to ignorance of the plant, partly to a literary celebrity presupposing an unproven frequency in art.

Egyptian surface design in preservation is confined to religious art, as far as pictures go. The tomb paintings which show realistic views are now known to represent the life of the defunct in the spirit world; hence the pictures of trades, husbandry, and natural objects. These paintings are best known in bulk at points remote from the Delta, where the cultivation of the papyrus was especially affected (Note 9). The papyrus requires a marshy ground and water throughout the year. It cannot spring up, like the lotus, in a pool dependent on the inundation; for the roots of the latter plant are known to live in dry ground for a year or two (Note 1, p. 27). If a large number of tomb-pictures were known from the Delta, realistic views of the papyrus might possibly be found; but no tomb-paintings are known from the Delta. Therefore, considering that the palm is a dominant feature of Egyptian landscape, and that pictures of it are extremely rare in tomb-paintings, it is not difficult to understand the present deficiency of pictures of the papyrus as growing in a state of nature.

This deficiency is also explained by the fact that the larger proportion of paintings in which the papyrus might presumably occur as a background or accessory, relate to the procuring of food for the spirit of the defunct (hunting water-fowl, &c.). The supposition that the Egyptians allowed a carefully cultivated exotic (Note 9) to be trampled down in such hunting occupations in real life is highly improbable.

The presumption that the *Cyperus Papyrus* grew wild throughout Egypt like bulrushes and water-reeds is by no means probable in view of the extinction of the plant. It grew plentifully where it was carefully cultivated and tended, like wheat or rye and other cereals, and was doubtless always rare in Egypt in a wild condition (Note 9). In the time of Strabo the cultivation of *Cyperus Papyrus* was a government monopoly.

Rosellini has pointed to the lack of paintings showing the cultivation, reaping, or manufacture of papyrus (Note 6). His solitary supposed illustration of such culture is that of two men carrying bundles of the conventional outline (M.C. xxxvi. 3), but there is no reason why paintings showing the papyrus should not yet be found.

LOTUS FORMS MISTAKEN FOR PAPYRUS.

It may be asked, what then are the plants invariably called papyrus, which are represented as growing in marshes at Beni Hasan (Figs. 14, 15); which are

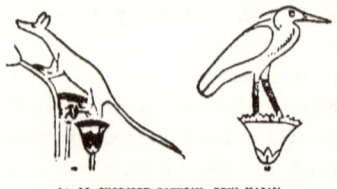

14, 15. SUPPOSED PAPYRUS, BENI HASAN.
From Rosellini.

seen growing in the tomb of Tih, at Sakkara, &c.? At Beni Hasan they are painted green, and are represented with interior lines (although not with separated filaments). At Beni Hasan they are found, moreover, growing beside normal lotuses, which is certainly presumptive evidence that they represent a distinct plant.

The answer is a curious one. As it is decisive for the entire question, I shall naturally reserve it until the more obvious errors and inconsistencies of Egyptology in the matter of the papyrus have been pointed out in the Plate illustrations. Meantime, the cuts adjacent of the plants in question indicate either gross indifference to nature or a supernatural point of view on the part of the designer. The birds and quadrupeds calmly standing on them are impossibilities for either realistic papyrus or lotus.

It is another question why the papyrus does not occur in typical ornament. We can only say that all Egyptian ornament is religious symbolism, and that the papyrus, if it were a religious symbol at all, which remains to be proved (and this is a distinct question from the one of its sacred character), was not a symbol of a sufficiently definite, ancient, and powerful nature to create an ornamental type. As a matter of argument from the standpoint of decorative adaptability, we can appeal to the fact that the scarab, the hawk, the lion, and other symbols did not create an ornamental type. The symbolic asp is, perhaps, the only living form, aside from lotus motives, which became a currently repeated pattern. As for the amulet form, frequently called papyrus, in shape of Fig. 16 (conceiving the hawk as removed and the column as thickened), it is just as frequently called a lotus, is constantly detailed as a lotus, its associations when supporting various gods and divine animals are all explained by the known symbolism of the lotus, and it would be impossible to base an argument for the papyrus on it. The reference of Brugsch to this symbol as papyrus when supporting a hawk, as in Fig. 16, has been noticed (p. 44), but the details, v. 6, 7 [p. 65], have been

16 GOD HORUS ON THE LOTUS COLUMN.

LOTUS FORMS MISTAKEN FOR PAPYRUS.

selected to show that the Sun-hawks on the lotus stelès fully explain the association v. 5. The related amulet is called "lotus" by Maspero.[10]

Considering its deserts, the lotus has been a much-neglected plant, notwithstanding its fame. It has been recently mistaken for "garlic,"[11] for a "branch,"[12] for an "Assyrian tulip,"[13] for a "daisy,"[14] for a "pig-tail,"[15] for "palm fronds,"[16] for a "fan-shaped flower,"[17] for "the branch of a tree,"[18] and for a "triad."[19] Worse than all, it has been confounded with the lotus of the "lotus eaters,"[20] i.e. with the jujube tree, by the author of a book on sun-worship.[21] Grotesque misconceptions of its forms have been entered as realistic pictures in Webster's Dictionary[22] and in a popular history of Egypt.[23] Lotus motives have been mistaken for a "mussel,"[24] for a "bent stick,"[25] for a "knop and flower" pattern,[26] for a "honeysuckle,"[27] for an "egg-and-dart" moulding,[28] for an "ivy leaf,"[29] for a "fleur-de-lys,"[30] for the "silphium plant,"[31] for a "pine-cone,"[32] for

---

10. *Archæology*, translated by Miss Edwards, p. 241 and Fig. 207. "The little lotus-flower column in green fieldspath symbolized the divine gift of eternal youth."

11. MENANT, *Cylindres*, &c., referring to the seal of Sargon. See xxxvi. 4 [p. 247] and p. 175.

12. MENANT, *Cylindres*, &c., referring to Cylinder xliv. 1 [p. 285]. See p. 175.

13. LAYARD's *Discoveries*, p. 184; an error adopted by BABELON in LENORMANT's *Histoire*, &c., v. p. 341.

14. ERNEST BABELON, *Manuel d'Archéologie Orientale*, on the rosette, as "fleur de marguerite," p. 340. DIEULAFOY, as quoted by PERROT, mistakes xx. 1 [p. 153] for a "double marguerite," PERROT ET CHIPIEZ, v. p. 558.

15. SCHUCHARDT, *Schliemann's Ausgrabungen im Lichte der heutigen Wissenschaft*, referring to the Sphinx head, xxxiv. 2 [p. 227]. "Das Haar scheint zum Theil in einen langen Zopf geflochten."

16. SCHLIEMANN's *Mycenæ*, p. 309. FURTWÄNGLER and LOESCHKE, *Mykenische Vasen*, have mistaken "Mycenæ" types, liv. 13, 15 [p. 325], for palms. Text, p. 46, as one instance.

17. F. ADLER's Preface in SCHLIEMANN's *Tiryns*, referring to li. 9 [p. 319].

18. *Gazette Archéologique*, 1888. "En train de brouter un rameau d'arbre," referring to xxxix. 7 [p. 253].

19. See INMAN's *Ancient Pagan and Modern Christian Symbolism*, matter for his Pl. xiii.

20. "The fruit of *Ziziphus lotus*, a small tree that grows in Barbary. This is something like a date or plum in appearance, has a delicious flavour, and the Arabian poets ascribe to it a lethal influence similar to that felt by Homer's *lotophagoi*." Dr. J. S. NEWBERRY, in *Food and Fibre Plants of the North American Indians*, Note to p. 9. See also *Encyclopædia Britannica* (ninth edition), on the "Lotuseaters" and the "Jujube Tree."

21. COX's *Sun Worship*, ii. p. 120.

22. The illustration for "lotus" in WEBSTER's *Dictionary*, specifies the white lotus, but represents the leaves as growing on stems out of water. Compare p. 27.

23. Compare p. 39 and Fig. 11.

24. Compare matter for the Cypriote "boss" (xlvii., xlviii. [p. 303]), with Mycenæ derivative, liii. 2 [p. 323]. Specified as a mussel by FURTWÄNGLER and LOESCHKE, *Mykenische Vasen*, Text, p. 61.

25. Compare liii. 4 [p. 323]; Mycenæ motive from the Cypriote "boss"; specified as a "gebogene Stiele." F. and L. *Myk. Vasen*, p. 59.

26. BIRDWOOD, *Industrial Arts of India*, p. 424.

27. "Honeysuckle" is a current designation for the Greek Anthemion.

28. Compare matter for pl. xxi. [p. 159].

29. Compare matter for pl. xxii. [p. 165].

30. Current designation of the trefoil lotus.

31. MÜLLER, *Numismatique de l'ancienne Afrique*, p. 11, Fig. 17, mistakes four trefoil lotuses for "quatre pousses de silphium."

32. LÉON DE VESLY, in matter for the "egg-and-dart" moulding. See p. 155.

"the Syrian flower" and "Phenician Bouquet,"[33] for "oak leaves and acorns,"[34] for a "Fleuron"[35] &c. When we find an archæologist of the distinction of Longpérier referring to the most familiar lotus border of Egyptian ornament (xxi. 12 [p. 159]) as "a pattern found at Kuyunjik,"[36] we cannot wonder that the lotus has been mistaken for *Nelumbium* and for papyrus.

The argument of Plates iv. [p. 63] and v. [p. 65] is mainly apparent from the descriptions of the pieces as given with the plates. For instance, the papyrus has no leaf, and the cleft leaves of iv. 3 and iv. 7 specify the lotus.

The symbolizing methods which show a lotus leaf supported by the flower, as in Figs. 17, 18, enable us to understand a typical form shown by Plate xi. 7 [p. 107], which has a summary repetition in iv. 5. Therefore iv. 5 designates a lotus.[36A]

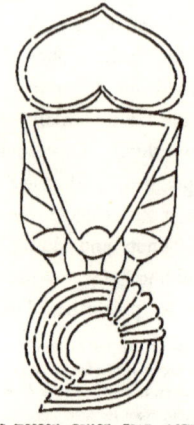

17. WOODEN TOILET TRAY, LOTUS SUPPORTING A LEAF. (Rosellini.)

18. LOTUS SUPPORTING A LEAF. (Prisse.)

Although in nature each bud is supported by a separate stalk, there is a symbolizing method which attaches the bud to the stalk of the flower (iv. 9). Unpublished relief panels in the temple-portico at Denderah, show many cases of Hathor carrying normal lotus flowers with long stems to which buds are attached. Fig. 19 is from a photograph taken for the author. This peculiarity is seen on Cypriote vases at xlvii. 13 [p. 303], and at xlix. 10 [p. 307]. It is seen in Egyptian originals at iv. 12 and iv. 14 [p. 63]. (In the latter example the natural position of the bud is reversed, as frequently found in instances like xi. 7 [p. 107].) Therefore iv. 12 and iv. 14 are proven to be lotuses. We see "tabs" on stems of the normal lotuses iv. 10, and iv. 15, which are thus explained as a conventional remnant of buds. The "tabs" therefore designate as lotuses the so-called papyrus forms iv. 4, iv. 6, iv. 8, and iv. 11. The right-hand stem

33. LUDWIG VON SYBEL, *Weltgeschichte der Kunst*, p. 63, referring to motive ix. 5 [p. 91].

34. PERROT ET CHIPIEZ, vol. v., have published Fig. 88 [p. 129] under this title.

35. DE LUYNES, *Num. et In. Cyp.*, referring to xxxii 5 [p. 223].

36. LONGPÉRIER, in *Musée Napoléon III.*; matter for Rhodian vases. The motive undoubtedly occurs at Kuyunjik, but only because it is the commonest of all Egyptian lotus-borders.

36A. For the peculiar leaf of Fig. 18, with cleft above round base, see foot of p. 106.

LOTUS FORMS MISTAKEN FOR PAPYRUS. 51

of iv. 1 supports a lotus. The two other plants of the same design are specified by the same trait of the tabs.

19. Detail from the temple-portico, Denderah. Isis-Hathor bearing lotus stems with attached buds. Sketch from photograph.

The argument from association is also obvious by comparison of iv. 13 and iv. 16; by comparison of v. 1 with v. 4 [p. 65]; and by comparison of v. 8 with v. 10. The downward broken stems of the buds are the same in both cases. In v. 3 the left asp wears the crown for "the North," and is twined about a form which is supposed to be papyrus as sign for "the North," but the parallel asp of v. 2 with crown for "the North" is twined about a normal lotus, which is thus proven an equivalent variant. The Sun-hawk on the lotus, v. 7 (an association repeated at xliii. 3, 9 [p. 283]), leads by transition through v. 6, where petals and sepals are indicated at the base (in symbolizing fashion), to v. 5, the form supposed by Brugsch to be Horus on the papyrus (Note 1).

This last demonstration solves the question of the campaniform capital (Fig. 20). It has been frequently specified as a lotus, and also stoutly held to be papyrus, notably by Mariette.[37]

20. CAMPANIFORM LOTUS CAPITAL (Karnak). From LEPSIUS, *Denkmäler*.

The goddess Neith (v. 9) holds the staff common to many gods, which is alternately specified as a "papyrus-sceptre" and a "lotus-sceptre," according to the mood or chance attitude of the individual expert; an indecision which is as misleading in result as the constant error would be.

The confusion which has so far made a hopeless riddle of the subject of the lotus and papyrus (so-called) in Egyptology results from inattention to one simple fact, viz. that in solid material the lotus was often represented by a bell-shaped form and frequently without detail.[38] The solid

---

37. Compare PERROT ET CHIPIEZ, *Égypte*, p. 582.
38. Remembering that Egyptian art did not admit of projected relief detail on stone capitals until the Ptolemaic time, it will be obvious that a lotus flower could only be represented in solid stone by a bell-shaped form, and that the same point of view will hold for porcelain.

LOTUS FORMS MISTAKEN FOR PAPYRUS.

bell-shaped form was then copied in surface rendering and became an independent lotus motive in pictorial art. This solid bell-shaped form was the origin of the hieroglyphic which has been mistaken for "papyrus." In other words, the so-called "papyrus" form does not represent a lotus, but it represents a lotus amulet (the word amulet being used without restriction as to size).

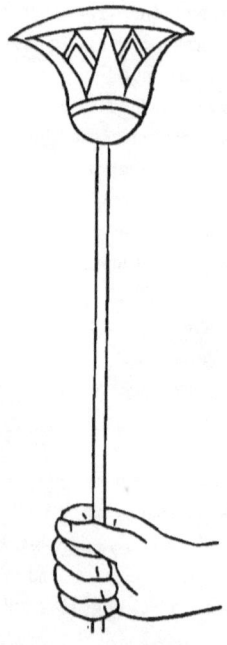

21. Lotus-sceptre held by Isis-Hathor, Denderah. From Author's sketch.

In making this fact obvious we may begin with the object last mentioned by the text, viz. the sceptre. This sceptre may still be seen in solid material in stone statues of Sekhet, and projected in front of the body in high relief. In such cases the sceptre is rarely detailed as a lotus, but a case may be quoted from the Turin Museum where the sceptre is detailed and has been specified by Rossi as a lotus.[39] When the sceptre is transferred to pictorial art, it is also rarely detailed with sepals and petals. We may quote, however, the large reliefs on the outer rear wall of the Hathor temple at Denderah, where the sceptre of Isis is fully detailed as a lotus in at least two cases (Fig. 21).[40]

As regards the colonette amulet and the bell capital in architecture, both are conclusively proven lotuses by the Turin Papyrus numbered 10, which shows the bell-shaped flower *detailed with perpendicular lines* (supposed to represent, at Beni Hasan, the filaments of a papyrus) and connected with a lotus leaf (Fig. 22) and lotus bud.

22. From Turin Papyrus No. 10. So-called papyrus form specified as lotus by the leaf. From Author's sketch.

The same Papyrus shows the bell capital with similar detail (Fig. 23) and the colonette amulet (framed as represented) with exactly similar detail

---

39. "Cinque Statue leontocefale di diorite, rappresentanti ancora la dea Sekhet, che, ritta in piedi, tiene colla mano sinistra appoggiata al seno, lo scettro a fior di loto."— FRANCESCO ROSSI, *I Monumenti Egizi del Museo d'Antichità di Torino*, p. 9.

40. Personal sketch, and also specially photographed.

LOTUS FORMS MISTAKEN FOR PAPYRUS.

(Fig. 24). The head of the Sacred Bark is represented on the same papyrus in the same way (Fig 25).

In the case of the colonette amulet (Figs. 24, 27) the decoration of lotus sepals and petals at the base of the column deserves especial attention, because it has been confounded by Wilkinson, by Owen Jones, and by various other writers and observers, including botanists, with the enveloping leaves sheathing the base of a papyrus stalk.

23. From Turin Papyrus No. 10. Bell capital specified as a lotus by Fig. 22, same Papyrus. From Author's sketch.

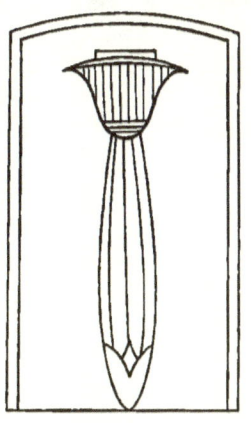

24. From Turin Papyrus No. 10. Colonette Amulet (so-called papyrus) specified as a lotus by Fig. 22, same Papyrus. From Author's sketch.

The hieroglyphic form called papyrus is a direct copy of the form of Fig. 24. It appears, for example, in large dimension among the hieroglyphics in the tomb of Rahotep, at Maydoum (IIIrd or IVth Dynasty) as an accurately represented lotus colonette or lotus column of the same shape (Fig. 26), with the distinction that it shows, instead of perpendicular lines on the flower, a sheath of lotus sepals and lotus petals at the base of the flower (as in Fig. 23). As this sheath of sepals and petals has been confounded with an imitation of the sheath at the base of the papyrus head, it is necessary to insist on the fact that lotus detail in Egyptian art frequently deviates from nature on this point by a conventional method, which presents the sepals and petals as rising only to some intermediate point between the top of the flower and its base (Figs. 28, 29). In Fig. 27 we have the hieroglyph from a Theban Tomb (Tomb No. 6, Tombs of the Kings), which also shows the derivation from a colonette original (compare Fig. 24).

25. From Turin Papyrus No. 10. Head of the Sacred Bark, so-called papyrus form specified as a lotus by Fig. 22, same Papyrus. From Author's sketch.

Insisting on the fact that Figs. 22, 23, 24, and 25 are all from one Turin Papyrus, we now recur to the point that the original so-called papyrus form was a bell-shaped lotus in solid material, an amulet column or colonette. The proof lies in the outline representation of a solid top which all these figures show by the upper double curve, viz. 22, 23, 24, 25. Compare Fig. 23 with Fig. 22. Therefore it appears that the outline lotus (Fig. 22) belongs to a class of pictures which first represented a solid form.

We have next to consider the colour by which this lotus amulet is generally represented, either in pictures of unmistakably solid forms (for instance, architecture, Figs. 28, 29), or in surface designs which are hence derived. This colour is green generally, with red or yellow top line and red or yellow petal sheath.

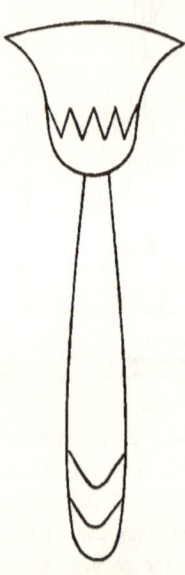

26. Hieroglyphic in Ra-hotep's tomb, Maydoum. From Author's sketch. So-called papyrus, specified as lotus by Fig. 24. Coloured green, with black outline and red detail.

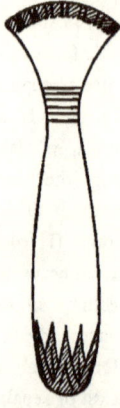

27. Hieroglyphic, Tombs of of the Kings. From Author's sketch. So-called papyrus, specified as a lotus by Fig. 24. Coloured green, top and lower detail yellow, with red lines.

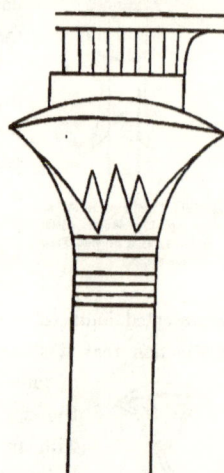

28. From Turin Papyrus No. 51. Lotus capital, coloured green, with red top. From Author's sketch. Compare Fig. 23.

The pictures of Turin Papyrus No. 10 are without colour, but there are many Turin Papyri with pictures of lotuses which are green throughout and fully detailed with sepals and petals. It is not surprising, therefore, that in the Turin Papyri we also find the lotus bell capital detailed with green body, dark green perpendicular lines, red top line, and yellow petal sheath. These are the colours of Fig. 28, from the Turin Papyrus numbered 51, and of Fig. 29, from the Turin Papyrus numbered 7.

LOTUS FORMS MISTAKEN FOR PAPYRUS.

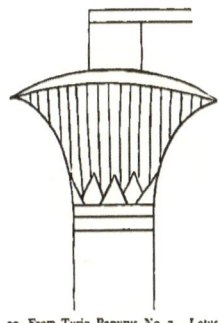

29. From Turin Papyrus No. 7. Lotus capital, coloured green, with red top and yellow petal sheath. From Author's sketch. Compare Fig. 23.

Such green lotuses, with red or yellow (or also red *and* yellow) top and red or pink petal sheath at the base of the outlined flower, are also common in the Theban tomb bouquets which have done so much to confuse the study of Egyptian botany from the monuments. Fig. 30 represents a photograph of such coloured flowers from the Tombs of the Kings (Ramesid Tomb No. 6, XXth Dyn.). The flowers are specified as lotus by the leaves placed over them (compare Figs. 17, 18), and by a variant form of the leaf (like Plate iii., type 2, p. 41) attached to the stem.[41]

That we are dealing here with pictures derived from solid forms actually existing as ceremonial amulet staves is apparent from the following observations. In Theban tombs and in the reliefs of Dehr-el-Bahri we constantly find figures bearing a lotus staff, to which artificial lotus leaves or lotus buds are attached. Figs. 31 and 32 are from sketches made by me in a Theban tomb at Abd-el-Kourneh (Tomb 125). In the more carefully detailed reliefs of ceremonial processions at Dehr-el-Bahri, it is apparent, as here, that a ceremonial staff, and not a natural plant, is represented. This point is accentuated by the fact that naturally detailed lotus flowers with pliant bending stems are frequently held in one hand, and conventional forms on a straight staff in the other (Fig. 31).[42]

41. This form is natural to young leaves, as first made known to me by Mr. Percy E. Newberry. At p. 31 I have erroneously referred to such pointed leaves as an Egyptian conventional departure from nature. Compare xi. 2 [p. 107].

42. The development of the "tabs" (Plate iv. [p. 63]) is

30. Lotuses from Tombs of the Kings, Thebes, supporting leaves (compare Figs. 17, 18) and with leaves attached to the stem. The flowers are green with yellow top, crossed with red lines. The upper leaves are coloured in the same way, lower leaves blue. From photograph for the Author.

LOTUS FORMS MISTAKEN FOR PAPYRUS.

The hieroglyph now denominated "papyrus" (Figs. 26 and 27) has the significance "to be green, fresh," also "to despatch, deliver over, to give,"[42] and its colour is green in Figs. 26 and 27, with red (or red and yellow) detail. Whether the original form was the blue-green porcelain amulet now known in Museums,[44] and the colour is thence derived, or whether the solid form in other materials was painted green for decorative or for hieratic reasons, is of course not for me to say,[45] but it has already been noted that normal lotuses are very frequently painted green throughout, in Papyri exhibited at Turin, and it has been shown that details like Figs. 28 and 29 are habitually painted green, and that they are demonstrated by the Turin Papyrus No. 10 to be lotuses.

As regards the hieroglyphic, we now recur to the evidence that the sign for "the North," although called a "papyrus,"

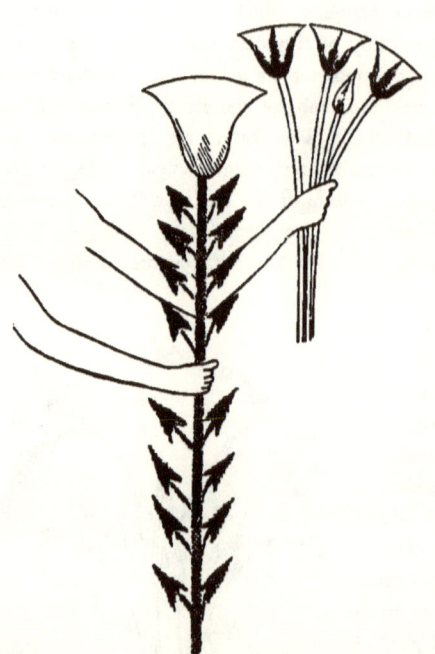

31. From Author's sketch in Tomb No. 125, Abd-el-Kourneh. The staff is green with pink sepals. The bouquet has green sepals, white spaces, and yellow tops.

thus explained as being from leaves as well as from buds, and can be demonstrated in Theban tombs from paintings which show a hurried and careless or off-hand representation of these ceremonial forms, as for instance in Fig. 32. The ceremonial lotus staff with attached artificial leaves, as in Fig. 31, has been mistaken by Wilkinson for "Convolvulus."

43. BRUGSCH, *Mythologie*, Zweite Ausgabe, p. 314. "Syllabarisches Schriftzeichen, welches *ut* lautet und die Grundbedeutungen eines Verbalstammes in sich schliesst; "grün, frisch sein" und "entsenden, überliefern, spenden."

And p. 328. "Man legte dem worte *ut* die darin enthaltene Nebenbedeutung von *grün sein, grünen*, unter; mit besonderer Anwendung auf das frische Grün der Pflanzenwelt im Frühjahr."

44. Sometimes of very large dimensions, as in the Polytechnic at Athens—colonette supporting the head of a hawk.

45. BRUGSCH, *Mythologie*, Zweite Ausgabe, p. 325. "The colours white, yellow, green, blue, red, and black, in cases of the dominant colour of deities and sacred animals, of sun and moon, were not chosen haphazard, but

LOTUS FORMS MISTAKEN FOR PAPYRUS.

can be proven a lotus variant by the evidence of v. 2 [p. 65] as compared with v. 3. On the rear exterior wall of the Hathor temple at Denderah there is also found the asp with crown for "the North" (Fig. 33), twined about a normal lotus, and facing an asp with crown for "the South" on the opposite end of the same wall, twined about a trefoil lotus.[46] The sign for "the North" was held to be a lotus by Champollion.[47]

32. From Author's sketch in Tomb No. 125, Abd-el-Kourneh. The bouquet is green with yellow tops, crossed with red bars. The tabs are derived from lotus buds; compare Fig. 19.

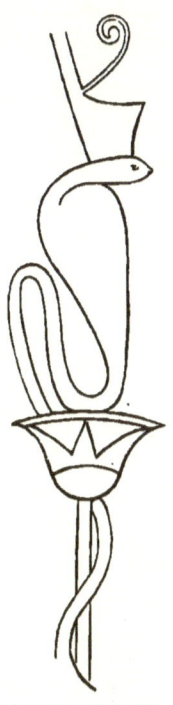

33. Asp with crown for "the North," resting on a lotus as sign for "the North." Denderah. From Author's sketch.

We are now able to move to the curious conclusion that as early as the IIIrd or IVth Dynasty the amulet form had been transplanted to the world of nature and represented as an actual living growth. In the tomb of Ra-hotep at Maydoum, where the hieroglyph, Fig. 26, is found, we may also see, on the opposite wall, a picture of a fisherman seated under a group of plants, of which Fig. 34 represents a detail. The body of the flower is green, the outline is black, and the sheath of petals at the base is red (compare colours of Fig. 26). Thus is solved the problem of the supposed papyrus marshes at Beni Hasan (Figs. 14, 15)

---

according to the symbolic significance which the Egyptians were accustomed to attribute to each colour, ... the idea of joy was connected with white and green."

46. To this evidence we may add two cases of the current representation of "water-plants" on either side of the god Nilus, or as independent bouquets, these "water-plants" are supposed to be papyrus and lotus respectively, as signs for "the North" and "the South." On the granite Naos, facing the entrance of the Florence Egyptian Collection, the gods Nilus both hold stems with the supposed papyrus forms, showing that one and, consequently, both are lotus variants. The same fact may be observed for the plants on a throne of Isis-Hathor at Denderah (west exterior wall).

47. *Panthéon Égyptien.* Matter for Pl. vii. b. "Le bouquet de lotus, formant l'emblème d'Égypte inférieure, est ici d'une couleur et d'une espèce qui diffèrent assez

and at Sakkara. For the spirit world, at least, the Egyptian represented his lotus amulets as actually growing plants. As his tomb-paintings always represent the spirit world, it is impossible for us to say whether he would have committed, or did commit, this absurdity in realistic art—impossible to say—because it remains to be proven that the Eygptian ever had a realistic art.

It would apparently result from the foregoing matter that the papyrus is unknown to Egyptian Art, but this I think is not the case. I think it is clear that realistic pictures of growing papyrus have not yet been pointed out in publication, that the conventional outline form is derived from the lotus, that the campaniform capital, the sceptre, and the hieroglyph, all represent the lotus—but it does not follow that the papyrus does not occur because it has not yet been specified correctly. I have said that papyrus symbolism has not yet been demonstrated from the monuments, but I think that it can be demonstrated.

I have quoted at Note 9, p. 46, a reference from the English translation of Hehn's "Wanderings of Plants and Animals" to the studies of the Florentine Botanist Parlatore. The translation is somewhat inadequate, and Hehn himself has scarcely succeeded in explaining the point made by Parlatore. The edition of Stallybrass says—as quoted by Note 9—that Parlatore "first distinguished between two species of the plant—the old Egyptian papyrus still living in Nubia and Abyssinia, which he calls *Cyperus Papyrus*, and the Sicilian papyrus growing much taller, spreading at the top into a plume and not into a cup, which was a native of Syria," &c. In this

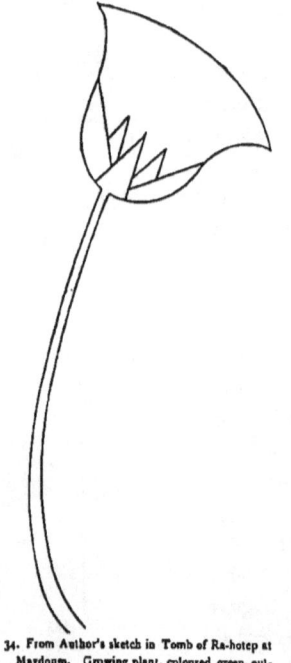

34. From Author's sketch in Tomb of Ra-hotep at Maydoom. Growing plant, coloured green, outline black, detail red.

essentiellement de celui qui exprime la même idée dans la planche précédente; mais différence d'espèce et de forme, soit de la plante, soit de la fleur seulement, ne porte aucune espèce de modification dans le sens de ces groupes. J'ai eu une foule d'occasions de me convaincre de leur parfaite identité."

translation the word "cup" especially attracted my attention as being an impossible word for any supposable meaning and as being an undoubted translation from the German "Kelch," which sometimes means "cup" and sometimes means a calyx. I therefore had recourse to the original German, which used the word "Kelch," as I had expected, and which is not especially successful in explaining Parlatore's meaning, but which had the great merit of furnishing the reference to his publication. This is omitted by the English edition, which is professedly an abridgment in matters of detail.

Parlatore's publication was made in the "Mémoires" of the Paris "Académie des Sciences" for 1854 (Vol. XII.). As an Italian botanist it was naturally his duty to study the Sicilian papyrus, hence his publication. Parlatore's point is entirely obscured by the English translation of Hehn. It is the head of the papyrus now growing on the Upper Nile, which is a plume (neither the word "cup" or "Kelch" would carry this meaning), and he shows that this plume is either erect or a plume drooping in one direction (generally the latter), and never umbelliferous or spreading. Parlatore shows that the head of the Sicilian papyrus is spreading and umbelliferous and not a plume. To make this point clear he publishes a picture of the Sicilian papyrus. This picture corresponds to the plant at Kew and to Fig. 13 (borrowed from Perrot). Beside this picture he places the one, made by Bruce in the eighteenth century, of the *Cyperus Papyrus*, which also appears in the Encyclopædia Britannica and in Webster's Dictionary, together with a drawing expressly forwarded to him by a friend on the Upper Nile. The latter is a schematic view of the erect plume of the *Cyperus Papyrus;* the former shows the bending plume, with all filaments pendant to one side (and not umbelliferous) as it generally appears in nature.

We shall now observe that, according to Parlatore, there was only one correct original picture of the true papyrus in existence, down to 1854, viz., the one made by Bruce in the eighteenth century. Since 1854, Parlatore's investigations have been apparently unknown to persons treating on the papyrus in Egyptian Art, who have been misled by the *Cyperus Syriacus* of Sicily, and who have all proceeded on the assumption that the head of the *Cyperus Papyrus* is umbelliferous, whereas it is not. Granted that the head of the *Cyperus Papyrus* is not umbelliferous, the entire argument for the conventional outline as a naturalistic *Cyperus Papyrus* fails to the ground.

I shall now return to the point that the papyrus is probably not unknown to Egyptian art, and probably not unknown to Egyptian symbolism on the monuments. The only difficulty has been that the conventional outline has so abundantly supplied the sentimental demand for a papyrus in Egyptian art that the true plant has been overlooked.

Fig. 35 is from a sketch of a picture in the Turin Papyrus, No. 10—Sebak before an altar surmounted by a lotus. He holds a plant which corresponds to Parlatore's schematic illustration for the *Cyperus Papyrus*.

Pliny says, after enumerating various uses of the papyrus, that its head had no value except to crown the statues of the gods (p. 44). Now on most of the altars of offerings of the Old Empire, which are represented by reliefs in the Gizeh Museum, there is a representation of a plant which corresponds to the plume of the *Cyperus Papyrus*, as it would appear when laid sideways on such objects. In the New Empire this representation has become more schematic (Fig. 36). According to my view, here is the true papyrus. A similar representation is also found erect (Fig. 36), and will pass for a schematic representation of a plume, handed down by tradition and conventionalized. Such plumes occur frequently with the lotus as associated with statues of Khem and in other ways, and they appear sometimes with and sometimes without detail.

35. SEBAK HOLDING THE TRUE CYPERUS PAPYRUS before an altar crowned by the lotus. From Author's sketch of a picture in the Turin Papyrus, No. 10.

36. Photograph from an Altar of Offerings at Dehr-el-Bahri, with a conventional papyrus plume laid on the altar and another erect beside it.

LOTUS FORMS MISTAKEN FOR PAPYRUS.

For the latter case see iv. 13, where these forms appear to be buds, but really are not. According to this view the papyrus should be classed with the Persea Tree as occurring frequently in Egyptian symbolic art.

But there is still a point to be made on this difficult topic. It appears from the Greek text of the decree of Canopus, as made known to me by Professor R. S. Poole, that the Greeks of the Alexandrine Period compared the sceptre of the goddesses to a papyrus. This makes it possible that the Egyptians themselves had occasionally mistaken their amulet form (also when represented as a growing plant) for papyrus. That the sceptre was really a lotus is proven by Fig. 21, and by the relation of the hieroglyphic form to the lotus (Figs. 22, 24, 26, 27). The mistake will be more comprehensible if we remember that the *Cyperus Papyrus* was not the only *Cyperus* that grew in Egypt. The Sicilian papyrus was brought from Syria by the Arabs, but there is every likelihood that it once grew in Egypt. Inferior kinds of papyrus are mentioned by ancient authors (p. 46, Note 9), and we have no grounds for assuming that they were not also sacred plants. The umbelliferous shape of the head of the *Cyperus Syriacus* may have been compared to the shape of the sceptre, or confused with it, as it has been by the moderns. It is clear from the Decree of Canopus that the comparison was made by the Greeks. Their mistakes in such matters were so numerous that the point is not serious.

The authorities at Kew have classed the Sicilian and Syrian species with that of the Upper Nile, and their growing specimen is from Syria. The distinction pointed out by Parlatore may not warrant the creation of a new botanical species, but it is quite sufficient to cast one more stumbling block in the way of those who consider the conventional outline a papyrus. It also assists, according to my view, the specification of papyrus forms which have been overlooked. Not wishing to debate a question of Botany, I have borrowed the illustration of Perrot, but the true papyrus of the Nile appears to be more correctly represented by the Encyclopædia Britannica, and by Webster's Dictionary.

PLATE IV.

LOTUS FORMS MISTAKEN FOR PAPYRUS.*

1. Typical forms; showing lotus stems with tabs derived from lotus buds. Cows (Hathor) and the lotus. Detail of a painted vase, from PRISSE D'AVENNES, *Amphores, Jarres, et autres Vases.*

2, 3. Typical associated decorative details, showing the so-called papyrus form, but having lotus leaves. Detail from Esneh. *Description de l'Égypte,* A. I. 85.

4. Typical detail, showing lotus stems with tabs derived from buds. Hathor (the cow) and the lotus. From PIERRET, *Panthéon Égyptien,* p. 42.

5. Typical lotus forms (so-called papyrus), supporting leaves of the lotus partly concealed by the flower. (Compare XI. 7 [p. 107], and Figs. 17, 18.) From LEPSIUS, *Denkmäler,* VIII., 3, 244.

6. Typical so-called papyrus, showing tabs derived from lotus buds. Decorative detail from ROSELLINI, M.C., LXXXIII.

7. Typical so-called papyrus, with lotus leaf. Detail from Tell-el-Amarna, XVIIIth Dyn. PRISSE D'AVENNES, *Offrandes au Soleil.*

8. Phenician seal, showing so-called papyrus form, with tabs derived from lotus buds. From CESNOLA, *Cyprus,* KING'S Appendix for Gems, XXXI. 11.

9. Lotus, with buds attached to stem of flower; a conventional symbolism, contrary to nature, and explaining the tabs previously illustrated. Detail from a Cypriote vase in New York. Compare Plates xlv. 13 [p. 287]; xlvii. 13 [p. 303], and xlix. 10 [p. 307].

10. Typical Egyptian detail, showing lotus with tabs as above explained. From NAVILLE, *Todtenbuch,* LXXII., A. 10.

11. Typical Egyptian detail, showing a so-called papyrus form, which is specified as lotus by the tabs. From an Egyptian vase in the New York Museum, Maspero Collection.

12. Typical Egyptian detail, showing so-called papyrus form, with lotus buds attached to the stem. The buds are reversed; a common decorative arrangement, as in Plate xi. 7 [p. 107]. From PRISSE D'AVENNES, *Amphores, &c.*

13. God Khem, with lotus crowning a shrine. To be compared with No. 16. Detail from CHAMPOLLION, IV., cccxlviii.

14. Mummy, with lotus, having buds on the stem (to illustrate origin of the tabs). Detail of a stone sarcophagus from P. Q. VISCONTI, *Collection of Egyptian Antiquities, Property of G. Athanasi,* XV.

15. Lotus with tabs. Detail from a Cypriote vase in New York.

16. God Khem, with lotus (so-called papyrus form), crowning a shrine. Compare No. 13. Detail from ROSELLINI, M.d.C., XLI.

---

* This heading specifies the argument of the plate rather than all its individual examples.

Pl. IV., p. 63.

PLATE V.

LOTUS FORMS MISTAKEN FOR PAPYRUS.*

1. The Genii of Amenti, on the lotus. Compare No. 4. Detail from ROSELLINI, M.C., CXXXV. 2.

2. The asp and the lotus, in two forms. The asp on the left wears the crown for "the North." Compare No. 3. Detail from Thebes, XVIIIth Dyn. PRISSE D'AVENNES, *Piliers Isiaques.*

3. The asp and the lotus, in two forms. The asp on the left wears the crown for "the North," and rests on the form now held to be "papyrus" as hieroglyph for "the North." Time of Trajan. Compare No. 2. Detail from PRISSE D'AVENNES, *Décoration de la niche de l'Emisi.*

4. The Genii of Amenti, on the lotus. Compare No. 1. From MARIETTE, *Album du Musée de Boulaq,* XIII.

5. Sun-hawk on the so-called papyrus stelè. Compare Nos. 6 and 7. From ROSELLINI, M.D.C, XXI., 11.

6. Sun-hawk on the lotus. Compare Nos. 5 and 7. Detail from PRISSE D'AVENNES, *Monuments,* XXXI. (*Petit édifice de Tahraka.*)

7. Sun-hawk on the lotus. Compare Nos. 5 and 6. Detail from MARIETTE, *Dendérah,* II., 44. Additional illustrations, xliii. 3, 9 [p. 283]. See also list of unpublished monuments, p. 24.

8 and 10. Alternating decorative details, showing lotus buds in each design. Ptolemaic or Roman. From PRISSE D'AVENNES, *Bases et Soubassements.*

9. Goddess Neith, with so-called "papyrus-sceptre." Edfou. From the *Description de l'Égypte,* A. III. cxxxvii. 4.

---

* This heading specifies the argument of the plate rather than its individual pieces.

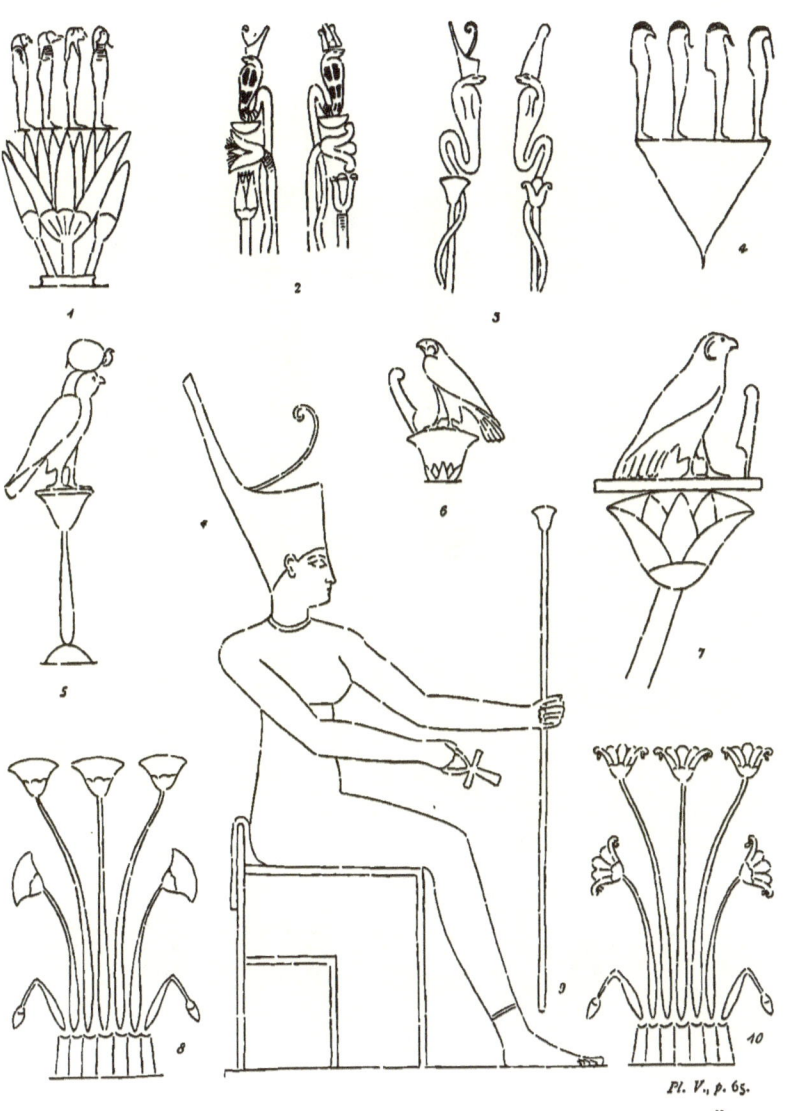

Pl. V., p. 65.

APPENDIX.

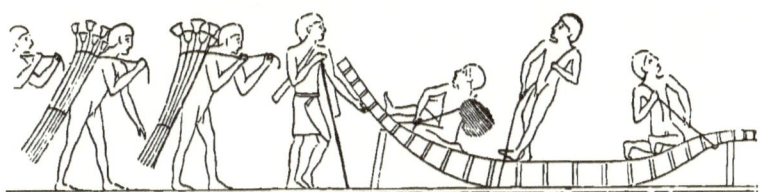

37. Picture in Lepsius, *Denkmäler* (Ab. II. 12), supposed by Wilkinson to represent making a boat of papyrus.

FINALLY we have to mention the problem of the picture from Lepsius, Denkmäler (Fig. 37), which is supposed to represent the making of a papyrus boat. I have never seen an Egyptian fresco with the plant form which is carried by these figures which was without detail. On this point the picture is undoubtedly inexact, and the small size of the copy would excuse this lapse by an artist trained to believe that the conventional outline represents papyrus. The tombs opened by Lepsius near the Pyramids and by Mariette at Sakkara, have been mostly sanded up or ruined. This picture is no longer accessible. It undoubtedly complicates the problem. It leads us to ask whether the lotus may not have been occasionally used to represent water-plants in general. The decision of this question is outside my jurisdiction. It is sufficient for me to have proven that all the forms which have been hitherto called papyrus are lotuses in derivation, in association, and in ordinary symbolic use. Baedeker's "Egypt" mentions a picture of the culture of papyrus in the tomb of Ptah-hotep, at Sakkara. This tomb is now sanded up. I offered a large sum of money to the Scheik at Sakkara to have it opened, but without success.

38. Demonstration for the hieroglyph called papyrus as being a lotus, by association with the leaf. From Birch, *Antiquities in the British Museum*. Plate 32.

39. So-called papyrus supporting a lotus bud inverted (compare Fig. 45, p. 73). From Prisse d'Avennes.

39A. Lotuses of the IVth Dynasty (to compare with Fig. 39B). From Prisse d'Avennes.

39B. Conventional outlines of the XVIIIth Dynasty (to compare with Fig. 39A). From Prisse d'Avennes.

EGYPTIAN LOTUS CAPITALS.

(PLATE VI., PAGE 69.)

THE types illustrated by Plate vi. are those familiar to all students. Type vi. 3 is intended to indicate and include the campaniform capital of heavier proportions (Fig. 20). We have seen that this capital, which is still in debate as regards the motive, must be positively assigned to the lotus. The decorative petals and sepals of Fig. 20 and of vi. 3 deserve attention because similar ornament at the bases of columns (lix. 1, 6, 12, 15 [p. 345]) has been ascribed to imitation of the sheathing leaves at the base of the papyrus stalk,[1] and also because it has been mistaken for an indication of lotus sepals from a realistic point of view.[2] The fact is, as may be seen by reference to lix. 1, 6, 12, 15, that this ornament does not relate in Fig. 20 (or vi. 3) to a naturalistic conception of an individual flower, for in this case the representation would be as in the lower member of vi. 6. The representation of sepals and petals, or of petals alone, or of sepals alone, grew into a running ornament of successive overlapping triangles which is used by the decorator without reference to naturalism. Thus we understand the surface ornament of the middle member of vi. 6. The form of this member will be explained by the next Plate. The upper member is a lotus form like vi. 3, and having a similar ornament of overlapping sepal triangles.

The capital vi. 5 has been correctly specified by Reber,[3] but its relation to vi. 4 (a bundle of lotus buds) as a conventional derivative has been generally overlooked.

The types of Plate vi. indicate fairly all those in general use, as known by surviving examples, down to the Persian Conquest about 525 B.C., assuming that the three members of vi. 6 may also be taken to represent distinct capitals. One capital clearly distinct from those illustrated, in earlier use, is that with the heads of the goddess Hathor, as indicated by i. 7 [p. 21]. This capital is mainly

---

1. By OWEN JONES, *Grammar of Ornament*, Pls. for Egyptian ornament, and by many others.
2. DIEULAFOY. See Notes 8, 9, p. 72.
3. *History of Ancient Art*, translated by JOSEPH THACHER CLARKE; Harper & Bros., N.Y.

distinctive for the Greco-Roman time, and is only found in exceptional cases at an earlier date. It appears therefore that the colonnade architecture of ancient Egypt was one of lotus columns and lotus capitals, whose symbolical relation to the national cult has been explained. From translations of Professor Maspero[4] it appears that the word for lotus indicates an architectural capital when reference to architecture is in question.

4. In *Histoire Ancienne des Peuples de l'Orient.*

PLATE VI.

EGYPTIAN LOTUS CAPITALS.

1. Typical lotus capital in wood, from a tomb-painting. PRISSE D'AVENNES, *Constructions en Bois.* Similar capitals under the IVth Dyn.

2. Typical lotus bud capital in wood, from a tomb-painting. PRISSE D'AVENNES, *Constructions en Bois.*

3. Typical campaniform lotus capital. Detail in stone relief, Karnak. From PRISSE D'AVENNES, *Piliers, Thothmes III.*

4. Typical lotus capital, representing buds bound together. Beni Hasan, XIIth Dyn. From CHIPIEZ, *Histoire des Ordres Grecs.*

5. Typical lotus capital (type under the XVIIIth and XIXth Dyns.); derived from the foregoing type. Detail from PRISSE D'AVENNES, *Temple de Menephtehum.*

6. Typical combination capital, of the description shown by tomb-paintings; which, being of wood and metal, have no surviving examples. From PRISSE D'AVENNES, *Colonettes en Bois.*

7. Typical lotus bud capital; same reference as No. 5.

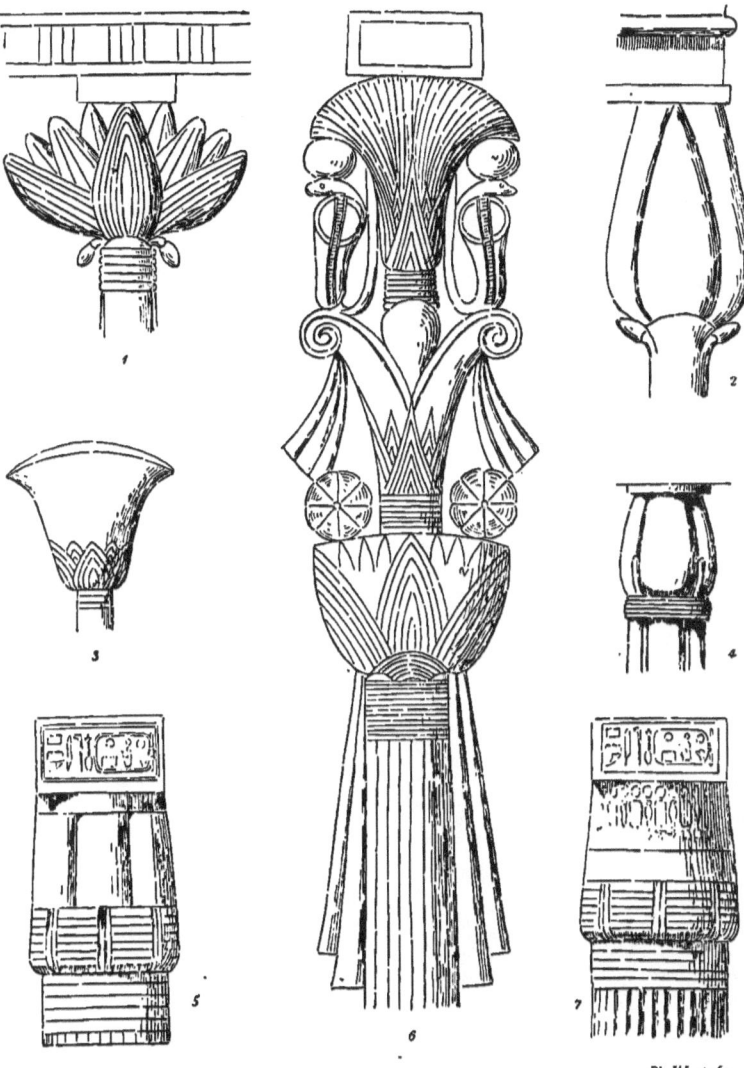

Pl. VI., p. 69.

EGYPTIAN LOTUS IONIC FORMS.

(PLATE VII., PAGE 79.)

An Ionic capital is generally presumed to have the form of Fig. 41, with volutes joined at the top by connecting lines, which in the best Greek examples have a slight downward bend towards their centre, but this depression is attributed to a delicate Greek preference for the curving line as more graceful than one which

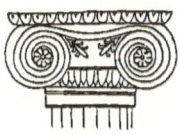

41. GREEK IONIC CAPITAL.

is straight. According to present views of the Ionic capital, the lines which join the spirals are in principle straight lines, and the original and typical form is supposed to have adhered to them, as nearly as the sentiment of beauty would allow.[1] Although the upper member of vii. 5 is so far in harmony with the type of the Greek Ionic, and is Egyptian art of the fourteenth century B.C.,[2] there has been no disposition on the part of authorities who have published similar capitals[3] to connect them with the Greek Ionic, which offers no dated examples of earlier time than the sixth century B.C.

The first published announcement of the Ionic capital as a lotus was made by the French archæologist, Georges Colonna-Ceccaldi, in 1875,[4] and he again

42. CYPRIOTE IONIC CAPITAL.

43. CYPRIOTE TOMBSTONE (Golgoi).

44. CYPRIOTE IONIC CAPITAL.

recurred to this point in 1877.[5] His references to the matter, made in essays

1. Otto Puchstein, *Das Ionische Capitell; Siebenundvierzigstes Programm zum Winckelmannsfeste der Archæologischen Gesellschaft zu Berlin.* Berlin, Reimer, 1887.

2. It dates from Menephthah, son of Ramses II.

3. A similar capital in Perrot et Chipiez, *Égypte*,

who adhere to the generally accepted view that the Ionic capital has an Assyrian origin (Fig. 317).

4. *Revue Archéologique*, vol. xxix. p. 24, 1875. Republished posthumously in *Monuments Antiques de Chypre.*

5. *Revue Archéologique*, vol. xxxiii. p. 176, 1877. Republished posthumously in *Monuments Antiques de Chypre.*

devoted to other subjects, were brief but positive. Although they related to a Cypriote tombstone (Fig. 43) and to Cypriote Ionic capitals (Figs. 42, 44), the universal assumption of archæology that any lotus motive points to an Egyptian origin, was undoubtedly present in his mind. As he makes no reference to Egyptian examples, it is uncertain whether he conceived the evolution of the Ionic form itself to have taken place in Egypt. Colonna-Ceccaldi, whose first reference was to the tombstone, Fig. 43, specified the volutes as representing curling petals, the central triangle as representing the ovary, and the upper introrse scrolls as representing stamens.

A specific reference to Egyptian Ionic forms was made by Hans Auer in 1880.[6] Sir Gardner Wilkinson published a detail resembling vii. 7, as original of the Greek Ionic, in 1857.[7] Neither author specified the Ionic form as lotus; but Wilkinson called it a "water-plant."

In 1885 Marcel Dieulafoy made the first systematic effort to connect the volutes of Egyptian lotus capitals with the volutes of the Greek Ionic, by way of appeal to details of Assyrian ivories, and to the intermediate Cypriote connecting links, tombstones and capitals, already specified as lotuses by Colonna-Ceccaldi.[8] The normal form taken as point of departure by Dieulafoy is the Karnak example, vii. 6, whose volutes he conceived to be petals curling downward under pressure, while the central intermediate member was supposed by him to represent the ovary.[9] The highly important examples, vii. 8, 9, are borrowed from his book. Without debating the interpretation of M. Dieulafoy in detail, it is sufficient to say that he was undoubtedly correct in his results, and fortunate in his citation of examples. However the lotus volute originated, it is clearly one aspect of the Egyptian lotus form. We can trace it from the slight decorative bend of the supposed papyrus form, as in iv. 5 [p. 63], or in the more definite bend of iii. 4 [p. 41], to examples like vii. 2, 3, 7 on the one hand, or examples like vii. 1, 4, 6, 9, 10 on the other.

Plate ix. 5 [p. 91] shows a case of an inverted bud between the two volutes, which finds many other illustrations in the monuments (see xi. 2, 3 [p. 107], and

6. *Zeitschrift für bildende Kunst*, 1880, No. 10; in important essays devoted to the Egyptian Proto-Doric Triglyphs.
7. *The Egyptians in the time of the Pharaohs* (published for the Crystal Palace Company), p. 157.
8. *L'Art Antique de la Perse*, IIIième *Partie*, pp. 34-55.

9. "En posant au-dessus de la fleur un abaque rectangulaire, les pétales s'écrasèrent, se retournèrent légèrement sur eux-mêmes et laisseront apercevoir, en s'ouvrant, l'ovaire placé au centre de leur corolle. Entre le corolle et la tige se distinguaient les enveloppes foliacées du calice."

EGYPTIAN LOTUS IONIC FORMS.

Fig. 45), and it is not certain whether the analogous intermediate member in vii. 1, 4, 6, 9 is always thus explained, or whether we have sometimes a reminiscence of the form iii. 4 [p. 41] in this member. I am obliged, at all events, to reject the suggestion that this central member represents an ovary, with all deference to M. Dieulafoy. Such an explanation would oblige us to assume an artificially manufactured conventional form, in which a cleft was introduced to show in a figurative way an interior portion of the flower. Taking, for the moment, vii. 4 as type of this supposed artificial presentation, it would be comparable in such a case to a modern botanical model showing partly the exterior sides and partly an interior central section of the flower, and a botanical model which would be incorrect, because the ovary of the white and blue lotus lies at their base. Now the Egyptian art constantly shows symbolizing associations of different entire portions of the lotus plant, for instance, a flower supporting a leaf (Figs. 17, 18), but it never indulges in artificial and figurative botanical sections. It shows the ovary, for example, by a rosette, i.e. by an actual picture of the ovary as seen from above (Figs. 5, 6, 8). We must consider the conventional lotus forms as decorative evolutions, not as ready-made artificial inventions. For the trefoil forms of Plate vii., we have already found a clear explanation in the three-spiked form emphasizing the sepals (Figs. 2, 3, and Plate iii.), and as especially illustrated by iii. 1, 4. As the central member of the conventional lotus trefoil is sometimes displaced by an inverted bud (Fig. 45), it is not possible to decide in all cases which is intended, but it is always one of the two.

45. EGYPTIAN IONIC LOTUS SUPPORTING AN INVERTED BUD.

We have, then, two phases of Egyptian lotus Ionic forms and volutes, one showing a straight or convex connecting line, as in vii. 5, 2, 3; the other showing more highly developed volutes rising from a cleft centre, as in vii. 1, 4, 10. An intermediate form, with developed volutes and a convex connecting line (like the Ionic of Bassæ), vii. 7, is an isolated and rare example, but undoubtedly based on an architectural model. It is probable that the forms which relate to the so-called papyrus form, vii. 2, 3, are decorative exaggerations of the conventional outline (Fig. 12), influenced originally by the lotus Ionic forms which rise from a cleft centre.

The most interesting and important detail of Plate vii. is No. 8, because it clearly distinguishes the volutes as belonging to the calyx leaves or sepals. (A similar example is the Cypriote tombstone, xxiii. 7 [p. 173]). These illustrations support the view that the cleft, simplified forms, vii. 1, 4, 6, 9, 10, exhibit in their volutes a conventional termination of the outer sepals or calyx leaves, a conclusion already reached through the three-spiked form in its trefoil stage, iii. 4 [p. 41].

We may now consider the suggestion of M. Dieulafoy, that these lotus Ionic volutes represent petals as curling downward under pressure (Note 8). As the petals of the lotus never curl over, and as the Egyptians clearly had no sentimental objection to representing petals erect under pressure (vi. 1 [p. 69]), we shall prefer an explanation based on the natural habits of the plant. Fig. 4 (p. 27), from nature, shows a peculiarity which has been mentioned. This flower corresponds to Fig. 3, with exception that the sepals have curled over, a frequent though not a constant appearance in the white and blue lotus, not found in the "Rose Lotus," whose sepals, however, are frequently pendant. That this detail did not escape the attention of ancient decorators is apparent from Cypriote vases, which frequently copy it (Figs. 46, 47, 48). In nature the sepals are also found pendant in advanced stages of the flower. A very fairly realistic representation of this peculiarity is offered by Fig. 49, from a notable Cypriote vase, to be found on xiv. 3 [p. 287]. More of the details from Cypriote vases, showing the curling sepals, will be found on xlvii. [p. 303], and two of peculiarly interesting relation to the Greek Ionic form appear on xv. 7, 13 [p. 139]. In "Mycenæ" pottery there is a distinct motive based on the pendant sepals, which has eluded the specifications of Professors Furtwängler and Lœschke. On liv. [p. 325] we shall find an obvious case in No. 15. Nos. 3 and 4 also retain the three-spiked form.[10] More remote examples are easily specified through these, viz., 1, 2, and 24. Nos. 10 and 19 are obvious cases of the lotus volute, and valuable proofs that in pottery motives also, the volutes were carried above the naturalistic point of departure from the line of the

46. CYPRIOTE VASE.
N. Y. Museum.

47. CYPRIOTE POTTERY LOTUS.

48. CYPRIOTE POTTERY LOTUS.

---

10. In *Mykenische Vasen*. The most obvious relation of this motive to Cypriote and Rhodian examples will be found at xxxix. 5 [p. 253], and Figs. 160-163; pp. 313, 314. The same treatment of the sepals occurs on a Greek "geometric" vase in the Louvre, which has been mentioned by Furtwängler, but without knowledge that the form is a lotus.

flower. In architectural examples this was a necessary consequence of the solid form and hard material.

Returning therefore to the detail vii. 8, we shall conclude that Egyptian decorators have derived the Ionic volutes of its lotus sepals, either from more realistic representations of the same peculiarity, or from such a transfer of natural resemblance (to Fig. 4) as seemed to them warranted by decorative conditions. One decorative deviation is apparent. In nature, the sepals generally, though not invariably, curl over together, in about equal degree. In the Cypriote details mentioned, and in the Egyptian detail, vii. 8, the central sepal is erect, and only the side sepals curl over. This is an obvious accommodation of actual facts to the decorative habit which forbade an illusive foreshortening of the central sepal, which in nature would be seen curling forward, as in Fig. 4. Hence, we may argue that when the Egyptian decorator represented the exterior curling sepals as still rising to the top of the flower, he was governed by the conditions of the material in which he was working, in view of the obvious difficulty or impossibility of other representation of the curling sepal in wood or stone. As for the Cypriote pottery lotuses with Ionic volutes (Figs. 47, 48 and Pl. xlvii.), where there was no difficulty of this kind, it will be observed that they are generally faithful to the fact that the sepals curl over from the base of the flower. The Cypriote flowers, however, continue to exhibit bounding outlines at the sides, which appear like the erect sepals of the usual three-spiked form.

According to the views above offered, the suggestions made by Colonna-Ceccaldi (p. 72) are also subject to revision in matters of detail. The supposed "ovary" (Fig. 43) is in reality the survival of the traditional central sepal. His view of the volutes as curling petals must also be abandoned. The upper introrse scrolls of Fig. 43 are not stamens, but represent a palmette or "honeysuckle," to be subsequently explained. Notwithstanding these corrections of detail, to Georges Colonna-Ceccaldi belongs the honour of the first announcement (1875) of the one main important fact, that the Ionic capital is a lotus, and to M. Dieulafoy belongs the honour of the first systematic demonstration of this fact (1885). My own observation, based on Cypriote vases in New York, was made in 1873.

It is not, however, assumed that this chapter demonstrates a connection between the Egyptian lotus Ionic form and the Greek Ionic capital. This demonstration is reserved, and we only claim to have indicated the existence of an

Egyptian lotus Ionic form, and to have related its volutes to the sepals of the lotus. We leave the problem here at the stage presented by vii. 9, observing that the only existing case of a stone Ionic form in Egypt (vii. 6) is in relief, against a solid pillar backing, which the detail does not reproduce. Otherwise the materials of proof as to actual architectural use are drawn from tomb-paintings of wooden capitals. The reasons why such wooden capitals are not themselves available for demonstration are obvious, and it is also obvious that the Egyptians did not consider the lotus volutes appropriate to capitals in stone. Their sentiment for the massiveness and solidity of fact and appearance in stone construction is an abundant explanation; but we have seen that their stone capitals also represent the lotus (Plate vi.). In contrast with the heavy solemnity of Egyptian stone architecture, the paintings of ædicules, shrines, and other buildings in wood, show a light and elegant system of construction to which the graceful lotus Ionic form was confined. It is the destruction of the monuments in wood which has so far obscured the Egyptian origin of the Ionic capital.

The derivation of the Ionic form from the curling sepals of the lotus was independently worked out by Mr. Percy E. Newberry in 1885 (then and now on the staff of the Egypt Exploration Fund), and was announced by letter to Professor Reginald Stuart Poole in that year. Mr. Newberry's matter was ready for the press [11] when it was anticipated by my own publication of 1888,[12] in consequence of which his intended announcement was abandoned. As Mr. Newberry is an expert botanist as well as an Egyptologist, it is very gratifying to be able to quote him, not only as concurrent authority, but also as independent discoverer of the true origin of the Ionic form. I use the words "Ionic form," as distinct from the Ionic capital, with purpose, for Mr. Newberry's observations, like my own, included surface patterns. They included the spiral scroll as a variant of the Ionic form, and consequently included the Mycenae spirals as Egyptian lotus derivatives, as announced by me in 1888.

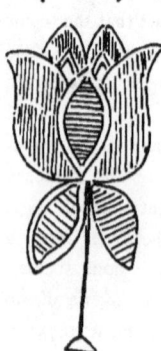

47. CYPRIOTE POTTERY LOTUS WITH PENDANT SEPALS. From a vase shown by Pl. xlv. 3 (p. 287).

The Ionic volute is not confined to the form of an architectural capital.

11. It was prepared for publication in the *Builder*.
12. *American Journal of Archæology*, Vol. iii, No. 4, "Egyptian Origin of the Ionic Capital and Anthemion"; and *American Architect*, 1889, six papers on "The Lotus in Ancient Art."

EGYPTIAN LOTUS IONIC FORMS.

Although the demonstration is easily offered through architectural examples, it depends upon and involves an infinitely larger fact, viz. that an apparently geometric spiral design in surface ornament was originally a floral motive. It can be proven to satiety that there is not one spiral in Greek ornament which is not a lotus derivative. This proof reacts on our conceptions of the ornamental art from which the lotus motive sprang, and of which it constituted the most essential part. It is impossible to admit the spiral as a lotus in Greek art and deny the spiral to be a lotus in the Egyptian art, from which the Greek ornament developed. I have devoted almost an entire volume to the proofs for the Greek spiral. For the Egyptian ornamental art our matter is more limited, because we have no monuments of its development and origin, and it is a curious fortune which enables us to specify this origin by an argument built on the art of a copying nation.

It thus happens that a preliminary treatment of Egyptian art obliges us to announce the extreme conclusions which can only be proven by a history of Greek ornament, viz. that the meander and concentric rings are both lotus motives as well as the spiral scroll. I should prefer not to speak of the chevron until the illustration is in evidence, but it may be mentioned here to show that the entire history of European prehistoric ornament, and therefore of European civilization, may receive a new direction from an observation based on the sepal of a water-lily.

Although a logical treatment of the subject forces us to consider the Egyptian patterns first, it is not till we reach the Plates for the Swastika and for Greek "Geometric" Pottery, that we can conclusively announce the meander to have been originally the copy of a lotus spiral (possibly in textile copy, to begin with). The demonstration for concentric rings is also derived mainly from European prehistoric ornament, but an initial announcement must be made in the following chapter.

FROM NATURE.

CYPRIOTE LOTUS.

RHODIAN LOTUS.

MELIAN LOTUS.

PLATE VII.

EGYPTIAN LOTUS IONIC FORMS.

The earliest dated example of Egyptian Ionic architecture belongs to the XVIIIth Dynasty, about 1600 B.C. (No. 6). The earliest dated Assyrian Ionic belongs either to the IXth or XIth century B.C. (Sippara Tablet xv. 9 [p. 139]; xxiii. 1 [p. 173]). The earliest dated Greek Ionic belongs to the sixth century B.C.

1. Typical lotus Ionic capital in wood. From a tomb-painting ; PRISSE D'AVENNES, *Constructions en Bois*.
2. Typical lotus Ionic form ; handle of a standard, in wood. ROSELLINI, M.C. lxxx.
3. Typical lotus Ionic form ; handle of a mirror, in wood. ROSELLINI, M.C. lxxxi.
4. Typical lotus Ionic capital, in wood, as represented in tomb-paintings. Detail from PRISSE D'AVENNES, *Constructions en Bois*.
5. Typical combination capital, in wood ; bud, flower, and two lotus Ionic forms, as represented in tomb-paintings. PRISSE D'AVENNES, *Colonnettes en Bois*.
6. Typical lotus Ionic capitals, in stone relief on pillar at Karnak, and mate to Fig. 50. PRISSE D'AVENNES, *Piliers, Thothmes III*.
7. Lotus Ionic form, wooden mirror handle representing an architectural column. ROSELLINI, M.C. lxxxi.
8. Typical lotus, with Ionic volutes. Porcelain amulet in the Louvre. DIEULAFOY, *L'Art Antique de la Perse*, Part III.
9. Typical lotus, with Ionic volutes. Porcelain amulet in the Louvre. Reference as above.
10. Typical lotus Ionic capital in wood, as represented in tomb-paintings. PRISSE D'AVENNES, *Constructions en Bois*.

50. CAPITALS IN RELIEF ON PILLAR AT KARNAK.

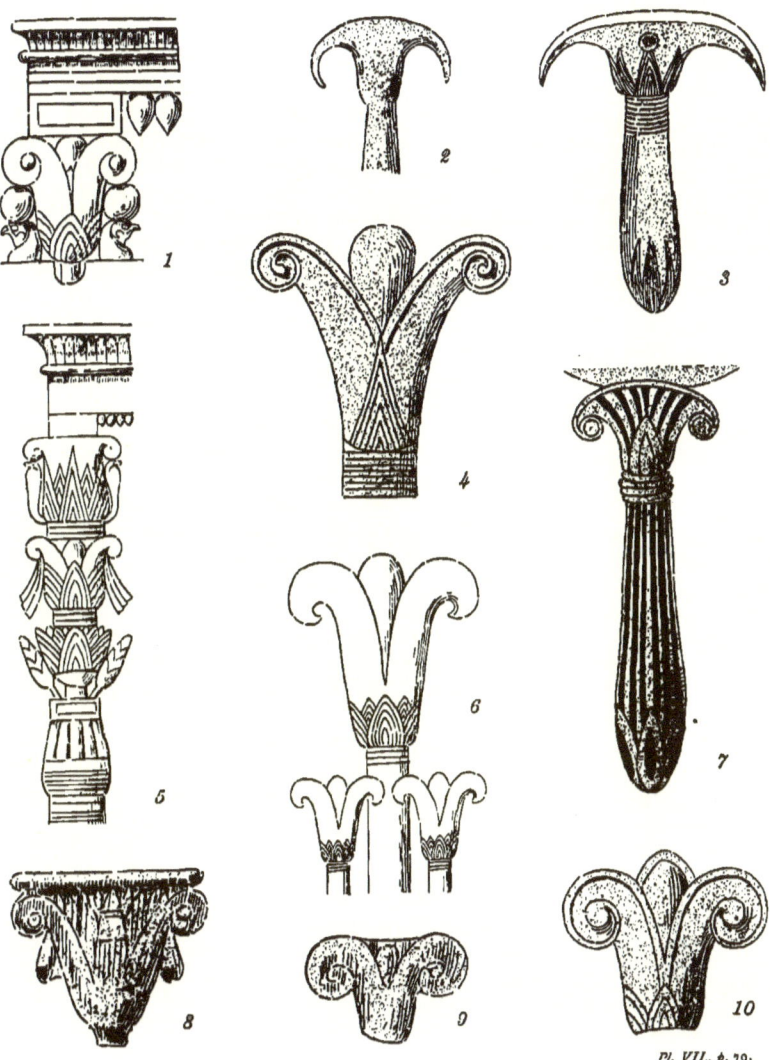

Pl. VII., p. 79.

THE PROBLEM OF CONCENTRIC RINGS.

(PLATE VIII., PAGE 87.)

THERE does not appear to be any published matter relating to the type of Egyptian scarabs decorated with concentric rings (viii. 21, 25). The gentleman who catalogued the Farman Collection of scarabs, lent to the New York Museum, is an accomplished Egyptologist and hieroglyphic scholar, and his translations and interpretations do not offer any suggestions for this type.[1] They are classed by Leemans under the heading of *Ornemens Fantastiques*.[2] As the scarab is the most distinctively sacred and significant amulet of Egyptian worship, it is impossible to suppose that the extremely numerous type of scarabs with concentric rings should be destitute of significance. The suggestion has been repeatedly made for the similar ornaments of Greek "geometric" and Cypriote vases, that they are derived from concentric rings connected by tangents, which in their turn represent conventional spirals.[3] This suggestion, which has not yet been made for Egyptian scarabs, is most obviously demonstrated for them by the lower numbers of Plate viii. No. 23 illustrates a traditional survival of disconnected tangents. No. 24 is a conventional method of representing a spiral scroll.

The spirals on Egyptian scarabs have not been absolutely neglected. They are mentioned by Mariette as representing the wanderings of the soul.[4] This interpretation may have been an afterthought of Egyptian antiquity, but Mariette does not quote texts for his interesting suggestion. The Cypriote Ionic capital,

---

1. Mr. Charles Edwin Wilbour, otherwise known as translator of Victor Hugo's *Les Misérables* and of Renan's *Life of Jesus*.

2. *Monuments Égyptiens du Musée d'Antiquités des Pays-Bas à Leyde*.

3. That concentric rings in Greek art are derived from Greek spirals is suggested by BÖHLAU in the *Jahrbuch des Archæologischen Instituts*, 1888, p. 374. A similar explanation has been offered by DUMONT ET CHAPLAIN, *Céramiques de la Grèce Propre*, in fascicule III. relating to Pl. v. 22. The same explanation in CESNOLA's *Cyprus*, p. 334.

4. 'Emblems of peregrinations of the soul,' *Album du Musée de Boulaq*, text for Pl. xvi. "Emblème des pérignations de l'âme dans l'autre monde," *Monuments d'Abydos*, p. 541.

THE PROBLEM OF CONCENTRIC RINGS.

viii. 14, offers another explanation supplementary to, or displacing, the above Assuming the demonstration, which follows in later pages, for the identity of the Greek Ionic form with the Egyptian Ionic lotus, it appears from this remarkable monument that concentric rings may represent an Ionic lotus; another instance is in the Naples Museum (p. 86, No. 14). This demonstration would include the spiral scroll, from which concentric rings were obviously evolved. Hence the question,—how does the Egyptian spiral scroll relate to the lotus?

As far as scarabs are concerned, the answer is suggested by the remaining and upper numbers of our Plate. From obvious lotuses or from obvious Ionic forms (Nos. 1—16 of Plate viii.) related to vii. 9 [p. 79] we pass to viii. 17, as illustrating the natural decorative method which in connecting together lotus forms with Ionic volutes would reverse one spiral. A simpler statement of the obviously decorative expedient, illustrated by viii. 17, is that each lotus is deprived of one Ionic spiral and represented with only one, which is connected with the following lotus. The pattern is derived as in Fig. 51. To obtain a pattern of lotuses in spiral scrolls, we have only then to design a lotus with one spiral, or Ionic volute, instead of two, and join it to a fellow, as in Fig. 51. Supposing the lotus scroll to be accepted as a conventional symbol, there are obvious reasons why the pattern on scarabs should have been simplified to the point of purely linear suggestion.

51. FORMATION OF THE SPIRAL SCROLL
FROM LOTUS WITH ONE VOLUTE.

The extremely small size, hard material, and rapid manufacture of large numbers of these amulets would explain any device to simplify and conventionalize the symbol. It is, therefore, to be observed that concentric rings are mainly confined, in remains of Egyptian art, to these amulets. Occasional exceptions are offered by small ivory objects, which are not numerous in the museums, but which frequently exhibit this pattern. The difficulty of working lotus spiral patterns on this material would again be obvious. There are also Egyptian instances in the British Museum of concentric rings on wooden rakes and combs.

From the study of scarabs it thus appears that concentric rings were a hieratic, sacred, and traditional symbol in Egypt. From the quoted Cypriote Ionic capital it appears that concentric rings were an equivalent of the Ionic spiral, and from subsequent demonstration it follows that they were an equivalent of the lotus. From the scarabs it appears that concentric rings are derived from concentric rings

THE PROBLEM OF CONCENTRIC RINGS. 83

joined by tangents, which are derived from spirals. That these spirals were a significant, hieratic, sacred, and traditional ornament, is proven by their use on an important class of amulets. That all existing scarabs represent traditional forms of high antiquity is conceded, and we are consequently justified in using the latest survival of a realistic method as original form of a pattern whose early examples may have disappeared. The earliest dated scarab of the Plate is No. 20, of the Vth Dynasty; No. 17, of the XIth Dynasty, is earlier than the majority of dated scarabs in Mr. Petrie's work, "Historical Scarabs." As indicated by the description which heads the Plate, the number of lotus Ionic forms on scarabs is very large. The rarity of the style of No. 17 would be explained by the difficulty of cutting the delicate details of the flower on a hard material in so small a compass. The Museum of Leyden contains a related example in which the rudiments of

52. LOTUSES AND SPIRAL SCROLL.   53. RUDIMENTARY LOTUSES WITH SPIRAL SCROLLS.   54. ANKHS WITH SOLAR HIEROGLYPHICS.
Scarab in Leyden.   Scarab in Leyden.   Scarab (Kl proth).

three-spiked lotuses appear (Fig. 53). From the Leyden Museum is also the example Fig. 52, showing the habitual Egyptian association of the lotus and the spiral, which appears in other ways on Plate viii. Related instances are very numerous. The association of the *Ankh* with solar hieroglyphics (Ra) (Fig. 54) is a distinct design. The existence of a porcelain amulet type for concentric rings is a very important fact. It appears among the "Miscellaneous Porcelain Objects" of the Fourth Egyptian Room, British Museum (No. 7688).

According to Maspero, "the subjects engraved on scarabæi have not yet been classified, nor even completely catalogued."[5] We may conclude, therefore, that there is still place for these suggestions relating to Ionic forms, to spiral scrolls, and to concentric rings, as found on these monuments. We may add the following

5. *Egyptian Archæology*; English translation by MISS AMELIA B. EDWARDS, p. 243.

quotation from the same author and work:—"The object of decoration was not merely to delight the eye. Applied to a piece of furniture, a coffin, a house, a temple, decoration possessed a certain magical property, of which the power or nature was determined by each being or action represented, by each word inscribed or spoken at the moment of consecration. *Every* object was therefore an amulet as well as an ornament."[6] The italics are my own.

This belief in the magical power and importance of decoration, or rather the magical use of what we call ornament, with an entirely different purpose, was by no means confined to the ancient Egyptians. The modern Zuni Indians of New Mexico, whose culture is a remarkable survival from prehistoric times, do not use a single form or line in their pottery decoration which has not magic significance. Even a break in a line of colour may affect the "life" of the vase.[7] It is obvious that such symbolic use in pattern ornament, of any natural form, promotes a conventional treatment. The letters of the alphabet, as derived from hieroglyphics, lost their original pictorial character because any symbolic abbreviation of the form served the use as well. The same fact explains the history of the lotus in ornament.

As concentric rings on scarabs have not been specially noticed by Egyptologists, it is natural that concentric rings on Egyptian ivories should also have been neglected, and consequently natural that concentric rings on the ivories of the ancient Mediterranean art should not have been connected with them. Nothing could be more palpable than this connection, if it be looked into. I have collected a mass of notices from a number of museums on this point.[8] The largest united collection of such ivories is in the British Museum, from Camirus, Rhodes, found and exhibited with quasi-Egyptian enamel objects.[9] Combs were thus decorated, both in Egypt and in Mediterranean localities, where the finds otherwise show Egyptian influence.[10]

Small pottery coffee cup holders decorated with concentric rings are still sold

6. Maspero, *Egyptian Archæology*, p. 97.

7. My authority is Dr. J. Walter Feukes, secretary of the Natural History Society of Boston; now in charge of the Hemenway Expeditions to the Zuni Indians.

8. For instance, concentric rings on Egyptian ivory boomerangs, Case A, 3, Fourth Egyptian Room, British Museum. Concentric rings on ivories from Spata, Polytechnic, Athens ("Mycenæ culture"), with other indications of Egyptian influence. Concentric rings on ivories, associated with objects showing Egyptian influence, from prehistoric tombs, Museum of Bologna. Concentric rings on ivory cylinder, from Cambridge, Anglo-Saxon Room, British Museum, &c., &c.

9. First Vase Room. The objects are mainly small oblong plaques, and sticks of square section; uncertain use.

10. Concentric rings on wooden combs; Fourth Egyptian Room, British Museum, Case E, and in the Egyptian Collection at Florence.

THE PROBLEM OF CONCENTRIC RINGS.

at Assouan, and this ornament is one of three motives by which the earliest decorated incised pottery of prehistoric Europe is everywhere distinguished.[11] The concentric rings on prehistoric pottery are derived from those which the bronzes and gold and silver vessels associated with the pottery finds also exhibit.[12]

These metal objects can be traced, by study of their patterns, from Scandinavia, Ireland, England, Germany, France, Switzerland, and the Tyrol (Hallstadt), to early Italian art, and to the "Mycenæ" culture—in which two latter arts both concentric rings and spirals are dominant motives. The meander and the chevron travelled the same road, also carried by the arts of metal. In the metal vessels (gold, silver, and bronze) of Mycenæ and of prehistoric Italy we can relate the disconnected concentric rings to others joined by tangents,[13] and these latter to the spiral scrolls on metals of the same art. The spirals of these vessels can again be connected with Egyptian originals, as copied in the tomb-paintings (x. 8 [p. 97]).

The argument derived from these facts may be illustrated by a modern parallel. If we are advised to-day of spiral scrolls as being found in the ornament of Salt Lake City, we can predicate the fact with absolute certainty that these spiral scrolls show a Renaissance influence and belong to Renaissance art. We do not assert that the artist of Salt Lake City could not independently invent a spiral scroll, but we assert as a matter of fact that he never does. This is because it is easier for him to borrow his patterns than it is for him to invent them, also because he is part of a civilization which borrowed its spiral scrolls from the Renaissance, and did not invent them.

There is nothing to show that early races were more original than we are in such matters. As far as their civilization was derivative their ornament was also derivative. The first great step in history was that which passed from the use of stone implements to implements and vessels of metal. The history of patterns demonstrates the history of metals. Both arts were derived from Egypt.

11. Plates lvi.-lix. (pp. 339-345). The other two motives are the chevron and the meander, illustrated by the same Plates.

12. Compare the metal vessels on the Plates specified by Note 11. The most interesting gold and silver examples are in the Schliemann collection at Athens. The finest bronze examples are in Vienna, from prehistoric tombs of Hallstadt (Tyrol).

13. Fine example from Dodona, prehistoric bronze plaque in the Louvre; a similar example in the Polytechnic, Athens. Concentric rings joined by tangents, on ivory, from Menidi ("Mycenæ culture"), Polytechnic, Athens, &c., &c. Compare Plate lvi. 7 [p. 339] for pottery. Concentric rings on pottery are most largely represented by Cypriote art. in which there is a distinct and very numerous class of vases so decorated; but none of these show tangents (lvii. 1, 10 [p. 341]).

PLATE VIII.

THE PROBLEM OF CONCENTRIC RINGS.

ALL figures of this Plate, except No. 14, represent Egyptian scarabs. All scarabs selected are types having numerous examples (compare Leemans, *Musée des Antiquités de Leyde*), excepting Nos. 17 and 23, which are rare. The references to Klaproth indicate the publication of DOROW AND KLAPROTH, *Collection d'Antiquités Égyptiennes*, Paris, 1829. The earliest dated examples are from PETRIE'S *Historical Scarabs*, Vth Dynasty (No. 20), and XIth Dynasty (No. 17). Concentric rings on scarabs are dated to the XIIth Dynasty (PETRIE, *Historical Scarabs*, No. 182).

1. KLAPROTH, XXV. 135. Scarab, showing one lotus with Ionic volutes, and two small lotuses.
2. KLAPROTH, II. 73. Scarab, showing three lotuses in conventional outline.
3. Farman Collection, New York Museum. Scarab, with lotus having Ionic volutes.
4. *Tanis*, II. viii. 29. Scarab, showing four lotus Ionic forms.
5. KLAPROTH, II. 82. Scarab, showing six lotus Ionic forms.
6. KLAPROTH, II. 74. Scarab, showing one lotus Ionic form.
7. KLAPROTH, I. 46. Scarab, showing one lotus Ionic form.
8. KLAPROTH, II. 75. Scarab, showing a central lotus, two introrse scrolls, and two lotuses in conventional outline.
9. KLAPROTH, VI. 313. Scarab, showing four lotus Ionic forms.
10. KLAPROTH, I. 52. Scarab, showing one lotus Ionic form and two spiral scrolls.
11. KLAPROTH, II. 77. Scarab, showing two lotus Ionic forms. The little tabs are a mark of the lotus. Compare vii. 8; ix. 1, 2, 3, 5. They may be originally inverted buds, or simply streamers, in which shape they also frequently appear, as in vii. 5.
12. KLAPROTH, II. 64. Scarab, showing four connected lotus Ionic forms.
13. KLAPROTH, II. 75. Scarab, showing two lotus Ionic scrolls, and two lotuses in conventional outline.
14. Cypriote Ionic capital, with volutes in form of concentric rings, New York Museum. CESNOLA, *Atlas*, I. 3. In the basement of the Naples Museum is a small Roman tomb relief, showing Ionic capitals with concentric rings in place of volutes.
15. KLAPROTH, II. 65. Scarab, showing four connected lotus Ionic forms, and two conventional lotuses.
16. KLAPROTH, XXV. Scarab, showing two lotus Ionic forms, best viewed from the side.
17. PETRIE, *Historical Scarabs* (XIth Dyn.). Scarab, showing lotuses in lotus spirals.
18. RENAN, *Mission de Phénicie*, p. 161. Scarab, showing connected spirals, of arrangement like the foregoing.
19. RENAN, *Mission de Phénicie*, p. 163. Scarab, showing disconnected spiral scrolls.
20. PETRIE, *Historical Scarabs* (Vth Dyn.). Scarab, showing connected spiral scrolls.
21. KLAPROTH, II. 107. Scarab, showing concentric rings.
22. KLAPROTH, II. 86. Scarab, showing concentric rings, connected by tangents.
23. Barringer Collection, New York Museum. Scarab, showing concentric rings with disconnected tangents.
24. KLAPROTH, II. 85. Scarab, showing concentric rings connected by tangents. Compare No. 19.
25. Farman Collection, New York Museum. Scarab, showing concentric rings.

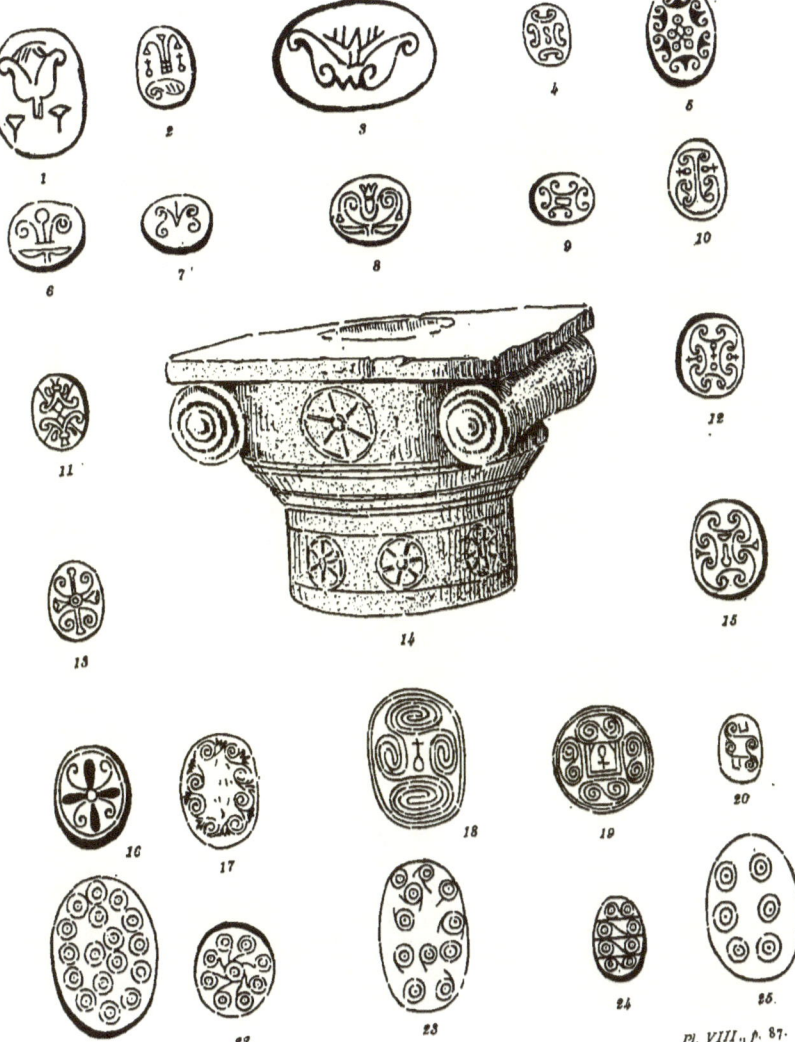

Pl. VIII., p. 87.

EGYPTIAN INTRORSE SCROLLS.

(PLATE IX., PAGE 91.)

Assuming a point, still to be proven, that the Egyptian Ionic lotus and the Greek Ionic capital are one and the same, it must be observed that the question at stake involves a pattern in Greek art which has been named by German students the "Herzblatt," the "heart-leaf," i.e. the heart-shaped leaf. Some of its forms have been confused with the ivy.[1] The pattern in Greek art is shown by xix. 4 [p. 147]. It is also shown at xiv. 4, 5, 10 [p. 133]. The identity of problems is indicated by the curious and otherwise unknown form of the Greek Ionic capital shown at ix. 4. Hence, it is taking a step forward to prove that there is a scroll in Egyptian ornament of precisely similar character, which is an evolution from the lotus. I have specified this ornament as the "introrse scroll." As illustrated by ix. 1, it results from the decorative inversion of a voluted or Ionic lotus. A similar motive, in gold and enamel, at ix. 3, is clearly an inverted repetition of the supporting lotus with scrolls turned inward. The entire pattern is placed upside down at ix. 6 in order to show the correspondence of the heart-shaped pattern with the Ionic capital, ix. 4. The decorative border, ix. 5, shows in alternate sections the Ionic lotus supporting an inverted bud, and in alternating sections an introrse pattern, which is purely a decorative variant. The entire pattern is inverted at ix. 8 in order to show its relation, aside from the bud, to ix. 4. Finally, the similar ceiling pattern from a tomb is shown at ix. 7, as being a type explained by the following Plate.

Ludwig Von Sybel has mistaken the elementary form of ix. 5 for the "Syrische Blume," or "Syrian flower," a plant which is not mentioned in works on botany.[2]

---

1. The resemblance of the "Herzblatt" in Greek art (for instance xiv. 5 [p. 133]) to the pattern in Greek art commonly called "ivy" (xxii. 9 [p. 165]), is very obvious. But the pattern called "Herzblatt" must not be confused with the pattern called "ivy." The patterns have not been confused by students; both have been erroneously attributed to the "ivy," but the attribution has been rarely made for the "Herzblatt," and has been invariably made for the pattern xxii. 9.

2. P. 50, Note 33.

PLATE IX.

EGYPTIAN INTRORSE SCROLLS.

THE earliest dated pattern of the introrse scroll was formerly at Beni Hasan (XIIth Dynasty); a ceiling motive resembling ix. 7. See descriptive matter below for that number.

1. Handle of a toilet tray, illustrating the introrse scroll as a lotus. The lower member shows the typical Ionic lotus. The member next above shows the decorative inversion of the same form, a correspondence marked additionally by the repetition of the tabs or streamers, which are one of the formal signs of the Ionic lotus. These tabs are possibly derived from buds. Compare other figures of this Plate. From CHAMPOLLION, II. clxvii.

2. Pendant architectural ornament, illustrating the Egyptian Ionic lotus when inverted. From PRISSE D'AVENNES, *Colonettes en Bois*.

3. Detail from a gold and enamel bracelet (shown at xxxi. 8 [p. 221]), and illustrating the introrse scroll as a lotus. From PRISSE D'AVENNES, *Bijoux*.

4. Greek Ionic stele, illustrating the introrse scroll inverted; from the sanctuary of Artemis Limnatis. SEMPER, *Der Stil*, II. p. 421. The demonstration for the Greek Ionic form (Plates xii., xiii., xiv., xv. [pp. 113, 121, 133, 139]), includes this type and proves it a lotus.[1]

5. Ceiling ornament (original in colour), showing the origin of the introrse lotus scroll. The intermediate member is a decorative variant of the Ionic lotuses above and below it. From PRISSE D'AVENNES, *Plafonds*.

6. Repetition of No. 3, inverted, to show the origin of the Ionic capital from the sanctuary of Artemis Limnatis.

7. Ceiling pattern (original in colour), showing a combination of introrse scrolls from PRISSE D'AVENNES, *Plafonds*; compare No. 5. A similar pattern from Beni Hasan (XIIth Dynasty) was published by the *Description de l'Égypte*, A. iv., 64, but is now destroyed, and the oldest pattern of this class now extant is at Siout; tomb of Meri-ka-ra, XIIIth Dynasty. The demonstration for this form in Greek art as a lotus (for instance as at xix. 4 [p. 147]) is positive. The demonstration reacts on the original Egyptian forms, whose history is more obscure, and whose earliest evolution is unknown.

MELIAN DOUBLE LOTUS.    MELIAN LOTUS DERIVATIVE.

8. Repetition of No. 5, inverted, to show the origin of the Ionic capital from the sanctuary of Artemis Limnatis.

Pl. IX., p. 91.

EGYPTIAN MEANDERS AND SPIRAL SCROLLS.

(PLATE X., PAGE 97.)

THE "Meander," "Fret," or "Key" pattern is habitually mentioned as "Greek," and in the latest contributions to the history of Greek ornament by the most distinguished German archæologists, this erroneous presumption still exists. The plates of Rosellini and Prisse d'Avennes render any argument on this topic needless. We can only say that the tomb patterns in which this Egyptian ornament occurs have been overlooked by most scholars, and especially that the habit of looking in Egyptian art for the original types of Greek ornament has not been cultivated. It is not always that we find what we are not looking for.

Prisse d'Avennes has suggested that the Egyptian spiral is derived from the meander. As the tendency of traditional ornament is to simplify rather than elaborate, I suggested (in 1888[1]) that the exact converse of this proposition was the true one. The same suggestion has been subsequently made by the German archæologist Böhlau,[2] as regards the derivation of the Greek meander from the Greek spiral, but with oversight of the original home of these patterns. We will accept the proposition of Böhlau and apply it to the Egyptian forms. Plate x. 9, showing the Swastika meander,[3] will therefore be an adaptation in straight lines and rectangles of the more elaborate spiral pattern, x. 7, and the various other forms of the meander will have developed from spirals of varying arrangement. The fact that such patterns are found as decorative variants in the same tomb, suggests an additional cause for the development of the meander in the natural wish to substitute a decorative variant for a motive which has become monotonous by repetition. It is also the natural form of a continuous spiral scroll for textiles.

---

[1] "Egyptian origin of the Ionic Capital and Anthemion." *American Journal of Archæology*, vol. iii., No. 4.

[2] *Jahrbuch des Archæologischen Instituts*, 1888, p. 349.

[3] The designation "Swastika meander" is intended to indicate that form of meander in which the lines intersect. Compare Plate lx. [p. 359].

94   *EGYPTIAN MEANDERS AND SPIRAL SCROLLS.*

The question may then be asked, "Is there any ground for assigning a symbolical significance to the Egyptian meander, which would correspond to that which must be conceded to the Egyptian spiral, in view of its use on scarabs? (viii. [p. 87].) To this it may be answered that the Swastika (lx. [p. 359]) is most positively, in origin, a section of the Egyptian meander, and that the solar and generative significance of this symbol are well known (p. 354). The meander is a rare pattern on scarabs, because of their generally oval outline, to which a device of straight lines and rectangles is unsuited; but one scarab of the British Museum (No. 17,538, Fourth Egyptian Room) is proof of the hieratic significance of this pattern, and the scarab in question has an oblong rectangular outline.[4] An additional corroboration for the derivation of the meander from the spiral pattern is offered by the corresponding association with lotus rosettes in both these patterns, as found in the tomb decorations (x. 7, 9).

In the lotus spirals of Plate x., No. 6 is an illustration of the normal form, and 1, 2, 3, 4 must be viewed as combinations based upon it. This may be most readily conceived by supposing them to be composed of patterns like No. 6, placed vertically, and side by side. As the pattern of No. 6 is cut to show only one spiral, it will be well to recur to the explanation of p. 82, showing that a running pattern of lotuses in spiral scrolls consists really of a series of flowers having one spiral volute instead of two. Thus the pattern of No. 6 consists of lotuses with one spiral, indefinitely repeated (Fig. 55). In No. 6 the pattern is doubled. The origin of the Egyptian Ionic volute in the curling sepal (Plate vii. [p. 79] Fig. 4, and pp. 73-77) therefore explains this pattern. The most curious corroboration of an original floral unity in the Egyptian lotus spiral patterns is furnished by a comparison of lotuses on Cypriote, Rhodian, and Melian vases. Plate xvi. 2 [p. 144] shows a Melian doubled lotus whose spirals are related to those of the Rhodian lotuses, xvi. 1, 4, 5. These again are clearly related to the Cypriote, xvi. 3, and this must be referred to Fig. 4 from nature: It is fortunate that we are able to identify the introrse scroll or "Herzblatt" as a lotus motive through the Greek Ionic form ix., 4 [p. 91] and other details there shown. It will now be noticed that we may also obtain the "Herzblatt" (as at ix. 7) from parallel spirals like x. 6, arranged as in x. 1, 2, 3. This explains the "Mycenæ"

55. EVOLUTION OF THE SPIRAL SCROLL.

---

[4] It is corroborated by an "Eye" amulet with meander, No. 17,943, in the same room, and by a Turin scarab (No. 2165).

EGYPTIAN MEANDERS AND SPIRAL SCROLLS.

pattern, lii. 6 [p. 321]. We are able to carry back the "Herzblatt" to an Egyptian tomb-pattern of the XIIth Dynasty at Beni Hasan. (Reference for No. 7, p. 90.)

The patterns x. 4 and 5 are variants from the same tomb, and the substitution of the Ionic lotus in x. 5 for the lotus proper in x. 4, is an interesting variation. It also explains how the original element of the lotus pattern may be dropped, leaving only linear ornament. No. 8 is an indication in the same direction, showing how traditional designs in metal will naturally simplify and diminish, and ultimately eliminate, the floral element in favour of the linear. Rudimentary survivals of the floral element may be traced considerably farther than the stage of x. 8. In the British Museum, for instance (First Vase Room), there are some enormous Rhodian terra-cotta *pithoi*, with relief spiral scrolls showing lotus rudiments in the shape of small intermediate triangles. An exactly similar pattern occurs in colour on an Egyptian box for the preservation of funerary jars, in the Maspero collection of the New York Museum.[5] It is, therefore, important to observe that, at a given period, the floral detail of an Egyptian spiral pattern will vary with the material conveying the pattern; that a scarab or metal decoration (known by tomb-painting copy) will preferably present the spiral scroll, without the floral detail, at the time when the large tomb pattern in colour preferably retains it. It is, therefore, a very desirable test, open to the expert, to count up the tomb spirals in the publication which has given them largest illustration (Prisse d'Avennes), and to observe that the floral element of the lotus predominates in them, that the "Herzblätt" patterns generally include small lotuses (ix. 7 [p. 91]), and that the linear spirals and meanders almost invariably exhibit the rosette. This ornament will, therefore, be treated in the following chapter.

5. On this important point see descriptive matter (next page) for x. 7 with account of the distortion perpetrated by the artist of Prisse d'Avennes.

56. ORCHOMENUS LOTUS SPIRALS WITH ROSETTES (SCHLIEMANN). "Mycenæ" culture.

PLATE X.

EGYPTIAN MEANDERS AND SPIRAL SCROLLS.

THE earliest dated instance of lotus and spiral appears to be at present of the XIth Dynasty (viii. 17 [p. 87]). The isolated spiral scroll can be dated to the Vth Dynasty (viii. 20). Published examples of types of this Plate can be dated from the XVIIIth Dynasty, but the pattern ix. 7 [p. 91] can be dated to the XIIth Dynasty: pattern from Beni Hasan in the *Description de l'Égypte*, A. iv. 64. This tomb detail has been destroyed, but the pattern can still be dated to the XIIIth Dynasty in the tomb of Meri-ka-ra at Siout. The earliest dated meander is in the same tomb.

1, 2, 3, 4, 5, 6. Lotus spirals (in colour); ceiling patterns from tombs. PRISSE D'AVENNES, *Plafonds*. The animal heads, mistaken by Prisse d'Avennes for *Bucrânes*, i.e. the skulls of sacrificed animals, are the cow-heads of Hathor (supporting rosettes).

7. Typical spiral (in colour), with rosettes, PRISSE D'AVENNES, *Plafonds*. To illustrate the derivation of the Egyptian meander. This important pattern, from Tomb No. 33, Abd-el-Kourneh, at Thebes, shows in the original perfectly separate and distinct lotus rudiments in the shape of triangles in solid colour. These triangles have been enlarged and united by the artist of Prisse d'Avennes in such a way that they appear to be a filling in around the rosette, and are so copied in my Plate illustration. Compare the cut below from a sketch personally made in the tomb. The three-spiked rudiments of Fig. 53 are a parallel to this phenomenon of the rudimentary triangles, which is well explained by No. 8.

8. Typical lotus spiral; decoration of a metal vase from a design at Kourneh. CHAMPOLLION, II. cxci.

9. Typical Egyptian meander, fret, or key pattern, with rosettes; to illustrate derivation from type of x. 7. PRISSE D'AVENNES, *Plafonds*. The Egyptian meander is by no means confined to the type with intersecting lines.

EGYPTIAN TOMB SPIRAL.

LOTUS RUDIMENTS IN SPIRALS. To compare with x. 8. Sketch from the original tomb pattern misrepresented by the artist of Prisse d'Avennes, as copied at x. 7.

MELIAN SPIRAL SCROLL.

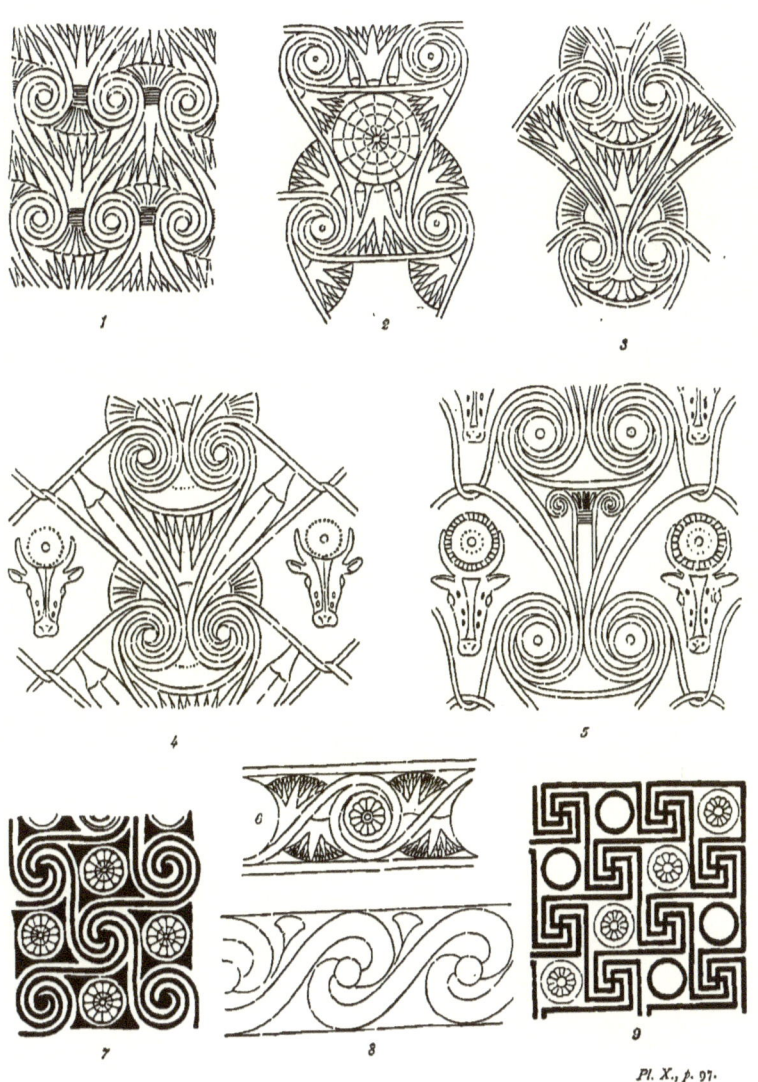

Pl. X., p. 97.

THE ROSETTE.

(PLATE XI., PAGE 107.)

THE most curious prejudice of modern archæology is the one which considers the rosette to be a distinctively Assyrian or Babylonian ornament.[1] As long as this prejudice continues, it will render a true science of ancient history impossible, for it exactly reverses the true relations of Assyria to Egypt in matters of ornamental influence, and therefore in those questions of civilization which an ornamental influence implies. Of the fundamental dependence of Assyrian civilization on the Chaldean there can, of course, be no question; but the history of antiquity after the eighteenth century B.C. resembles the history of Europe after the fifteenth century A.D. We do not deny that the history of Spain, France, Germany, and England is a continuous national history, when we observe that these countries were swept by a wave of Italian Renaissance influence after 1500, which absolutely obliterated the Gothic style and ornament and all mediæval externals. We do not deny that the modern constitution and institutions of England were founded in the Middle Ages, when we assert that its seventeenth-century architecture and ornament came from Italy, or when we assert that this Renaissance influence profoundly modified English literature, music, dress, diplomacy, business, manners, customs, and habits of thought. France and Spain (including the Spanish Netherlands) were the countries through which this Italian influence penetrated into England. Syria was the country through which a corresponding Egyptian influence penetrated Mesopotamia.

It does not weaken our estimate of the influence of Italian Renaissance civilization upon modern Europe, to observe that the House of Anjou ruled

---

1. VON SYBEL, *Kritik des Aegyptischen Ornaments*, speaks of the rosette as occurring only under the New Empire, and as derived from Assyria. Von Sybel is quoted by WINTER in a paper on the "Grabmal von Lamptrae," *Mittheilungen aus Athen*, and the rosette is invariably referred by German archæologists to Assyria. Professor A. S. MURRAY quotes the rosette as Assyrian in CESNOLA's *Cyprus*, p. 394. Professor SAYCE refers the rosette on the silver cow-head of Mycenæ (xxvii. 7 [p. 197]) to Babylonian origin.

Naples and Sicily in the thirteenth century, and that the House of Aragon ruled Sicily, and ultimately Naples, afterward; that Spain was mistress of all Southern Italy after 1500, and that France had conquered Milan at the same time. It does not weaken our estimate of the influence of Italian Renaissance civilization upon modern Europe to know that there was not one principality in Italy after 1530, outside of Venice, which was not ruled or controlled by a foreign dynasty, and that even the elections of the Popes were influenced by the rivalry of France and Spain. In like manner it does not affect the question of Egyptian influence upon Mesopotamia to observe that Assyrian armies penetrated to Meroe,[2] that the campaigns of Nebuchadnezzar reached into Egypt, and that Egyptian rulers had begun to intermarry with Hittites, Semites, or Assyrians from the XVIIIth Dynasty downward.

In the eighth and seventh centuries B.C., when Assyrian military power controlled the fate of Western Asia, and influenced that of Egypt; in the sixth century B.C., when Babylonian power did the same, until the Persian supplanted it, and overthrew Egyptian independence—we have repeated the experience of Italy with France and Spain in the sixteenth century. French and Spanish armies overran the country, and foreign dynasties controlled its destinies, but it was because Italy was the magnet of barbarism, and the focus of art and letters, the centre of luxury, and the home of modern civilization.

The relation of Egypt to Assyria was that of China to the Tartars who now rule that country; it was the relation of Greece to Macedonia in the fourth century B.C., and of Italy to Rome at the same time; the relation of Rome to the Germans in the fifth century; of Byzantium and Persia to the Arabs in the seventh century; of the Arabs to the Turks in the eleventh century; and the relation of India to many foreign races since the eighth century B.C. down to the present time. All history repeats the story of an expanding civilization, weakened by expansion and by luxury, and tempting barbarism by its weakness and by its luxury; until that barbarism, in its turn civilized, experiences the like destiny. Assyria was flaying defenceless captives taken in war, not far from the time when an Egyptian king had abolished the penalty of death as a punishment for crime.

But Assyria played its *rôle* in two directions, and it had overrun Chaldea

---

2. *Proceedings, Society of Biblical Archæology*, May, 1880. The Assyrians marched as far as Meroe in the times of Tarharqa and Assurbanipal

before it invaded Egypt. Assyrian letters, religion, art, and civilization were Chaldean, and we cannot estimate the civilization of Mesopotamia by the cruelty of a military caste which reigned at Nineveh. What we have to consider, then, in the character of Assyrian ornament, is a glaze or crust of ornamental fashion, like that Renaissance ornament which conquered Germany in the time of Luther. Holbein was a Protestant, but his Virgin stands in a niche whose fashion came from Italy. The style of a Jesuit church is that of St. Paul's Cathedral, and controlled it. To one who appreciates the absolute erasure which Gothic ornament suffered throughout Europe in the sixteenth century, and the absolute dominance of the Classic Renaissance style from that time until 1750, the problem of the rosette offers no great difficulties.

The history of civilization may explain, but it cannot prove the history of the rosette. What, then, are the facts about it? They are simply these—that the earliest excavated Assyrian palace dates from the ninth century B.C., and that not even isolated cases of rosette ornament can be named in Assyria for an earlier date at present. It does not appear that a single instance can be dated at present, either in Assyria or Chaldea before the twelfth century B.C. (p. 106, descriptive matter). On the other hand, kings of the XVIIIth Dynasty had brought Assyria inside the Egyptian frontier soon after 1700 B.C., and Thothmes III. had probably reached India by way of Mesopotamia at this time, according to the view of Dr. Birch (p. 15). The rosette appears in Egypt two thousand eight hundred years before it appears in Mesopotamia, according to present record. This is the difference in time between the head-band of Nefert and the robe of Merodach-idin-akhi.[3] If we appeal to the periods of abundant reference, the time of the earliest Assyrian palace is eight hundred years later than the time of the XVIIIth Dynasty, under which the Egyptian rosette is in demonstrably habitual use. And if it be suggested that excavations may reveal an earlier date for the rosette in Mesopotamia, we can only answer that excavations, or observations, may do the same for Egypt. Apparently the excavations just now needed should be made in Rosellini and in Prisse d'Avennes.

It has been supposed that the rosette is an ornament foreign to Egypt because it appears on vases at Kourneh brought by the "Kefa."[4] Exactly the same argument would prove that the Renaissance Majolica patterns of Italy were derived from the

---

3. DIEULAFOY, L'Art Antique de la Perse, I. pl. ix. Also illustrated in PERROT ET CHIPIEZ, Assyrie. For illustration and date of Nefert's head-band see Note 7.

4. For instance, by LONGPÉRIER, in Musée Napoléon III.

"ware of Henri Deux." According to this view a possible present from Louis XIV. to an Italian pope would prove that the Renaissance style spread to Italy from France, and the tomb of Henry VIII. would prove that the Renaissance style came from England. The argument would prove that Torrigiano had never worked in London, and that Benvenuto Cellini had never been in France. Moreover, those who have commented on the rosette as appearing on vases of the "Kefa" have never suggested that the Kefa made or inspired the tomb paintings of the XVIIIth and XIXth Dynasties, and it is not clear that their details have ever attracted the attention of such students. If, as Renan says, "Phenicia became a province of Egypt"[5] in matters of religion, it is clear that the same fact will explain Phenician ornament, and the style of the vases from Cyprus or Syria "brought by the Kefa."

This brings us to the question—"If the fact is patent, as would appear from Plate xi., that the rosette is a familiar feature of Egyptian ornament, and as early a feature as the earliest dated remains of other ornaments, how is it that this patent fact has been overlooked?" The answer apparently is, that the rosette is mainly known to publication in Assyrian relief slabs from Nineveh, and very abundantly known in this way, and that architectural surface carvings in Egypt, which have been also abundantly published, are almost absolutely destitute of rosette ornament. It is the tomb paintings which abundantly exhibit the rosettes. This source of information has been neglected by the friends of the "Assyrian" rosette. As compared with both Assyrian and Persian carved relief ornament, Egyptian ornament is almost an absolute blank for repeated patterns in stone carving. The force was exhausted on the hieroglyphics. Consequently, the painted patterns of the tombs are a necessary authority, not only for the rosette, but for many other motives of Egyptian ornament.

The rosette form belongs, however, to the series of mortuary amulets, among which it is very frequent, and it can be dated as an amulet to the XIIth Dynasty by Mr. Petrie's recent excavations. This date is written by his own hand on a card of amulets at Manchester (Owens College), which includes this form in several examples. The rosette is included in the plate for typical mortuary amulets in Mariette's *Album du Musée de Boulaq*.

It will be difficult for any one who examines the plates of Prisse d'Avennes to

---

5. *Mission de Phénicie.* "De plus en plus dans la suite de cette ouvrage nous verrons la Phénicie devenir sous le rapport religieux une province d'Égypte," p. 70.

THE ROSETTE.

consider the rosette as distinctively Assyrian, in view of the priority of dates so heavily in favour of Egypt, as above noted. Hence we may turn to the nature of rosette ornament as distinct from the question of its original home. That the rosette is a lotus-motive is, in the first instance, made probable by the invariable lotus associations which attend it. These are exhibited by Plate xi., as specified in detail in the descriptive matter. The alternations show in related patterns a lotus supporting a lotus leaf, and a rosette supporting a lotus leaf (xi. 7, xi. 4); a flower supporting a rosette, and a bud supporting a rosette (xi. 3, xi. 1); a flower supporting a bud and a bud supporting a bud, in one pattern with a rosette supporting a bud (xi. 5); a leaf, flower, bud, and rosette in one design (xi. 7); a flower, bud, and rosette in one pattern (xi. 10); a leaf supporting a bud (xi. 11); and rosettes supporting a bud (xi. 6, 8, 9).

These associations lead to the question, "What is the rosette?" The most obvious answer is found in the ovary stigma of the white and blue lotus as figured in the *Histoire Naturelle* of the *Description de l'Égypte*, from which Figs. 5, 6 (p. 28) are borrowed, or as shown by the design of a dried ovary stigma taken from nature (Fig. 8). But there are three other lotus combinations from which the rosette is derived. It appears as the flower with petals spread out, and as seen from above (xx. 1, 5, 18 [p. 153]); as a group of buds in radiating arrangement (xx. 2, 4, 8, 10, 21); and as a group of lotus flowers in radiating arrangement (xx. 11, 13). In xx. 13 it is the central rosette of the side of the sarcophagus and of the cover which exhibits this combination. The earliest dated rosettes (with normal lotuses),[6] on the head-band of Nefert,[7] are so highly conventional that no assistance is offered by them as to the theory of original derivation. All forms and arrangements may have been practically simultaneous. An obvious explanation would start from the flower "in plan." A more obvious explanation would start from the ovary stigma, for the reason that the rosettes with pointed petals (the flower "in plan") appear to be carefully distinguished from those with rounded blunt radiations (the ovary stigma) (xx., p. 153), that the rosettes of buds appear to give a wider spacing to the divisions of the rosette (xx., p. 153), and also that the rosettes of combined flowers (xx. 11, 13) are not numerous. The brilliant

---

[6]. They have been mistaken by W. J. LOFTIE for roses and leaves—"a ribbon or snood ornamented with roses and leaves."—*A Ride in Egypt*, p. 211.

[7]. Statue of the IVth Dynasty, in the Gizeh Museum, from the tomb of Ra-hotep at Maydoum. See MASPERO'S *Archæology*, translated by MISS EDWARDS, Fig. 190.

THE ROSETTE.

yellow rays of the ovary stigma in both blue and white lotus may have assisted or inspired the primary symbolic association of the lotus with the sun.

My own observation for the rosette was first suggested by the ovary stigma as illustrated in the *Histoire Naturelle* of the *Description de l'Égypte*, and as far as publication goes I am probably the first to have made this designation.[8] The observation for the ovary stigma was first made by Mr. Percy E. Newberry (Staff of the Egypt Exploration Fund) in 1885.[9]

8. *American Journal of Archæology*, 1888. "Egyptian Origin of the Ionic Capital and Anthemion."
9. Personal advice. Mr. Newberry had the matter prepared for publication and was about to publish, when my papers in the *American Architect* on the "Lotus in Ancient Art," fell into his hands. It is much to be regretted that this anticipation led him to abandon publication, because his standing as an expert botanist, as well as in Egyptology, gives the designation a weight which my name could scarcely secure for it.

57. GOLD CEREMONIAL VASE WITH STEMS SUPPORTING ROSETTES IN SYMBOLIZING FASHION.
Compare xx. 7 (p. 153) and explanatory matter, p. 152. Theban tomb-painting; from Prisse d'Avennes.

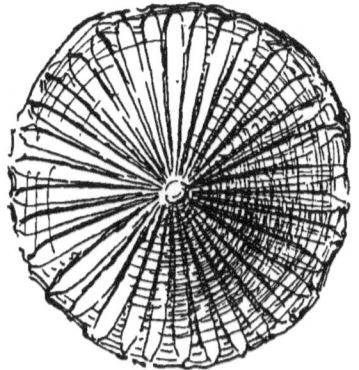

DRIED OVARY STIGMA OF THE LOTUS BULB AFTER SEEDING.
From Nature. Repeated from p. 29.

PLATE XI.

THE ROSETTE.

THE earliest dated Egyptian rosettes occur, with other lotuses, on the head-dress of Nefert, statue of the IVth Dynasty (4000 B.C.) The earliest dated Babylonian rosettes are on the dress of King Merodach-idin-akhi, XIIth century B.C.

1. Lotus buds supporting rosettes, and Ionic lotus supporting an inverted bud (a variant of No. 3). Detail repeated with variants on all the columns at Esneh. From PRISSE D'AVENNES, *Bases et Soubassements*.

2. Lotus variants, one form trefoil, with inverted bud and leaves bent over; rosette in the field. From PRISSE D'AVENNES, *Couronnements*.

3. Lotus flowers supporting rosettes, and Ionic form supporting an inverted bud. Detail repeated with variants on all the columns at Esneh. From PRISSE D'AVENNES, *Bases et Soubassements*.

4. Rosettes supporting lotus leaves (a variant of the cleft form, compare Nos. 7, 11, and matter at the foot of this page), and trefoil lotuses. From PRISSE D'AVENNES, *Frises Fleuronnées*.

5. Lotus supporting bud inverted; rosettes supporting buds erect; bud supporting bud inverted. Reference as above.

6. Rosettes supporting lotus buds. Reference as above.

7. Portion of a toilet tray in wood (coloured), showing a lotus leaf partly concealed by a flower, buds inverted on the stalk (decorative filling in more successful by this arrangement), and rosettes on stalks. From PRISSE D'AVENNES, *Art Industriel, Utensiles de Toilette*.

8. Lotus bud, with inverted buds supported by rosettes. From PRISSE D'AVENNES, *Frises Fleuronnées*.

9. Flowers; bud on rosette. Reference as above.

10. Flower, bud, and rosette. Reference as above.

11. Lotus in trefoil outline; leaf supporting bud; lotus in conventional outline. Reference as above.

All above are in colour. All but No. 7 are details borrowed from patterns which are mainly confined to tombs or shrines.

A peculiar shape of the leaf in many Egyptian patterns is seen at 4 and 11. It also appears at Fig. 18 (p. 50). The lower portion of the leaf is rounded, and the cleft is figured above. Compare xi. 7, where the leaf is partly cut off by the flower, while the cleft still appears, which should properly be the base of the leaf. The form is explained by amulets (British Museum) of enamel and other hard materials, which made the representation of an actual cleft at the base of a leaf so connected with a lotus impossible. Hence the cleft is indicated in surface design over the actual joint. It is therefore clear that designs in surface colour were borrowed from amulets, a very important point as bearing on the symbolism of the colour patterns.

The leaf amulet has been dated by Mr. Petrie to the XIIth Dynasty (Collection of Owens College, Manchester). There is an amulet form of the Persea fruit somewhat like it.

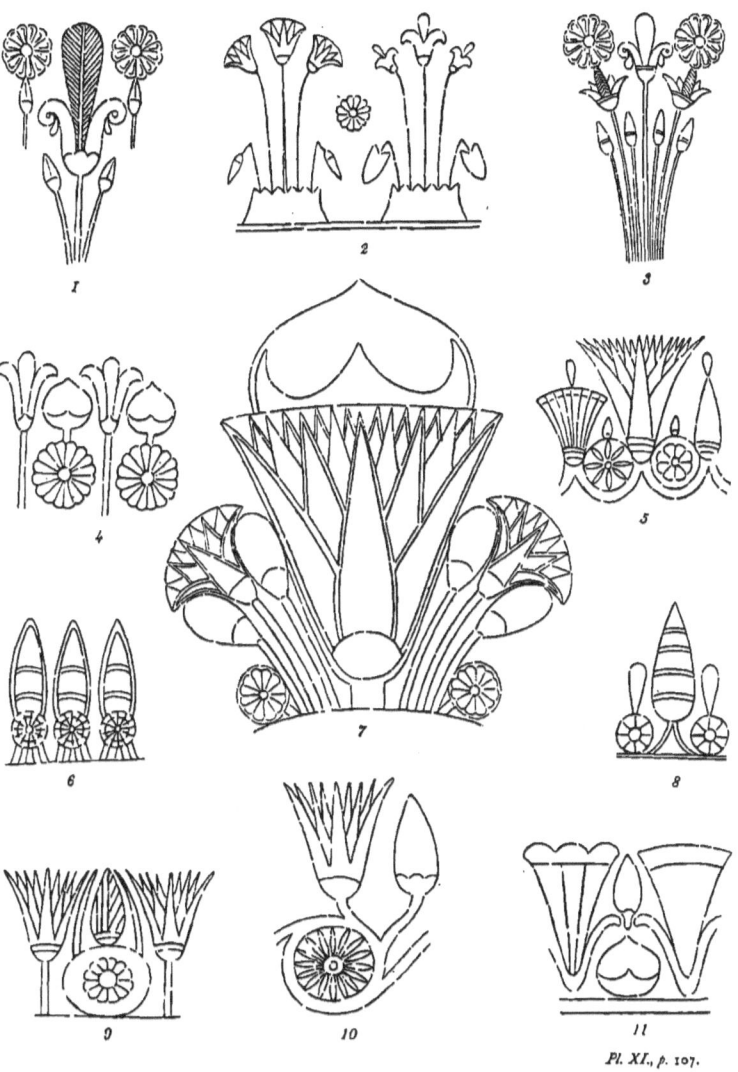

Pl. XI., p. 107.

THE EGYPTIAN LOTUS PALMETTE.

(PLATE XII., PAGE 113.)

IN the tomb-ceiling patterns of Prisse d'Avennes there is a frequently recurring motive, illustrated by Fig. 58. The motive also occurs with a conventional outline for the palmette portion, as in Fig. 59, which also includes an inverted bud. The tabs, generally found pendant from the volutes, have been mentioned at p. 86 (No. 11), as being either buds inverted or pendant streamers, and appear

on the important Ionic lotus, vii. 8 [p. 79], and elsewhere. As there is no doubt that Figs. 58, 59 represent lotuses, the origin of the palmette crown deserves consideration, and is explained by the rosette.

58. EGYPTIAN LOTUS PALMETTE. Hence the details of Plate xii. Com- 59. EGYPTIAN LOTUS PALMETTE. binations like xii. 1 and 2 are rare, and the individual examples offered are Ptolemaic, but xii. 3 dates the combination from the XVIIIth and XIXth Dynasties, and Mr. Petrie has dated the amulet forms of this design (xii. 16-19) to the XIIth Dynasty (Collection of Owens College, Manchester.)

As we have already found an analogous combination for the leaf (xi. 7 [p. 107] iv. 5 [p. 63], and Figs. 17, 18), there is no difficulty in solving the problem of the Egyptian lotus palmette. It represents the combination of the ovary stigma (or lotus rosette, as otherwise explained) with the flower. It does not follow that the combination denotes a supposed concealment of a portion of the rosette; we may rather assume the abbreviation of one half the rosette to be suggested by decorative considerations. The sacred standard, or *flabellum* (xx. 20 [p. 153]), shows that a half-section of the lotus rosette was a familiar object to the Egyptian.

The details regarding the *provenance* of the patterns illustrated by Plate xii. are connected with their descriptive matter, and indicate the fact, supported by many instances not illustrated, that the pattern was familiar to the Phenicians, Etruscans, Cypriote Greeks, Assyrians, and Persians. It was from this form (as shown by xii. 5 or 11) that the Assyrian palmette (Figs. 60, 61, 62) was derived.[1] The counterpart of xii. 5 is found on Phenician bronze *pateras* from Nineveh, and the tabs are an easy identification of the purely Egyptian form. The Assyrian palmette dropped the tabs (as they are also frequently dropped by the Egyptians and Phenicians), but otherwise developed from the Egyptian forms by stages which are still traceable, by various traditional survivals, in Ninevite remains, and which are especially visible in the Egypto-Phenician ivory plaques of the British Museum.

It has escaped the notice of Dr. E. B. Tylor, in an interesting contribution to the subject of the Sacred Tree,[2] that xii. 14 is a palpable lotus. The palmette

60. ASSYRIAN PALMETTE WITH LOTUS BULB.[3]
From fresco, British Museum.

61. ASSYRIAN PALMETTE WITH LOTUS BUD.
From fresco, British Museum.

combination makes the recognition of the rosette as a lotus a matter of special importance, but it also assists this recognition, since an arbitrary and fanciful addition of this palmette form to the Ionic lotus is not to be assumed. The addition calls for an explanation, and can find no other solution. It is not to be forgotten that this form constitutes a funeral amulet. Three of these palmette amulets, in blue enamel ware (xii. 18), are the central feature of a photographic plate, arranged by Mariette from objects in the Boulak Museum, which is exclusively devoted to amulets found in tombs. Among these the rosette is also represented. The conclusion is obvious that both were Egyptian tomb symbols.

---

1. The dependence of the Assyrian palmette on an Egyptian original is announced by DIEULAFOY, *L'Art Antique de la Perse*, IIIème Partie. Dieulafoy's illustration and matter are confined to the type of the *flabellum* (xx. 20) [p. 153] overlooking the real original, viz. xii. 3, 11, &c.

2. *Proceedings, Society of Biblical Archæology*, June, 1890. "The winged figures of the Assyrian and other monuments." Reference is to his Fig. 17.

3. The lotus bulb has been mistaken for a pomegranate. Mr. P. E. Newberry coincides with my designation (p. 181).

THE EGYPTIAN LOTUS PALMETTE.

Two very important "Mycenæ" pottery motives are imitations in outline of Egyptian lotus palmettes as copied from bronze or other metal. Neither motive has been previously specified as a lotus. One has been mistaken by Professors Furtwängler and Loeschke for a palm motive. As a palm motive always implies Assyrian influence, the correction is important for the history of the "Mycenæ" civilization. Plate liv. [p. 325] shows, among other patterns, some of the two in question. Nos. 7 and 11 on Plate liv. are repetitions of the original motives in metal, to assist the eye. From type No. 7 in bronze are derived the pottery motives 5, 6, 8, 13, 14. From type No. 11 in bronze are derived 9, 12, 16, 17, 18, 20, 21, 22, 23.[4]

I believe that my explanation of the Egyptian lotus palmette is new, as it depends on a preceding recognition of the rosette.[5] When first published (1888) I did not myself recognize the identity with the Greek anthemion,

6a. ASSYRIAN PALMETTE.
Textile ornament, on stone relief. From Layard.

Detail on Bronze. From the Regulini-Galassi Tomb.

having been misled on this point by a study of Greek pottery lotuses to the conclusion that the Greeks had independently developed the "honeysuckle" from their own lotus forms. After inspecting the large relief patterns on bronze in the Vatican and in Florence, the later conclusions reached from the study of publications are confirmed, that the exact original of the Greek anthemion was on imported metals. The bronzes in question[6] are undoubtedly Phenician; the tabs are an unmistakable indication of Egyptian ornament. The forms have exact counterparts on Greek monuments (xiii., p. 121).

Repetition of xii. 12. Detail on Bronze, from the shield of Amathus.

4. Since penning the above I have found the exact original form of the last-named type among the gold objects from Spata ("Mycenæ Culture") in Athens. See p. 324.

5. The Egyptian palmette appears to have been entirely overlooked and neglected, and it certainly does require some research to connect the published Egyptian forms with the published Greek and Phenician counterparts. The only attempt to explain the Egyptian palmette which I have found was made by COLONNA-CECCALDI, who supposed xii. 12 to represent a lotus surmounted by a segment picture of the sun—"un emblême qui paraît représenter le soleil (figuré en demi-pâquerette, comme celui de la nef isiaque) s'épanouissant en sortant du calice d'un lotus."—*Monuments de Chypre*, p. 148.

6. Etruscan Museum of the Vatican : bronzes from the Regulini-Galassi tomb. Etruscan Museum of the Museo Archæologico, Florence : bronzes from the Tomba del Duce. I have sketches of close counterparts of these designs from unpublished details of the First Temple Court of Karnak, and from amulets in Bologna and Turin.

PLATE XII.

THE EGYPTIAN LOTUS PALMETTE.

THE earliest dated Egyptian palmettes (amulets at Owens College, Manchester, Mr. Petrie's excavations) belong to the XIIth Dynasty (about 3000 B.C.). Lotus palmettes in conventional outline can be dated to the IVth Dynasty (Fig. 39C), about 4000 B.C.

1, 2. Details, from Plate xi., 1, 3 [p. 107].
3. Ionic lotus with tabs, supporting rosette. Detail from PRISSE D'AVENNES, *Sièges* (XVIIIth and XIXth Dyns.).
4. Ionic lotus with tabs or streamers, supporting demi-rosette. Egypto-Phenician. Detail in bronze from finds at Cære (Regulini-Galassi tomb). From the *Museo Etrusco-Vaticano*, I. xvii.
5. Pattern of minimized Ionic lotuses, with tabs, supporting demi-rosettes. Reference as above.
6. Ionic lotuses, supporting demi-rosettes. Detail of Egyptian gold jewellery; from PRISSE D'AVENNES, *Bijoux, &c.*
7. Ionic lotus with tabs, supporting demi-rosette. Detail in colour; from PRISSE D'AVENNES.
8. Ionic lotus with tabs, supporting demi-rosette. Egypto-Phenician detail, in bronze, from the Regulini Galassi tomb. Reference as with No. 4.
9. Ionic lotus, supporting demi-rosette. Detail in bronze, from the *Museo Etrusco-Vaticano*, I. ii. 3.
10. Ionic lotus, supporting demi-rosette. Detail in stone carving from Cyprus; decorating handles of the enormous stone bowl in the Louvre. Illustration in LONGPÉRIER, *Musée Napoléon III.*, xxxiii. 2.
11. Pattern of minimized Ionic lotus (larger than No. 5), with tabs, supporting demi-rosette. Same reference as No. 4.
12. Conventional lotus (not Ionic), supporting demi-rosette. Detail in bronze, from the shield of Amathus. COLONNA-CECCALDI, *Monuments de Chypre*, ix.
13. Ionic lotus, supporting an elongated demi-rosette. Portion of a tray handle, as supposed, in gold, originally enamelled, found at Tell-Defenneh. In the Boston Museum. From *Tanis*, II. xli. 10.
14. Persian multiple lotus detail, supporting demi-rosette. (This form has only been published for the Persian period, but it occurs on Assyrian ivories from Nineveh, in the British Museum, of the IXth century B.C.) From PERROT ET CHIPIEZ, V. p. 528. Tile ornaments of stairway at Susa. Dieulafoy excavations.
15. Ionic lotus, supporting demi-rosette. Egypto-Phenician detail in bronze, from the *Museo Etrusco-Vaticano*, I. lxiv. 10.
16. Ionic lotus, supporting demi-rosette. Link of a necklace, blue glazed ware, in the British Museum. XIXth Dyn.
17. Similar amulet in the Boston Museum.
18. Ionic lotuses, supporting demi-rosettes. Funerary amulets, in blue glazed ware, from MARRIETTE, *Album du Musée de Boulaq*, xvii. Plate for funerary amulets.
19. Similar amulet, with tabs (one broken off), in the Boston Museum.

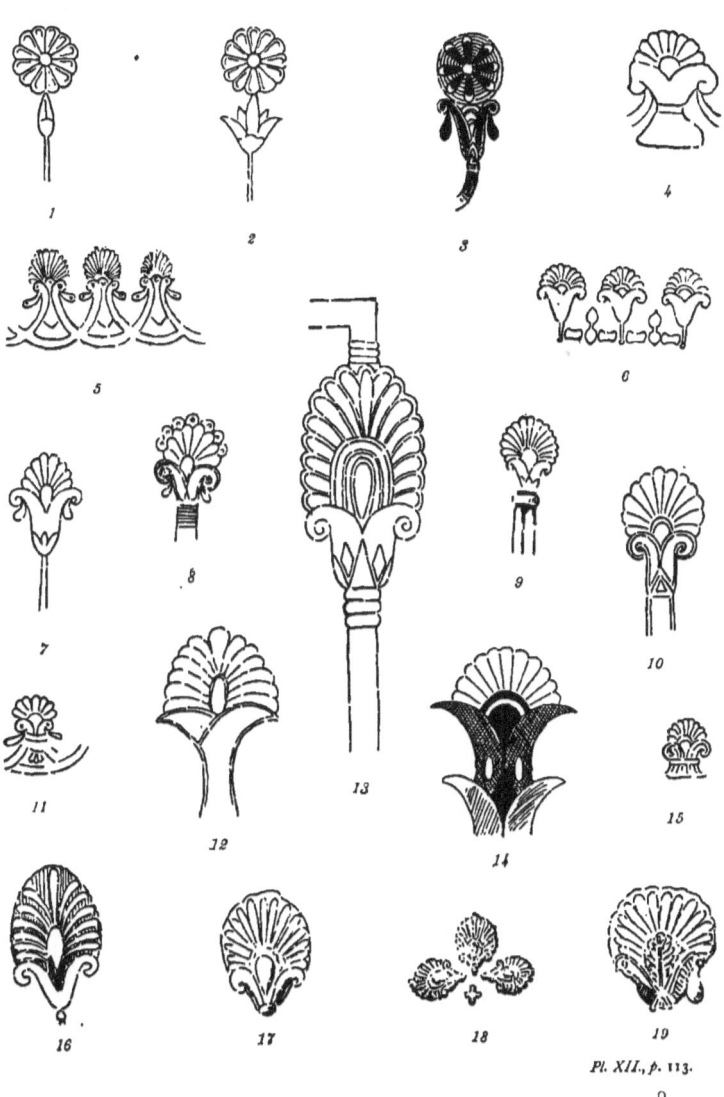

Pl. XII., p. 113.

GREEK IONIC AND ANTHEMION FORMS.

(PLATE XIII., PAGE 121.)

IT will scarcely escape the notice of experts in Greek ornament that certain phases of the Egyptian lotus palmette (xii. [p. 113]) are exactly identical with certain phases of the Greek anthemion form. From the detail of the Greek vase of Sidon (xiii. 1), or from the anthemion of a Greek vase (xiii. 4, see also Fig. 66), we pass to details of Plate xii.—8 and 10, for instance—without noting one distinction. The temptation would be almost irresistible to a sceptic, who denies the Greek anthemion to be a lotus, to hold that the Egyptian forms quoted are derived from Greek. He might even gather breath for a moment, when noting that xii. 8 is from Italy and xii. 10 from Cyprus, and vow that this was the case. Let us observe the results of such a possible position. It would oblige the sceptic to prove that the Ninevite ivories (xiii. 2, 3, 5) are also Greek, and so far the tendency of Greek archæology has been to derive Greek ornament from Nineveh rather than Ninevite ornament from Greece. It would oblige the sceptic to prove that a motive like xiii. 4, which cannot in that form be carried back of the fifth century B.C. in Greece, was the original of a form, xii. 7, which occurs in Egypt more than twenty-five hundred years before that time (XIIth Dynasty begins about 3000 B.C.). So far, only one case of the "tabs" (ix. [p. 91]) has been published for the whole range of Greek art, and it occurs in the third or fourth century B.C. on the Greek vase from Sidon (xiii. 1). Did it produce the palmette tabs of the XVIIIth Dynasty?

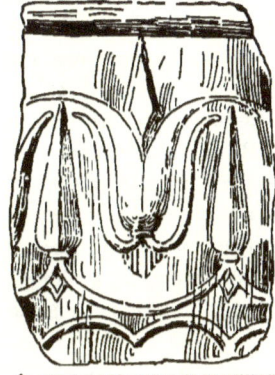

63. GREEK NECKING ORNAMENT OF A COLUMN FOUND AT NAUKRATIS.

On the whole, we may say that the case is proven for the Greek anthemion, with all the consequences which flow therefrom.

The motive xiii. 4 was published by M. Dieulafoy in 1885, with the simple subscription, *Ornament lotiforme*.[1] A simultaneous announcement was made by Mr. W. M. Flinders Petrie, based on the Naukratic relief ornament herewith (Fig. 63), that the Egyptian lotus was the original of the so-called "honeysuckle" ornament (or anthemion) on the column necking of the Erechtheium.[2] As Mr. Petrie's observation did not include the Ionic form, his point of view was defective on this side as M. Dieulafoy's is weak on the side of the palmette portion (see Note 1). A really solid foundation for the study of the anthemion was first offered by Dr. Joseph Thacher Clarke; in calling attention to the fact that the anthemion is simply a phase of the Ionic form.[3] Although Dr. Clarke moved from the old theories of Assyrian palm origin, his demonstration of the identity of the anthemion with the Ionic form must henceforth be taken as the basis for the lotiform point of view in treating the anthemion. Hence my arrangement of Plate xiii., whose pieces are grouped about the Capital of Neandreia (xiii. 9).

The argument of Plate xiii. is self-apparent. Its anthemions are all variants of an Ionic form. Its Ionic forms are all variants of an anthemion. It is impossible to say where one motive begins and the other ends, and whether we begin with the largest volutes or the largest palmette as the starting point, we can still refer to

---

1. *L'Art Antique de la Perse*, IIIième *Partie*. M. Dieulafoy's matter on the Greek anthemion is somewhat vague, but his convictions as to the Ionic volutes carried him to a just conclusion. As far as the palmette part of xiii. 4 is concerned, he offers no suggestions as to derivation, and is apparently ignorant of the existence of an exact original in Egyptian art. He offers no reference whatever to the Egyptian palmette as found in amulets and frescoes, but applies the words "Egyptian palmette" to the *flabellum* or standard, consisting of one half the lotus flower as seen in plan. Not having reached the solution of the rosette, which M. Dieulafoy calls Anthemion, he naturally could not offer the exact explanation of the Egyptian, and consequently of the Greek, palmette form.

2. *Annual Report of the Egypt Exploration Fund*, 1885, with report of Mr. PETRIE's lecture announcing his discovery.

"In architecture, although we have as yet only gleaned the scraps left by the Arabs, from one building we have obtained invaluable results. Hitherto not a single early Greek building was known in Egypt—nothing before Ptolemaic times. We have now before us fragments of one of the earliest Greek temples that is known, that of Apollo of the Milesians; enough to show the style of the architecture and the nature of its decoration. The building was Ionic, but peculiar in many respects. The volute, which I only saw before its destruction by the Arabs, had no droop in its lines where they pass over the echinus, but was like the form in the Aqueduct of Hadrian, to take a late example. The column had a sculptured necking above the flutings, which is very unusual, and this necking is ornamented *with the lotus pattern in a form which seems like a prototype of the Greek honeysuckle*," pp. 25 and 26.

3. JOSEPH THACHER CLARKE, "A Proto-Ionic Capital from the site of Neandreia."—*American Journal of Archæology*, Vol. ii., No. 1. Figured at xiii. 9.

Egypt for originals. Among these types are illustrations for Asia Minor, for Athens, for Etruria, and for Nineveh. The Assyrian types (2, 3, 5) are from ivory plaques, which are specified by all authorities as of Egypto-Phenician work and style, and their Egyptian character is unmistakable (compare xxiv. 10 [p. 183].) No. 5 is a direct counterpart of the Egyptian xii. 4 [p. 113.]

The earliest dated Greek anthemions are of the eighth or seventh century (xix. 3 [p. 147]). The "Mycenæ" pottery copies from metal [p. 111] are earlier, but are not Greek and not connected with the Greek development. The earliest known Assyrian palmettes are of the ninth century. The earliest dated Egyptian detailed palmettes are two thousand years older (XIIth Dynasty, Owens College, Manchester, see p. 109), but an outline lotus palmette can be dated to the IVth Dynasty (Fig. 39c).[4] This form has been mistaken by Perrot for lotus leaves.[5]

The supposed origin of the Greek anthemion is from the palm-tree by way of the "Assyrian palmette."[6] The palm-tree was a symbol in Assyria,[7] but there are no indications of its having developed into the decorative pattern of the anthemion or of the "Assyrian palmette" (Figs. 60, 61, 62). The upper part of the palm-tree,

---

4. An outlined lotus palmette is also held by a figure in a painting of the Old Empire, LEPSIUS, *Denkmäler* (reference wanting, memory distinct). The outline Egyptian palmette is found in Ninevite ivories, PERROT ET CHIPIEZ, *Assyrie*, 535. It has been mistaken by COLONNA-CECCALDI for the "fruit" of the lotus. The word fruit probably means the Nelumbium seed-pod. *Monuments de Chypre, Une Fatère de Curium*.

5. PERROT ET CHIPIEZ, *Égypte*, p. 515.

6. CLARKE in *American Journal of Archæology*, vol. ii., No. 1. "A Proto-Ionic capital from the site of Neandreia." SEMPER, *Der Stil;* RAWLINSON in *Ancient Monarchies;* BIRDWOOD, *Industrial Arts of India*, p. 430 (South Kensington Series); and German archæologists generally. Birdwood says, "Its form (the Greek honeysuckle) is derived originally from the date *Hom*, but it really represents conventionally a flowering lotus, as the Bharhut sculptures enable us to determine" (p. 128). This is coming dangerously near the truth, according to the natural theory that conventional types have developed from the natural forms which they represent.

The words "Date *Hom*" need explanation. The "Hom," or Indian soma-tree, has nothing to do with the date palm, but the Sacred Tree of Lotus Buds (xxiv. 15) is supposed by Birdwood to represent a soma-tree, hence the word Hom is used by him to mean the Sacred Tree in general, and consequently the sacred palm—hence the expression "Date *Hom*."

7. A. H. SAYCE, *Hibbert Lectures*, p. 240, referring to texts, says that the "cedar-tree is identified with the 'Tree of Life,'" and that the palm is "possible," "later." The palm is undoubtedly a symbol on Chaldean and Assyrian cylinders, as abundantly illustrated by LAJARD'S *Culte de Mithra*; but it does not appear from the above quotation that the texts would give much support to the theory of an ornamental palm symbolism in Assyria. According to LENORMANT, *Divination*, p. 86,—"Le palmier était aussi dans une partie de la Chaldée l'arbre sacré par excellence ; voyez mon Commentaire sur Bérose, p. 330." According to ROBERTSON SMITH, *Religion of the Semites*, p. 176,— "The palm was a symbol of Astarte." It appears on Carthaginian coins, PERROT ET CHIPIEZ, *Phénicie*, p. 365. Its most significant use is in the Syrian caves described by RENAN, *Mission de Phénicie*, p. 652 (with illustration). In the quoted cases the naturalistic form is perfectly obvious. It also appears in rudely naturalistic form on several Cypriote vases. It was a symbol of Apollo in Delos, and at Delphi.

as represented in the scenery of Assyrian reliefs, has occasionally a close resemblance to the decorative palmette form; but the trunk of a tree is rather a serious thing to dispose of in a decorative pattern, and there ought to be some traces of its gradual decorative elimination if it produced a pattern without a trunk. So far from there being any such transitional forms, there is not even any evidence for patterns of natural palm-trees in Assyria. By the word pattern we understand a repeated motive as distinct from an isolated naturalistic representation. In symbolic use (and every appearance may be considered symbolic where it is not a palpable landscape accessory) the palm-tree is always isolated. Whether in rude or in artistic rendering on the cylinders which are our main reference for the palm as a symbol, the indications of the natural tree are always positive and distinct. There is not one instance of a pattern in Assyrian art which cannot be directly referred to Egypt, and no pattern for which examples, conceded to be Egyptian, are not abundantly found in Assyria (xxv.). It is useless to appeal to the deficiency of excavations and to future possible discoveries. The Persian art is a direct continuation of the Babylonian and Assyrian, and its remains are very abundantly known and published. All Oriental art has a traditional and conservative character which perpetuates and re-copies its original motives, and the Persian, Babylonian, and Assyrian ornament may, therefore, be fairly judged by the evidences which date from the ninth century B.C. If Egypt were swept clear of every relic dating before the Greco-Roman period, we could reconstruct the entire history of the lotus motive from the traditional survivals of all its primitive forms, and there is no reason which could explain the utter disappearance, from the known Persian, Assyrian, and Babylonian examples, of such Oriental traditional survivals. Moreover, in cylinders, monuments of a high antiquity can be brought in evidence, and so far from antagonizing the matter-of-fact evidence cited on the subject of the palm-tree, it is mainly the cylinders which supply it.

The traditional and constant combinations of the palmette with the lotus bud and lotus flower (Figs. 61, 71, 74, 76, 77, 82, 83, 86, 88) are not only significant as furnishing an argument drawn from association. They also imply, on the supposition that they represent a palm motive, that realistic and normal palms should be at least as frequent as normal and realistic lotuses, whereas they are of the greatest rarity, and, roughly speaking, almost unknown on the surviving ancient monuments, aside from Assyrian scenery backgrounds.

GREEK IONIC AND ANTHEMION FORMS.

Mr. Percy E. Newberry's independent conclusions regarding the "honeysuckle" and the lotus, reached in 1885, although unpublished, must not be passed over. His point of view included the Ionic form, and must be considered superior to Mr. Petrie's on this account,[8] for although the "honeysuckle" occasionally appears in Greek art without the supporting volutes, it never so appears in the archaic forms (xix, 3 [p. 147]) which must be the logical point of departure for a consistent theory, neither does it so appear in any large number of typical examples. The volutes are an essential portion of the necking ornaments of the Erechtheium (Fig. 118 [p. 171]), but they do not appear on the necking ornament of Naukratis (Fig. 63), which was Mr. Petrie's point of departure.

MELIAN ANTHEMION.
Repetition of xix., 3.

This Naukratic ornament really belongs to the type which produced the Egg-and-Dart moulding (xxi. [p. 159]) and was so entered on my plate for this moulding, published in the *American Journal of Archæology*, in 1888.

Mention must also be made of the announcements regarding the anthemion, of Mr. John Pennethorne,[9] who derives an anthemion pattern resembling Fig. 64, and found on the "Cyma of the pediment cornice of the Parthenon," from a "lotus and papyrus ornament," published by him, which is the counterpart of Fig. 65.[10] Mr. Pennethorne failed to cut the Gordian knot which has so far bound together the papyrus and the lotus, but his perception of the unity of the ornaments in question is the earliest which I have met. His matter is weakened by not knowing that the volutes at the base of the anthemion are the same volutes which form the Ionic capital (Plate xiii.).[11]

64. Type of the anthemion considered to be "lotus and papyrus" by Mr. John Pennethorne.

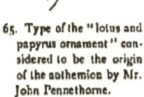
65. Type of the "lotus and papyrus ornament" considered to be the origin of the anthemion by Mr. John Pennethorne.

---

8. In the *Annual Report* of the Palestine Exploring Fund for 1890, Mr. PETRIE still adheres to the old notion of a derivation of the Ionic capital from the horns of a ram, and supposes that "the Greeks borrowed the Ionic volute from Asia."

9. *Geometry and Optics of Ancient Architecture*, 1878.

10. Originally published by OWEN JONES, *Grammar of Ornament*, as "a kind of lotus," but what kind of lotus, Owen Jones does not say.

11. PENNETHORNE remarks that "The only exceptions to the above statement [regarding the Egyptian origin of Greek ornament] are the spiral lines of Greek architecture, such as the volutes of the Ionic capital . . . and of these no trace appears to be found in Egypt—they belong to a later period of art," p. 173. This was written by an architect of wide information, the discoverer of the horizontal curves of Greek architecture, in 1878.

PLATE XIII.

GREEK IONIC AND ANTHEMION FORMS.

1. Greek anthemion. Detail from the handle of a Greek bronze vase, from Sidon. *Jahrbuch*,* 1888.
2. Phenician ivory detail of an Egyptian palmette, from Nineveh, in the British Museum. From CLARKE in *American Journal of Archæology*, 1886.
3. Similar detail, same reference.
4. Greek anthemion, head of a funeral stelè, in a vase painting. From CHIPIEZ, *Histoire des Ordres Grecs*, p. 273.
5. Phenician ivory detail of an Egyptian palmette, same reference as Nos. 4 and 5.
6. Ionic capital, found at Athens. From TROWBRIDGE, in *American Journal of Archæology*, 1888.
7. Greek incised detail in bronze. From the *Museo Etrusco-Vaticano*.
8. Etruscan Ionic detail, from MARTHA, *L'Art Étrusque*. In Florence, from Chiusi.
9. The Ionic capital of Neandreia (Chigri), Asia Minor. From CLARKE, in *American Journal of Archæology*, 1886.
10. Greek anthemion, stone relief. From HEUZEY, *Mission de Macédoine*, xxvi.
11. Greek anthemion, with introrse scrolls, stone relief. Reference as above, xlii.
12. Greek anthemion, stone relief. Same reference, xxviii. 3.
13. Ionic capital, found at Athens. From TROWBRIDGE, in *American Journal of Archæology*, 1888.
14. Greek anthemion, with introrse scrolls, terra-cotta antefix. From SCHLIEMANN, *Tiryns*, p. 295.
15. Ionic capital, found at Athens. From the *Jahrbuch*, 1888, iii. Fig. 17.

Nos. 13 and 6 have also been published by the Imperial Archæological Institute. No. 13, in the *Jahrbuch* for 1888, and No. 6, in the *Antike Denkmäler* for 1889.

---

* All references to the *Jahrbuch* indicate the journal, published under that name, of the Imperial Archæological Institute of Germany.

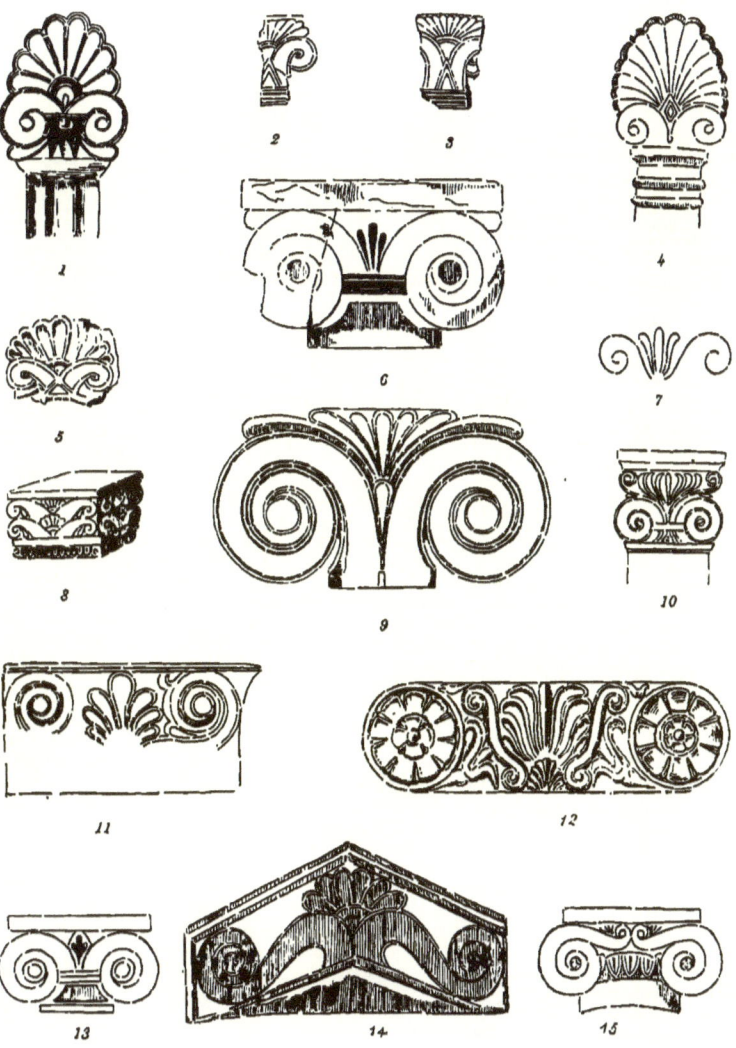

Pl. XIII., p. 121.

GREEK POTTERY ANTHEMIONS, ROPE PATTERNS, AND "HERZBLATTS."

(PLATE XIV., PAGE 133.)

66. GREEK TERRA-COTTA ANTHEMION.

ACCORDING to the illustrations offered by Plate xiii. [p. 121] for the Greek anthemion, it appears that the Greek types directly borrowed from Egyptian art are in hard material, stone, bronze, or terra-cotta (xiii.; 1, 4). It is also easy to understand that the originals most easily accessible to Greeks of the mother-country were in hard material, jewelry or bronze. From the eighth century B.C. there were large numbers of Greeks in Egypt,[1] and although they were ultimately confined to Naukratis, as a trading port and port of entry, this did not interfere with their individual presence and in large numbers, as soldiers, or otherwise, elsewhere. Still it may be that portable objects carried to the mother-country, and at an earlier time than the eighth century, rather than surface colour patterns, were the point of departure for the Greek anthemion. In Egypt the same original form is found in the colour patterns (xii. 7 [p. 113]), and in the motives of bronze and jewelry. In Greece the painted decoration of pottery, which art was first practised there in perfection and large amount, led to a development of variants from the original of complex and dissimilar character and often of remote resemblance. The Greek anthemion in stone or terra-cotta generally retains the severe outline of Fig. 67 from the Parthenon or of the motives

---

1. MASPERO, *Histoire Ancienne*. Two hundred thousand Greeks were transferred from the Pelusiac settlements to Naukratis. They were employed especially in the capacity of mercenaries, and in this capacity (with the Carians) so far displaced the native Egyptian forces that these, on one occasion, migrated in mass to Ethiopia as the only protest left them. The ultimate restriction of the Greeks to Naukratis, as a trading port of entry, placed no restriction on their individual presence as sight-seers, students, or traders, in other sections. Maspero mentions Milesians at Abydos, and Samians in the Great Oasis.

Fig. 66, and Plate xiii. 4 [p. 121] (which is a vase-picture of a tombstone), through the fifth century B.C. After that date it tends toward the complexity of such later examples as Figs. 68, 69 (tombstone ornaments), and 70.

The students of ornament and of architecture are well aware that here and elsewhere there has been a regulated

67. ANTHEMION OF THE PARTHENON.

68. ANTHEMION, FROM AN ATHENIAN TOMBSTONE.

69. ANTHEMION, FROM AN ATHENIAN TOMBSTONE.

evolution from the simple to the complex and the elaborately ornate; which is dependent, historically speaking, on sequence of time. Hence the facility, easily acquired, of dating objects according to style in Greek and Italian art, and in the Byzantine, Romanesque, Gothic, and Renaissance styles. This facility fails us on the other hand in Chinese, Hindu, Arab, and other Oriental art, and in the Egyptian. Where the civilization has been stationary its ornament remains unchanged. Hence the freedom with which we can dispense with the question of dates, under certain restrictions for the Greco-Roman period, in matters of Egyptian art. Every motive, whatever the individual date, represents an unknown antiquity of the original form. On the other hand

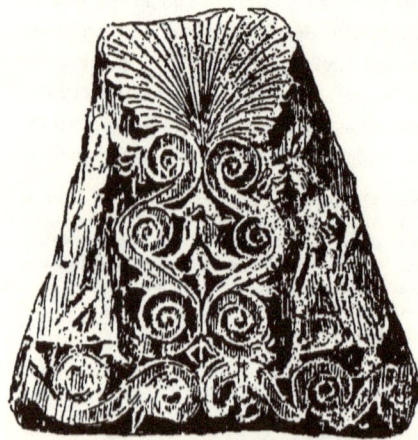
70. LATE ANTHEMION, MACEDONIA. From Heuzey.

GREEK POTTERY ANTHEMIONS, ROPE PATTERNS, &c.   125

the movement is so rapid in Italian art in the early sixteenth century that tombstones, for example, can be dated for that period within ten years on the basis of style, and according to the simple, ornate, or highly elaborate character. The movement is as rapid in Greek ornament between 430 and 330 B.C.

The pottery ornament of Greek art naturally developed in greater freedom and rapidity (although it bears a distinct relation to contemporary style in hard

71. RHODIAN VASE.   From Salzmann.

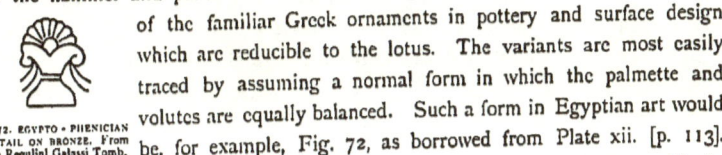

material), because it used the brush instead of the chisel or the moulder's stick, or the hammer and point of a workman in *repoussé*. Plate xiv. indicates some of the familiar Greek ornaments in pottery and surface design which are reducible to the lotus. The variants are most easily traced by assuming a normal form in which the palmette and volutes are equally balanced. Such a form in Egyptian art would be, for example, Fig. 72, as borrowed from Plate xii. [p. 113]. For Assyrian remains of Egypto-Phenician art such a form would be

72. EGYPTO - PHENICIAN DETAIL ON BRONZE. From the Regulini Galassi Tomb.

Fig. 73, as borrowed from Plate xiii. [p. 121].' For Greek pottery art such a form would be xiv. 6, which is directly borrowed from the above types; or it would be the alternating palmettes of Fig. 74 or Fig. 83.

73. EGYPTO-PHENICIAN IVORY DETAIL FROM NINEVEH. British Museum.

The assumed normal form is also well illustrated by the Melian pattern, xix. 3 [p. 147].

We will move then directly to the extreme development in size of the spiral volute as shown by xiv. 14. After this

74. GREEK ETRUSCAN DETAIL. Bronze Repoussé.

point is reached the entire disappearance of the palmette is the next abbreviation. As extreme case of a palmette without supporting volutes, we may name the alternating forms of xiv. 11. A highly important example of the palmette without supporting scrolls is shown at xxii. 8, 10 [p. 165]—important, because these details

represent an extremely frequent vase-pattern of the sixth century. The minimum of the scrolls as supporting the palmette is illustrated by Figs. 75, 76, 77, or by the case where there is only one pair of volutes for two palmettes, as in xiv. 8. This fine pattern, from a Greek vase found in Italy, has been chosen as a general type of some of the variations which have developed in Greek and modern ornament from the Egyptian lotus motive. The relations of certain details of this pattern to Byzantine scrolls,

75. GREEK POTTERY ANTHEMION.

76. GREEK ARCHITECTURAL DETAIL IN COLOUR.

77. GREEK POTTERY DETAILS.

Arab trefoils, and Medieval "*fleurs-de-lys*" will not escape attention (Fig. 78).

It need not be said that Byzantine ornament develops from the Neo-Persian and Roman Greek, and that Arab ornament developed after the Arab conquest of Syria, Egypt, and North Africa, and in these Byzantine countries.

The "Herzblatt" is obtained in various ways (Plate ix. [p. 91] and text related), but one method is illustrated here. By comparison of xiv. 3 and 5, we see that the "Herzblatt" is obtained by enlarging the lower volutes of No. 3, minimizing the palmette, and carrying the prolongation of the volutes

GREEK POTTERY ANTHEMIONS, ROPE PATTERNS, &c. 127

over the palmette to a point. Nos. 4 and 10 show "Herzblatts" with introrse scrolls.

The guilloche (rope pattern) is shown at Nos. 2 and 7, with inverted lotus buds and lotus palmettes. These are not very common instances, but the association is significant. The guilloche is an abbreviated spiral scroll, as may be seen by reference to the upper running pattern of xiv. 11, or to the diagram Fig. 79. It does not appear to be originally Egyptian, but is an abbreviation common in Syria, Mesopotamia, and Cyprus, and is especially favoured by early Rhodian vases (xxxviii. [p. 251]). Its evolution from the central pattern of Fig. 79 may be most easily studied in Cypriote vases, but it is not very frequent on them in extant examples (several in New York). It occurs on pottery found in Egypt and dated to the XIIth Dynasty.[2] It is the form of spiral affected by Assyrian cylinders (hence proven to be originally a hieratic symbol, compare xxxvi. 7 [p. 247]); and for the reasons which explain the concentric rings of scarabs (viii. [p. 87]), viz., the small dimension and hard material. It has been specified as a symbol by Colonna-Ceccaldi, both in Cypriote vases and in cylinders.

78. SARACENIC ALGERIAN DETAIL. From Ravoisié.

Various text cuts of this chapter (Figs. 80, 88, 89, 90) will speak for themselves as variants of the anthemion motive and types of ornament common to ancient and modern times. In our own modern ornament the recent patterns of decorators have been especially influenced by the "Grammar of Ornament" of Owen Jones, and by the South Kensington and Decorative Art movement, which sprang from his connection with the Crystal Palace Exhibition of 1851. Before this "Decorative Art" movement our conventional patterns were drawn from the

79. EVOLUTION OF THE GUILLOCHE.

---

2. FLINDERS PETRIE, *Catalogue of the Antiquities discovered in Egypt and Palestine*, 1890, "XIIth Dynasty, found at Kahun. piece of black pottery (Italian?) with guilloche pattern";

"Greek Revival" (late eighteenth and early nineteenth centuries), and before that, from the Italian Revival and Renaissance of the fifteenth and sixteenth centuries, and hence in both cases were classic. Although the preceding Gothic

80. GREEK ANTHEMIONS, MACEDONIA. From Heuzey.

time, whose ornament was absolutely rejected by the Renaissance, had developed an ornamental naturalism of its own, it retained many traces of the older Romanesque patterns. These again go back to the Byzantine and Greco-Roman.

81. ASSYRIAN.   82. ASSYRIAN.   83. GREEK POTTERY.   84. SINDH POTTERY.

Throughout the Middle Ages, Hindu, Moresque, and Arab patterns had filtered into Europe, especially through textiles; but these patterns again recur to Byzantine or Neo-Persian, under the conditions already described (Figs. 78, 84, 85).

85. SINDH TILES.   86. GREEK POTTERY.   87. RENAISSANCE CARVING.

From the fourth century B.C. onwards, and especially in the Roman-Greek period, there are distinct traces of an ornamental naturalism, which supplemented,

GREEK POTTERY ANTHEMIONS, ROPE PATTERNS, &c.   129

modified, and mistranslated the fundamental patterns of Greek art. How far the original elements of Greek and later classic decoration are contained in the illustrations offered, or to be offered, I leave the expert to decide, but some of the later mistranslations are eminently curious. The known instance of the transformation of the lotus bud in necklaces into an amphora will serve as an example. These mistranslations have not been confined to Roman and Alexandrine Antiquity, but have found their way into modern interpretation of ancient patterns to an alarming extent. Figs. 81-85 are borrowed from Birdwood's "Industrial Arts of India" (South Kensington Museum Art Handbooks), where they are used as illustrations of the "Knop and Flower" pattern, and although the Egyptian lotus element is recognized in the flower of Fig. 81, the lotus bud is interpreted as the "fruit of the *Hom*" (p. 424). The lotus bud of Birdwood's illustrations is otherwise disguised by the designation of "Knop." It is true that these buds

85. LOTUS BUDS AND ANTHEMIONS, ASIA MINOR. From Perrot.

are not obvious lotuses until the "honeysuckle" has been recognized as such, and these illustrations have also been introduced to mark the prevalence of the lotus bud, with the flower or palmette patterns; the bud having been largely omitted from my Plates, as being an obvious motive. The pattern 86 is supposed by Birdwood to be borrowed from the Assyrian "Tree of Life" (Fig. 121), although it is an obvious case of a doubled lotus. The palmettes and lotus buds of Fig. 88 have been noted by the eminent authority of Perrot as "oak leaves and acorns."[3] The traditional "honeysuckle" still grows rankly on the pages of our books on decoration, and the "palm" (without a trunk) flourishes like a green bay-tree on the pages of German archæology. Such mistakes have been common to the ancients and the moderns. They were made frequently by the decorators of later ancient times, who were almost as far removed as we are from

3. PERROT ET CHIPIEZ, v., p. 191, "Feuilles et Glands de Chêne."

the hoary antiquity of the lotus motive, from the stern and simple symbolism which suffered no encroachment on its sacred ground; from the time when the pictorial hieroglyph was restricted to religious uses, and "decorative art" was a thought unknown; from the time when art was religion; and when religion was national and individual existence, life and death, combined.[4]

_{4. ROBERTSON SMITH'S *Religion of the Semites* gives a valuable account of the connection between ancient religions and the local, communal, and national interests.}

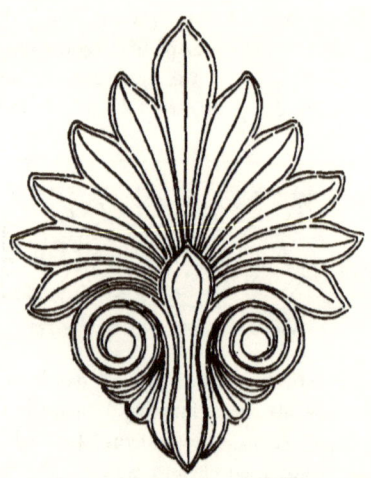

89. GREEK ANTHEMION, SICILY. From Hittorf.

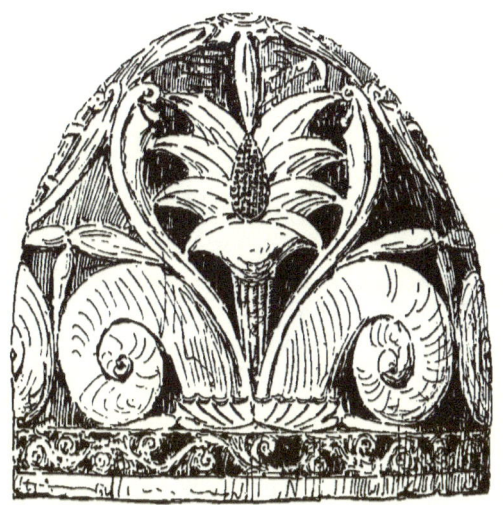

90. GRECO-SCYTHIAN GOLD HELMET FROM KERTCH. St. Petersburg.

PLATE XIV.

GREEK POTTERY ANTHEMIONS, ROPE PATTERNS, AND "HERZBLATTS."

1. Pottery anthemion. From a Greek vase in the *Monumenti Inediti*, X., xxv.
2. Rope pattern (guilloche) with palmettes. Detail from the terra-cotta sarcophagus of Clazomenæ, in Vienna. *Antike Denkmäler*, 1889.
3. Pottery anthemion. Rhodian vase in SALZMANN'S *Nécropole de Camire*, xxxiii.
4. "Herzblatt" with palmettes. From the *Antike Denkmäler*, 1889, i. 44.
5. "Herzblatts," in bronze *repoussé*. From ADOLPH BŒTTICHER, *Olympia*, Fig. 29.
6. Pottery anthemion. From STOCKBAUER AND OTTO, *Ornament antiker Thongefässe*, x.
7. Guilloche, with lotus buds. Pottery motive, from *Tanis*, II., xxxi. 6.
8. Pottery anthemion. From a Greek vase in the *Monumenti Inediti*, XI., xv.
9. Pottery anthemion. From a Greek vase in the *Monumenti Inediti*, X., viii. 5.
10. "Herzblatt" motive, painted terra-cotta at Olympia. From SEMPER, *Der Stil*, I., iii.
11. Lotuses and palmettes, spiral scroll above. Greek-Etruscan bronze *repoussé*. From the *Museo Etrusco Vaticano*, I., xxxix. 3.
12. Greek pottery lotus. From a vase in the *Monumenti Inediti*, XI., x. 2.
13. Border of palmettes and inverted lotuses. Greek-Etruscan bronze *repoussé*. From the *Museo Etrusco Vaticano*, I, xxxix. 2.
14. Spiral scrolls and palmettes. From a Rhodian vase in SALZMANN'S *Nécropole de Camire*.

Pl. XIV., p. 133

LOTUS IONIC CAPITALS AND DETAILS,

SHOWING THE SEPAL VOLUTES WITH AND WITHOUT THE CENTRAL SPIKE.

(PLATE XV., PAGE 139.)

The Egyptian palmette is the obvious original of the anthemion; hence a treatment of the Greek Ionic capital, which proves the identity of the two Greek motives is the most convincing. But there are not less than three original sources of the Greek Ionic capital; aside from the possibility or probability that volutes joined by a straight line at the top were directly copied by the Greeks in Egypt from capitals like vii. 7 [p. 79], or the upper member of vii. 5.

The honour of demonstrating the identity of certain Ionic capitals with the anthemion, within the limits of Greek art, belongs to Mr. Joseph Thacher Clarke,[1] and his essay on the Capital of Neandreia (xiii. 9 [p. 121]), which he discovered, gave a death-blow to the "palm-tree" (which he supposed to be the original anthemion form, in agreement with the generally accepted view) by linking the anthemion with the history of the Ionic capital, which is undoubtedly an Egyptian lotus. But we are by no means confined to the palmette form of the Ionic capital in our demonstration of its lotus origin.

The convincing point of M. Dieulafoy's demonstration is the relation of the lotus to certain Cypriote Ionic capitals and tombstones (xv. 15, 17). He also published the detail xv. 1; Egypto-Phenician detail of an ivory plaque from Nineveh, in the British Museum—as a lotus explaining the triangles of xv. 15 and 17. There is another capital in the Louvre with triangle, like 15, and another tombstone like 17 (Plate xli. 3 [p. 263].) There are two similar tombstones in the New York Museum (Fig. 43.)[2]

---

[1]. *American Journal of Archæology*, Vol. II., No. 1. "A Proto-Ionic Capital from the site of Neandreia."

[2]. The upper introrse scrolls of these tombstones are explained by the "Phenician palmette" (Plate xli. [p. 263]), and also through variants of the "honeysuckle" aspect of the lotus-palmette.

Colonna-Ceccaldi had already mentioned these triangles as related to the lotus (p. 72), although his interpretation did not exactly hit the point. This triangle is the central sepal spike (compare the Cypriote lotuses xv. 7, 13). Colonna-Ceccaldi had suggested an ovary. M. Dieulafoy specifies the triangle correctly as a "calyx leaf" (sepal), but by considering the outer scrolls as petals, he failed to give a logical account of the form. In my own original publication I made the reverse mistake, interpreting the scrolls correctly, but considering the central triangle to be an enlarged petal. My own mistake and M. Dieulafoy's were caused by inattention to the Egyptian three-spiked form and by confounding the Egyptian Nymphæas with the "Rose Lotus," which has not this peculiarity of the four sepal spikes or three in profile view (Plate iii. [p. 41] and related text).

The prominence of the central spike in the Cypriote lotuses (Plate xlvii, [p. 303]) makes them valuable references for the Cypriote capitals and tombstones ; therefore two of them have been given a central place on Plate xv.[3] The curling volutes of these flowers have already been explained (Fig. 4, of the flower from nature, with curling sepals); therefore we will immediately notice the rudimentary survivals, aside from Cypriote Ionic capitals and tombstones, of the central spike in Ionic capitals and Ionic forms.

The central sepal spike appears for instance in the Assyrian Ionic (xv. 9), which has been considered the original of the Greek,[4] and which is thus proved to be itself Egyptian. It survives in Greek Etruscan art of the third century B.C. (xv., 12), as dated by style of the relief from which it is taken. It appears on a mirror handle at Olympia (xv. 14) which cannot be dated far from 500 B.C. It appears on the Egypto-Phenician detail xv. 1, and is much repeated on Melian vases (xv. 8; variants, xvii. [p. 145], xviii. [p. 146]). As regards vases, the motive xv. 8 can be traced back, by way of xv. 6, 16, to the Cypriote pottery lotus.

The interesting capital xv. 10 is mentioned in descriptive details concerning the Plate (p. 138) and has an obvious connection with the floral forms placed above and below it.

We have then, finally, to notice the Ionic capitals which have neither spike

---

3. Their pendant exterior lines are explained by xlvii. 1. [p. 303] as rudimentary survivals of pendant lotuses.

4. By all authors of compendious works on the History of Art. To the exceptional views of Colonna-Ceccaldi, Dieulafoy, and Hans Auer (p. 72), we may add the Danish Archæologist, Julius Lange, who has, according to Puchstein's reference (p. 71), derived the Ionic capital from the "Papyrus" (apparently about 1877). This would be a case of just perception under mistaken verbal designation.

LOTUS IONIC CAPITALS AND DETAILS, &c.

nor palmette rudiment of the lotus, and whose volutes rise from the neck of the capital instead of meeting at the top. For these capitals, the original Egyptian Ionic is decisive reference. It is easily apparent how the capitals vii. 1, 4, 6, 9, 10 [p. 79] were reduced to forms like xv. 3, 4, 5, respectively Etruscan, Greek, and Syrian. Plate xv. 11 shows a Syrian capital, of uncertain date, in which one mode of transition to the Greek Ionic is clearly illustrated.

The dates of these capitals are not important. They exhibit survivals, in any case, of earlier traditions.

91. ASSYRIAN IONIC. RELIEF, KHORSABAD.

Plate xv. 2, ivory detail from Nineveh, is related to vii. 8 [p. 79] and to the inner detail of x. 5. Fig. 91 is a reminder of the Ionic of Khorsabad (from a relief) which has figured so largely in histories of art as proof of the Assyrian origin of the Greek capital.

The Syrian Ionic capital of Maschnaka (Fig. 92) is borrowed from Renan's "Mission de Phénicie." It is also figured by Reber, who has come very near to the correct explanation of the Ionic form.[5] The addition of the one word "lotus" to his account would have made it quite accurate.

92. SYRIA.

We must not overlook the bearing of these observations on the Persian Ionic (xxvi. 10 [p. 193]). For these Ionic volutes in Persian art we have earlier reference in certain "Mycenæ" pottery details (liv. 3, 4 [p. 325]). Diculafoy has correctly specified the lower member of this capital as a lotus, and with references to Assyrian ivory details in the British Museum which represent its original derivation. The pendant leaves suggest pendant sepals, and the entire lower member is suggestive of Hindu lotus treatment and of its Assyrian and Persian origin.[6]

---

5. REBER, *History of Ancient Art*; translated by Joseph Thacher Clarke (Harper). "There is reason to suppose that the double helix was not the primitive and normal form of the Assyrian [Ionic] capital, but was rather an abbreviation of the leaved calyx, so frequently met with in Phenicia, Palestine and Cyprus, and that the rolled ends of the leaves originally suggested the volutes of the capital and the various spiral forms occurring upon carved Assyrian furniture" (p. 70). At p. 231 Reber alludes to the Assyrian origin of the Ionic capital, which it would have been impossible for him to do if he had observed that the "leaved calyx" is a lotus.

6. This lower member has been mistaken by Perrot for "palmier" in matter relating to his illustration in Vol. V., PERROT ET CHIPIEZ. The enormous bases of these columns are covered with normal lotus details, apparent in Perrot's illustration, but still more obvious on the original in the Louvre (Diculafoy excavations).

T

PLATE XV.

LOTUS IONIC CAPITALS AND DETAILS, SHOWING THE SEPAL VOLUTES, WITH AND WITHOUT THE CENTRAL SPIKE.

1. Detail of an Egypto-Phenician ivory plaque from Nineveh, in the British Museum. From DIEULAFOY, *L'Art Antique de la Perse*, Part III. (Entire plaque in LAYARD'S Plates, First Series, 90 ; and in PERROT ET CHIPIEZ, *Assyrie*, p. 435.)
2. Egypto-Phenician ivory detail from Nineveh, in the British Museum. DIEULAFOY, as above.
3. Etruscan Ionic capital. Tomb at Cervetri. From MARTHA, *L'Art Étrusque*.
4. Ionic capital. From the *Monumenti Inediti*, VI., lix.
5. Proto-Ionic capital, Jerusalem. From PERROT ET CHIPIFZ, *Phénicie*.
6. Detail of No. 16. From a Rhodian vase in the British Museum.
7. Cypriote pottery lotus. From a vase in the New York Museum.
8. Detail of a Melian vase (compare xix. 1. [p. 147]). From CONZE, *Melische Thongefässe*.
9. Assyrian Ionic capital. Detail from the "Sippara Tablet." CLARKE, in *American Journal of Archæology*, 1886.
10. Cypriote Ionic capital. From COLONNA-CECCALDI, *Monuments de Chypre*. Published posthumously as a *Dessin Inédit* and without comment, except the word "Dali" (Idalium in Cyprus), followed by an interrogation mark. The present whereabouts of this capital does not appear, but measurements are attached to the design.
11. Syrian Ionic capital (uncertain date) at Deir-el-Kalaah, near Beyrout. From the *Revue Archéologique*, 1846-47.
12. Greek Etruscan Ionic capital. Detail of a relief not earlier than 3rd century B.C. From CONESTABILE, *Monumenti di Perugia*, LXVI., xcii.
13. Cypriote pottery lotus. From a vase in the New York Museum.
14. Detail of a bronze mirror handle found at Olympia, *Olympia*, IV., xxii.
15. Cypriote Ionic capital, in the Louvre. From DIEULAFOY, *L'Art Antique de la Perse*, Part III. (also published by LONGPÉRIER, *Musée Napoléon III.*, xxxiii., and in PERROT ET CHIPIEZ, *Cypre*, p. 116.
16. Shield with lotus Ionic forms. Detail of a Rhodian vase in the British Museum. From SALZMANN'S *Nécropole de Camire*, liii.
17. Cypriote tombstone in the Louvre. Compare Fig. 43 and Plate xli. 3 [p. 263]. From LONGPÉRIER, *Musée Napoléon III*.

Pl. XV, p. 139.

THE LOTUS SPIRAL ON CYPRIOTE, RHODIAN, AND MELIAN VASES.

(PLATES XVI., XVII., XVIII., XIX., PAGES 144, 145, 146, 147.)

THE type of Greek vases known as "Melian" is extremely limited in number as regards modern finds, but there is no doubt of its singular importance and significance for the history of Greek pottery. The force and individuality of the decoration speak for themselves and as distinct from those "Geometric" vases which show the Greek art struggling out of barbarism as regards design of the figure, the Melian vases are, with some Rhodian pieces, the earliest which show that art fully launched on its independent career in figure design. The published pieces herewith are supposed to date from the seventh century B.C.[1]

Professor Conze, of the Berlin Museum, was the first to point out the importance of the Melian vases, and his publication of them in colour is the most sumptuous work of Greek archæology as regards the scale, execution, and colouring of the individual pieces presented. In my own study of the Ionic volute as derived from the curling lotus sepal I chanced to pass from the study of Cypriote examples (xlvii. [p. 303]) to the publication of Professor Conze. It was impossible for me not to recognize the enormous spiral volutes of xvi. 2 (doubled lotus form) as a development of the Cypriote lotus (3), and this led me to look for the Rhodian connecting links which are also represented on the Plate.

The Rhodian lotuses 1 and 4 show a Grecianizing and decorative treatment of the Cypriote lotus (compare xlvii. [p. 303]). No. 5 (supporting demi-rosette) from a vase of Thera (Rhodian style) shows a related palmette form, with central spike. The Melian lotus numbered 2, showing the spiral volute in still more

[1] By references in DUMONT ET CHAPLAIN, *Céramiques* 1861, p. 9; and by DE WITTE, *Rev. Arch.*, 1862, t. vi., *de la Grecè propre*, p. 220; in article by CONZE, *Bulletino*, p. 403.

142 THE LOTUS SPIRAL ON CYPRIOTE, RHODIAN, & MELIAN VASES.

elaborate rendering, carries us to Plate xvii. where the palmette displaces the petals, or to Plate xviii. where the lower spirals are inverted.

On Plate xix. we have a Melian vase and examples of additional scroll and spiral motives summarizing results already reached. The value of the Melian vases for the history of the lotus lies in the fact that they unite on individual pieces all the variants which are in question as the basis of scroll and spiral in Greek art; as, for example, in xix. 1; and that in these individual vases it is impossible not to recognize the unity of design and of origin for all the forms. These vases also exhibit normal lotus patterns and rosettes.

On a given vase, for instance xix. 1, it is impossible not to refer the various details, including the concentric rings, to the larger types on the neck and on the body of the vase (shown in detail, xvi. 2 and xviii.). It is again impossible not to refer the spirals of these larger details to the Rhodian and Cypriote volute. The latter must be assigned to the curling sepal (Fig. 4). Hence the Cypriote, Rhodian, and Melian vases offer a parallel and corroboration to the explanation offered for Egyptian Ionic forms (vii. [p. 79]), concentric rings (viii. [p. 87]), spiral scrolls (x. [p. 97]), and "Herzblatts" (ix. [p. 91]).

One origin of the "Herzblatt" is demonstrated by xix. 4, as compared with xix. 3. The spiral scroll, as shown by xix. 5, appears on the vase below the handle with only rudimentary rings to mark the displaced palmette and on the foot of the vase without this rudiment. In xix. 3 we see the normal form of the Greek lotus-anthemion; normal in the sense that the proportion of volute to palmette is balanced, and that according to the development of one or the other, either the Ionic form or the "honeysuckle" is result.

EGYPTIAN LOTUS SPIRALS.   From Prisse d'Avennes.

THE LOTUS SPIRAL ON CYPRIOTE, RHODIAN, AND MELIAN VASES.

PLATE XVI.

1. Rhodian lotus, showing spirals derived from the type No. 3. Detail of a vase in SALZMANN'S *Nécropole de Camire*. Compare the vase of Plate xxxviii. [p. 251].
2. Melian double lotus, with one flower inverted, showing spirals derived from type No. 1. Detail of a vase in CONZE, *Melische Thongefässe*. Compare neck of the vase, Plate xix. 1. [p. 147].
3. Cypriote lotus, showing original type of Nos. 1, 2, 4, and 5. From the neck of the vase figured on Plate xlvii. 11. [p. 303]. In the New York Museum.
4. Rhodian lotus, derived from type No. 3. From the vase in the Louvre, figured Plate xxxviii. [p. 251].
5. Lotus supporting demi-rosette, related to type Nos. 1 and 3. From a vase of Thera. *Monumenti Inediti*, VIII., v.

PLATE XVII

The Melian vases illustrated are in the Polytechnic at Athens.

Detail from CONZE, *Melische Thongefässe*. Double lotus palmette, one inverted, and inverted Ionic lotus above. A variant of xvi. 2.

PLATE XVIII.

Detail from CONZE, *Melische Thongefässe*. Double lotus palmette related to Plate xvii, but showing lower reversed scrolls like the "Herzblatt." Ionic lotus forms beneath the horses.

PLATE XIX.

Vase and details from CONZE, *Melische Thongefässe*.

1. Vase showing double lotuses, like xvi. 2, on the neck. From this vase is taken the large detail, Plate xviii.
2. Detail showing spiral lotus scrolls. Compare the spiral scrolls under the handle of No. 1, where only rings indicate the eliminated palmette. On the foot is a spiral scroll, from which all trace of the palmette has disappeared.
3. Normal form of the Greek anthemion, showing Ionic spirals and the palmette in balanced proportion.
4. Illustration of the "Herzblatt" motive, for comparison with No. 2, and with the detail between the horses of No. 1. The original repeats the details in a longer pattern.
5. Illustration for the spiral scroll as obtained by reversing one spiral of the type No. 3.

Pl. XVI, p. 144.

Pl. XVII. p. 145.

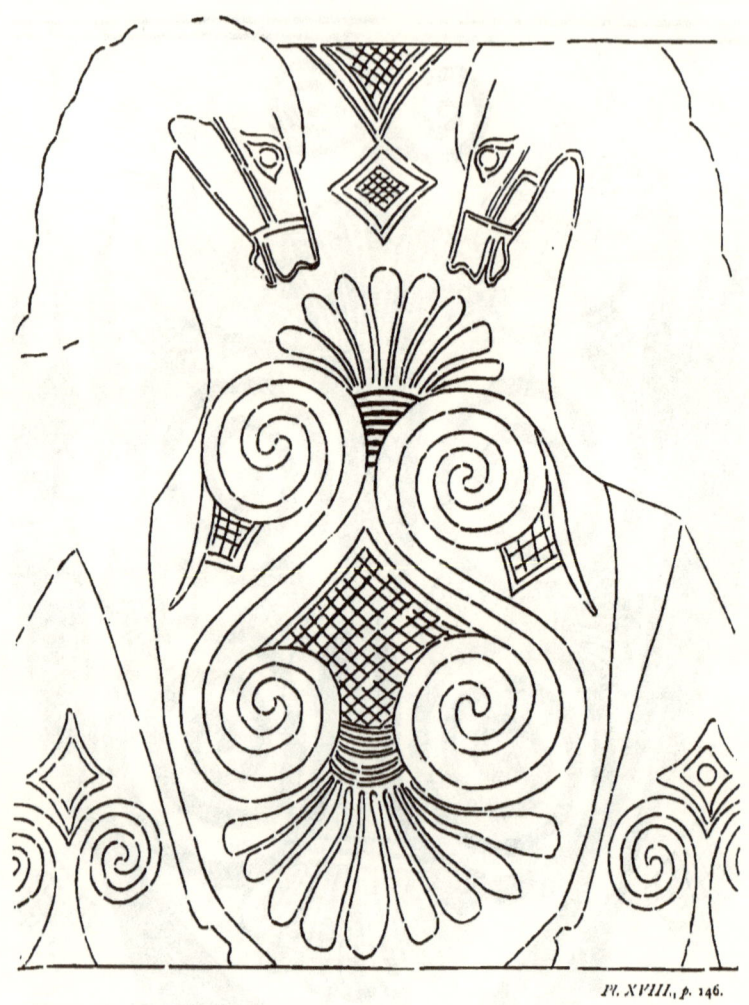

Pl. XVIII., p. 146.

Pl. XIX., p. 147.

THE ROSETTE.

(PLATE XX., PAGE 153.)

CONTINUED FROM PAGE 99 AND PLATE XI. (PAGE 107).

The Rosette is a constant feature on Cypriote vases (xx. 19, and xxxvii. 12 [p. 249]); on Melian vases (xix. 1 [p. 147] above the horse); on Rhodian vases (xx. 3, 8); on Naukratic vases (xxx. 2, 10 [p. 211]); and on "Corinthian" vases (so-called). It is rare on " Mycenæ" vases (lv. 18 [p 327]), but familiar to " Mycenæ" ornament (xxvii. 7 [p. 197]), and perhaps unknown to the oldest Greek " Geometric " style (lvi. [p. 339]). Its association with the Ionic capital at the centre of the volutes (Fig. 41 [p. 71]), and on Persian Ionic variants (xxvi. 10 [p. 193]) is an indication of its lotiform derivation, to which instances we may add the text-cuts 93, 94, 95, as examples of significant juxtaposition.

The Rosette is not to be confounded with certain diagrams of Cypriote, Rhodian, and Melian vases, like lvii. 12 [p. 341], which are independent solar diagrams related to the Egyptian hieroglyph *Ra*.

Aside from the above references to vases, the following numbers of Plate xx. belong to Greek art:—No. 13, Syrian Greek; No. 22, Cypriote Greek; No. 16, Alexandrine Greek ; No. 17, Naukratic Greek ; No. 5, Greek Etruscan ; Nos, 4, 21, Greco-Roman ; and No. 6, Greco-Buddhist.

Having found the theory of the Assyrian origin of the Rosette unfounded (p. 99), and having specified the four distinct lotus combinations or representations which explain it (p. 103), we have only to mention the confusion and chaos which the supposed Mesopotamian origin of the Rosette has created in Greek archæology and history.

Since our knowledge of early Greece and the origins of its culture is so largely dependent on the character of ornament and mainly dependent on the history of pottery, it will be impossible to found a science of Mediterranean history while this prejudice continues.

As the Rosette is an important feature of Assyrian ornament there is no reason for disputing a reactive influence on Greek art from Assyria, which reactive influence may also be conceded to the Assyrian palmette. But to magnify the importance of this reactive influence is to displace the centre of history, from the beginning of the XVIIIth Dynasty onwards.

Who has ever dreamed of suggesting that the Renaissance civilization of Italy was controlled by the armies of Germans, French, and Spaniards, who overran the country in the days of its glory? As little cause have we to assume that the Hittites, Phenicians, Assyrians, Carians, Libyans, Greeks, and Sardinians, either in their character of foreign foes or of Egyptian mercenaries, influenced the civilization of Egypt. It was they, on the contrary, who thus obtained their own civilization.

Before the Greek factory of Egyptian scarabs for export, with unreadable hieroglyphics, was discovered at Naukratis,[1] the presence of Egyptian scarabs in Italian tombs, or in Greeks tombs, was always attributed to the Phenicians. In so far then a historic prejudice was dispelled by this discovery. In a similar way the Phenicians themselves have suffered from a historic prejudice. Wherever the palmette and the rosette have been found in Mediterranean art, they have been attributed to Assyrian influence; but if the Assyrian palmette and rosette were borrowed from Egypt, they were borrowed by way of the Phenicians and the Hittites, whose palaces are recorded by Assyrian inscriptions to have been copied by Assyrian kings.[2] The whole theory of Phenician art, as at present accepted, falls to the ground if the rosette and the palmette be Egyptian. Phenician art is a supposed bastard combinatian of Assyrian and Egyptian. This theory is no longer tenable. It was Egypto-Phenician art which controlled the ornament of the Assyrian. Hence a reactive influence of Assyrian art by way of Asia Minor or Syria, or of the Phenicians themselves, can have had no great importance. It would simply mean, to recur to the example of the Renaissance, that English Renaissance art came from Italy by way of Spain rather than by way of France.

The illustration of the Buddhist "Trisula" (xx. 6) shows a combination of two trefoil lotuses with two buds and a rosette. Lotus spirals are frequently

---

1. FLINDERS PETRIE, *Naukratis*, I. They were imitations for export trade.

2. Verbal advice of Professor A. L. Frothingham, Junr., of Princeton.

THE ROSETTE.

introduced between the stems of the trefoils.³ This publication appears to be the first modern recognition of the "Trisula" as a lotus,⁴ although the lotiform symbolism of the Buddhists is a matter of commonplace knowledge. The most highly venerated idol of Krishna in all India has been proven to be a defaced and unrecognized Trisula.⁵ The relation of the lotus rosette to the pedestals of Hindu deities has been mentioned (p. 37).⁶

94. CYPRIOTE LOTUS.

3. Sanchi Tope at Bhopal, early first century A.D. Casts in the India Museum, South Kensington. Two fine cuts of the Trisula in the *Archæological Survey of Southern India*, by JAMES BURGESS, I. p. 47. See also JAMES FERGUSSON, *Cave Temples of India*, pp. 73, 74, and SIR ALEXANDER CUNNINGHAM, *The Stûpa of Bharhut*, Plate vii. and p. 36.

4. "The Trisula not yet satisfactorily explained."— BURGESS, *Archæological Survey of Southern India*, I. p. 47. . . . . "Shield ornament not yet explained,"—JAMES FERGUSSON, *Cave Temples of India*, p. 74.

5. BIRDWOOD, *Industrial Arts of India* (South Kensington Series). "In the Madras Presidency it would appear to be always Krishna, who is represented under the form of Vishnu. His most famous form is Jagan-natha, 'Lord of the World,' under which he is worshipped in association with his brother Balarama, and his sister Subhadra, at Puri, near Cuttack, in Orissa. This image has no legs and only stumps for arms, and its head is very large. Krishna, it will be remembered, was accidentally killed at Dwaraka, and the story at Puri is that some pious person collected his bones and put them in a box, in which they remained until King Indradyumna was directed by Vishnu to make an image of Jagan-natha, and put Krishna's bones into its belly. Viswakarma, the architect of the gods, undertook to do this, on condition that he should be left undisturbed until completion of the work. But the king, after fifteen days, losing all patience, went to see how he was getting on, when Viswakarma at once went off in a huff, leaving Jagan-natha without hands or feet. Such is the explanation given by the Brahmans of this hideous idol. The true one is General Cunningham's, who has proved that the image has been concocted of the *trisula* of a Buddhist tope, which was erected at Puri B.C. 250. Before this monstrous shrine all distinctions of caste are forgotten, and even a Christian may sit down and eat with a Brahman. In his work on *Orissa*, Dr. W. W. Hunter says that at the 'Sacrament of the Holy Food' he has seen a Puri priest receive his food from a Christian's hand" (p. 76). . . . "General Cunningham considers that the *trisula* represents *Dharma*, the Law; more probably it represents *Buddha*; but these were all in their origin sun and phallic symbols. . . . Every native of India would at once recognize the *trisula* as a symbol of the generative power. . . ." (p. 105).

6. There are many recognitions of the Rosette in CUNNINGHAM'S *Bharhut*; for instance —"In the flowered medallions the central portion is always a many-leaved lotus," p. 116. In reality the "many leaves" of the rosettes mentioned consist of flowers closely ranged side by side. This point in Hindu rosettes has been correctly noticed by BURGESS, *Archæological Survey*, I. p. 37—"Half disk, outer border half-blown lotus blossoms." The normal Egyptian lotuses of Indian patterns have not been noticed by these authors, for instance, *Bharhut*, Plates xxi., xl.

95. IONIC CAPITAL WITH ROSETTE. Macedonia. From Heuzey.

PLATE XX.

THE ROSETTE.
CONTINUED FROM PAGE 99 AND PLATE XI. (PAGE 107).

1. Rosette, showing the expanded flower "in plan," as spread out and seen from above. Detail of a bronze door from Susa (Dieulafoy excavations). Mistaken by Dieulafoy and Perrot for a "double daisy" (p. 49, Note 14). From PERROT ET CHIPIEZ, v., p. 557.
2. Rosette of lotus buds, Greek pottery. *Naukratis*, II. xxvi.
3. Rhodian vase, showing normal rosettes of the highly conventional form supposed to be based on the ovary stigma (Figs. 5, 6, 8).
4. Rosette of lotus buds. From a cake stamp. *Naukratis*, I. xxix
5. Rosette, showing the expanded flower "in plan." From an Etruscan bronze *Cista* (Præneste). *Monumenti Inediti*, VIII. xxvi.
6. Rosette, supporting buds and trefoil lotuses. From the "foot-print of Buddha" in SCHLIEMANN'S *Troy*, p. 103. This is the famous Buddhist emblem called the *Trisula*, and has not previously been recognized as a lotus motive. Original design in *Archæological Survey of Southern India*, I., p. 98.
7. Rosettes, on stems, with tabs. Portion of a "bouquet," or symmetrically arranged group. From an Egyptian tomb-painting. ROSELLINI, C. lxxiii. The bouquet is balanced by another, partly shown at No. 9, and repeating the type and illustration explained for Plate iv. 6 [p. 63]. The demonstration for the stem of iv. 4 specifies our design as a lotus. See p. 50.
8. Rosette of lotus buds, from a Rhodian vase. *Jahrbuch*, 1889, iv., p. 93.
9. See matter for No. 7.
10. Terra-cotta whorl or disk, with rosette of lotus buds; concentric rings on reverse. *Naukratis*, I. xxxvii. 2.
11. Rosette, composed of four lotuses alternating with buds. Detail from PRISSE D'AVENNES, *Vases en or émaillé*.
12. Goddess Sekhet (lioness-headed) and rosette; an amulet also called the "Aegis of Pakht" or Bast. Bronze; from BIRCH, *Antiquities in the British Museum*.
13. Syrian sarcophagus (Greek period) showing two central rosettes (cover and side) composed of lotuses and buds, and other rosettes of conventional form. LONGPÉRIER, *Musée Napoléon III*., xxx.
14. Bronze Isis on wheel-shaped rosette of conventional form. BIRCH, *Antiquities in the British Museum*. The spokes of this rosette are shown to be made of lotuses by a similar amulet in PETRIE, *Kahun, Gurob, Hawara*, x. 77; of XVIIth or XVIIIth Dynasty.
15. Conventional rosette (Persian coloured tile). PERROT ET CHIPIEZ, V., Fig. 344.
16. Conventional rosette in stone relief. From the Greek sarcophagus of a child; from Alexandria. In the New York Museum.
17. Sepulchral stone image carved in recess. Lotus flowers, buds, and rosette. *Naukratis*, I.
18. Rosette form of the flower "in plan" (compare 1 and 5). Blue enamel *patera* from Cyprus, in the New York Museum.
19. Cypriote lotus (from the vase of Plate xlvii. 11 [p. 303]), showing lotus association for the rosette.
20. Type of the "Flabellum" (Sacred Standard). Demi-rosette of the type 1, 5, 18. ROSELLINI.
21. Rosette of lotus buds, turned in alternate opposite directions. Cake stamp, Roman period. *Naukratis*, I. xxix.
22. Ivory whorl from Cyprus, in the New York Museum.

Pl. XX., p. 153.

THE EGG-AND-DART MOULDING.

(PLATE XXI., PAGE 159.)

THE Egg-and-Dart moulding was announced as a lotus border by Owen Jones in 1856 in his "Grammar of Ornament." The announcement was repeated by M. Léon de Vesley in 1870.[1] The interpretations were incorrect in detail, but no archæologist has so far taken the trouble to correct them or to give a single word to this important subject.

96. LOTUS BORDER WITH BUNCHES OF GRAPES.
From Rosellini.

According to Owen Jones, a lotus border with intervening bunches of grapes (Fig. 96) was the origin of the motive, and the grape bunches were the basis of the egg (the inversion of the pattern is to be assumed always). Bunches of grapes are a rare appearance in Egyptian lotus borders. They certainly have nothing to do with the Egg-and-Dart moulding.

M. Léon de Vesley has based his explanation of the Egg-and-Dart moulding on a supposed border of "pine-cones" and lotuses. There are no "pine-cones" in Egyptian ornament, but a similar mistake has been made regarding the lotus bud in Assyrian art (Plate xxv. [p. 185]).

Neither bud, cone, nor grapes have anything to do with the moulding of the egg, which is derived from the commonest and not the rarest lotus border of Egyptian art. This commonest border is a lotus border pure and simple (xxi. 12), and although the intermediate bud appears here, and also *on* early examples of the "egg," it has nothing to do with its shape, form, or existence.

For clear explanation we will assume the two lotuses of xxi. 12 brought close together, with tips touching; the bud dispensed with. Reduce the lotuses to

---

1. *Société Centrale des Architectes: Annales*, 1871.

THE EGG-AND-DART MOULDING.

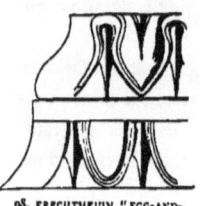

97. CYPRIOTE LOTUS.

the simplified three-spiked form (Fig. 97) and invert them. The Egg-and-Dart moulding will then appear "in flat." This was its original use in Egypt—a flat lotus border in colour.

When the Greeks incised the flower (xxi. 1), a rounded projection appeared as result between the flowers, as seen by the deeper cutting of xxi. 3; when the flower is inverted we have the ultimate moulding (xxi. 2, xxi. 4). The bud frequently appears in indication on the oval as reminiscence of the original border; for instance in the upper detail of the Erectheium moulding (Fig. 98), or in xxi. 1, 2. The bud in this detail corresponds to a natural appearance which is mentioned in the *Histoire Naturelle* of the *Description de l'Égypte*.

98. ERECHTHEIUM "EGG-AND-DART" MOULDING.

In this case the bud resembles the four-sided and sharp-edged bud of the blue lotus (Fig. 2, from nature). In the flat, painted border, xxi. 7, the rudimentary reminiscence of the bud is similar to that of the Erechtheium.

It appears from the foregoing matter that the three-spiked form of the Egyptian lotus again vindicates itself as the key to many problems; the "dart" being simply the remnant of the central spike. For non-professionals it may be as well to remark that the "egg" is in element only a half oval (not an entire egg), and so frequently appears (Fig. 98).

The tendency to an entire oval, as seen at xxi. 6, is not especially typical of the original or later moulding, although it also appears in the shape of an entire egg. In this case the Cypriote vase No. 8 will explain the doubled pattern as the one to be assumed.[2]

It was by these two Cypriote vases that my solution of the "Egg-and-Dart" moulding was suggested. The corroborations were then sought and found in Naukratic carvings (1, 2, 3, 4), and the anticipations of Owen Jones and Léon de Vesley were subsequently discovered.

The lotiform derivation of the "Egg-and-Dart" moulding was independently worked out by Mr. Percy E. Newberry in 1885. (Compare pp. 76, 104, 119.)

Although the conventional examples 5 and 6 belong to Persian art, they are

---

2. The doubled bud is represented on this vase by one outline; explained as junction of two buds, one inverted. This explanation is indicated by the upper border of No. 10.

THE EGG-AND-DART MOULDING.

typical of the Greek, Roman, Renaissance, and modern use. From the slightly indicated darts of No. 5, Greek art already passed to a moulding in which their omission had obscured every trace of the true origin of this ornament and the "egg" moulding, pure and simple, is also thus derived (see lxvi. 14 [p. 399]). An

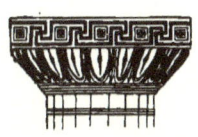  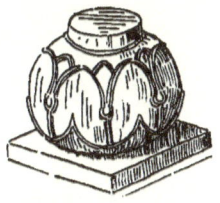

99. DORIC CAPITAL (original surface designs in colour).   100. BRONZE DETAIL. OLYMPIA. From Furtwängler.   101. ASSYRIAN BASE. From Place.

equally obscured inverted lotus border was used in colour surface ornament by the Greeks, and forms the painted pattern of the Doric capital (Fig. 99).

Fig. 100, Greek ornament in bronze, shows one early stage of the normal pattern, without intervening buds. For the moulding in position on a Greek monument, see xxxiii. 4 [p. 225].

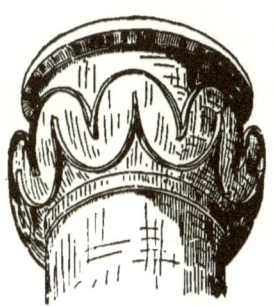

102. ASSYRIAN CAPITAL. From Place.

The Assyrian base[3] and capital[4] herewith have an interesting relation to our immediate subject, and have also the interest of being the only base and capital of actual architectural Assyrian use which have been so far published.[5] The base offers an obvious lotus border, related to the Egg-and-Dart moulding type of lotus border in surface design. The capital is an equally obvious derivative from a motive like that of the base.

3. From PLACE, in PERROT ET CHIPIEZ, *Assyrie*, Fig. 82.
4. From PLACE, in PERROT ET CHIPIEZ, *Assyrie*, Fig. 74.
5. Actual columnar members are great rarities in Assyrian finds. The excavated architecture was one of walls and not of columns, excepting in so far as they were made of wood and have entirely disappeared. Our knowledge of Assyrian columnar architecture is derived from pictorial reliefs, which do not always represent Assyrian buildings; but which argue, at least, familiarity with the forms represented (Fig. 91, and xv. 9 [p. 139]). There are a few other columnar members known, but only those above have been published. The lotus border of the base is repeated above an Assyrian Sphinx, figured by PERROT ET CHIPIEZ, *Assyrie*, and originally published by GEORGE SMITH.

PLATE XXI.

THE EGG-AND-DART MOULDING.

1. Stone carving; lotus incised, leaving projected "egg," on which is a bud. Compare Nos. 9, 11, 13. *Naukratis*, I. xiv.
2. The same fragment reversed, to show the origin of the Egg-and-Dart moulding.
3. Similar fragment (*Naukratis*, I. xiv.), the lotus more deeply incised and showing projecting fragments of the "egg" in higher relief.
4. The same fragment reversed, to show the origin of the Egg-and-Dart moulding.
5. Typical Egg-and-Dart moulding in conventional form. DIEULAFOY, *Monuments Antiques de la Perse*, Part III.
6. Typical Egg-and-Dart moulding in conventional form. Reference as above.
7. Typical Egg-and-Dart motive in colour design, showing an inverted lotus and angles on the ovals, derived from buds. Painted terra-cotta. *Monumenti Inediti*, XI. x.
8. Cypriote vase in the New York Museum, showing doubled lotuses, whose bounding outlines form continuous ovals. The lozenges on the ovals represent doubled buds. Compare the neck border of No. 10.
9. Greek pottery fragment (*Naukratis*, I. vii.), showing the lotus border origin of the moulding (before inversion).
10. Cypriote vase in the New York Museum, with lotus border, showing the pattern of the Egg-and-Dart moulding before it is inverted. The central spikes represent the "dart" (petals to be eliminated); the buds are on the oval which represent the "egg." Lotus bud border below.
11. Greek pottery fragment (*Naukratis*, I. vii.), showing the lotus border original of the moulding (before inversion).
12. Greek Rhodian pottery motive. (SALZMANN, *Nécropole de Camire*, xxxii.) Lotus border original of the moulding, with lotuses more widely spaced. In the exact original border the bounding lines of the flowers connect, the petals are eliminated, the central spike becomes the "dart," and the border is reversed.
13. Greek pottery fragment (*Naukratis*, I. vii.), indicating the constant use of this lotus border in Naukratic and Rhodian vases.

Interesting Phenician examples are seen at lxvi, 5, 11, 13, 14 [p. 399], showing that the motive may appear as a series of chevrons, and also illustrating the egg moulding pure and simple.

Compare also Figs. 165, 166 [p. 334] for the related Egyptian border of lotus chevrons.

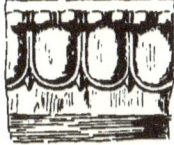  

Pl. XXI., p. 159.

THE SO-CALLED "IVY LEAF."

(PLATE XXII., PAGE 165.)

My suspicion that the "ivy leaf" (so-called) of Greek ornament is a lotus leaf was first suggested by a Rhodian vase (detail xxii. 5) pictured in Salzmann's "*Nécropole de Camire*," and now in the British Museum. This suspicion has been confirmed. Plate xxii. 6 (from Rosellini) repeats the cleft leaf of heart-shaped pattern already shown in other Egyptian illustrations (Plate iii. 2, 3, 5, 6, 8, 12 [p. 41], and Fig. 2, from nature [p. 26]).

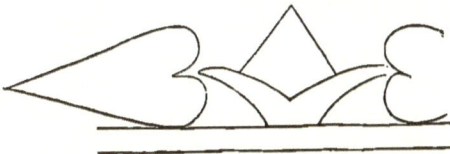

103. DETAIL FROM A STONE RELIEF. MUSEUM OF BOLOGNA. LOTUS WITH SO-CALLED "IVY LEAVES." From Author's sketch.

The long pliant stems of this leaf, as at li. 7 [p. 319] on an Italian tombstone at Bologna, forbid the suggestion of an ivy leaf.

The associations of this leaf with the lotus, as at xxii. 2, 10, and with the lotus palmette, as at xxii. 8, 10, are conclusive. An equally conclusive association is that of the leaf and lotus of the Cypriote coin, xxxii. 5 [p. 223]. Fig. 103 shows a detail from the Museum of Bologna, which also unites this leaf with the lotus.

The ornament first appears, as far as known monuments outside Egyptian patterns are concerned, on "Mycenæ" vases (xxii. 1, 3, and lii. 9 [p. 321], from the "Sixth Tomb"), but there is not one indication in "Mycenæ" art of an independent ornamental pattern, and this one must have been borrowed either in Egypt, Syria, or Cyprus, in which latter countries it can also be definitely traced, but not on dated monuments.

The pattern can be dated on "Mycenæ" vases from Egypt to the XIXth or XXth Dynasty.¹ It is rare as a running pattern on the distinctive Cypriote vases, but it occurs in Cyprus both in Cypriote "Mycenæ" pottery and otherwise.² It does not occur in the Greek "Geometric" style. It is the only pattern which is common to "Mycenæ" pottery and to Greek art (the Greek spirals are not connected with the Mycenæ patterns),³ but must have passed into Greek use by way of Rhodes, or Cyprus, as it is not common on Greek pottery before the fifth century B.C., and therefore could not have been borrowed from "Mycenæ" vases, in which case it would appear on the earlier Greek pottery.

The designation of an "ivy leaf" is traditional, but absolutely arbitrary and without foundation. The diagrams frequently combined with this pattern (xxii. 7) are the ordinary solar diagrams, but these do not appear in the "Mycenæ" use as so far known to publication.⁴ The combination, as at xxii. 7 was translated in Roman art into a pattern of grapes and vine leaves, and so appears on a Roman stone vase of the British Museum.⁵

Curious variants of the leaf on Mycenæ vases are shown at lii. 1, 2, 7 [p. 321].

It is so far not noticed by students that examples of the "ivy" pattern in the Museum of Bologna (Figs. 103, 104, and li. 7 [p. 319]) are connected with the art of Mycenæ. It is the typical ornament of Bologna tombstones, and it is only here, within my knowledge, that it is largely represented on stone reliefs. Many tombstones which show the pattern are as late as the fourth or third century B.C., but there is a positive connection between these and, the prehistoric Celtic

---

1. FLINDERS PETRIE, *Catalogue of the Collection of Antiquities discovered in Egypt*, 1890. From a tomb of the XIXth or XXth Dynasty. "Greek pottery, of buff with red ivy pattern, of the same work and form as the Greek vases with cuttle-fish, found in Egypt," p. 8. From my own observation of this piece, as may be argued from the comparison of the cuttle-fish vases, which belong only to the "Mycenæ" pottery, it is one of pure "Mycenæ" style, by which I understand the Carian style of the Archipelago (lii -lv. [pp. 321-327]). [Since writing the foregoing note, I have Mr. Petrie's verbal assurance that he used the word "Greek" as implying Ægean character in contrast with Egyptian, and that in any other sense the use of the word was an oversight.]

2. See CESNOLA, *Cyprus*, for illustrations of the "large stone vase found at the entrance to the temple, Golgoi," p. 145, and of the terra-cotta coffin, p. 190.

3. The continuous spiral scroll of the "Mycenæ" type is not common in Greek art, and is quite unknown to early Greek pottery. The meander and the guilloche only are employed, but the guilloche is not found in the early "Geometric" style.

4. It is probable that the pattern was mistaken for ivy or some other plant by the Greeks, whose vases sometimes represent the solar diagram as berries with stems (Greek vases in the Etruscan Museum of the Vatican). The stems of xxii. 7, 9 also indicate this misapprehension. For the solar diagram, see p. 149, p. 200 (Note 4); Plates xxxiv. 2 [p. 227]—xxxviii. [p. 251]—xlv. 3 [p. 287]—xlvi. 10 [p. 289]—xlviii. 8 [p. 305]—L 3, 6 [p. 309]—lvii. 12 [p. 341]—lx. 8 10 [p. 359]—lxi. 4, 10, 11 [p. 365].

5. Room left of the Mausoleum Room. On a sarcophagus under the middle window.

monuments of Bologna. This appearance of the "ivy leaf" at Bologna unites with other obvious indications of a connection between its prehistoric art and that of the "Mycenæ culture," which was probably also Celtic.[6]

I have generally avoided mention of the corroborations furnished by the

104. STONE RELIEF DETAIL. MUSEUM OF BOLOGNA, SO-CALLED "IVY LEAF," WITH SPIRAL.
From Author's sketch.

second division of this book, but will specify here the remarkable reliefs from Bologna figured from my sketches under the "Lion and the Lotus" and the "Sphinx and the Lotus" (Figs. 128 [p. 206] and 129 [p. 214]).

6. ZANNONI has emphasized this connection by entering on one of his Plates a number of objects from the Schliemann excavations at Mycenæ; *Scavi nella Certosa di Bologna*. His Plates do not, however, indicate the prominence of the "ivy" pattern which a visit to the Museum of Bologna reveals.

105. Seed-pods of the "Rose Lotus." Flowers of the White Lotus (European Variety). Leaves of the Blue Lotus. Leaves of the "Rose Lotus." Buds of the "Rose Lotus."

PLATE XXII.

THE SO-CALLED "IVY LEAF."

1. "Mycenæ" vase. Showing the lotus leaf and stem. Compare No. 6. FURTWANGLER and LOESCHKE *Mykenische Vasen*, xxi. 152.

2. Cypriote pottery lotus, with lotus leaves. The shape here approximates to that of a bud, but there are no buds on Cypriote vases with the indication of a cleft base. Such elongated lotus leaves are common in Egyptian art. Compare the elongated form at iii. 5 [p. 41], at Fig. 30 [p. 55], and at xi. 2 [p. 107] (leaves with bent stems).

3. "Mycenæ" vase. FURTWANGLER and LOESCHKE, *Mykenische Vasen*, xvii. 121. Showing the lotus leaf with spirals.

4. Typical Greek vase border of lotus leaves. STOCKBAUER and OTTO, *Ornament Antiker Thongefasse*, xlvi.

5. Lotus leaves (horizontal neck border). Rhodian vase in the British Museum. SALZMANN, xlvi. The drawing repeats the appearance of the leaves as seen in perspective on the rounding body of the vase, where they are horizontally arranged.

6. Egyptian design from a tomb-painting showing the lotus leaf. ROSELLINI M.C. xl. 6. Compare Plate iii. 2, 3, 5, 6, 8, 12 [p. 41].

7. Typical Greek vase border of lotus leaves and diagrams of the sun. STOCKBAUER and OTTO, as above.

8. Details from a Greek vase (*Monumenti Inediti*, I. li.), showing association of the so-called "ivy leaf" with a lotus palmette.

9. Typical Greek vase border. STOCKBAUER and OTTO, as above.

10. Detail from a Greek vase (*Monumenti Inediti*, I. li.), showing two so-called "ivy leaves," with a lotus flower and a lotus palmette.

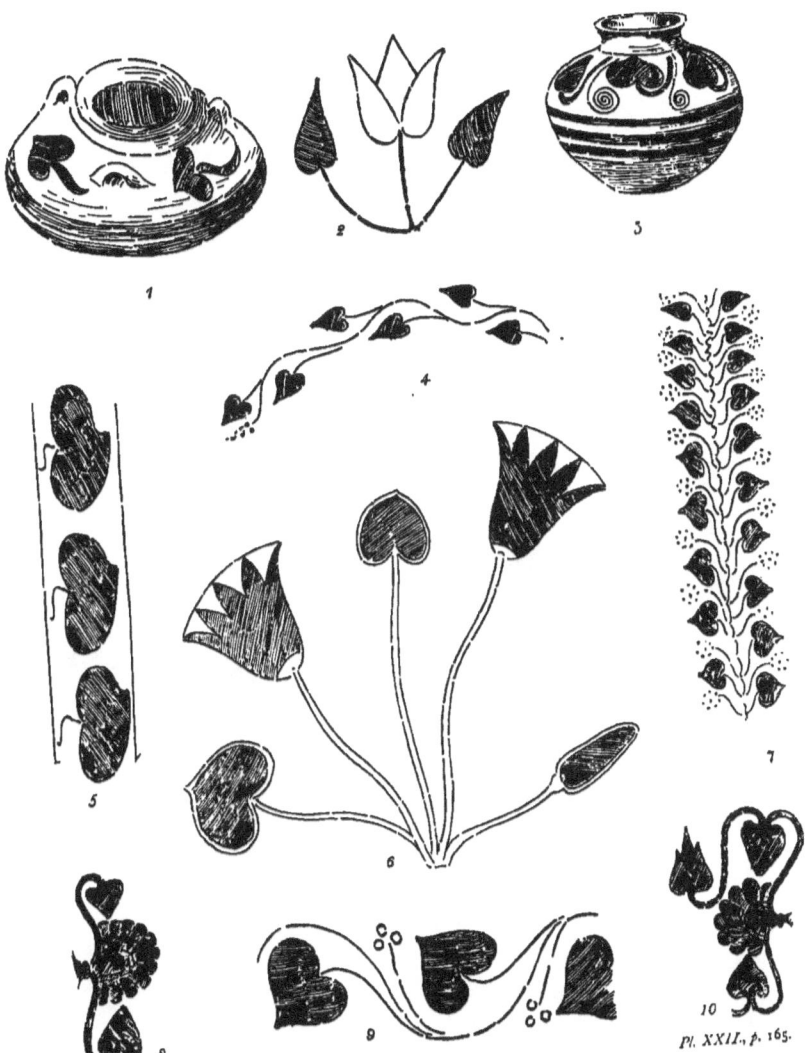

Pl. XXII., p. 165.

PART II.

ASSOCIATIONS OF THE LOTUS MOTIVE.

SOLAR SYMBOLISM IN IONIC FORMS.

(PLATE XXIII., PAGE 173.)

HAVING proven the lotus and the Ionic form to be identical, the question inevitably arises, were they co-extensive as symbols? The answer is undoubtedly affirmative, as far as Egypt was concerned. The Ionic form of Egypt (Figs. 106-109) is to our observation a palpable lotus, and it was equally so to the observation of an Egyptian. The symbolism of the lotus undoubtedly lasted as long in Egypt as the religion whose worship it reflected.

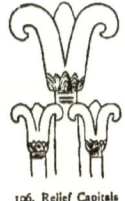

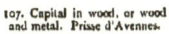

106. Relief Capitals at Karnak.
107. Capital in wood, or wood and metal. Prisse d'Avennes.
108. Egyptian mirror handle.
109. Capital in wood, or wood and metal.

All our present notions of Greek art are adverse to considering its ornament as significant of anything but decorative and artistic feeling, and the view that all the original motives of Greek ornament are sun symbols does not necessarily involve the view that they were regarded as sun symbols by the Greeks. The various strange travesties of Egyptian beliefs and divinities which found their way into Greek mistranslations are best indicated by the much-quoted transformation of the youthful Horus of Egypt into Harpocrates, a Greek god of silence.[1] The Siren and the Harpy, the Sphinx and the Gryphon, are all derived

---

1. DE ROUGÉ, *Notice Sommaire, &c.* "Horus enfant, c'était un symbole de l'enfance qu'on a pris mal à propos en Égyptien *Harpo chrate*, portait le doigt à la bouche; pour le signe du silence," p. 142.

170   SOLAR SYMBOLISM IN IONIC FORMS.

from Egyptian sources and are all found in strange disguises, both of myth and form, in their first European home. That the Greeks borrowed every fundamental motive of their decorative art from Egyptian sources is quite clear. That their religion, or their symbolism, as far as they had any, corresponded to the Egyptian in any exact sense is doubtful. But when we speak of the Greeks we speak of them as we know them. The millenium before 500 B.C. is still an obscure period. A thousand years was as long a period in Greece as it was in Medieval Europe. There was as much reason for the obliteration of traditions and the oversights of time. There was a Classic Revival in the fifteenth century, but it was not till the eighteenth century that Europe paid its debt to the memory of the Greeks. It may be in the twentieth century that it will realize the debt of the Greeks to the Egyptians. I do not speak in forgetfulness of Asia Minor, of Syria, or of Chaldæa, but all these countries were so saturated by Egyptian influence from the XVIIIth Dynasty on, that the phrase will pass. The proof lies in the history of the lotus.

It is impossible to doubt that the lotus was a sun and moon symbol, a generative symbol, and a mortuary symbol to the Phenician, the Hittite, and the Assyrian, and as impossible to doubt that the Ionic form was a co-extensive and equivalent symbol to the same nationalities. Colonna-Ceccaldi was the first to

110. Repetition of xxiii. 3. Ionic lotus supporting sun and moon. From an Assyrian cylinder.

111. Repetition of xxiii. 2. Ionic lotus associated with the symbols of sun and moon. Cypriote capital.

112. Repetition of xv. 17. Ionic lotus associated with the symbols of sun and moon. Cypriote tombstone.

113. Repetition of xxiii. 7. Lotus supporting the head of Hathor. Cypriote tombstone.

appeal to the cylinder whose detail is presented in Plate xxiii. 3, in his reference to the Ionic Capital as a lotus and a sun-symbol. He also specified the solar disk and crescent as appearing on the Cypriote Ionic form (xv. 17; [p. 139] xxiii. 2; xli. 3 [p. 263]). The head of Hathor, Moon Goddess[3] and equivalent of Astarte,[4] on the lotus in Cypriote art, was also mentioned by him (xxiii. 7).

2. *Monuments de Chypre.*
3. BRUGSCH, *Mythologie,* i. p. 84. Identity of Isis and Hathor. *Ibid.,* i, pp. 6, 12; for Isis as the moon.
4. COLONNA-CECCALDI, *Monuments de Chypre,* p. 97.

SOLAR SYMBOLISM IN IONIC FORMS.

To these instances we will add the sun disk of the Sippara Tablet on the Ionic Capital (1), the Hittite winged disk of Boghaz Keui on Ionic Capitals (4), the head of Hathor on the Ionic Capital of Carthage (6), and the Ionic lotus and the moon of "Umbrian"[5] art (8)—all of Plate xxiii.

114. Repetition of xxiii. 1. Ionic lotus supporting the sun. Detail from the Sippara tablet.

115. Repetition from xxiii. 4. Ionic lotuses supporting the winged solar disk. From Hittite relief of Boghaz-Keui.

These indications are all initial, and the evidence will swell in following pages, till no scholar can deny that the lotus variants which have been so far specified must have all been recognized or traditional equivalents of the original symbolism of this flower in the Tigris-Euphrates valley, in Asia Minor, and in Syria. Rhodes and Cyprus are included in the demonstration.

116. Repetition of xxiv. 7. The sun, the worshipper, and the lotus flower. Assyrian seal.

117. Repetition of xxiv. 11. The Moon-god, the worshipper, and the lotus flower, with buds. Assyrian seal.

The indications of lotus symbolism (normal form) on Plate xxiii. for the Cypriotes (5 and 10), the Hittites (?), (9), and the Carthaginians (11) are self-apparent. That the Cypriote stelès (Fig. 43 [p. 71], Fig. 112, &c.) were tombstones, must be considered as an illustration of mortuary symbolism.

> 5. The word "Umbrian" is applied by HELBIG to the Prehistoric Celtic Art of North Italy, as developed from Etruscan and other Italian influences.

118. IONIC CAPITAL OF THE ERECHTHEIUM.

PLATE XXIII.

SOLAR SYMBOLISM IN IONIC FORMS.

1. Ionic capital, supporting the sun disk. Detail from the "Sippara Tablet." PERROT ET CHIPIEZ, *Assyrie*, Fig. 71 ; also in MENANT, *Cylindres, &c.*

2. Cypriote Ionic capital, with sun and lunar crescent between the volutes. Compare xv. 17 [p. 139]; xli. 3 [p. 263]. LONGPÉRIER, *Musée Napoléon III.*, xxxiii.

3. Ionic capital, supporting sun and lunar crescent. From a cylinder shown at Plate xxxvi. 7 [p. 247]. LAJARD, *Culte de Mithra*, lii. 6.

4. Ionic columns, supporting winged solar disk. From the Hittite relief at Boghaz Keui, Asia Minor. LAJARD, *Culte de Venus*, xxii. 2.

5. Lotuses below the Sun-bark and winged solar disk. Cypriote seal, CESNOLA, *Cyprus;* KING'S Appendix ; Gems, vii. 11.

6. Ionic capital, supporting head of the goddess Hathor. PERROT ET CHIPIEZ, *Phénicie*, Fig. 16 (Carthage).

7. Ionic lotus supporting head of the goddess Hathor. (The Hathor head-dress is distinct in the original.) Cypriote stone tablet in the New York Museum. CESNOLA, *Atlas*, I. xviii. 26.

8. Ionic capital and lunar crescent. Details from an Italian bronze *cista.* ZANNONI, *Scavi nella Certosa di Bologna*, cl.

9. Figure holding lotuses under sun and lunar crescent. From a Hittite (?) cylinder. LAJARD, *Culte de Mithra*, xxxvii. 6.

10. Lotus, with sun and lunar crescent. Central sepal spike or triangle, of a Cypriote Ionic tombstone in New York (inverted here, to show the lotus without inversion, compare Fig. 43 [p. 71]). CESNOLA, *Atlas*, c.

11. Lotuses, with sun and two lunar crescents. Phenician relief slab from Ebba, Algeria. PERROT ET CHIPIEZ, *Phénicie*, p. 311.

Pl. XXIII, p. 173.

THE LOTUS AND THE SACRED TREE.

(PLATES XXIV., XXV., PAGES 183, 185.)

THE study of cuneiform inscriptions is undoubtedly the most exacting one to which the human intellect has ever been subjected. That the cuneiform scholar should have overlooked the evidence of minor monuments for the normal lotus as an ordinary symbol of Assyrian worship is not surprising.

The work in which this evidence is found was published before the conquest of cuneiform was made,[1] and hence has rather passed from notice. Its author was unaware himself of his contribution to the study of the lotus. Lajard's great work, "Le Culte de Mithra," contains the word "lotus" only once.[2] He did not live to undertake the division assigned to plants, but his Plates were published complete and his references to them in the completed portion of his text do not indicate that this unwritten section would have filled the gap for lotus symbolism on seals and cylinders.

Menant's designation of the normal lotus on the seal of Sargon (xxxvi. 4 [p. 247]) as "garlic," though entered with a mark of interrogation, shows that the greatest expert of our day in seals and cylinders has not surpassed the perceptions of his great predecessor on this point. Menant specifies the normal lotus xxiv. 8 as "a flower,"[3] and the lotus xliv. 1 [p. 285] as "a branch."[4] Perrot has quoted xxv. 14 as evidence for Layard's thoroughly erroneous view,[5] that the lotus is not found in the earlier Assyrian art.[6] The British Museum designates the relief from

---

[1] The text of LAJARD's *Culte de Mithra* appeared in 1847.

[2] In unimportant matter referring to Plate xviii. 7, of his work, p. 546.

[3] *Cylindres*, &c., ii. p. 68. "*Une fleur a la main*" designates xxiv. 8.

[4] *Cylindres*, &c., ii. p. 117. "*Un rameau s'élève d'une sorte de corbeille*" designates xliv. 1 [p.   ].

[5] The minor relics from the palace of Assur-nazir-pal in the British Museum, which is the earliest excavated, exhibit an abundance of normal lotus motives, which could not have been familiar to Layard as such. His "Assyrian tulip" and his "fleur-de-lys" are evidence.

[6] *Assyrie*, p. 318. (Referring to xxv. 14) "Dans les bas-reliefs anciens on ne rencontre que des fleurs probablement copiées sur nature, fleurs dont l'aspect est assez différent [from a lotus] (!). On en jugera par ce bouquet [xxv. 14] que tient en main un génie ailé dans le palais d'Assour-nazir-pal." The quoted case shows normal lotuses.

which xxv. 14 is taken as a priest offering "a branch." Clearly, then, the Assyrian lotus is a virgin field. The seals and cylinders borrowed from Lajard's Plates will tell their own story on Plate xxiv. Additional Assyrian seals and cylinders, showing the normal lotus and the winged sun disk, are entered on Plate xxxii., Nos. 6, 11, 12 [p. 223]; an Assyrian Sacred Tree of normal three-spiked lotuses at xxxvi. 6 [p. 247].

It is not simply the minor monuments which have escaped attention. Can any scholar look at the array of ceremonial branches on Plate xxv., as confined simply to the normal lotus (1, 3, 5, 6, 8, 14), and deny that the lotus was an important emblem of Assyrian worship? As far as these normal forms are detailed, they exhibit the Egyptian and Egypto-Phenician type, and no one has ever questioned that the Assyrian normal lotus patterns are borrowed from the Egyptian. Let us add to these ceremonial branches (held by gods more often than by worshippers) the lotus-palmette (4) and the lotus-rosette (12), and turn to the question of the Sacred Tree.

Examples of normal lotuses connected with acts of worship are found on Cypriote vases (xlv. 1, 3 [p. 287]). The only Sacred Tree of rosettes which has ever been published is on a Cypriote vase (xxxvii. 5 [p. 249]; xlvi. 2 [p. 289]—two views of the same vase). The much published ivory plaque from Nineveh (xxiv. 10) (several repetitions in the British Museum) has never found its obvious reference to solar worship, which immediately appears when confronted with the seal directly above it, on the Plate.

According to demonstrations for the rosette (p. 99) and the palmette (p. 109), the acts of worship or symbolical associations of xxiv. 4, 9 come under the same explanation. The class of Sacred Trees with buds (xxiv. 15, 16, 17) finds its explanation in the habitual Assyrian treatment of the lotus bud in normal patterns (xxv. 9, 11, 13). The congruity of a representation of lotus buds with lotus palmettes speaks for itself (13).

A decisive reference for the Sacred Cone is furnished by 14, as compared with 10. A similar representation of the lotus bud is quite frequent in Egyptian amulets and enamels, and is occasionally found in Egyptian surface design in colour. It should not be overlooked that Layard's patterns are very largely drawn from the ornament of robes (in relief pictures). We are dealing, therefore, not simply with an art of sculpture, but with the traditional weaving patterns of Assyrian art.

THE LOTUS AND THE SACRED TREE.

The general dependence of Assyrian art on Egypt was already noted by the trained eye of Owen Jones,[7] and we may value on this head the opinion of an expert in design, as not less important than that of an expert in archæology, or in cuneiform. No one can undervalue the marvellous naturalistic instinct of the Assyrian in pictorial art. His ornament has also undoubted qualities of national and distinctive decorative feeling, but he was not as successful as the Greek in disguising an Egypto-Phenician source of inspiration, and he was not less dependent on it. The oldest dated Phenician seal was found beneath a winged bull at Khorsabad,[8] and the minor works of Assyrian art in the British Museum are saturated with Egypto-Phenician traits and style. That a Chaldean mythology and elementary civilization underlay this glaze is not disputed, and I have stated my views of the historic relation of Egypt to Assyria in an earlier chapter (pp. 99-101).[9]

119. STONE CONE, a common terminal ornament of Cypriote tombstones.

120. CYPRIOTE TOMB STELÉ, showing an abbreviated cone, like Fig. 119.

It is by no means denied that the palm was a "Sacred Tree" in Assyria. The fact is patent that it was. It has been observed

---

7. *Grammar of Ornament*, text for Assyrian Plates; where the Assyrian art is considered as having a debased Egyptian style.

8. The seal, found by PLACE, is dated by this position of ceremonial deposit. It shows the Egyptian asp, sun-hawk (Horus), and winged solar disk. MENANT, *Cylindres*, ii. p. 234. There is also an ivory relief of Horus on the lotus from Nineveh, in the British Museum (Layard's Plates for Ivories).

9. The native barbarism of the Assyrians proper, in distinction from the higher civilization of the earlier Chaldeans, whom they subjugated, is well recognized. "Malgré l'éclat et les raffinements de leur civilisation extérieur ils démeurèrent toujours des barbares"—MASPERO, *Histoire Ancienne*, p. 283. Under Assour-nazir-habal they had the habit of covering walls with the flayed skins of captives (MASPERO). A relief of the British Museum shows Assur-bani-pal at a banquet, with salted head of an enemy hung up as a trophy (MASPERO). It was not such a people which developed the pattern ornaments of all later history. Aside from this barbarism, as rendering the Assyrians subject to the foreign influences of more highly developed civilizations, we must remember that relations between Chaldea and Egypt have been asserted for the IVth Dynasty (MENANT, "*Cylindres*" ii. pp. 197-200). OPPERT finds in the inscriptions of the Chaldean king Gudea (IVth Dynasty period), proof that stone for statuary was then brought from Egypt [Sinai Peninsula]. PERROT ET CHIPIEZ, *Assyrie*, p. 588. SAYCE, *Hibbert Lectures*, also makes reference to the inscriptions at Tell-loh [King Gudea] showing that the diorite of his statues came from the Sinai Peninsula. BRUGSCH (*Die Lösung der alt-Aegyptischen Münzfrage*) has proven that the Egyptian Sexagesimal system preceded the Babylonian and was "die uralte Grundlage der gesammten späteren Numismatik"; *Zeitschrift für Aegyptische Sprache, Band xxvii., Erstes Heft*, May, 1889. The province of Assyria was territory of the Egyptian Monarchy under the XVIIIth Dynasty; and Thothmes III. is thought by Dr. BIRCH to have reached India (note 70, p. 15). The most important relations between Egyptian and Mesopotamian civilization were those resulting from the contact with Phenicia and Syria, and from the Assyrian conquests in Syria and in Egypt. The Assyrian campaigns reached to the Soudan (note 2, p. 100).

by Menant that many plants were sacred to the Chaldeans [10] and that it is pure hypothesis to suppose that representations of the "Sacred Tree" were confined to one plant.[11] According to texts the cedar must also be admitted to the category; and according to appearances the cedar cone might also solve the problem of the "Sacred Cone" for which so many suggestions have been made.[12]

The argument from association and from the identity of the two forms as represented in Assyrian art seems, however, to specify the Sacred Cone as a lotus bud, and the absence of the cedar tree from symbolic ornament, or associations with the cone, must also be admitted. The cone which frequently surmounts Cypriote tombstones (Fig. 120) would appear to represent also the lotus bud (compare Fig. 119). In the matter of lotus ornament and lotus symbolism Assyria is best compared with India, where there are innumerable "sacred plants," according to Brahman testimony;[13] where the patterns are all lotus motives largely of foreign derivation; and where the dominance of the lotus over other symbols, both in art and literature, is simply overwhelming.

According to the evidence of the monuments the lotus must have been as prevalent a symbol in Assyria as it was in India. Two things have interfered with the recognition of this fact by Assyriology. The first is the inattention of Egyptologists to the natural forms of the flower and to the normal representations of it. It cannot be expected that Assyriology should be wiser in this matter than students of the Egyptian lotus motive. Until the three-spiked treatment of the Egyptian normal form (Pl. iii. [p. 41]) and its relation to the three-spiked form

---

10. *Cylindres*, &c., ii. pp. 65, 66. "Si nous consultons les fragments liturgiques qui nous sont transmis par l'Assyrie sur les anciens coutumes de la Chaldée, nous voyons que toutes les plantes étaient l'objet d'une adoration particulière et figuraient à différents titres dans les cérémonies réligieuses, telles l'ail, la mandragore; c'est ainsi que nous avons la *homa* chez les Perses et le lotus dans l'Inde et sur les bords du Nil."

11. *Cylindres*, &c., ii., p. 65. "Il est certain que la défiguration symbolique de l'arbre sacré ne procède pas d'un type unique, et que chaque type peut répondre dans le même culte a des idées bien différentes."

12. For references to the palm and the cedar as Sacred Trees see p. 117, Note 7. A recent suggestion for the cone is that of Dr. E. B. Tylor: "The object resembling a fir-cone is the inflorescence of the male date palm, as it appears when freed from its sheath, ready to have its pollen dusted over the sacred flowers. This artificial fertilization, indispensable to the production of a crop of edible dates, is the operation which the winged deity is seen sometimes about to perform, sometimes actually performing, and he carries a fresh supply of flowers in his basket;" letter in *Academy*, June 8, 1889, p. 396. Dr. Tylor's development of this thesis appeared in the *Proceedings of the Society of Biblical Archæology*, June 3rd, 1890: "The Winged Figures of the Assyrian and other Monuments." The cone is supposed by Birdwood, *Industrial Arts of India*, p. 430, to be a bunch of dates bursting from its spathe. According to recent publications in the *Babylonian and Oriental Record* the cone is a citron.

13. A partial list fills three pages of Birdwood's *Industrial Arts of India*, pp. 85, 86, 87, 88.

THE LOTUS AND THE SACRED TREE. 179

of the natural flower (Fig. 3) have been recognized, it is impossible to expect the prompt recognition of the normal lotus motives on cylinders and seals by experts. In other words it is the assumption of a *Nelumbium Speciosum* as being found in Egyptian ornament which has made a science of the lotus impossible (p. 39).

The recognition of the lotus in Assyrian art and by Assyriology has also been retarded by the problematic rendering of cuneiform texts and the absence of a word for the lotus from the Assyrian and Accadian dictionary, as at present known to students. The testimony of one of the great fathers of Assyriological science and author of several cuneiform "Word-lists," that the absence of this word from the Assyrian dictionary does not imply its absence from the texts, and that its unrecognised presence among the texts is to be taken for granted, is therefore of peculiar interest.[14]

It is hardly fair to refer to provisional theories of the Sacred Tree as found on the monuments, which are supplanted by new demonstrations for the palmette and bud forms, or to quote the name of any particular author in a matter where all have made mistakes, unless they have said nothing. Sir George C. M. Birdwood's treatment of the subject of the Assyrian Sacred Tree in the "Industrial Arts of India" (South Kensington Museum Series) may, however, be quoted as a type of the prevalent allusions to the Soma tree of India, as the original of xxiv. 16, and as being intertwined with the date palm in Sacred Trees like Fig. 121.[15]

The weakness of the theory regarding the Soma tree (the much-quoted "*Hom*"), is not only the weakness of the "palm-tree" theory; which is, that no transitional forms between the "palmette" and palm can be shown in Assyrian art —but the additional weakness that the Soma tree has no naturalistic renderings at all in Assyrian art, that it is not native in Assyria, and not known to have grown there.[16] It would also be desirable that some student who quotes the Soma tree should offer a drawing of it, to make his point more obvious; but we are not favoured in this way within my observation.

---

14. Rev. J. N. STRASSMAIER, S. J., author of various Assyrian Dictionaries, has favoured me with the following communication: "I am sorry to say that I do not know any word in Assyrian or Accadian which might mean lotus. Moreover, I think, no one could prove such a meaning if a word were found in a list. I believe that there must be a word in the many lists, but certainly no one can identify it."

15. Pages 430, 431. As usual in such matter, normal lotus forms pass without recognition. Both BIRDWOOD and TYLOR have quoted and published the Greek pattern of xxxiii. 6 [p. 225] without being aware that the central portion is a duplicated variant of the normal lotus.

16. BIRDWOOD, pp. 430, 431.

THE LOTUS AND THE SACRED TREE.

We have only to turn to the Assyrian renderings of already recognized lotus buds (xxv. 9), and to observe the pliant long stem of the lotus, to understand xxiv. 16. As to the supposed artificial date-palm examples (Fig. 121), they must share the fate of the palmette in ornament. The constant association of the palmette form in ornament with the lotus flower and lotus bud has been mentioned (p. 118). According to the prevalence of these associations there ought to be a realistic palm-tree motive corresponding in prevalence to the realistic lotus. So far from being prevalent, not one case of an ornamental pattern of realistic palms can be quoted at present for ancient Assyrian, Babylonian, or Persian art.[17]

121. ASSYRIAN "SACRED TREE."

The artificial representations of the lotus bud and lotus palmette (Fig. 121), which appear among the Assyrian "Sacred Trees," undoubtedly require an explanation. This is furnished by Biblical mention of the "*Asherah*" or "Grove," and the connection of this "*Asherah*" with the Assyrian Sacred Tree is already commonplace to students. The forms of the Sacred Tree on Assyrian reliefs indicate actual originals in metal, by the pliant yet highly conventional treatment of the detail. Ceremonial metal branches of the lotus are also clearly indicated by the reliefs (xxv).

122. HORUS, WITH LOTUSES.

Some forms of the "*Asherah*," therefore, were artificially constructed symbolic "Trees of Life," which were used in shrines. The word "grove" would easily apply to multiple combinations of the lotus, which are also familiar in Egyptian art, and which also imply very frequently actual metal originals,[18] at least for the plant form (Fig. 122). It does not at all lie within our province to assert that the realistic palm or cedar were not additional models for the "*Asherah*,"[19] and there is moreover evidence for a brazen palm in the Apollo shrine at Delphi (p. 17, Note 78).

17. By the word "pattern" we understand a repeated motive as distinct from an isolated naturalistic representation. See p. 118.

18. A positive case of such combination is furnished by the stelè supporting hawk and a "grove" of lotuses, which could only be imagined in metal original, in the *Description de l'Égypte*, A. iii. 60 (Karnak).

19. SAYCE, *Hibbert Lectures* (p. 409), mentions "bare tree trunks which symbolized Asherah the goddess of fertility and Baal the sun god." ROBERTSON SMITH, *Religion of the Semites* (p. 176), does not credit the existence of a Syrian goddess named Asherah as above supposed, but mentions the "*Asherah*" as "a tree or tree post," and as a phase of "tree worship." He suggests that the draping and anointing of a sacred stump were practised, and in connection mentions the palm as a symbol of Astarte.

THE LOTUS AND THE SACRED TREE.

An Assyrian ornamental motive, so far unmentioned, is the so-called "pomegranate" (associated with the palmette, Fig. 60 [p. 110]). The illustrations from Assyrian ornament (Figs. 123, 124) are exaggerations of a form frequently found on Egyptian monuments, which represents the seed-bulb of the lotus (Fig. 7). In this view I have the concurrence of Mr. Percy E. Newberry. The statue of Hapi, the Nile God, in the British Museum, includes such representations (Fig. 125).

123. LOTUS BULB TILE ORNAMENT. From Perrot et Chipiez.

124. LOTUS BULB TILE ORNAMENT. From Perrot et Chipiez.

A very curious corroboration on this point is offered by an unpublished anthemion in Bologna (Fig. 126), where the argument from association is obvious. The so-called pomegranate on vases from Cyrene is included in this demonstration.

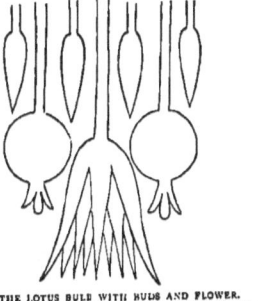

125. THE LOTUS BULB WITH BUDS AND FLOWER. Detail from a statue of the Nile God in the British Museum.

126. LOTUS BULBS WITH ANTHEMION. Tombstone in Bologna. From Author's sketch.

PLATE XXIV.

THE LOTUS AND THE SACRED TREE.

1. Lotus supporting the winged solar disk. Detail from a cylinder shown at xliv. 1 [p. 285]. LAJARD, *Culte de Mithra*, xxxviii. 4.
2. Lotuses below the winged solar disk. Assyrian seal. LAJARD, *Culte de Mithra*, xxx. 6.
3. Lotus below the winged solar disk. Assyrian seal. LAJARD, *Culte de Mithra*, xvii. 26.
4. Assyrian winged deities, facing the Rosette. Detail of enamel in colour. PLACE, xv.
5. Lotuses, with lunar crescent and star. Phenician seal. LAJARD, *Culte de Mithra*, x. 19
6. Lotuses and the Moon-god. Assyrian seal. LAJARD, *Culte de Mithra*, xlvi. 16.
7. Lotus, worshipper, and winged solar disk. Assyrian seal. LAJARD, *Culte de Mithra*, xxxi. 3.
8. The worshipper, the ibex, and the lotus. Assyrian relief. MENANT, *Cylindres*, &c., II., p. 68.
9. The palmette and the winged solar disk. Assyrian relief detail. LAYARD, Plates, *First Series*, xxxix.
10. The worshipper and the lotus. Ivory plaque from Nineveh, in the British Museum. PERROT ET CHIPIEZ, *Assyrie*, p. 222. Also in LAYARD, Plates; and DIEULAFOY, *L'Art Antique de la Perse*.
11. Lotus and the Moon-god, an eight-rayed star, equivalent of the sun.* Assyrian seal. LAJARD, *Culte de Mithra*, xliv. 1.
12. Lotus and buds with lunar crescent. Phenician seal. MENANT, *Cylindres*, &c., II., viii. 3.
13. Lotuses. Phenician seal. LAJARD, *Culte de Mithra*, xlv. 3.
14. Lotus and two buds, with lunar crescent. Detail of an Assyrian or Phenician seal. LAJARD, *Culte de Mithra*, xvii. 5.
15. Sacred Tree of lotus buds. Assyrian cylinder. MENANT, *Cylindres*, viii. 3.
16. Sacred Tree of lotus buds, under the winged solar disk. From LAYARD'S Plates.
17. Sacred Tree of lotus buds, and Sun-god. Assyrian cylinder. MENANT, *Cylindres*, II., p. 64.

For additional examples of the normal lotus and the winged sun disk, see Plate xxxii. 6, 11, 12 [p. 223], and Figs. 200, 202. For an Assyrian Sacred Tree of normal three-spiked lotuses, see xxxvi. 6 [p. 247].

---

* The eight-rayed star is quoted as a symbol of the sun by KING, *Gnostics*, p. 126. It is quoted for the goddess Istar by MENANT, *Cylindres*, &c., p. 245. It is quoted as a sign for "deity" by SAYCE, *Hibbert Lectures*, p. 400.

Pl. XXIV., p. 183.

PLATE XXV.

THE LOTUS AND THE SACRED TREE.

1. Ceremonial branch (copy of an original in metal) of lotuses and rosettes, held by a winged deity. Assyrian relief detail LAYARD, *First Series*, xxxvii.
2. Multiple lotus palmette and bud, rosette border. Persian relief detail of the stairway, Susa. PERROT ET CHIPIEZ, V., p. 543. The bud mistaken for a tree by Perrot.
3. Ceremonial branch of lotuses and rosettes, held by a winged deity. Assyrian relief detail. LAYARD, *First Series*, xxxviii.
4. Ceremonial branch of lotus palmettes, held by a winged deity (with deer). Assyrian relief detail. LAYARD, *First Series*, xxxv.
5. Ceremonial branch of lotuses. Assyrian detail. MENANT, *Cylindres*, II., p. 61.
6. Ceremonial branch of lotuses. Assyrian detail. BOTTA, II., 105.
7. Assyrian relief detail. Inverted lotus colonette amulet and buds, over winged deity. LAYARD, *First Series*, l.
8. Ceremonial branch of lotuses. Detail of xxiv. 8. BOTTA, I. 43.
9. Lotus border; buds with hatched lines in Assyrian style. Detail from LAYARD, *Second Series*, lvi.
10. The Sacred Cone. Detail from LAYARD, *First Series*, xxxvi.
11. Lotus border; buds with hatched lines, in Assyrian style. LAYARD, *First Series*, ix.
12. Ceremonial branch of lotus rosettes, held by adorer. LAYARD, *Second Series*, 5.
13. Lotus palmettes and lotus buds, large and small; rosette border. Assyrian ornamental detail. LAYARD, *First Series*, ix.
14. Ceremonial branch of lotuses on rosettes; buds with hatched lines, in Assyrian style. Compare No. 10. PERROT ET CHIPIEZ, *Assyrie*, p. 318.

Pl. XXV., p. 185.

THE BULL AND THE LOTUS.

(PLATE XXVI., PAGE 193.)

IN 1855, Kenrick wrote in the preface of his "Phenicia" as follows:—" No Phenician sepulchre has yet supplied a relic of antiquity to illustrate the manners and history of the nation. Phenician archæology is almost an entire blank." Notwithstanding the number of Phenician monuments which have been brought to light since these words were penned, it is still true that scholars have little knowledge of Phenician art in its original Syrian home. It is in Cyprus, in Sardinia, in Italy, in North Africa, or in Mesopotamia, that its acknowledged remains have been most largely found, and of Syrian Phenician art we can still learn more in Egyptian tomb-paintings, of vases and the like, than from existing remains found in the mother country.

The causes which have brought about the destruction of Phenician monuments in Syria have been considered by Renan (*Mission de Phénicie*), but it is by no means certain that lack of excavation is not the most important explanation. However this may be, scholars are united, and justly so, in recognizing the monuments which have been found exterior to Syria as characteristic and typical for those lacking in the mother country. Phenician art as thus known is conceded to be largely Egyptian in inspiration and exterior forms, and largely Egyptian in mythological foundation. No original quality has so far been asserted for it.

In so far as Phenician art is supposed not to be Egyptian, it is supposed to be Assyrian. This supposition is based mainly on theories of the history of ornament, which can be proven erroneous.

Aside from the frequency of the palmette and rosette, it is difficult to see even an apparent indication of Assyrian quality in Phenician art, and the recognition of these forms as original to Egypt would carry with it the art with which the forms are associated; not to the extent of asserting the art to be absolutely Egyptian, but to the extent of asserting it to be Egypto-Phenician. We should concede then to Assyrian art, as known to us, an undoubted national quality and distinction, but we should reverse the view which has considered Phenician art as intermediate dependency of Egypt and Assyria combined, and assign to it an active motive quality as acting on Assyria rather than as re-acted upon by that country.[1]

This view concedes that every nation of antiquity had a distinct and peculiar national religion, and that every locality had a distinct and essentially original local cult. It concedes that the original Phenician religion was, as being Semitic, more closely allied to Assyria and Chaldæa than to Egypt; but it asserts that the ornamental art and active motive civilizing force of Phenicia was more directly influenced by Egypt than by Mesopotamia from the time of the XVIIIth Dynasty; and that a movement of culture, focussing in Egypt, passed through Syria to the Euphrates-Tigris country, after that time.

So far from being disposed to minimize the Semitic element or the Mesopotamian element in history, I am positive that the history of the lotus will tend to raise our estimate of that influence as regards the Greeks. The history of an Egyptian motive will be found in later pages to demonstrate in many points a Syrian and Semitic influence on Greek history, independent of the Egyptian, and in matters of religion hostile to it; just as Dutch Protestants carried to America with the "Colonial" Renaissance style an indication of Italian influence which largely came to them from the Spanish Netherlands and from Spain; a country with which they had been in deadly antagonism.

As far as these remarks depend on demonstrations still to be offered (and especially through the history of the lotus as associated with the deer, gazelle, and ibex) they cannot have value here, but they point to one fact which can be immediately related to a demonstration already given.

In so far as the indications of a lotus cult in Assyria have been neglected (and it cannot be denied that even the normal lotus in Assyria has been absolutely neglected, aside from pattern ornaments), in so far the lotus cult of Phenicia and Syria is also magnified and emphasized by calling attention to

[1]. In DUMONT ET CHAPLAIN, *Céramiques de la Grèce propre*, there is a very fair admission as to the unknown quantity which lies in debate between Phenician influence on Assyria and the counter hypothesis, pp. 133 and 136.

this neglect. In so far as Syria does not furnish the evidence for its own lotus cult, it is only because the monuments have perished. In so far as the Egyptian lotus appears in Assyrian art, in so far we are obliged to concede that it must have appeared in Syrian art, because it travelled through Syria. Therefore, as we began our history of the lotus motive exterior to Egypt, by showing that its presence in Assyria has been ignored in palpable instances, let us follow this by noting the same point for Phenicia.

The Sphinx and Gryphon are forms of Horus (pp. 8, 9). Wherever we find the Gryphon and the lotus, or the Sphinx and lotus in Mesopotamian art, we are dealing with a fact of Phenician history and the fact, namely, of Phenician influence on Mesopotamia. Observe that there are massed on Plate xxxii. [p. 223] thirteen cases of the Sphinx or Gryphon lotus association, and that seven of these instances are absolutely normal forms; and observe that not one of these normal lotus forms has been pointed out by the publications from which they are taken.

The cult of the sun and moon at Carthage, under the names of Baal Hamman and Tanith, is attested by inscribed votive tablets, on which the normal lotus constantly appears. On Plates lxvi. [p. 399], and lxvii. [p. 401] there are seventeen instances of the lotus from seventeen different votive tablets dedicated to the sun and moon. Seven of these cases are immediately recognizable normal lotuses, lxvi. 4, 6, 12; lxvii. 2, 4, 6, 10. The Egg-and-Dart motives, lxvi. 5, 11, 13, 14, must also be conceded—the anthemions 5 and 10 likewise. We have also on the two Plates cases of the rosette, bud, and simple outline lotus, which need not detain us now.

Phenician scholars are best able to say what notice has been taken of the significance of the normal lotus on such Phenician votive tablets. I have failed to discover any mention of this significance, or even of the appearance of the flower, in the publications from which these details are taken. These lotuses are all Egyptian forms; they all represent a condition of civilization in Syria, although they come from Carthage.

In the series of collocations exhibited by the Plates xxvi.-xlvi. [pp. 193-289], and beginning with the "Bull and the Lotus," we are obliged in general to assume counterparts in Syrian art for which existing material is often at best only supplied by gems or coins. This material is however frequently supplemented by facts derived from literary sources and historic tradition. It is not necessary to quote this material beyond the limits of the problem suggested by a given Plate.

In the case of the "Bull and the Lotus" (xxvi.), our object is simply to illustrate for Assyrian art the significance of certain combinations which have so far been published as purely ornamental. In Assyrian mythology, as derived from Chaldæan, the bull is a well-known solar animal,[2] and hence an animal of the Chaldæan Zodiac[3]—a form of the sun-god Merodach[4] and of his equivalent the Syrian Baal.[5] He is the animal also of the Phœnician moon-goddess Astarte[6] and of her equivalent Europa.[7] The winged bulls of Assyrian palace portals are Genii,[8] of whom little or nothing is otherwise known, and we are not authorized at present to assume that the winged bulls of Plate xxvi. are anything else.

As the bull is a solar emblem in general, we are not obliged to move beyond the present known facts of Assyriology regarding the special meaning of individual examples, excepting to observe that the bull unicorn and palmette (No. 11), bull unicorn and rosette (No. 9), bull unicorn and Sacred Tree of cones (No. 8), must henceforth be recognized as instances of symbolic lotus association.

Although the significance of the bull in Egyptian religion is widely recognized,[9] it is not presumed that Egyptian associations like Nos. 1 and 3 indicate any direct transmission of the bull and lotus combination from Egypt to Assyria. The Chaldæan mythology would forbid this assumption. The worship of the solar bull in Egypt and Chaldæa is a fact of coincidence, as far as present historical information enables us to judge, or of original derivation from one source. But the forms of the lotus, including the palmette and rosette, which appear in the

---

2. SAYCE, *Hibbert Lectures*, p. 107. The sun was termed by the Accadians "*Gudibir*," the Bull of Light.

3. ROBERT BROWN, Jun., *Proceedings of the Society of Biblical Archæology*, 1890. "The solar interpretation of the sign [Taurus] goes back to the far-off time when the year began with Taurus, and the sun was conceived as a bull entering upon the great furrow of heaven, as he ploughed his way among the stars."

4. SAYCE, *Hibbert Lectures*. Merodach, "the Bull of Light" (p. 48). Merodach originally a Sun-god, proven by texts (p. 100). Merodach, the primitive Bull-god (p. 286).

5. SAYCE, *Hibbert Lectures*. Merodach an equivalent of Baal (pp. 92 and 110), and of Zeus (p. 109).

6. ROBERTSON SMITH, *Religion of the Semites*. Astarte referred to as figured with a bull's head (p. 292).

7. *Ibid.* The bull of Europa counterpart of Astarte (p. 292).

8. SAYCE, *Hibbert Lectures*. Winged bulls, genii of the household (p. 286).

9. BRUGSCH, *Mythologie, &c.* In Egyptian cosmogony the beginning of all things is the watery element (*Das Urwasser*) which was personified by Noun, whose equivalents were Ptah, Amon, and Khnoum (p. 108). Noun=the bull, which also represents the male creative force of elemental water (p. 116). In Greek mythology the bull belongs to river-gods. For references as to the solar bull in Egypt, see p. 8, Notes 22, 23, 24.

representations of the Assyrian bull, were derived from Egypt. Aside from inattention to obvious Assyrian associations of the normal lotus with the sun, it may be that inadequate knowledge of cuneiform texts, or imperfect translations (p. 179, Note 14) have obscured the fact that lotus symbolism was as strongly rooted in Mesopotamia as in India, and possibly in times antedating Egyptian influence. We have seen that Egyptian lotus ornament reached India not later than the third century B.C. (pp. 35, 36; 151, Note 6). It was widely diffused in Assyria in the ninth century B.C. (p. 175, Note 5). It must have been mainly through Assyria that the Egyptian ornament reached India (p. 36, Note 16).

The association of the bull and the winged solar disk on Cypriote coins (No. 4) is undoubtedly Phenician in direct origin.[10] The bull was sacred to Venus in Cyprus and in Syria,[11] and the Phenician bull symbolism appears to be rather Semitic than Egyptian in origin, for the association of the bull which is quoted for the "Assyrian Venus," belongs to the male gods of Egypt.

The Mongol solar bull (No. 2) is of late date, and it is not within our knowledge to say whether this symbolism was native or whether it was borrowed in countries of Mongol conquest.

Persian texts are very explicit and numerous for the symbolism of the bull,[12] and we cannot doubt that the Ionic form on Persian bull capitals has significance. The lower member of the capital xxvi. 10, has a lotus form already known to Assyrian ivories of the ninth century.[13] Certain forms of Hindu art and architecture are so strongly indicated by it, that we cannot but suggest a Persian and Assyrian influence as explaining the resemblance. That this influence should have preceded that conceded to the Greeks is natural. It has been so far overlooked that the patterns on the enormous bases of these Persian columns are from the normal lotus, as may be observed in the Louvre or in the published illustrations.[14]

---

10. KELLER, *Thiere des Classischen Alterthums in Kulturhistorischer Beziehung*, p. 70, attributes the presence of the zebu (*Bos Indicus*) in ancient Cyprus to introduction for religious reasons. The zebu is generally known as the sacred bull of the Brahmans, but a variety of zebu was also known in Egypt, according to Keller, p. 67. See ii. 5, p. 23.

11. See reference (Note 6) to Astarte. Lucian's matter for the bull as sacred to the Assyrian Venus and as nourished by the priests at Hierapolis in Syria (*De Deâ Syriâ*) is quoted by LAJARD, *Culte de Mithra*, p. 503.

12. LAJARD, *Culte de Mithra*. The bull was an emblem of generation and of life in Persian myth (p. 56). The bull was the first created being (p. 49). Slain by Ahriman, his soul became the germ of all later creation (p. 50).

13. In the British Museum. DIEULAFOY has recognized this form, and has illustrated these ivories in his matter on the lotus, *L'Art Antique de la Perse*, IIIième Partie.

14. PERROT ET CHIPIEZ, V.

PLATE XXVI.

THE BULL AND THE LOTUS.

1. Apis bull and lotus. Detail, MARIETTE, *Serapeum de Memphis*, iii. 21.
2. Solar bull. Detail, Mongol coin. WARING, *Ceramic Art in Remote Ages*, xxxi. 6.
3. Bull in the lotus bower. Denderah. From a photograph taken for the Author, of a panel on the wall of the temple-portico.
4. Bull, *Ankh*, and winged solar disk. Cypriote coin. DE LUYNES, *Num. et In. Cyp.*
5. Bull, or cow, and lotus. CESNOLA, *Cyprus;* KING'S *Appendix for Gems*, viii. d.
6. Bull, or cow, and lotus. Scarab from Nineveh. BOTTA, II., 154.
7. Bull unicorn and Sacred Tree of lotus buds. Assyrian relief known as the "Aberdeen Stone." INMAN, *Ancient Pagan and Modern Christian Symbolism*, p. 49.
8. Bull unicorn and Sacred Tree of lotus buds. Assyrian relief. LAYARD, *First Series*, xlvi.
9. Bull unicorn and rosette. Assyrian enamel detail. LAYARD, *First Series*, lxxxvii.
10. Persian capital. Bull unicorns and lotus Ionic volutes, supported by a lotus (pendant sepals). PERROT ET CHIPIEZ, v. p. 493.
11. Bull unicorn and palmette. Assyrian relief detail. LAYARD, *First Series*, xliii.

For additional examples of the bull (zebu) and the lotus, see ii. 1 [p. 23] ; lii. 10 [p. 321] (Mycenæ); lxv. 5 [p. 393].

The bull unicorn is generally conceded to be a representation of the natural bull with profile view of the horns, one concealing the other; a point mentioned in LAJARD'S *Culte de Mithra*.

THE COW AND THE LOTUS.

(PLATE XXVII., PAGE 197.)

THAT the Phenicians should, apparently, have derived their symbolism of the bull from Mesopotamian sources, and their symbolism of the cow from Egypt, is easily explained. Although the bull symbolism of Egypt was not confined to the Sun-god Ptah of Memphis (p. 8, Note 23), and his incarnation of the Apis, it was especially distinctive for him, and the Phenicians were more influenced by a cult which was common to the entire country. For their deities borrowed from Egypt were especially Horus (the winged solar disk and hawk) and Isis or Hathor (the cow and the fish). To these Osiris may be added, whose myth was connected with the Syrian Byblus, and whose worship was assimilated to that of Adonis and of Tammuz.[1]

The associations of Plate xxvii. include three illustrations for the Phenician cult of Hathor or Isis—No. 1, marked as Phenician by its inscription; No. 4, marked as Phenician by the location of the find (Sardinia); and No. 9, marked as Phenician by Egyptian testimony (a tribute from "the Kefa"). As between the bull and cow we have little difficulty in deciding the head to be that of a cow in

127. HATHOR WITH COW-EARS AND LOTUSES. From Prisse d'Avennes.

this last case, since the Phenician Isis cult was so universally connected with the latter animal. Four other monuments in doubt, all exhibiting the normal trefoil lotus, have been distributed between Plates xxvi. and xxvii. (xxvi., 5, 6; xxvii., 3, 6).

The interest of Plate xxvii. centres especially in the famous silver and gold monument of Dr. Schliemann's excavations (No. 7). The attribution of this piece to Hathor, and identification of Juno (Hera) with this deity, have been made by good authority, and are generally conceded.[2] We have only to point out that the rosette, considered by Prof. Sayce of Babylonian origin, belongs as a lotus form to the cow-goddess.

1. Among many references for this identification see KENRICK, *Phenicia*, p. 313.

2. SCHLIEMANN's *Mycenæ*, p. 213. A point also noticed in Mr. Gladstone's Preface.

THE COW AND THE LOTUS.

The argument from association, which shows two other Egyptian Hathor cow-heads with rosettes, will be apparent. In No. 8 we observe a rosette form composed of four flowers and four buds.

The supposed papyrus form of No. 2 has been restored to its proper interpretation in earlier pages (Plates iv., v. [pp. 63, 65]).

Fig. 127 shows an additional instance of the cow-goddess and the lotus.[3]

---

3. For Fig. 127, see i. 7 [p. 21]. For Hathor as a "*Nebengestalt*," i.e. equivalent form, of Isis, see BRUGSCH, *Mythologie*, and Note 61, p. 13. For Astarte as an equivalent form, see COLONNA-CECCALDI, *Monuments de Chypre*, pp. 95, 97. All above titles designate Moon-goddesses by unanimous authority. For Isis as Moon-goddess see BRUGSCH, *Mythologie*, I., pp. 6, 12.

PLATE XXVII.

THE COW AND THE LOTUS.

1. Hathor cow and the lotus. Phœnician seal. LEVY, *Phœnizische Studien.*
2. Hathor cow in sacred bark, and lotuses. Detail, Ipsamboul. ROSELLINI, III., v. 1.
3. Cow and two lotuses, one springing from the mouth. Compare xxxiv. 3 [p. 227]; xxxix. 4, 6, 7 [p. 253]. Bronze *repoussé* detail of the "*Situla d'Este*," *Gazette Archéologique*, 1888, xii.
4. Hathor cow, calf, and the lotus. Egypto-Phenician enamel seal, Sardinia. PERROT ET CHIPIEZ, *Phénicie*, Fig. 182. For Horus as calf, see BRUGSCH, *Mythologie*, I. p. 160.
5. Hathor cow-head, supporting rosette. Detail from Plate x. 4 [p. 97]. PRISSE D'AVENNES, *Plafonds.*
6. The cow (Hathor) and the lotus. Egyptian scarab. KLAPROTH, xx. 2067.
7. Cow-head (Hathor) in silver (gold horns), with rosette. SCHLIEMANN, *Mycenæ*, p. 216.
8. Cow-head (Hathor) on lotus and two rosettes of lotuses. Top of a vase in gold, from an Egyptian tomb-painting. PRISSE D'AVENNES, *Vases en Or.*
9. Cow-head (Hathor) and rosette. Detail of a vase from an Egyptian tomb-painting. PRISSE D'AVENNES, *Vases des Tributaires de Kefa.*

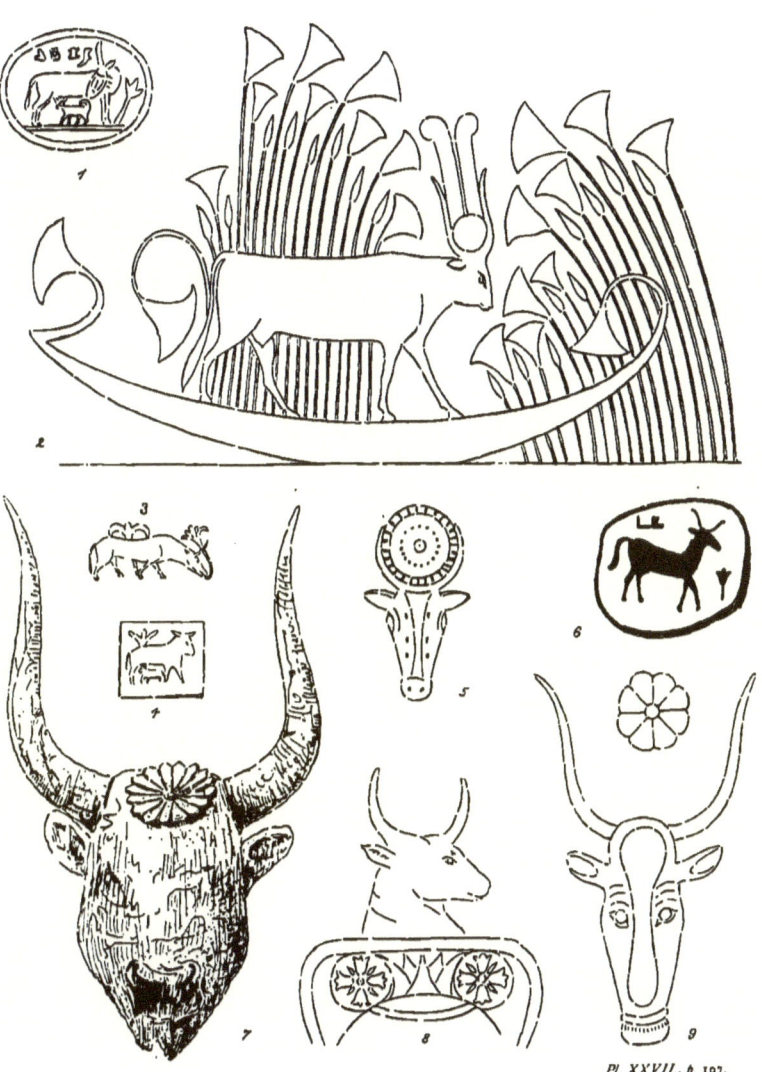

Pl. XXVII., p. 197.

THE RAM AND THE LOTUS.

(PLATE XXVIII., PAGE 203.)

IN his publication of Cypriote coins, De Luynes speaks of the ram as follows:—
"There is nothing surprising about the type of the ram for Amathus, where the worship of Venus was dominant. Sacrifice was made to her there of a ram covered with its fleece, and this practice had been transferred to Corinth."[1]

In Enmann's publication "Cyprus and the Origin of Aphrodite Worship,"[2] the Greek Venus is held to have been originally a Moon-goddess, a goddess of death and of fertility. This essay is quoted with approval by Professor Dümmler as bearing on the independence of the Greeks from supposed Phenician influence, and was written by Enmann with this motive. Since the Cyprian Aphrodite is the most universally quoted instance of a Greek deity borrowed from foreign nations, to prove the Cyprian Aphrodite a Greek goddess is to meet the supporters of foreign gods in Greek mythology on their chosen battle-ground. But the points of Enmann's essay lead to the curious result that the independent Greek goddess corresponded exactly to the significance of the Assyrian and Chaldean Venus whose worship in Cyprus was practised by the Phenicians. Therefore, lest the bearing of my later illustrations be considered as arguing a wholesale importation by the Greeks of foreign gods, it is best noted here that an assimilation of corresponding deities is quoted for all points where the Greeks came in contact with foreign nations. For the argument of this work an assimilation comes to the same thing as a derivation, and will explain the phenomena as well.

In the case of the Rhodian vase (Ram, &c.) which takes the central place in Plate xxviii., we have reached the first instance of a problem which will recur

---

1. *Num. et In. Cyp.*, pp. 5, 6. Quoting "Joann. Lyd., De Mensib. 4, 45."
2. ENMANN, *Mémoires de l'Académie Royale des Sciences de St. Petersbourg*, 1886. "Kypros und der Ursprung des Aphrodite cultus." "Wir dürfen sie als einen Tod und Zeugung regelnden Mondgeist definiren und ihren Namen auf die Bezeichnung als Mondanzündenden deuten."

under many forms in following pages, viz. as to the symbolism of the remote anthemion lotus derivatives of Greek art.

It would be possible to ignore this question or avoid it, were it not for the associations of the lotus with the solar or divine animals, but the flower itself occurs with, and specifies, many solar animals, within the limits of Greek art and under circumstances which make the supposition of mechanical copy impossible. When, therefore, the anthemion occurs in a like association it is difficult to dispute the possibility of a corresponding symbolism. On this point the evidence of Carthaginian votive tablets to the sun and moon is of value, because their anthemions belong to a late period of Greek influence as regards date and style, and because these tablets exhibit the normal flowers as well as most of the hitherto unrecognized variants of the plant (lxvi., lxvii., pp. 399, 401).

The ram is the equivalent of Amon and of Khnoum. He appears on Cypriote coins directly associated with Aphrodite;[3] on others with the sun, the moon crescent, and the solar diagram[4] with lotuses (Nos. 6, 8); and on others still, with the solar diagram and lotuses (Nos. 4, 5). He was sacrificed in Cyprus to a goddess who was a Moon-goddess, according to the view of one archæologist (Enmann), which asserts the independent Greek character of Aphrodite—who was certainly a Moon-goddess, according to an assimilation with the Phenician Astarte,[5] which was undoubtedly made in Cyprus. The ram is moreover the first sign of the later Chaldean Zodiac, and his place in the Zodiac is owing to his solar character.[6]

When therefore we find a Rhodian vase (xxviii. 7) which associates the ram with an inverted form of the lotus anthemion (type of xiii. 11 [p. 121]), it is impossible not to assume or suggest that they were, or had once been, associated symbols either of the Zodiac or of a Sun-god or Moon-goddess, who had been either derived from, or assimilated with, a foreign deity.

Whether such an anthemion was recognized as a lotus is another question. It may have been a sun-symbol as matter of tradition, without reference to its origin.

---

3. De Luynes, *Num. et In. Cyp.*, Plate v. 3. Coin of Salamis. Venus leaning on the ram; reverse, a bull.

4. The designation of a circle of dots surrounding a central dot (or without this dot in small objects), as a solar diagram, is susceptible of demonstration and will be authenticated in later pages. The diagram is a form of the Egyptian sign, *Ra*, for the sun; a circle surrounding a dot.

5. The relations of the Phenician Ashtoreth or Astarte to the moon, which are quoted by all authorities, are also quoted by Enmann in his essay.

6. Robert Brown, Jun., *Proceedings, Society of Biblical Archæology*, 1890.

It is also within the range of possible suppositions that the association was traditional without significance, as dating from an earlier time of significance which had been lost sight of.

According to the negative evidence of published monuments the association of the ram (as an animal form distinct from the ram-headed gods) and the lotus was a rare one in Egypt.[7] No published case has met my observation. It is positive that a direct copy from an Egyptian work of art cannot be assumed, even in the case of the Greek vase found in Egypt (No. 1). The ram and the lotus could never have been combined in Egyptian art as we find them in this example. This makes the theory of an absolutely misconceived or mechanically made direct imitation impossible. Both elements of No. 1 can be explained from Egyptian or from Mesopotamian symbolism; one element at least, the lotus spiral, was originally Egyptian. But when the ram and the lotus were combined in Egypt it was certainly never done by placing a lotus spiral under the nose of the animal.

Hence there can be only two theories for No. 1 or No. 7. One would be that Greek art accidentally combined two things; one of which it had borrowed; without conceiving significance for either. The other theory would be that Greek art consciously combined two symbols, both of which it had borrowed, in a perfectly comprehensible but absolutely novel manner. This last is my own view.

The proposition that the lotus spiral scroll and the Egyptian meander are identical (Plate x. 7, 9 [p. 97]) is re-suggested by the Swastika meander of No. 7, and the lotus scroll of No. 1.

The Hittite ram with gazelle relief (No. 2) will gain significance when the gazelle-god has had attention. Till then we will leave it in its proper association on this Plate.

The ram was no less a Chaldean than an Egyptian sun-symbol (note 6), and later matter will show that the lotus was often connected in Greek art with animals which were Typhonic in Egypt and peculiarly sacred in Mesopotamia. It is therefore by no means to be assumed that the Rhodian vase designates a distinctively Egyptian influence. It is most probable that the ram appears on it as a solar sign of the Greek Zodiac, and with lotus association abundantly explained by later matter for the deer, gazelle, oryx, ibex, wild goat, bird, and lotus.

7. An unpublished instance in Turin. Rams facing the lotus; limestone stelè, No. 188.

PLATE XXVIII.

THE RAM AND THE LOTUS.

1. Ram and spiral scrolls, two rudimentary lotuses in the scrolls. Detail of a Greek vase. *Naukratis*, II. ix. 5.

2. Colossal stone ram (Hittite), with gazelle in relief. At Kumbet, Phrygia. (Ramsay explorations.) PERROT ET CHIPIEZ, V., p. 170.

3. God Khnoum (ram-headed) and lotus buds. Repeated from Plate ii. 7 [p. 23]. Esneh. *Description de l'Égypte*, A., Vol. I., 86, 10.

4. Cypriote coin, ram. DE LUYNES, *Num. et In. Cyp.*, xii.

5. Reverse of No. 4. Cross supporting solar diagram, four lotuses in corners.

6. Ram, sun, and lunar crescent. Cypriote coin. SCHMIDT, *Cyp. In.*, x. 1.

7. Rhodian vase, British Museum. Ram above inverted lotus anthemion with introrse scrolls (type of xiii. 11 [p. 121]); Swastika meander, and other diagrams. SALZMANN, *Nécropole de Camire*, ii.

8. Reverse of No. 7. Cross supporting sun diagram. Four lotuses in corners.

Pl. XXVIII., p. 203.

THE LION AND THE LOTUS.

(PLATES XXIX., XXX., PAGES 209, 211.)

THE lion is a well-known form of Horus[1] and of Sekhet (xx. 12 [p. 153], Lion-goddess[2] and spouse of Ptah; and a solar equivalent under various other names.[3] Even the temple-roof water-spouts of the Greco-Roman time, which were sculptured in lion form, are inscribed as symbols of the summer sun in the Zodiacal sign of the lion.[4] The familiar Egyptian representation of two lions sitting on the hind-quarters, back to back, and supporting the sun disk, has been lately explained by M. Le Page Renouf. They are the Sun-lions "to-morrow" and "yesterday"—the day that is to be, and the day that was, otherwise Ra and Osiris (p. 8, Note 5).

The solar significance of the lion and the lotus associations on Plates xxix. and xxx. is thus apparent. An additional example is found at Plate ii. [p. 23]. A rare little amulet in the British Museum shows the lion wearing the lotus as crown upon his head. There is a similar one in the Polytechnic at Athens.

Although the lion was a solar animal and a sign of the Zodiac in Chaldea and Assyria, the associations of the lion and the lotus in Greek art unite with those for the lotus and the Sphinx in pointing to direct and indirect Egyptian influence—indirect influence by way of Syria, Cyprus, and Asia Minor, and direct influence through the Greeks in Egypt.

The continuous and abundant presence of the Greeks in Egypt from the eighth century onwards, produced a style, both in Greece and Italy, which is frequently mistaken for "Assyrian." Thus we find in Plates xxix., xxx., corroborative evidence for the rosette as a lotus, in monuments which are at the same time transferred by this association from the assumed Assyrian or Assyro-

---

1. For various references to the solar lion see p. 8.
2. An equivalent form of Bast or Pakht (British Museum designations).
3. The lion was a symbol of Apollo in Lycia. WELCKER, quoted by DAREMBERG ET SAGLIO, *Dictionaire des Antiquités Grecques et Romaines* (Hachette, 1873).
4. BRUGSCH, *Mythologie*, II., p. 349. "Die in der Griechisch-römischen Epoche der Denkmäler an den äusseren Tempelgewänden unmittelbar unter dem Dache angebrachten Regengossen in Gestalt liegender Löwenkörper aus Stein (Tentyra, Thebes, Edfu, Philae) werden in den darauf eingemeisselten Inschriften geradezu als Sinnbilder der Sommerlichen Sonne im Zodiakalbilde des Löwen aufgefasst."

Phenician category to that of Greco-Egyptian (xxix. 4, 7; xxx. 2, 10). The Greek archaic vases which have been so abundantly published by German archæologists in recent years, take a new place in the history of art when their lotus forms are specified. As long as the lotuses of xxx. 1, 4, 8, are "palms" or unrecognized plants, the significance of the lions is also obscured and the Egyptian element of the art is unrecognized.

For the association of the lion with the normal lotus in Etruria and in Greece two monuments are offered in evidence (xxix. 3; xxx. 5). The lotus has not been noticed by the Antiquarian who published the vase.

The peculiar interest of such monuments is that they combine two elements which are both Egyptian, in a style which finds no parallel in Egyptian art, either as regards style in the narrower sense or the manner of association. If there are two lions with the lotus in Egypt, they are placed back to back (ii. 4, [p. 23]), not confronting one another. We can specify lions with lotus on the head in Egyptian art, but no lions with lotuses placed under the body. Thus, as in the case of the ram (xxviii. 7 [p. 203]), the hypothesis of a mechanical copy, indifferent to the symbolic sense of the corresponding original, cannot be assumed.

128. DETAIL OF A TOMB-RELIEF IN THE BOLOGNA MUSEUM. Demonstration for the so-called "ivy leaf" as a lotus leaf. From Author's sketch. (Compare Plate xxii., pp. 161-165.)

We have, then, the alternative of two theories. One theory would be that the Greeks accidentally combined two separate forms, both of which they had borrowed, without reference to a symbolizing combination of these forms in the art from which they were borrowed. The other theory would be that the Greeks combined two symbols whose sense was known to them as related to the sun, or to Apollo, and that in this combination they followed the meaning, without following the exterior style, of the nation from which the symbols were borrowed. The latter is my own view.

The lion was a symbol of Apollo in Lycia (Note 3), and there is abundant evidence for the lion as a solar emblem in Cyprus; the tomb-stelè, xxx. 7 (lions on the winged disk), being one of many similar tombstones. Therefore it is interesting to observe the anthemion association in cases like xxx. 3. We shall find that the disposition to accept the Cypriote art as dominantly Greek is that of the best authorities (p. 294, Note 3).

The style of the *patera* from Crete, from which the detail xxix. 8 is taken, would be called "Assyrian" according to present standards; that is to say, it is approximately like the Phenician *pateras* which have been found at Nineveh, and which are conceded to be Phenician. It is mainly from such Ninevite remains of Phenician decorative art—fragments of ivories admitted to be Phenician, bronzes admitted to be Phenician, &c.—that the standards of "Assyrian style," as found in Mediterranean art, are derived. These objects are mainly in the Cases of the British Museum, and their Egyptian quality is open to the observation of every expert. In the Assyrian stone reliefs, where a national quality is much more obvious, a relation to the so-called Assyrian style of Greece or Italy is almost absolutely lacking. A suggestion sometimes found in publication, that the horizontal bands of animals on Greek vases are related to the horizontal bands of Assyrian relief, shows more attention to the appearance of these reliefs in publication than it does to their former appearance on an Assyrian palace.

The "Herzblatt" of xxix. 9 should be compared with xxxix. 3 [p. 253]. Both are possibly related to a similar Mycenæ pattern which is connected with lii. 3, 5, 7 [p. 321] and derived from a lotus leaf.

As for the minor monument, xxx. 9, it is a scarab from a publication made before the time of Egyptian science and also before the time of Egyptian counterfeits. Presumably from Egypt, it is not positive that this scarab may not represent a Phenician, Greek, Lycian, or Carian mongrel art. It belongs to a series of eccentricities in which the lotus is attached to a symbolic animal form in various ways. For the Gryphon with tail ending in a lotus we can appeal to Rosellini for a picture of the XIIth Dynasty (tombs of Beni Hasan), not only in the published picture but also according to his own designation in text.[5]

The lion and lotus can be specified in Hindu art, a fact which will become significant when the Hindu instances of the deer and lotus and of the "bird" and lotus have been made known.[6]

---

5. ROSELLINI, M.C. xxiii. 4. Gryphon standing, with tail ending in a lotus flower, and so specified by Rosellini's text.

6. SIR ALEXANDER CUNNINGHAM, *The Stûpa of Bharhut*, Plate viii., lions and lotus rosettes (third century B.C.).

PLATE XXIX.

THE LION AND THE LOTUS.

1. Lion and lotus. Detail, Philae. *Description de l'Égypte*, A., I. 13, 1.

2. Lions and lotuses. LEPSIUS, *Denkmäler*, X., v. 2.

3. Lion and lotus. Etruscan gem, Vulci. *Museo Etrusco-Vaticano*, I. lxxii.

4. Lions rampant, facing a trefoil lotus which rests on a rosette. Etruscan bronze *repoussé* detail, Caere. *Museo-Etrusco-Vaticano*, I. xv.

5. The Lions "To-morrow and Yesterday," otherwise Ra and Osiris, supporting the solar disk. Detail from P. LE PAGE RENOUF, in *Proceedings, Society of Biblical Archæology*, Dec., 1888.

6. Egyptian lotus capital with lion heads. PRISSE D'AVENNES, *Colonettes en Bois*.

7. Lions rampant, facing rosette, lotus palmettes above. Cypriote relief fragment in the New York Museum. CESNOLA, *Atlas*, xxvii. 84.

8. Lions facing lotus bud. *Repoussé* bronze detail of a *patera* found in Crete. *Museo Italiano di Antichità Classica*, Taf. III., "*Antichità dell' Antro di Zeus Ideo in Creta.*"

9. Lion and "Herzblatt." Greek pottery detail. BÖHLAU, *Jahrbuch*, 1887.

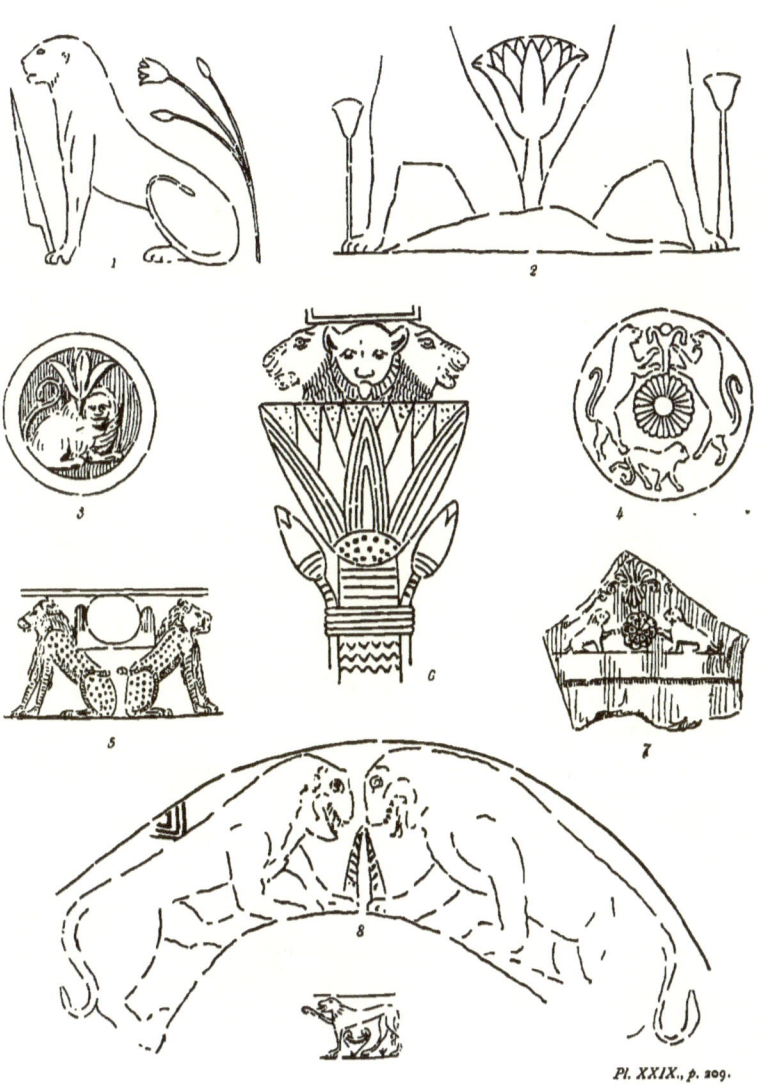

Pl. XXIX., p. 209.

PLATE XXX.

THE LION AND THE LOTUS.

1. Lions rampant, facing lotus palmette with birds. (Compare matter for the Bird and the Lotus, Plates xliii.—xlvi. [pp. 269-289]). Detail of an early Attic vase. BÖHLAU, in *Jahrbuch*, 1887, Taf. III.

2. Lion and rosettes. Pottery fragment. *Naukratis*, II. v. 7.

3. Lion and lotus anthemions. Cypriote tombstone in the New York Museum. CESNOLA, *Atlas*, xvi.

4. Lions rampant and lotus anthemion; Swastikas. Vase from Athens, in the British Museum. BIRCH, *Pottery*, p. 184.

5. Lion and lotus. Greek vase in the Louvre. The lotus is not noticed by BENNDORF, *Vasengemälde*, vi.

6. Lion. Egyptian scarab. KLAPROTH, xiii. 673. For references to "KLAPROTH" see p. 86.

7. Lions on the winged solar disk. Tombstone in the New York Museum. CESNOLA, *Atlas*, cxxii.

8. Lion and archaic lotus palmette. Detail, early Theban vase. BÖHLAU, in *Jahrbuch*, 1887, Taf. 4.

9. Lion with triangular lotuses pendant from tail and projecting from paw. Compare the fish, Plate xlii. 2, 4 [p. 267], especially No. 2. Compare also ROSELLINI, M.C. xxiii. for hawk-headed lion with normal lotus at the end of the tail (which is so specified by Rosellini in his text).

10. Lion and rosettes, Swastika and sun diagram above. Greek pottery fragment. *Naukratis*, II. viii. 1.

Among the Cretan gems of the British Museum is a lion and trefoil lotus, Case R, No. 150.

Pl. XXX., p. 211.

THE SPHINX AND THE LOTUS.

(PLATES XXXI., XXXII., XXXIII., XXXIV., PAGES 221, 223, 225, 227.)

THE Egyptian Sphinx is a solar lion with human head, a form of Horus, and an image of the Sun-god under which the deified Pharoah was especially represented.[1] Hence the Sphinx presents the portrait of the reigning Pharoah and takes the female human head in the case of a reigning queen.[2] The Sphinx with head of the ram is an equally obvious and well-recognized solar combination, as is the Sphinx with head of a hawk, generally known as the Gryphon.[3]

The Gryphon can be dated to the XIIth Dynasty. It is specified by Egyptian texts as a form of Horus,[4] (compare ii. 8 [p. 23], Gryphon with Osiris). The winged Sphinxes have been thought to show Mesopotamian influence, but they can be dated many centuries earlier than any known monuments from Mesopotamia, i.e., to the XVIIIth and XIXth Dynasties, and to a period beginning nine centuries earlier than the earliest excavated Assyrian palace, which is of the 9th century B.C.

The riddle of the Greek Sphinx is a riddle still. It is conceded that the Theban myth has no general bearing on the problem as to what the Sphinx in Greek art meant to the Greeks, and recent writers on the subject have succeeded in showing mainly that not much is known about it.[5]

The general attitude of Greek archæology is that all the "Oriental Monsters" of Greek vases and Greek art are decorative adaptations for decorative uses, and with about the same relation to Greek history as the unicorn of the British coat of arms

---

1. References at pp. 8, 9, Notes 32, 33.
2. WILKINSON's statement that the female Sphinx does not occur in Egyptian art (*Ancient Egyptians*, II., p. 94, 3rd Edit.), is qualified by his own illustration (III., p. 310) of "the Queen Mut-netem as a female Sphinx." Compare Plate xxxi. 2 [p. 221].
3. A stone Gryphon of the XIXth Dynasty from Ipsamboul, in the British Museum, "sacred to Mentu." A painted Gryphon of the XIIth Dynasty at Beni Hasan (p. 207, Note 5).
4. ROSELLINI in text (p. 151) for M.D.C. xxii.) detail, Plate ii. 8 [p. 23]).
5. MILCHHŒFFER, in *Mit. aus Athen*, iv., p. 45. MARX, in *Jahrbuch*, 1889, "Der Stier von Tiryns."

has to the present religion of Great Britain. A recent publication of a sepulchral Sphinx at Athens takes the ground that the given Sphinx has no sepulchral significance, or, in other words, that the Greeks, who were notoriously reverent and circumspect in matters of the tomb, chose their tomb decoration without the amount of sentiment which inspires the monuments of a modern cemetery.

To deny significance to the Sphinxes of Cypriote tombstones will be impossible after the associations noted by this chapter have been considered and other tombstones are involved in these conclusions. There are two points in the problem of the Greek Sphinx. First, given a meaning related to the Egyptian original, why is the Greek Sphinx female, when the Egyptian original is generally male (since there were not many reigning queens)? Second, how is the meaning related to the original?

There does not appear to have been any subtle purpose in the Greek habit of designating the typical Sphinx as a woman. It is simply the same mistake which transformed the *Ba* into a Siren or a Harpy.[6] The Sphinx came originally to the Greeks by way of Phenician ivories and metal decoration, and we can still detect a sufficient amount of female resemblance in these Phenician originals to explain the error; for instance, in xxxii. 8, 13, which are Phenician ivories from Nineveh of a type also familiar to the Greeks; or in type xli. 7 [p. 263], in bronze from Cyprus; or in the type xli. 12 [p. 263], in stone carving from Syria.

129. "THE SPHINX AND THE LOTUS." Demonstration for the so-called "Ivy leaf" as a lotus leaf. To compare with Plate xxxiv. From a tomb relief in Bologna. From Author's sketch.

In such examples it is the Egyptian head-dress with its pendant flaps (xxxi. 1, 3; xli. 1, 12) or the Egyptian wig with pendant locks, as in xxxii. 8, 13), which have been mistaken for the long hair of a woman. It is only in the later Greek Sphinxes that we find the hair knotted on the head (xxxiii. 5, 7). The early Greek Sphinxes have the pendant locks which show the starting point of an easy transformation (xxxiii. 2, 6, 8, 9).

The distinctly male Sphinx made his way as far as Hallstadt (xxxiii. 10) and North Italy (xxxiv. 3). The Cypriote Greek Sphinxes are not all distinctly female (xxxiii. 11). The Greek tendency to beautify *(zum verschönern)* is one

6. Dr Rougé, *Notice Sommaire*, p. 101, ("l'âme, toujours représentée par un épervier a tête humaine." This transformation is conceded.

unquestionable cause of the transformation; as in the type of the later Gorgon, or in the transformation of the goose of Leda and of Jupiter to a swan.[7]

For the meaning of the Sphinx in Greek art we remark that it is a typical ornament of tombstones and sarcophagi (xxxiii. 1, 3, 4, 11, 12), and that it is mortuary because it is solar [p. 9]. When it appears on vases (xxxiii. 6, 8, 9; xxxiv. 9), it is very generally in that duplicate rampant arrangement which points to a Phenician bronze original like xli. 7 [p. 263]. In both originals and copies of the rampant type, the intervening lotus, or derivative, point to a solar significance.[8]

In the Phenician originals the Sphinx is solar, as in its Egyptian home. The value of the lotus in assisting this determination is of great importance when we reach the Greek copies. That the worship of Horus was directly affected by the Phenicians is attested by Cypriote bronzes (xliv. 2 [p. 285]) and Phenician seals (xliv. 5); and by the numerous instances of the winged solar disk in Syria (xliii. 6, [p. 283]) and on Phenician seals (lxvii. 3 [p. 401]), &c. The fact is, indeed, commonplace information. In Egypt the winged solar disk is distinctly Horus as apart from other Sun-gods. It is not at all clear, however, that Horus symbols derived from Egypt had the same limitation, and the positive contrary may be fairly asserted from the associations of the winged sun disk in Mesopotamian, Hittite, and Phenician art (xxiii. 4, 5 [p. 173]; xxiv. 1, 2, 3, 7 [p. 183]).

Phenician worship, as natural to mariners, was much devoted to the visible appearance of the heavenly bodies, as well as to the derivative personifications, if we may judge by the frequent indication of the sun and moon in union which is peculiar to their art (lxvi., lxvii. [pp. 399-401]). This fact might be explained by their Semitic affiliations with the distinctly celestial and stellar aspects of Babylonian cults, and from the general fact that Phenician worship was of a grosser and more naturalistic character than that of Egypt.

We have therefore every reason to suppose that the Solar Sphinx, as borrowed from Egypt, was borrowed as a Solar Sphinx in general rather than a Horus Sphinx in particular. The Egyptian habit of deifying the Pharoah under the form of Horus (which included the young Horus on the lotus, as well as the Sphinx), would have made this solar generalization an easy one. However the Sphinx was

---

7. O. KELLER, *Thiere des classischen Alterthums in culturhistorischer Beziehung*, p. 288; quoting STEPHANI.

8. Where not rampant and isolated, as on Rhodian vases, the same significance is determined by associations with the deer, goose &c. to be presently accounted for.

THE SPHINX AND THE LOTUS.

first borrowed, this general solar symbolism was its ultimate foreign symbolism, as long as it remained a symbol.

The Gryphon, which is identical with the Sphinx in Egypt and which is an equivalent symbol in foreign Syrian, Mesopotamian, and Greek use, assists the explanation of the Greek Sphinx, for we have explicit information as to the relations of the Gryphon with Apollo.[9] It would therefore appear that the Greeks were led astray by their own mistake in the matter of the female sex of their typical Sphinx— and having no female deity to represent the sun, could not, in later historical times, explain the Sphinx to their own satisfaction.

For the Sphinx in Greek art we have then simply to fall back on the Sun-lion, which is its original and essential character—the addition of the human head being a subordinate point, which is made clear by the fact that the Sphinx may also appear with the head of a solar ram or the head of a solar hawk. We find in the lion the same sepulchral use, the same union with the lotus, and the same association with the solar disk or sun and moon crescent. Compare xxx. 3, 7 [p. 211] (for which there are many Cypriote instances), with xxxiii. 1, 3, 4, 11, 12. As general result, then, it is clear that the winged Sun-lion with the lotus (xxxii. 9; or xxxii. 12) is the equivalent of the Sphinx of the Greek Cypriote coin, xxxii. 5.

The sepulchral use of both Lion and Sphinx in Greek art is a phase of the same idea which places the lotus anthemion on a tombstone (Figs. 43 [p. 71] 68, 69 [p. 124]; xiii. 4 [p. 121]), and which places the lotus anthemion on the Lion and Sphinx tombstones (xxx. 3 [p.211]; xxxiii. 3, 4, 11, 12).

This idea has been sufficiently developed in matter for the Egyptian lotus (pp. 9, 10), and it applies to every ancient solar emblem. With the worship of the sun was united a worship of creative force and generative power. With the cult of the dead and the theory of the spirit world was united the belief in the recreative-life-giving, and life-sustaining power of nature. This fact is summed up in the

---

9. As the Egyptian Gryphon is a combination of the Sun-hawk and Sun-lion (two forms of Horus), and is identified with Horus by Egyptian texts (p. 9, Note 34), it is interesting to observe that the relations of the classical Gryphon both to the sun and to Apollo were still familiar to the times of Ovid and of Apollonius of Tyana. According to Ovid as quoted by LAJARD, *Culte de Mithra*, "the God called Apollo by the Greeks is represented by a combination of the Hawk and Lion." In the life of Apollonius of Tyana (as quoted by LAJARD, p. 383), Gryphons are sacred to the sun, and their home has been transferred to "Media." According to WELCKER, "Gryphons belong to Apollo (the sun) by all traditions," quoted by LAJARD (p. 390). Gryphons are also quoted for the sun by KING, Appendix for Gems, in CESNOLA's *Cyprus*, p. 357.

Egyptian belief which assimilates and identifies the blessed dead with Osiris. However distinct the Greeks may have been, and were, from the Egyptians, they were like them in their reverence for the tomb. To say that our Greek vases and pottery fragments [10] are derived from tombs in the immense majority of cases is not to imply that other decorations and other art less known to us may have been used for the living; but the entire art of the Greeks in its foundation and original bearing is religious, and we may as well deny that the landscape art of modern Europe [11] began with exclusively religious pictures, as assert that the later art of Greece was independent of its earlier religious basis.

To say that the Greek knew his anthemion to be a lotus is quite another matter. It is known that the normal lotus was a recognized tomb-symbol in the Greco-Roman art (p. 10, Note 41), but this does not prove that the anthemion was known to the later Greeks as a lotus, and it appears to me improbable that it was so known. That it was to them a religious symbol I consider proven. That they were conscious of the originally lotiform character of the symbol at some time and in some places, viz., the time and places of early transition, appears, to say the least, highly probable.

The significance of the Gryphon illustrations of the four Plates under consideration is indicated by the matter for the Sphinx, but quotations and references are much more accessible. The Gryphon was a symbol of the distinctive Greek Sun-god Apollo (Note 9), and his association with the lotus in Greek art (xxxiv. 4) has an all-apparent relation to similar associations of Egyptian and Phenician art (xxxi. 7, 8, 9, compare matter for the tabs, iv. [p. 63]; xxxii. 4, 10; xxxiv. 1, 5). To the same effect are his associations with the sun disk (xxxi. 6), with the *Ankh* (xxxii 7, and lxv. 3 [p. 393], and again with the lotus (lxv. 4 [p. 393]).[12]

Earlier matter for the spiral, the spiral scroll, and for the identity of the spiral scroll with the meander, finds corroboration in Plate xxxiv. Among the eccentricities of solar symbolism is the one of attaching the lotus to the head of

---

10. Large masses of pottery fragments are frequently found directly exterior to the tomb. Such pottery was probably used in the periodical banquets commemorating the memory of the dead, and then broken.

11. Landscape pictures exclusively devoted to landscape were first painted (since the time of Antiquity) in the 17th century, and developed from the landscape backgrounds of religious paintings.

12. KING, *Appendix for Gems*, CESNOLA'S *Cyprus*, p. 357, says of the Phenicians, "All their gems served the double purpose of signets and talismans, all embodying religious ideas."

the solar animal. In pure Egyptian art the gods Nefer-toum and Nilus are the only ones who habitually wear the lotus as a head-dress (i. 11, [p. 21]), but cases

130. GREEK VASE IN THE LOUVRE.

can be quoted in Egyptian art for this symbol on the head of the Sun-lion and the Sun-hawk. The Sphinx xxxi. 4 is also an instance, and the Sphinx xxxi. 2 wears a crown surmounted by the lotus.

We can quote the Phenician Gryphon xxxiv. 5 (from Cyprus) as having the normal three-spiked lotus on the head. The illustration of the Sphinx xxxiv. 6, with trefoil lotus on the head, is from the Regulini-Galassi tomb and also Phenician. The Gryphon, xxxiv. 4 (from a Greek vase) has a lotus, with exaggerated central spike, attached to the head. The instance of the lotus palmette xxxiv. 1 is Etruscan or Phenician, and the instance of the lotus palmette xxxiv. 9 is Greek.

131. DETAIL ON BRONZE. From the Regulini-Galassi Tomb.

The "ivy leaf" of Fig. 129 [p. 214] is one more case of the lotus head-ornament.

The head-ornament of the early Greek pottery Sphinx from Troy (xxxiv. 2) is an Ionic lotus, and has been mistaken by Schuchardt for a pig-tail.[13]

We shall not hesitate therefore to designate the spirals attached to the heads of xxxiv. 7, 8 as lotuses also. In xxxiv. 8 the co-extensive value of the spiral scroll and the meander is apparent, and we may turn to the twisted stems, ending in spirals, of xxxiii. 8 as another interesting evidence of the mutability of the lotus. In such a case we know what it is because it can be nothing else. There is no doubt that the peculiar limitation of ancient symbolic floral ornament to one plant explains its curious mutability and unrecognizable degraded forms. As long as only one plant was represented it made no difference whether it corresponded in any sense to natural appearance.

13. See p. 49, Note 15.

THE SPHINX AND THE LOTUS. 219

The corroborations of Plate xxxiii. for the palmette (No. 6); the Ionic capital (5, 7), the anthemion (3, 4, 11), for the Sacred Cone (9), and for the introrse scroll (12, compare ix. 5 [p. 91]), are self-apparent.

The instances of the normal lotus (2, 6, 12) can be indefinitely multiplied, and the lotuses of prehistoric Hallstadt (10) have yet to receive their recognition from archæologists.

We cannot leave these Plates without remarking that the Assyrian and Phenician examples of the normal lotus on seals and cylinders as related to sun-worship (xxxii. 4, 6, 9, 11, 12, and xxxiv. 5) have been absolutely ignored by the men of learning who have published them. Corroborations for the Sacred Cone (xxxii. 1), for the "Assyrian" palmette (2, 8, 13, 14) and rosette (3), will not be overlooked.

An obvious case of rosette association is offered by the large Syrian Sphinx (xxxi. 3). Analogous instances are frequent in the paintings of necklace collars on mummy-cases.

132. THE SPHINX AND THE LOTUS. Persepolis. From LAJARD. Compare xii. 14 (p. 113).

PLATE XXXI.

THE SPHINX AND THE LOTUS.

1. Sphinxes and lotuses. Detail of an Egyptian vase, from a tomb-painting. PRISSE D'AVENNES. *Vases, Règne de Thothmes III.*

2. Female winged Sphinx, crowned with introrse lotus scrolls, buds, and lotus; necklace with rosette. PRISSE D'AVENNES, *Types de Sphinx.* This Sphinx represents the Queen Mut-netem of the XVIIIth Dynasty. (Compare WILKINSON, *Ancient Egyptians*, 3rd Ed., III., p. 310.)

3. Granite Sphinx, Oum el Aouamid, Syria. Detail from an entire view in RENAN, *Mission de Phénicie*, lvi. Showing necklace in three hands, buds and lotus flowers, rosettes, and lotus buds inverted. Demonstration from association, for the rosette as lotus. Many parallel instances on the collarettes of mummy-cases.

4. Female winged Sphinx, wearing a crown with conventional outline lotus and two buds; necklace with projecting rosette pendant, compare No. 2. PRISSE D'AVENNES, *Types de Sphinx.*

5. Sphinx over doorway, and lotuses. Detail of a gold vase; from a tomb-painting. PRISSE D'AVENNES, *Vases en or emaillé.*

6. Hawk-headed Sphinx (Gryphon), supporting sun disk. CESNOLA, *Cyprus;* KING'S *Appendix for Gems*, v. 17.

7. Hawk-headed Sphinx (Gryphon) on the lotus. ROSELLINI, III., xxxix. (Edfou).

8. Hawk-headed Sphinxes (Gryphons), facing lotus details. Gold and enamel bracelet, in the Louvre. PRISSE D'AVENNES, *Bijoux.* Compare the enlarged detail ix. 3 [p. 91].

9. Hawk-headed Sphinx (Gryphon) and lotuses. Style of the Phenician and Syrian adaptations. Detail of a vase from an Egyptian tomb-painting. PRISSE D'AVENNES, *Vases du Tombeau Ramses III.*

Pl. XXXI, p. 221.

PLATE XXXII.

THE SPHINX AND THE LOTUS.

1. Sphinx, goat, and lotus bud. LAYARD, *First Series*, iv. 33.
2. Sphinx, winged sun disk, lotus palmette. Phenician or Assyrian seal. LAJARD, *Culte de Mithra*, liv. c. 22.
3. Hawk-headed deity, Sphinx and rosettes.
4. Hawk-headed Sphinx (Gryphon) and lotus. Phenician seal. LAJARD, *Culte de Mithra*, lvii. 2.
5. Cypriote coin; lotus, lotus leaf, *astragalus;* flower mistaken by DE LUYNES for "*fleur-de-lys*," leaf mistaken for "*feuille de lierre.*" Reverse, Sphinx on the lotus, flower and bud. DE LUYNES *Num. et In. Cyp.*, xii. 4.
6. Winged Sun-god, Sphinxes, and lotus. Assyrian cylinder. LAJARD, *Culte de Mithra*, xlii. 7.
7. Hawk-headed Sphinx (Gryphon) and *Ankh.* Cypriote seal. CESNOLA, *Cyprus;* KING'S *Appendix for Gems*, viii. c.
8. Sphinx, lotus, and lotus palmette. Egypto-Phenician ivory from Nineveh, British Museum. LAYARD, *First Series*, lxxxix. 12.
9. Winged lion and lotus. Phenician seal. PERROT ET CHIPIEZ, *Assyrie*, p. 689.
10. Hawk-headed Sphinx (Gryphon) facing a lotus. Egyptian or Phenician scarab. KLAPROTH, ix. 496.
11. Winged sun disk, Sphinxes, and lotus. Assyrian or Phenician seal. LAJARD, *Culte de Mithra*, lvii. 3.
12. Sun-god, winged lions, and lotus. Assyrian cylinder. LAJARD, *Culte de Mithra*, liv. A. 13.
13. Sphinx, facing lotus-Ionic stelè, which supports a lotus palmette. Egypto-Phenician ivory from Nineveh, British Museum. WARING, *Ceramic Art in Remote Ages*, xlv. 2.
14. Sphinx, winged deity, and lotus palmette. Assyrian relief detail. LAYARD, *First Series*, xliv. 8.

Pl. XXXII., p. 223.

PLATE XXXIII.

THE SPHINX AND THE LOTUS.

1. Sphinxes over sun disk and moon crescent. Cypriote tombstone in the New York Museum. CESNOLA, *Atlas*, xvii.
2. Sphinxes facing lotus. Greek pottery detail. *Monumenti Inediti*.
3. Sphinxes and lotus anthemions. From the cover of the sarcophagus of Amathus, New York Museum. CESNOLA, *Cyprus*, p. 267.
4. Sphinxes and lotus anthemions. Cypriote tombstone, New York Museum. Inverted lotus border (Egg-and-Dart" moulding, xxi. [p. 159]). PERROT ET CHIPIEZ, *Cypre*, Fig. 151.
5. Sphinx on the Ionic capital. Tombstone, Greek pottery detail. *Monumenti Inediti*.
6. Detail of Sphinxes rampant, facing lotus motive of a double flower, anthemions, palmettes, and introrse scrolls. Greek pottery detail. *Monumenti Inediti*, IV. lvii.
7. Sphinx on the Ionic capital. Tombstone, Greek pottery detail. *Monumenti Inediti*, VIII. xliv.
8. Sphinxes facing lotus spirals. Greek pottery detail, Daphnæ ware. *Tanis*, II., xxvi. 9a.
9. Sphinxes rampant, facing lotus bud. Greek pottery detail. *Archæologische Zeitung*, 1881, Taf. III.
10. Male Sphinx and lotus. Bronze *repoussé* detail from Hallstadt, prehistoric Celtic tombs. VON SACKEN, *Das Grabfeld von Hallstadt*, xxi.
11. Sphinxes rampant and lotus anthemion. Cypriote tombstone, New York Museum. CESNOLA, *Atlas*, civ.
12. Sphinxes on lotuses, facing introrse lotus scrolls (compare ix. 5 [p. 91]) which rise from an Ionic lotus. Cypriote tombstone, New York Museum. CESNOLA, *Atlas*, c.

Pl. XXXIII. p. 225.

PLATE XXXIV.

THE SPHINX AND THE LOTUS.

1. Sphinxes with lotus palmettes attached to the head. Phenician detail, Etruria. PERROT et CHIPIEZ, *Phénicie*, Fig. 625.

2. Sphinx with lotus attached to the head. Archaic Greek pottery detail. SCHLIEMANN, *Troy*, p. 55.

3. Sphinx with lotus springing from the mouth. *Repoussé* bronze detail from the "*Situla* d'Este." *Gazette Archéologique*, 1888, xii.

4. Gryphon head, with spiked lotus attached. Greek pottery detail. *Monumenti Inediti*, IV. lvii.

5. Gryphon, with lotus attached to the head. Cypriote cylinder. CESNOLA, *Cyprus*; KING'S Appendix for Gems, I., 9.

6. Sphinx head and lotus. *Repoussé* bronze detail. Caere. *Museo Etrusco-Vaticano*, I., xvii.

7. Sphinx head with lotus spiral attached. Greek pottery fragment from Egypt. *Journal of Hellenic Studies*, 1887, lxxix.

8. Sphinx with lotus spiral attached to the head, facing a Swastika of meander pattern, and spiral scrolls; inverted lotus anthemion, &c. Detail of a Meliar vase. BÖHLAU, *Jahrbuch*, 1887, xii.

9. Detail of Sphinxes rampant, facing lotuses and lotus palmettes. Lotus palmette attached to the head, "François" vase, Chiusi. *Monumenti Inediti*, iv.

Pl. XXXIV. p. 227.

THE DEER, GAZELLE, ORYX, IBEX, WILD GOAT, AND LOTUS.

(PLATES XXXV., XXXVI., XXXVII., XXXVIII., XXXIX., PAGES 245, 247, 249, 251, 253.)

ACCORDING to one authority, there is but one species of deer in Africa, indigenous to Barbary.[1] The antlered deer is pictured at Beni Hasan,[2] but the picture probably represents an imported animal, as it appears to be unknown to Egyptian symbolism. The deer is indigenous to Mesopotamia, and appears on the Assyrian monuments in connection with deities and sacred rites. The "Oriental" indications so generally assumed for the lion and Sphinx do not carry us beyond the range of Egypto-Syrian influences, but the problem of the deer and the lotus must be solved in Assyria and Chaldea.

From the study of the bird and the lotus on Cypriote vases, which subject I have reserved till the last of this particular series as offering the most crushing demonstration for the solar symbolism of the lotus in early Mediterranean art, I was led to the study of the deer and the lotus on Cypriote vases (xxxvii. 5, 7, 12; xxxix. 5), for which a very large number of examples can be cited in the New York Museum.

The way had been pointed here by Colonna-Ceccaldi in his citation of the Sacred Grove of the Curium Apollo with its sacred swans and sacred deer, and of the fable of Aelian relating to the latter,[3] and he was the first to make clear to me that the deer was an emblem of Apollo, and an emblem of Apollo distinctly recognized by the Greek worship of Cyprus. At the same time the reference in Engel[4] to the Cypriote king who sent a golden deer to the god at Delphi chanced

---

1. *Guide to the Galleries of Mammalia*, British Museum, South Kensington, p. 47. The animal is said by WILKINSON to have been seen in the neighbourhood of the Natron lakes of modern Egypt. *Ancient Egyptians*, 3rd Edition, I., p. 95.

2. ROSELLINI.

3. COLONNA-CECCALDI, *Monuments de Chypre*, p. 163; and *Revue Archéologique*, xxxiii., 1877; quoting AELIAN, *De Nat. Anim.*, lib. XI., cvii. See p. 240, this chapter.

4. ENGEL, *Cypern*.

to come in view. The Apollo and the deer of the sculptor Canachus were known to me, and on turning to a Dictionary of Antiquities [5] I found that the deer was a well-recognized symbol of the Greek Sun-god.

Later reference to the great work of Keller [6] has supplemented this information by a mass of classical authorities, among which the authorities for Artemis (the moon) are of course included. Within Keller's knowledge the deer was a "favourite of the gods in Western Asia." [7] On an island at the mouth of the Euphrates, in the time of the later Achemenidæ, were kept droves of deer and wild goats sacred to Artemis.[8] The prophetic doe of Sertorius in Spain is cited.[9] At the festival of Artemis held at Patræ in Achæa, the chariots were drawn by deer.[10] The deer was sacred to Apollo, and was sacred to Athene and Aphrodite as "Moon-goddesses." [11] The erotic significance of the deer is mentioned [12] together with his fabled love of music and consequent relations to Apollo.[13] The deer was sacred to "Isis" at Phocis,[14] to Athene Laodikeia in Syria,[15] and to Apollo at Delphi. Inscriptions of Delphi mention objects bought with "the gold of the deer," [17] and gold and silver deer were offered as presents to temples.[18]

It would therefore appear that the deer and the lotus on Cypriote vases as already quoted, and on Rhodian vases (xxxvii. 4), for which a large number of instances can be cited in the British Museum and the Louvre,[19] must be incorporated with the recognized monuments of Greek mythological art, a position which has not yet been conceded to them.[20] It would be in the highest degree unjust to lay the blame of this oversight on the shoulders of Perrot, who has given the most outspoken expression to the view that the pictures on Cypriote vases are without significance. In these utterances he has simply voiced

---

5. DAREMBERG et SAGLIO, *Dictionnaire des Antiquités Grecques et Romaines* (Hachette, 1873), under "Apollo," quoting for the doe and stag, PAUSANIAS, viii. 48, 2; x. 13, 2. The deer is also quoted for Apollo by LAJARD, *Culte de Mithra*, p. 631.

6. O. KELLER, *Thiere des classischen Alterthums in Culturhistorischer Beziehung* (London, David Nutt).

7. p. 75.—8, p. 75.—9, p. 89.—10, p. 90.—11, p. 94. 12, p. 96.—13, p. 93.—14, p. 96.—15, p. 96.—16, p. 96. 17, p. 96.—18, p. 97.

19. SALZMANN, *Nécropole de Camire;* and LONGPÉRIER, *Musée Napoléon III.*

20. PERROT et CHIPIEZ, *Cypre*. "Sur un autre vase de Citium c'est un cerf qui occupe la place que tient ici cette figure féminine avec la palmette centrale placée sous le bec de la cruche, et avec les deux cignes affrontés, il complète un décor auquel on aurait bien tort de vouloir assigner une signification quellconque.1 . . . Sur aucun des vases qui portent la marque de l'industrie Cypriote vous ne trouverez un tableau dont le sujet soit tiré de la Mythologie Grecque" (p. 709). At p. 706 of *Cypre* the animal designated by Perrot, "cheval ailé," is a deer (marked with rosettes).

THE DEER, GAZELLE, ORYX, IBEX, WILD GOAT, AND LOTUS. 231

an opinion of the specialists, whose views it has been his great mission to bring within the ken of the general public.

If we turn to another class of authorities, their references are equally explicit for the solar symbolism of the gazelle and the antelope. As being unknown to Europe we cannot expect to find large numbers of the latter animals figuring in European art otherwise than as borrowed forms, but as such they appear (xxxvii. 9; xxxix. 8).

According to Professor Sayce, the stag must be regarded as the equivalent of these animals in Babylonian mythology.[21] This view is supported by the monuments (xxxvi. 10, and in xxxvi. 5 a deer carried head downward by the ibex-headed gods); see also Note 33 for stag with lotus not recognized by Menant.

Our most obvious quotation for the stag on Assyrian monuments is the colossal relief of the British Museum, a winged deity bearing a spotted stag and a branch of lotus palmettes. The branch from this figure is shown at xxv. 4 [p. 185].

According to Chaldean mythology Ea was god of the primeval watery element, atmospheric and otherwise,[22] and father of Merodach,[23] a Sun-god.[24] Ea was called the "Antelope of the Deep," "the Antelope the Creator," "the Antelope the Prince," "the lusty Antelope."[25] "The name of Ea is sometimes expressed by an ideograph which signifies literally an Antelope,"[26] and the "ship" or ark of Ea, in which his image was carried at festivals, was entitled "the ship of the divine Antelope of the Deep."[27] Professor Sayce further states that Ea was equivalent deity to the Sun-god Mul-lil of Nipur,[28] who was equivalent of the Semitic (Phenician) Baal,[29] the younger Bel of Assyria, as against Merodach the Sun-god of Babylon, the elder Bel.[30] Egyptologists will remember that the sacred bark of Ptah-Sokar-Osiris bears the head of the oryx on its prow.[31]

It is also matter of record as bearing on the significance of the Semitic Antelope-god, that troops of sacred gazelles were kept at Mecca,[32] and the authority for this statement, Robertson Smith, mentions that the stag was sacred to Astarte (Phenician Venus) at Laodicea in Syria.[33] We have already found mention of a

---

21. PROFESSOR SAYCE has favoured me with the written advice that "in Babylonia the stag would be the equivalent of the antelope."

22. SAYCE, *Hibbert Lectures* (p. 104).—23, p. 104. 24, proven by texts, p. 100.—25, p. 280.—26, p. 280. 27, p. 280.—28, p. 145.—29, p. 147.—30, p. 147.

31. WILKINSON, *Ancient Egyptians*, III., p. 302, 3rd Edition. There are instances at Dehr-el-Bahri and at Dehr-el-Medineh (Thebes).

32, 33. *Religion of the Semites*, p. 447. In COLLECTION DE CLERCQ, II., Plate v, p6, stag, trefoil lotus (unrecognized), six-rayed star, "symbol of Istar."

THE DEER, GAZELLE, ORYX, IBEX, WILD GOAT, AND LOTUS.

similar fact for one of her later equivalents (the Oriental Artemis) at the mouth of the Euphrates (Note 8).

There is still another celestial animal to be included in this sketch. According to the evidence of Rhodian and Cypriote vases the ibex was a celestial equivalent of the deer. Both animals appear on the vase xxxvii. 4. Although the large Rhodian vase xxxviii. shows the ibex alone, a more common representation shows friezes of both animals on one vase. The ibex is also an equivalent of the deer on Cypriote vases (xxxvii. 6, 10), and on Hallstatt bronzes (xxxix. 4), and the most decisive evidence on this head is furnished by the cylinder xxxvi. 5.

133. DEITY WITH CEREMONIAL BRANCH AND IBEX, FACING A SACRED TREE OF LOTUS BUDS. From Layard.

As parallel to the Assyrian relief in the British Museum of the winged deity with branch of lotus palmettes and stag, we may mention also another relief from Nineveh, where the worshipper carries an ibex[34] and a ceremonial branch of lotuses (xxiv. 8 [p. 183]), and faces a sacred tree of lotus buds.[35]

According to Keller the ibex was "constantly" confused with the wild

---

34. The designation of "ibex" is authorized in this instance by MENANT, *Cylindres*, II., 65. At p. 68 he applies the word "chevreau" to the same animal. Although the horns of the goat and wild goat are with most species shorter and less curved than those of the ibex, there is a species of wild goat in Western Asia whose horns are exactly similar to those of a species of ibex found in the same locality; both instanced by examples in the Museum of Natural History, South Kensington. There does not appear to be any existing species of ibex with abrupt downward curve at the tip of a long horn, as found on the Rhodian vases, and on the cylinder, xxxvi. 7. These may represent an "extinct Lebanon species," quoted by Keller, or may be simply inaccurate copies either of the heavier and more regular curve of the "Nubian ibex," or of the slighter curve of the long-horned oryx. If it be always the oryx head which forms the prow of the sacred bark of Ptah-Sokar Osiris, then there is precedent for the exaggerated curve in Egyptian art (at Dehr-el-Bahri). In the tomb-paintings at Beni Hasan several varieties of antelope and gazelle are carefully distinguished from the ibex as regards the horns. The peculiarly heavy horns of the "Nubian ibex" are also distinctly represented on some very small monuments (the seal, xxxv. 11, for example), and are also distinctly shown by a Ninevite relief (Botta, II., 164). The horn of the Rhodian "ibex," as regards existing species, has no obvious counterpart, excepting that of the chamois, in the matter of curve, but the chamois horn is very short, and that of the Rhodian vase ibex is very long, nor does the habitat of the chamois answer the conditions. The body of an ibex resembles quite closely that of a deer, but it retains the beard of the goat. According to Zoölogy, the genus *Capra* is divided into two classes, ibexes and goats. The goats are divided into *capra hircus* (domestic), and *capra ægagrus* (the wild goat).

35. LAYARD, *Second Series*, 47, shows a similar subject with Sacred Tree, but the ibex is carried by the winged deity and the lotus branch is differently detailed (Fig. 133).

THE DEER, GAZELLE, ORYX, IBEX, WILD GOAT, AND LOTUS. 233

goat by the Greeks,[36] a fact which will not surprise a modern antiquarian who undertakes to study Natural History in the cause of the lotus. From this fact he concludes an equivalent significance for both animals. Neither the Latin "ibex" nor the Greek ἴξαλος are Indo-German,[37] with which the fact coincides that the presence of the animal cannot be proven as indigenous to ancient Italy or Greece, and it seems to have been rare with the Swiss Lake-dwellers, but it appears on the Greek islands.

An important fact for the history of the *Aegis* results from the foregoing, and is also explicitly stated, viz., that the Greeks confused the skin of the goat with the skin of the wild goat.[38] The appearance of the wild goat on Cretan coins is mentioned by Keller in connection with the *Aegis*[39] as worn by the Cretan Zeus, but here his advices mainly end, with the consoling information that beside the wild goat and the tame goat, the chamois, the ibex, and the "Paseng," there was probably still another Lebanon species which is now extinct.

It is the view of Professor A. S. Murray that the entire goat-skin was once worn by Athene. From Keller's matter relating to the ibex or wild goat of Cretan coins and the *Aegis* of the Cretan Zeus; from the evidence of Cretan gems with the ibex or wild goat; from the ibex on Rhodian and Cypriote vases (xxxvii., xxxviii.); from the Goat-gods and Sun-gods Mul-lil and Uz (Samas) as identified with the Phenician Baal (p. 234); and from the relations of the Astarte of Syria and the Oriental Artemis of Chaldea to the wild goat, it is difficult not to move to an explanation of the *Aegis*. That it came directly to the Greeks from Libya is reported by Herodotus, but Phenician cults were established here in early antiquity. The Chaldean Sun-god and Goat-god Uz was represented as dressed in goat-skins.[40]

According to Professor Sayce the Chaldean God Ea—"was at times regarded rather as a gazelle than as an antelope. It was then that he was entitled the 'Princely Gazelle,' 'the lusty Gazelle,' 'the Gazelle who gives the earth,' and Merodach his son [a Sun-god] is termed 'the mighty one of the Gazelle God.'"[41] . . . The gazelle, however, was more correctly appropriated to Mul-lil of Nipur [Sun-god and original of the Phenician Baal] who was specially called the Gazelle God."[42]

36. KELLER, *Thiere*, &c., p. 38.—37, pp. 35, 38.—38, p. 40.—39, p. 40.

40. ROBERT BROWN, Jun., *Proceedings, Society of Biblical Archæology*, 1890.
41. SAYCE, *Hibbert Lectures*, pp. 283, 284.—42, p. 284.

234   *THE DEER, GAZELLE, ORYX, IBEX, WILD GOAT, AND LOTUS.*

The gazelle "frequently takes the place of the goat, which was also sacred and exalted into the Zodiacal sign of Capricornus. Since Tebet, the tenth month, corresponds to the sign of Capricornus and was dedicated to Pap-sukal, it is possible that Pap-sukal, "the messenger of the gods," was himself the Goat-god. At any rate there was a deity called Uz, the Accadian word for a goat. . . . The archaic Babylonian form of the character Uz is glossed by Utuki "the great spirit" and explained to be synonymous with the Sun-god. . . . We may infer that Uz "the goat" was a title of the Sun-god of Šippara [Samas]."[43] It also appears that the "divine goat" was associated with the Sun-god Mul-lil,[44] and hence it once more appears that the goat [and wild goat or ibex] were equivalents of the gazelle.

This identity of symbolism is furthermore attested by the following facts. In the Egyptian Zodiac a species of oryx (a straight-horned gazelle) represented Capricorn (the tenth month).[45] In the Hindu Zodiac, which was introduced into Hindustan by the Greeks,[46] the sign for Capricorn is a gazelle's head [47] and the antelope, in India, is the "vehicle" of the Moon-god Chandra [48] and a symbol of Siva.[49]

According to Robert Brown, Jun., the elevation of various animals to a place in the Zodiac results from their divine relations to the gods who were considered patron deities of the various months and who represented the sun in various aspects or stages of his journey through the Heavens.[50]

To these abundant references which would explain the associations of the deer and the lotus, the gazelle or antelope and lotus, and the ibex or goat and lotus,

---

43. SAYCE, *Hibbert Lectures*, p. 284.—44, p. 286.
45. BIRCH, *Egyptian Antiquities in the British Museum*, p. 54. "In the Zodiac it represented Capricornus."
46. *Encyclopædia Britannica, Ninth Edition*, under "Zodiac." "The Greeks introduced the solar Zodiac into Hindustan." The older Hindu Zodiac was lunar and had twenty-seven divisions. (Article by Miss A. M. Clerke.)
47. *Encyclopædia Britannica*, as above.
48. BIRDWOOD, *Industrial Arts of India*, and MOOR, *Hindu Pantheon*. The latter quotes (p. 207) from Sir William Jones' translation of the Hitopadesa: "In driving away the antelopes, who are appointed keepers of the pool sacred to Chandra, thou hast acted improperly. We antelopes are its guardians."

49. Vishnu's relations to the moon are mentioned by BIRDWOOD, p. 60. Vishnu is connected with Egypt by the Puranas (MOOR, p. 30), and has been identified with Set or Typhon, whose sacred animals were the ibex, gazelle, and antelope, as subsequently shown. The consort of Siva has a striking resemblance to the Egyptian figures of Bes (Set), and this also has been noticed by PIERRET. Bes is related by Egyptian texts to Arabia, and the Semitic conception of Baal, with whom Bes (or Set) are identified, would probably explain the original traits of Siva, either by Arab, Chaldean, or Assyrian influence. According to an Egyptian text the god Bes came from Arabia (DE ROUGÉ, *Notice Sommaire*).
50. *Proceedings, Society of Biblical Archæology*, 1890.

THE DEER, GAZELLE, ORYX, IBEX, WILD GOAT, AND LOTUS. 235

in Greek, Assyrian, and Phenician art, we may add the curious negative evidence offered by the silence of Egyptian texts and the difficulty of securing authorities for the standing of the ibex,[51] gazelle, oryx,[52] and antelope[53] in Egyptian mythology. It has been a matter of considerable difficulty to secure the evidence furnished in the Notes that these animals were Typhonic, symbols of Set, and ultimately reprobated representations in Egyptian art, subject to the destruction which has made the statuettes of the Typhonic God himself of highest rarity in the Museums.[54]

It is well known that the God Set (or Typhon), brother and murderer of

51. A small bronze ibex of the Third Egyptian Room, British Museum, Case 77 (No. 1698A and 115850) bears the designation: "Ibex, animal devoted to Typhon." BIRCH, *Egyptian Antiquities in the British Museum*, mentions the ibex "as seldom, if ever, found with divine honours," and as "having been supposed an accursed animal." He makes reference to Aelian xiv. 16.

52. The oryxes are specified by Worcester's Dictionary as a genus including various gazelles and antelopes, including the White Antelope or *Oryx leucoryx*. The horns of this species are short and nearly straight, and resemble some illustrated on Plate xxxv. I have placed over the descriptive matter of this Plate an explanation as to the words "gazelle," "antelope," and "oryx," as I have personally used them. According to BIRCH, "This animal [the oryx] whose species have various names, was an animal devoted to Typhon, and does not appear in the monuments to have received divine honours." But this overlooks the evidence of the Denderah reliefs, where the short-horned oryx appears in the lotus bower on an equal footing with the goose, cow, and bull (Figs. 134, 140, 148). "Two representations show it being sacrificed. . . . [I have observed a number besides those mentioned.] It is the only animal sacrificed to the gods on sculptures. In the Zodiac it represented Capricorn, and its head is found on the boat of Ptah Socharis and embalmed." It was considered a representation of Set by CHAMPOLLION, and is mentioned by HORAPOLLO as an emblem of impurity. WILKINSON, *Ancient Egyptians*, III., p. 302, 3rd Ed.

53. See the quotation from BRUGSCH for the White Antelope as Typhonic at p. 12, Note 52. The most interesting evidence for the Typhonic character of the gazelle and antelope is furnished by monuments of the Leyden Museum. One of these is a bronze statuette, inlaid with gold, of Horus trampling under foot a gazelle. Illustration in LEEMANS' *Monumens Égyptiens du Musée d'Antiquités des Pays-Bas a Leide*: "Il foule sous ses pieds un oryx, animal Typhonien." Another statuette represents Bes (Set, Typhon, Baal) "sur une colonne, ornée d'un chapiteau à fleur de lotus; il foule sous ses pieds une gazelle dont il tient les cornes dans sa main gauche" (Ibid. I. xv. p. 13). The action of this statuette appears to be rather that of holding the animal as an emblem than that of trampling it under foot. This would be consonant with the Typhonic nature of Bes. The action of Horus is justly described. With these representations may be classed the ordinary Horus reliefs, of late epoch, of the god standing on a crocodile, surmounted by a head of Bes, and holding gazelles in both hands. These undoubtedly are emblems of his triumph over Set. In WILKINSON's *Ancient Egyptians*, 3rd Ed, III. p. 303, there is a note by BIRCH as follows: "Horus is sometimes represented holding a gazelle in the hand, supposed to explain his victory over Set; but a mummied gazelle, showing that it was a sacred animal, is in the collection of the British Museum, No. 6778A, *Antelope Dorcas*. It was called *Kahas*." Dr. Birch overlooks the fact that the worship of Set was in vogue under the XVIIIth and XIXth Dynasties. As to this worship, BRUGSCH says, "According to his essence a most ancient Egyptian creation, Set at one time gradually became the representative of all foreign countries—the god of the foreigners." *Egypt under the Pharaohs*, I. p. 212. There is a small temple at Denderah near the Hathor-temple, where the cult of Bes (Typhon, Set) was affected; as shown by the capitals and other indications, and this fact is probably related to the appearance of the gazelle in the unpublished reliefs of the Hathor temple-portico (Figs. 134, 140, 148).

54. A bronze of the Leyden Museum is supposed by LEEMANS to be the only statuette of Set extant. The head is partly broken away. "Cette petite statue est jusqu'à présent la seule qu'on sache être echappée à la destruction de toutes les statues de cette divinité" [1845].—I., Plate ii., 423, of Leemans' quoted work.

236   THE DEER, GAZELLE, ORYX, IBEX, WILD GOAT, AND LOTUS.

Osiris, was ultimately a deity banished from Egypt, that his statues were destroyed, his name erased from the monuments, and his symbols hated and despised. As representing the baleful and destructive heat of the sun he became a representative of evil. Set was identified with the Hittite Sutekh and with the Phenician Baal, whose own malevolent aspects are apparent in the human sacrifices which were made to him, and in other gross characteristics of his worship.

134. THE GAZELLE AND THE LOTUS. A lotus bower surrounds the animals. From a panel in the temple-portico at Denderah, photographed for the Author.

In spite of the generally antagonistic attitude of Egypt to Set, his cult had great vogue under certain sovereigns of the XVIIIth and XIXth Dynasties, under whom Mesopotamian influences were prevalent in various ways.

Aside from the deer, for which no evidence is forthcoming, as an animal probably not indigenous to Egypt, it appears that all animals treated in this chapter were Typhonic. Hence the illustrations for the ibex, gazelle, antelope, and lotus, in Egypt which have been collected on Plate xxxv., have the

135. THE IBEX AND THE LOTUS. From an Egyptian fresco fragment in Turin. The hieroglyphs read, "The divine soul of the Gods." From Author's sketch.

interest of representing an Egyptian lotus symbol as connected with a worship which was related to foreign influences, in so far as Set was considered counterpart of Baal, and ultimately banished from the country. Unpublished reliefs in

THE DEER, GAZELLE, ORYX, IBEX, WILD GOAT, AND LOTUS.

the temple-portico at Denderah prove, however, that here at least the gazelle was an important divine animal in the Ptolemaic period (Figs. 134, 140, 148, pp. 236, 250, 277). The Turin fresco (Fig. 135) is also a monument of great importance for the ibex.

The Mesopotamian influences in Greek history, as distinct from those of Egypt, can therefore be traced wherever the symbolic animals of this chapter are in question, and it is clear that the lotus symbol is the means of designating their importance and tracing the origins of their vogue.

Illustrations for the gazelle and lotus, ibex and lotus, from Egyptian art are rarities in collections and in publications. Nos. 1, 2, and 9, xxxv., are directly specified as of foreign Syrian art by the heraldic balance of the double animals No. 6 is equally foreign and carries with it the vase it decorates (4). No. 5 is of too late a date to come in question as a typical example, aside from the rarity of a representation otherwise unknown in publication. No. 11 is from the Delta, No. 8 is from Nineveh, No. 7 is Cypriote, and No. 10 is of unknown derivation. We have only the capital (3) remaining, also doubtless under Syrian influence, as reminder of the Typhonic cult of Egypt. A fine illustration of the ibex and the lotus, a blue enamel plate, dated to the XVIIIth or XIXth Dynasty, is among the recent finds of Mr. Petrie. The illustrations of the gazelle and the lotus from Denderah have never previously been published or mentioned in publication, within my knowledge.

Having vindicated, both by the exceptions in Egypt which prove the rule and by the monuments exterior to Egypt, the significance of the ibex, oryx, gazelle, and deer, in association with the lotus, it remains to point to a curious connecting link between Egyptian, Greek, and Syrian monuments of this description. Among the deities of Phenicia is the god Reshep.[55] He is identified by various Cypriote inscriptions with the Greek Apollo[56] of Amyclæ, and he is represented in Egyptian paintings with a head-dress decorated with a projecting head of an animal variously specified as an oryx, ibex, or gazelle.[57]

---

55. Read by WILKINSON, *Ancient Egyptians*, as Rampu. Variously spelled at present, Rassaf, Reshef, Reshep, Reschuf, &c. (Egyptian, Reschpu).

56. Two Cypriote inscriptions identifying Apollo with Reshep are so designated in the British Museum by the labels. The identification (translation by Euting) is noticed by BIRCH in CESNOLA's *Atlas*, text for Plate viii.; by ENMANN in the Essay noted at p. 199; by PIETSCHMANN's *Geschichte der Phönizier*, p. 150, &c. Apollo is also identified in Cyprus with Baal Melkarth, and a similar identification holds for Hercules (Note 65).

57. " Coiffé de la mitre blanche, orné d'une tête d'oryx,

238   THE DEER, GAZELLE, ORYX, IBEX, WILD GOAT, AND LOTUS.

That the cylinder xxxvi. 5 represents this god is possible, and it is in any case a highly important document in the history of the deer and ibex as solar emblems. An actually ibex-headed or deer-headed god is not otherwise known, and this monument has hitherto passed unnoticed in this particular.

The winged disk of this cylinder makes it clear that a Sun-god is in question. Both the *Ankh* and winged sun disk indicate an Egyptian influence, but both are so common on Assyrian cylinders as to leave the problem in debate between Assyrian and Phenician origin.

Hittite origin is also possible; for the antelope or gazelle was also a Hittite emblem, not only as seen on the ram (xxviii. 2 [p. 203]), but also as held by a Hittite deity at Boghaz-keui.[50]

On the Phenician cylinders of thoroughly Egyptian style, which are so far authority for Reshep on cylinders, he is associated with Set and Horus,[59] a farther indication of his solar character. Among the Cypriote statuettes in New York is one specified by Birch as having had the head of a deer with antlers broken away.[60]

136. "LE DIEU CORNU."
Detail from a Gallo-Roman tombstone. From the photograph of a cast in the Museum of St. Germain.

After reviewing the evidence for the deer as solar emblem it is difficult not to recognize the *Dieu Cornu* of the Gauls,[61] who appears on Gallo-Roman

de gazelle, ou de belier." PIERRET, *Panthéon*, p. 46. "Vor der Stirn als Abzeichen statt der Uræusschlange die den Stirnkopf der Aegyptischesn Gottheiten bildet, den Kopf einer Gazelle." PIETSCHMANN, *Geschichte der Phönizier*, p. 150; in ONCKEN'S *Allgemeine Geschichte*. The following references for Reshep in hieroglyphic inscriptions have been furnished by a friend: DÜMMICHEN, *Resultate;* MARIETTE, *Karnak;* SHARPE, *Egyptian Inscriptions*.

58. It is noticed by INMAN, *Ancient Pagan and Modern Christian Symbolism*, that the Hittite goddess at Boghaz Keui stands on a lioness and holds an antelope.

59. Published by PIETSCHMANN as above, and by MENANT, *Cylindres*, &c.

60. The figure is in CESNOLA'S *Atlas*, Plate xxiv., and it is here that the matter of Birch, who wrote the descriptions, occurs. The horns of the original are entirely broken away.

61. SALOMON REINACH, *Catalogue Sommaire du Musée des Antiquités Nationales au Château de Saint-Germain-en-Laye*, p. 123, "Très importante statuette des environs d'Autun, représentant un dieu barbu, cornu (les cornes sont brisées) portant un *torques* au cou, les jambes croisées sur un coussin, tenant sur ses genoux deux serpents a tête de belier et un *torques* placé entre eux. Au-dessus des oreilles du dieu, on aperçoit deux petites têtes collées au crâne ; c'est donc une divinité tricéphale."

THE DEER, GAZELLE, ORYX, IBEX, WILD GOAT, AND LOTUS. 239

monuments with antlered human head and with Apollo and Mercury[62] (Fig. 136) as a reminiscence of prehistoric deer-worship and old Phenician influences in France by way of Marseilles and otherwise. The votive deer transfixed by swords, of Sardinian-Phenician art, are also in point (Perrot et Chipiez, *Sardaigne* p. 82).

We can at all events trace the solar deer and ibex, with the lotus as solar indication, as far as the prehistoric monuments of Hallstatt.[63] Plate xxxix. 4 shows the ibex, and the deer occurs with lotus on the same *patera*. The deer also occurs with lotus spirals on metals of the Swiss Lake-dwellers.[64] Doe, antelope, and deer, are marked as solar by the lotus spiral on prehistoric Celtic bronzes of the Southern Tyrol (xxxix. 8), and we can trace them to the early home of Celtic art in Northern Italy (xxxix. 6, 7; lvii. 16, [p. 341]), and to the Greek "Geometric style" (lvi. 2, 6 [p. 339]; lvii. 2 [p. 341] ibex or wild goat).

The solar deer is also specified by the Swastika at Troy (lx. 1 [p. 359]). Other whorls without this indication are thus carried to the same score (xxxvii. 8). For the solar deer and the lotus in the circle of the "Mycenæ Culture" we have evidence in the gold objects found by Dr. Schliemann (xxxvii. 2, 11 [p. 249]).

Although the indications for Reshep as a Gazelle- and Ibex-God are supported by Egyptian paintings (quoted at Note 57), although his worship was affected in Cyprus, and although he was identified with Apollo in Cyprus, I have no intention of pushing his individual claims to have been the mediator and connecting link between the solar deer of Greece and of Mesopotamia, beyond the present evidence. The deer is apparently confined on later Cypriote coins to the type of Hercules, who is also a well-known Phenician Sun-god by derivation.[65] Great as

---

62. Ibid. p. 27. "Bas relief, 24, 414 . . . il représente le dieu gaulois cornu, Cernunnas, les jambes croissées à l'orientale, pressant de la main un sac, d'ou sortent des graines (?) assis entre un Mercure et un Apollon de style Grec, qui forment avec lui comme une triade." Other representations of this god are mentioned at pp. 28, 30, 33, 34, of the same Catalogue.

63. The most numerous and important finds of prehistoric metals in Northern Europe have been made at Hallstatt (near Salzburg). The tombs are considered Celtic, and are dated to the fourth century B.C., but many are earlier. Between 1847 and 1864 nine hundred and ninety-three tombs were opened, which furnished six thousand and eighty-four objects; of which three thousand six hundred and ninety-six were decorative objects in bronze, amber, glass, and gold; one hundred and eighty-two, vases of bronze, twelve hundred and forty-four, vases of pottery. No coins have been found; an indication of early dates. SALOMON REINACH, *Catalogue Sommaire*, p. 157. A fine illustrated publication has been made by VON SACKEN, *Das Grabfeld von Hallstatt*, but by far the most valuable reference, as showing a much larger selection of objects, is the exhibition in the Museum of St. Germain of the original colour sketches made by the director of the excavations (Ramsauer). The date of the fourth century is a minimum downward and much higher antiquity may be assigned to many tombs.

64. FERDINAND KELLER, *Lake Dwellings of Switzerland*, Plate cxxviii. 6. On iron from Marin.

65. DE LUYNES, *Num. et In. Cyp.*, Plate iv. Greek

240   THE DEER, GAZELLE, ORYX, IBEX, WILD GOAT, AND LOTUS.

was the number of sacred animals, they were not as numerous as the local gods of antiquity; and the deer, as Keller has shown us, belongs to many, even in Greece. He also belongs to several in Mesopotamia, according to texts and according to the equivalents which have been established for him in foregoing pages. There is no animal so frequently found with the Sacred Tree on cylinders (xxxvi. 6) and in other various phases of Assyrian art, as the ibex or wild goat. The antlered deer frequently occurs, and the antelope or gazelle may be indicated by many monuments, whose small dimensions and indifferent art lead the bewildered amateur in horns of animals to suspect an ibex.

137. THE IBEX AND THE LOTUS.
Detail of a Phenician bronze *patera* from Nineveh.
British Museum. From Layard.

In early days the worship of sun and moon united all the gods and all their symbols. With this worship they were all assimilated. From it many were derived. The significance of the lotus-symbol for history lies in the simplicity of its solvent power—in its implication of the essential facts underlying every ancient cult—in the sequence of history which it demonstrates. The lotus links the cults of Rhodes and of Cyprus with those of Greece and of Syria.

For Rhodes the worship of the sun as dominant cult is well attested. For Cyprus I have no wish to push the evidence for any single deity beyond the apparent facts. The lotus was not less the flower of Isis and of Astarte than it was the flower of Horus, of Baal Melkarth, and of Baal Merodach. The deer was a sacred animal of both Apollo and Aphrodite (p. 230), and we have found it quoted for Athene and Isis (p. 230), as well as for Artemis. The following facts must, however, be given due weight. Deer sacred to Apollo were kept at Curium and they were fabled to have swum from Syria (Aelian). A Phenician deity (viz. Reshep) is represented with a head-dress of horns on Egyptian monuments, and this deity has been identified with Apollo in Cyprus. The deer, or ibex, and lotus are one of the two favoured subjects of Cypriote vases, and the deer, ibex, and normal lotus are represented on Oriental monuments which no scholar will dare to say are not symbolic (xxiv. 8 [p. 183]; xxxv.; xxxvi. 4, 6; and the seal mentioned by Note 33).

Cypriote coins: Head of Hercules; reverse, antlered deer. Hercules is identified with Baal Melkarth at Corinth, and with the Chaldean Izdubar. ISAAC TAYLOR, *Origin of the Aryans*, p. 304. The Greek word Apollo may represent the Semitic "Ablu," a title of Tammuz, the Syrian Sun-god. Ibid. p. 104.

THE DEER, GAZELLE, ORYX, IBEX, WILD GOAT, AND LOTUS. 241

Conceding the associations of the deer, ibex or wild goat, oryx, gazelle, and antelope, with the lotus to be symbolic for sun or moon or both, it remains to indicate the importance of some monuments illustrated by the Plates and not yet noticed, or too rapidly passed by. The lotus and ibex on the seal of Sennacherib (or of Sargon according to Menant) (xxxvi. 4) have not been specified by experts, but Menant's lapse in calling this lotus "garlic" has been mentioned (Note 11, p. 49). The Cypriote cylinder xxxvi. 2, with antlered deer turned sideways, demonstrates the symbolism of the lotus-Ionic form for the original time and place of this monument. The solar significance of the Ionic capital xxxvi. 7 specified by Colonna-Ceccaldi (Note 4, p. 170), is reinforced by the ibex heads beside it (in detail xxiii. 3 [p. 173]). These again carry us to the well-known Assyrian instances xxxvi. 1, 8, 9, 10, and give them a significance which has not hitherto been claimed for them. We return then by way of a cylinder (6) showing the ibex with the Sacred Tree of normal three-spiked lotuses (hitherto overlooked by Assyriologists) to the cylinder showing the ibex on the normal lotus (4), as beginning and completing the argument of the Plate.

The number of instances where lunar crescents are associated with gazelles (xxxv. 10; xxxvi. 3), and where no other emblems appear, is considerable. There may be connection here with the fate which has so distinctively assigned the deer to Diana, and with the fact that the Hindu Moon-god Chandra (Note 48) rides in a car drawn by antelopes. The antelope is also a recognized and very frequent attribute of Siva, whose affiliations with Set and Baal have also been pointed out (Note 49). Siva is also represented with the lunar crescent.

The evidence for the rosette as a lotus, furnished by the solar deer of Cyprus (xxxvii. 7, 12), will not be overlooked. As for the Sacred Tree of rosettes xxxvii. 5, it is the only one known to publication. The right-hand Sacred Tree of this vase shows a rare example of a lotus palmette in Cypriote pottery of this style. The details are lotus buds and lotus scrolls. The vase is undoubtedly Greek, as are the other Cypriote examples. The number of Cypriote vases showing the deer or ibex in New York can only be estimated by those who have examined this collection of Cypriote vases carefully, and it will argue the deficiency of similar monuments elsewhere to say that not one was cited by the publication in the Journal of Hellenic Studies from which the vase xxxvii. 5 is taken, a publication which consequently failed to solve the problems raised. This

242 THE DEER, GAZELLE, ORYX, IBEX, WILD GOAT, AND LOTUS.

lack of the comparative Cypriote examples has also doomed the very numerous Rhodian vases of European Museums, which show the deer or the ibex with the lotus, to an inefficient obscurity.

Renewed demonstrations are offered by Plate xxxix. for the rosette (1), for the spiral scroll and meander (2), for the "Herzblatt" (3), (lotus leaf derivative, see p. 320), and for the spiral (8). The lotus has a faculty of proving its omnipresent existence by apparently absurd examples. Comparative study of the prehistoric Celtic or "Umbrian" art, from which other curious examples of Plate xxxix. are taken, will prove the animal with lotus pendant from the mouth to be the explanation of the spiral (8). Compare the cow (xxvii. 3 [p. 197]), the sphinx (xxxiv. 3, [p. 227]), and the horse (lxi. 9, [p. 365]), with other illustrations of this Plate.

The study of the gazelle and lotus association has led me to fix positively the origin of the sceptre called the *Tam*, carrying an animal's head which is so far unspecified (Fig. 139,A).[66] The Tam of the British Museum stone tablet, No. 886, in the Hall of Egyptian statues (time of Ptolemy Lathyrus), is the head of an antelope (Fig. 138). The Tam held before an altar in "Bruce's Tomb" at Thebes is the head of a gazelle (Fig. 139). A wooden Tam in the British Museum (No. 6173) shows the bend of the antelope's horn as seen in profile view. The ordinary Tam

138. THE TAM WITH ANTELOPE HEAD.
Detail of the stone tablet No. 886 in the Hall of Egyptian Statues, British Museum. From Author's sketch.

139. TAM IN BRUCE'S TOMB AT THEBES. From Author's sketch.

---

[66] DE ROUGÉ, *Notice Sommaire*, &c., says of two amulets in the Louvre: "Deux pièces extrêmement rares, en faïence bleue, font voir en détail la tête de l'animal qui surmonte les sceptres divins; ses longues oreilles lui donnent une grande analogie avec le lévrier." The "long ears" are in reality ears conventionally attached to short horns. There is an amulet in the British Museum corresponding to the two in the Louvre. I have examined all three, and find them corroborative for the gazelle head as thus conceived. WILKINSON suggests the "Harrier" as original animal. *Ancient Egyptians*, III., p. 352, 3rd Ed.

THE DEER, GAZELLE, ORYX, IBEX, WILD GOAT, AND LOTUS. 243

consists of a gazelle head showing in profile view one ear and one horn joined together. To support this proposition we need the evidence that there are gazelles whose ears either equal or exceed the length of the horn, to show that such representation was originally plausible. This evidence is furnished by the mummied gazelle of the British Museum, Third Egyptian Room, case, 52, No. 6783a.[67] It is therefore clear that the Tam is a survival of gazelle solar symbolism whose traditional form survived the antagonism to Set—either because the Egyptians had themselves forgotten what the conventional Tam represented, or because the sceptre had become a general attribute of solar gods, and was not identified with Set as was the animal itself.

67. The number of the mummy differs from that given by BIRCH (Note 53). The piece is the same. According to Birch, as quoted, this gazelle is the *Antelope Dorcas*. The horns differ from the account of the *Antelope Dorcas* in the Encyclopædia Britannica (8th Edition) under "Mammalia," where the horns are described as having numerous rings. The horns of the mummy are smooth.

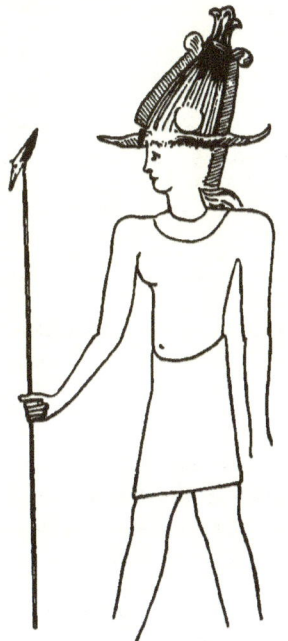

139A. DEITY BEARING THE TAM.
From the rear exterior wall of the Hathor temple, Denderah.

PLATE XXXV.

THE DEER, GAZELLE, ORYX, IBEX, WILD GOAT, AND LOTUS.

THE words "gazelle" and "antelope" are often used interchangeably, for instance, by the Encyclopædia Britannica (8th Edition), under "Mammalia." According to Worcester's Dictionary, both antelopes and gazelles come under the *genus* oryx, but the word "oryx" is often used without closer specification by Egyptologists, and it is mentioned by WILKINSON as "one of the antelopes" (*Ancient Egyptians*, III., p. 302, 3rd Edition), viz., the one having "long annulated horns tapering to a short point and nearly straight, with slight curve or inclination backwards," *Ancient Egyptians*, III., p. 94, 3rd Edition. To avoid confusion, I have used the word "gazelle" for the short-horned oryx, which use is justified by custom. I have used the word "oryx" for the long-horned oryx. I have used the word "antelope" for the gazelle with spiral horns, which are represented in profile view by a recurved bend.

All the illustrations of this Plate are supposed to exhibit Syrian influence.

1. Gazelles, with lotuses as collar pendants (compare Fig. 134), facing a "bouquet" of conventional lotuses. Detail from VILLIERS STUART, *Funeral Tent of an Egyptian Queen*. (Dehr-el-Bahri.)

2. Antelopes rampant and lotus "Sacred Tree." From an Egyptian box (for Canopic jars) in Bologna DÜMMLER, in *Mittheilungen aus Athen*, 1885. The animals are mistaken by Dümmler for goats. I have a carefully, and personally, made sketch of the original, which shows the recurved bend of the antelope horn as it appears when represented in profile. Compare frontispiece in BIRCH, *Catalogue of Egypt.an Antiquities at Alnwick Castle*.

3. Multiple lotus capital with gazelle heads. PRISSE D'AVENNES, *Colonettes en bois*.

4. Gazelle heads and inverted lotus supporting lotus trefoil. Cover of a vase, from a Theban tomb-painting. ROSELLINI, M.C. lviii. 3.

5. Figure bearing an antelope with lotuses. Detail from Dandour, time of Augustus. CHAMPOLLION, I. lvi. Compare Assyrian xxiv. 8 [p. 183].

6. Gazelle and lotuses, from the vase whose cover appears at No. 4.

7. Bird, fish, gazelle, and hand. Cypriote cylinder. CESNOLA, *Cyprus*, Gems, iii. 24.

8. Gazelle head, three-spiked lotus. Clay seal impression. LAYARD, *Second Series*, lxix. 18.

9. Gazelles rampant, lotus "Sacred Tree," sun diagrams. Detail of a vase from a tomb-painting. ROSELLINI, M.C. lxi. 3.

10. Running gazelle, moon crescent. Egyptian or Syrian Scarab. KLAPROTH, xxxii. 1705.

11. "Nubian ibex," three-spiked lotuses. Seal. *Tanis*, II. xli. 73.

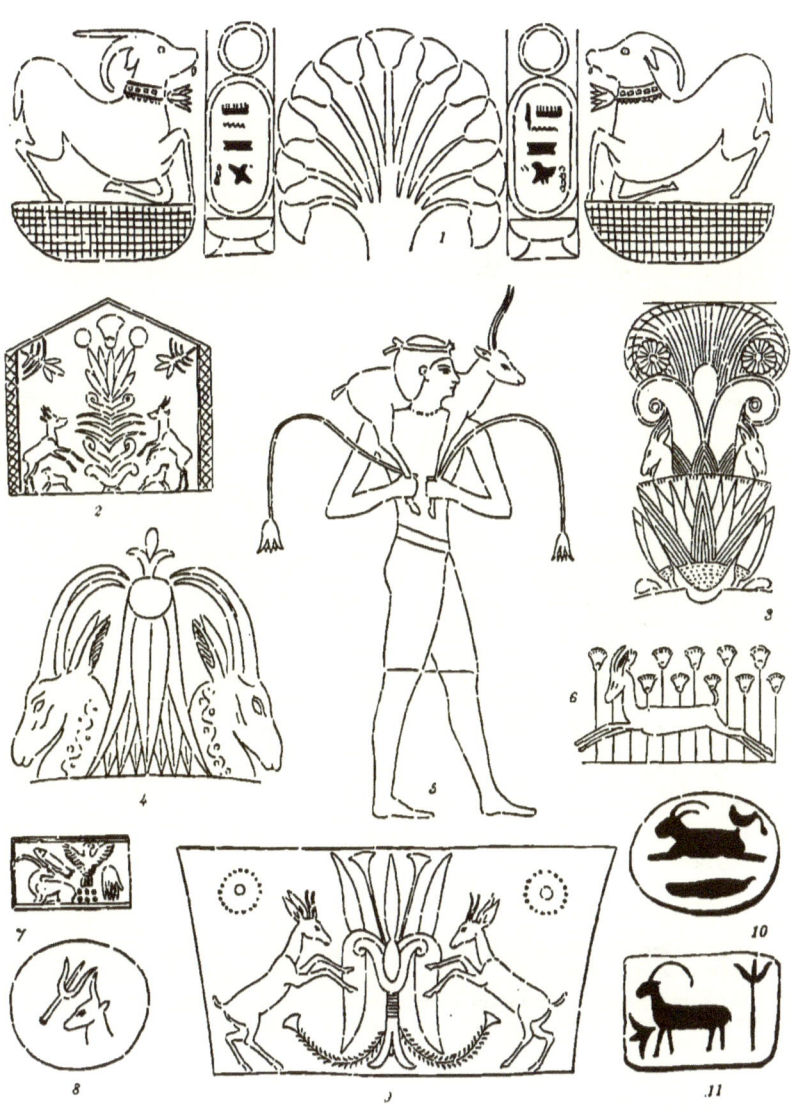

Pl. XXXV., p 245.

PLATE XXXVI.

THE DEER, GAZELLE, ORYX, IBEX, WILD GOAT, AND LOTUS.

1. Ibex,* lotus palmette. Assyrian detail. LAYARD, *First Series*, xliii.
2. Deer placed sideways, facing inward, Ionic lotus. Cypriote cylinder. A. D. CESNOLA, *Salaminia*, xiv. 33.
3. Antelope, two moon crescents. Assyrian or Phenician cone seal. LAJARD, *Culte de Mithra*, l. 2.
4. Ibex on a double lotus. Seal of Sennacherib, as specified by Layard and Perrot; assigned to Sargon by Menant. PERROT et CHIPIEZ, *Assyrie*, Fig. 69, also in LAYARD (text), and MENANT, *Cylindres*, ii. 79.
5. God, with head of an ibex or oryx† (Reshep, ?), and god with head of a deer (?) bearing a deer on a pole, one of them holding a gazelle; two worshippers bearing an antelope; next, a recumbent ibex; king or deity holding the *Ankh*, winged sun disk; worshipper holding an antelope. Uninterpreted cylinder published by LAJARD, *Culte de Mithra*, xxxvi. 13, and by KING, *Antique Gems*, Plate iii. 4, who notes "Egyptian influence."
6. Rampant gazelles, ibexes or wild goats; moon crescent, star, and Sacred Tree of normal three-spiked lotuses. Assyrian cylinder. LAJARD, *Culte de Mithra*, xxvi. 8.
7. Ionic column supporting sun and moon, with two ibex or oryx heads; hares below (sacred to Osiris); winged deities; eight-rayed star (the sun, p. 182); ibex over guilloche (compare p. 127); lion below. LAJARD, *Culte de Mithra*, lii. 6.
8. Ibex or wild goat on the Ionic lotus. LAYARD, *First Series*, xxx.
9. Ibexes or wild goats, rosette. Assyrian fresco fragment. BOTTA, ii. 97.
10. Deer on the lotus palmette, rosette above. Assyrian detail. LAYARD, *First Series*, xliv.

---

* I have observed at Note 34, p. 232, that there is a wild goat in Western Asia whose horns correspond to those of an ibex of the same region.

† The oryx horn has not as much bend in nature as here represented, but on the sacred bark of Ptah-Sokar-Osiris at Dehr-el-Bahri the supposed oryx horn has as definite a bend.

Pl. XXXVI., p. 247.

PLATE XXXVII.

THE DEER, GAZELLE, ORYX, IBEX, WILD GOAT, AND LOTUS.

1. The ibex and the lotus. The plants mistaken for papyrus by Cesnola. Detail, Curium *patera*. CESNOLA, *Cyprus*, p. 337.
2. Deer on the lotus. Plant mistaken by Schliemann for date palm. Gold ornament, from the "Third Tomb." SCHLIEMANN, *Mycenæ*.
3. Deer, does, swans, and lotuses. Plants mistaken for trees by Colonna-Ceccaldi. For the swans, compare Plates xliii.-xlvi. [pp. 282-289]. Detail, Curium *patera*. COLONNA-CECCALDI, *Monuments de Chypre*, p. 164; and in *Revue Archéologique*, 1877; also in CESNOLA'S *Cyprus*.
4. Typical Rhodian vase. Deer, inverted lotus, ibexes over lotus border. *Jahrbuch*, 1886, p. 138 (compare next Plate).
5. Cypriote vase. Sacred Tree of rosettes, deer, bird with lotus on the head (compare the "Bird and the Lotus"), deer facing a lotus, and a Sacred Tree of lotus palmettes and buds. Compare the top of the same vase at xlvi. 2 [p. 289], showing two Sacred Trees of rosettes, lotus palmettes, and bird with lotus on head. MAX OHNEFALSCH-RICHTER, in *Journal of Hellenic Studies*, v. p. 105.
6. Ibex and lotus, Cypriote vase. Another view at No. 10. PERROT et CHIPIEZ, *Cypre*.
7. Deer rampant, mistaken by Murray for goats;[*] Sacred Tree of an Ionic lotus supporting two buds; and an inverted Ionic scroll supporting triangle, which is surmounted by a trefoil lotus; lotus rosettes on one deer. Cypriote vase. CESNOLA, *Cyprus*, p. 55.
8. Deer on Trojan whorl. SCHLIEMANN, *Troy*, p. 121. Many repetitions (compare lx. 1 [p. 352]).
9. Antelope, Swastika. Detail of an early Attic vase, British Museum. BÖHLAU, *Jahrbuch*, 1886, p. 50.
10. Ibex and lotus. Cypriote vase in New York Museum.
11. Deer on the lotus. Gold ornament from the "Third Tomb." SCHLIEMANN, *Mycenæ*, Fig. 123.
12. Winged deer and lotus; rosettes on the deer. Detail from a Cypriote vase in New York; several similar examples.

For the ibex or deer, and lotus, on Cypriote vases, see also xxxix. 5 [p. 253]; xlix. 5 [p. 307].

[*] I am not clear as to whereabouts of this vase, and cannot find it in the New York Museum. Comparison with No. 12 will specify the animals.

Pl. XXXVII., p. 249.

PLATE XXXVIII.

THE DEER, GAZELLE, ORYX, IBEX, WILD GOAT, AND LOTUS.

TYPICAL. Rhodian vase; many examples in London and Paris. Ibexes and lotuses, geese and the lotus. Detail of the latter at Plate xvi. 4 [p. 141]. In many examples ibexes and deer alternate. Compare xxxvii. 4. SALZMANN, *Nécropole de Camire*. Similar vases in LONGPÉRIER, *Musée Napoléon III*.

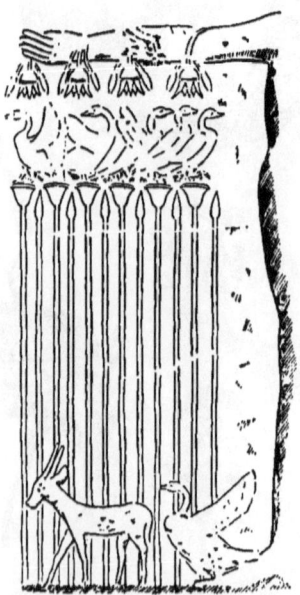

140. ISIS-HATHOR, THE GAZELLE, THE GOOSE, AND THE LOTUS.
From a panel in the temple portico at Denderah. Sketch from a photograph made for the Author.

PLATE XXXIX.

THE DEER, GAZELLE, ORYX, IBEX, WILD GOAT, AND LOTUS.

1. Doe and rosette. Detail, Bœotian vase. BÖHLAU, *Jahrbuch*, 1887, Taf. 4.

2. Ibex, or wild goat, facing spiral scroll; ibex, or wild goat, facing Swastika meander. Detail, Melian vase. Another detail from the same vase, xxxiv. 8 [p. 227]. BÖHLAU, *Jahrbuch*, 1887, p. 121.

3. Doe, "Herzblatt" (remote form of the leaf, compare Mycenæ leaf, Plate lii. 3, 5 [p. 321]). Bœotian vase. BÖHLAU, *Jahrbuch*, 1887.

4. Ibex, or wild goat, lotus springing from the mouth. The plant behind the animal is explained by Nos. 6 and 7. *Repoussé* bronze detail, Hallstatt. VON SACKEN, *Grabfeld von Hallstatt*, xxi.

5. Ibex, or wild goat, deer, and lotuses, lotus with pendant sepals. Detail, Cypriote vase. CESNOLA, *Cyprus*, p. 404.

6. Ibex, or wild goat, lotus springing from the mouth; lotus behind the animal. *Repoussé* bronze detail of the "*Situla* d'Este." *Gazette Archéologique*, 1888, xii.

7. Deer, lotus springing from the mouth. Plant mistaken by the publication for the branch of a tree—"*en train de brouter un rameau d'arbre.*" Lotus behind the animal. Same reference as No. 6 and originals of one scale.

8. Deer and antelopes, lotus spirals springing from their mouths; barbaric rosettes, border of inverted lotus buds. Detail of bronze vase, found in Southern Tyrol. Other details of same vase, horses with buds in the mouth, lxi. 9 [p. 365]. *Monumenti Inediti*, X. vi.

Pl. XXXIX., p. 253.

APPENDIX.

ADDITIONAL CITATIONS.

Antlered deer on a "Mycenæ" vase from the "Sixth Tomb," striking resemblance to the bronze detail xxxix. 8, from the Southern Tyrol, and apparently copied from a similar bronze; ill. in SCHUCHARDT, *Schliemann's Ausgrabungen*, Fig. 279.

ROSELLINI. Sacrifice of gazelle to Hor-Ammon by Amenophis III.

British Museum, Fourth Egyptian Room, No. 20761. Bronze gazelle or antelope on a lotus.

British Museum, Third Egyptian Room, "Miscellaneous Objects," No. 18073. Egyptian blue glazed ware; ibexes facing a lotus.

PETRIE, *Catalogue of Antiquities discovered* 1890, p. 9. "Blue glazed ware, half bowl with gazelle." Rather an ibex suckling young, and large lotus.

British Museum, Nimroud Gallery, Case F (N.D. 216). Ivory carving, ibexes facing a rosette.

British Museum, Nimroud Gallery. Bronze bowl, with rings of stags (E.N. 1.—N.G. 12).

British Museum, First Vase Room, Case 20, 21, A. 37. Rhodian vase, ibexes or wild goats, facing the anthemion.

British Museum. Gems from Crete. Ibex or wild goat and moon crescent. Case R.

British Museum. Gems from Crete. Ibex or wild goat with Ionic lotus and concentric rings.

ROBERT BROWN, Jun. *Proceedings, Society of Biblical Archæology*, 1890. Illustration, goat and inverted Ionic form. "Capricorn, from a Euphrates boundary stone."

Ibex and the Ankh, with Bes, Plate lxv. 10 [p. 393] of this work.

The ibex or antelope is the only animal habitually associated with the palm-tree on cylinders. LAJARD, *Culte de Venus*, iv. 12; xxxv.—xxxix, xxi. A. 23; *Culte de Mithra*, li. 2, and others.

MURRAY'S *Handbook for Egypt* (1888), p. 425. "In another large quarry [near Raâineh] ... two singular representations of the giant-god Antæus, accompanied by Nephthys, holding in his left hand a spear and an oryx. In one of these he has rays round his head like the Sun, and before him is a priest making offerings to him." An adjacent site is Gow-el-Kebéer, or Antæopolis—" Near Antæopolis the fabulous battle between Horus and Typhon was reputed to have taken place, and here Antæus is said to have been killed by Hercules in the time of Osiris."

WM. OSBURN, Jun.'s *Antiquities of Egypt* contains a quotation from the Confessional of "The Book of the Dead "—" I have not disturbed the gazelles of the gods in their pasturage."

VILLIERS STUART (*Funeral Tent of an Egyptian Queen*, p. 42) is aware that the Tam has the head of a gazelle, as he quotes the head of gazelle on a staff as "an emblem of purity." The Tam is generally quoted as meaning "strength," and, as far as we can judge, the gazelle itself was generally Typhonic.

SIR ALEXANDER CUNNINGHAM, *The Bhilsa Topes*, Plate xxxi. 10. Hindu Coin; the deer and the lotus.

JAMES BURGESS, *Archæological Survey of Southern India*, I. p. 50. (Illustration.)—Normal lotus border above "Worship of a Sacred Tree by Spotted Deer, from Bharhut." The Sacred Tree here is a real tree and the Hindu art is the only one which shows the worship of real trees.

THE LION, BULL, AND LOTUS.
THE CHIMÆRA AND LOTUS.

(PLATE XL., PAGE 259.)

ACCORDING to the eye-witness of Lajard,[1] then French Minister to Persia, the ceremony of turning a trained hunting lion loose, to run down and kill a bull in presence of the king, was observed in Persia at the time of the Vernal Equinox, as recently as the year 1808.

This interesting survival of an ancient astronomical symbolism supports Lajard's view that the bull and lion combat is a representation of the entry of the solar lion into the sign of the bull.[2] Another explanation has been offered, but it is also solar, and it does not appear that Lajard's curious contribution to matter-of-fact knowledge on this subject has been known to those who have given it currency.[3] As the representation is conceded to be solar we have only to call attention to its association with the lotus (xl. 1, 2, 3, 4) in ways which again corroborate the views advanced for the Egyptian and Phenician palmettes (xii. [p. 113]), for the tabs on lotus stems (iv. [p. 63]), for the rosette (xi., xx. [pp. 107, 153]), and for the Greek anthemion (xiii., xiv. [pp. 112, 133]). Our illustrations for the bull and lion are chosen from Cypriote (1, 3), Phenician (2), and from fairly developed Greek art (4).

A less generally noticed, more obscurely explained, and equally important subject of early Mediterranean art is the lion devouring a deer (Fig. 141, detail of

---

1. *Culte de Mithra*, p. 62.
2. Also the view of COLONNA-CECCALDI, *Monuments de Chypre*, "Rondache d'Amathonte," p. 148.
3. *Encyclopædia Britannica*, "Zodiac." "Izdubar's conquest of the winged bull was placed under Taurus; his slaying of the tyrant Houmbaba (the prototype of Geryon) in the fifth month, typified the victory of light over darkness, represented in plastic art by the group of a lion killing a bull, which is the form ordinarily given to the sign Leo on Ninevite cylinders." Reference is made to Lenormant.

256 THE LION, BULL, AND LOTUS. THE CHIMÆRA AND LOTUS.

141. LION DEVOURING DEER. Detail, Greek vase.

a vase shown at lxi. 3 [p. 365]). Important publications of this subject[4] have failed to give any explanation of it, which argues, in view of the learning and distinction of the scholars in question, a deficiency of material for reference.

The combat of lion and deer is mentioned, however, by Keller[5] as representing the struggle of light and darkness. This explanation, which has also been offered for the bull and lion combat (Note 3) is probably erroneous in view of Lajard's decisive reference for the Vernal Equinox in the latter case.

There is at least one monument which shows the lion devouring a

[4]. MENANT, *Cylindres II.*, p. 177; PERROT, in *Bulletin* of the French School at Athens, has also failed to cast light on the subject.

[5]. KELLER, *Thiere des Classichen Alterthums*, &c., p. 76, notes the subject on Syrian and Cilician coins as "Nacht im kampf gegen die Macht des Lichts."

THE LION, BULL, AND LOTUS. THE CHIMÆRA AND LOTUS.

bull, and the lion devouring a deer, on the same piece and in obvious association.[6] We are obliged therefore to look for an analogous explanation. It is mentioned by Professor Sayce that the antelope and gazelle were Babylonian equivalents for the goat in the sign of the tenth month (p. 234). The same authority has named the deer and antelope as equivalents (p. 231, Note 21), and we have ourselves found the deer an equivalent for the ibex and the wild goat.

The resulting presumption is that the lion attacking the deer represents the sun as entering the sign of the deer (viz. Capricornus), and is a sign of the Winter Solstice.

It would therefore appear that a similar representation should be found for the goat, and this is offered by the Chimæra. From this point of view the Chimæra is the equivalent of the lion devouring a deer, and symbolizes the sun as entering the sign of the goat, who is the equivalent of the deer. The lotiform associations of the Chimæra are represented therefore by xl. 5, 6; both being also significant for the rosette. As the Chimæra is already admitted to have solar reference,[7] the explanation is plausible and probably supplants that of Milchhöffer.[8] There is at least one monument which gives the "goat" of the Chimæra the horns of the oryx (Fig. 142).

The oryx (gazelle), according to Birch, represents the sign of Capricornus in Egypt.[9] The gazelle's head also represents the sign of Capricornus in the Hindu Zodiac which is derived from the Greeks. It would therefore seem that an instance of oryx horns in a representation of the Chimæra is an important corroboration of the view advanced.

6. *Monumenti Inediti*, Greek vase.
7. BAUMEISTER, *Antike Denkmäler*.
8. In *Anfange der Griechischen Kunst*, advancing the view that the Chimæra is a representation derived from gems in which the goat and lion were crowded together, one animal partly concealing the other.
9. P. 235, Note 52.

142. CHIMÆRA WITH GAZELLE HORN.
Engraved gem. Owens College, Manchester.

PLATE XL.

THE LION, BULL, AND LOTUS.
THE CHIMÆRA AND LOTUS.

1. Combat of bull and lion, lotus palmettes. From the shield of Amathus. COLONNA-CECCALDI, *Monuments de Chypre* ix. CESNOLA, *Cyprus*, xx.

2. Combat of bull and lions, normal lotuses, with stems having the tabs (compare Plate iv. [p. 63)]. Detail of metal plaque, Cære, *Monumenti Inediti* and PERROT ET CHIPIEZ, iii. p. 769.

3. Combat of bull and lion. Rosettes and pendant lotuses. Cypriote relief in New York Museum. CESNOLA, *Cyprus*, p. 159.

4. Combat of bull and lion, lotus anthemion. Detail, Greek vase. *Archæologische Zeitung*, 1883, Plate iii.

5. Chimæra on rosette, lotus below. Vase, Daphnæ. *Tanis*, II. xxvi. 8.

6. Chimæra, rosettes, and pendant lotuses. Cypriote relief, New York Museum. CESNOLA, *Cyprus*, p. 159.

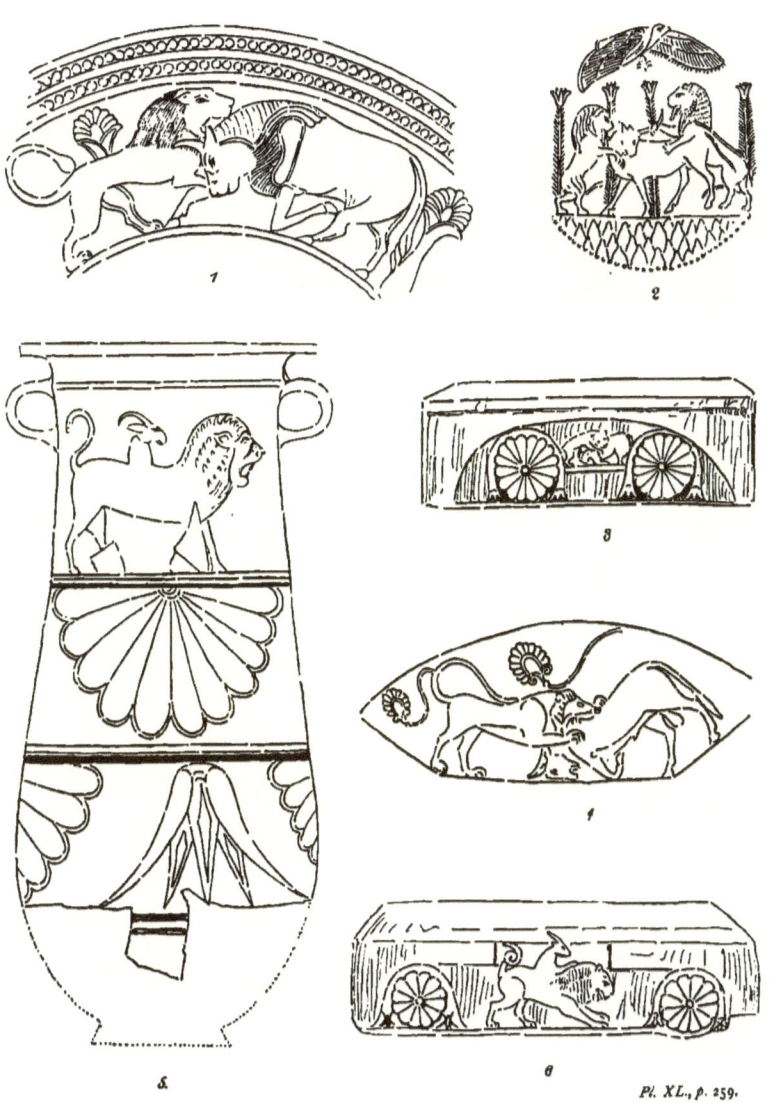

THE "PHENICIAN PALMETTE."

(PLATE XLI., PAGE 263.)

AMONG the early Mediterranean ornamental motives is one specified by archæologists as the "Phenician palmette." It is found on Greek vases[1] and in early Greek or Etruscan art otherwise (xli. 1), but is mainly confined to distinctive Phenician art (12, 14), Sardinian (2, 8, 11), Cypriote (4, 7, 10), Assyrian (13), or Cypriote Greek (3 and Fig. 43 [p. 72]). This text-cut carries us back to Colonna-Ceccaldi's suggestion that the stamens of the lotus were there represented by the upper scrolls and to the obligation then incurred of saying what the supposed stamens really are.

The ultimate conventional form of the "Phenician palmette" is simply a series of parallel upright bars, resting on a crescent-shaped support. The crescent is explained by the lower introrse scrolls of No. 5, or by the introrse scrolls of No. 9; which, in their turn, are included in the demonstration of Plate ix. [p. 91].

The upright bars are rudimentary survivals of lotus stems (compare 3 and 4, upper left-hand palmette, and 6). The abbreviated or outlined lotus palmette is the form shown by No. 6. Cases of lotus association with the highly conventional form are shown by 2, 8, 13. The demonstration is assisted by relations of the Sphinx-head (1) to xxxiv. [p. 227], of the Sphinx and Gryphon (12, 14) to xxxi.—xxxiii. [pp. 221—225], and of the ibexes or goats (10, 13) to xxxv.—xxxix. [pp. 245—253].

There are many forms of the Sacred Tree on Assyrian cylinders which are explained as lotus "trees," through Nos. 5 and 14 of Plate xli. The ever-present relation to the sun is marked by the winged disk of No. 5, by the sun disk and moon crescent of No. 3, and by the solar animals recently specified.

1. One such vase in GENICK and FURTWÄNGLER, *Griechische Keramik*.

143. GRYPHONS. Detail, Curium *patera*.

PLATE XLI.

THE "PHENICIAN PALMETTE."

1. Sphinx, " Phenician palmette " on the head. Detail, *Museo Etrusco Vaticano*, II. cvi. 16.
2. " Phenician palmettes," terra-cotta whorl, Sardinia. PERROT ET CHIPIEZ, *Phénicie*, p. 672.
3. " Phenician palmette," lotus bars, leaves, and lotuses over lotus of Ionic form. Cypriote stelè, Louvre. PERROT ET CHIPIEZ, *Cypre*, Fig. 53.
4. Curium *patera* detail, winged goddess holding two lotuses. Left upper palmette shows two normal lotus palmettes in outline, otherwise only bars appear. COLONNA-CECCALDI, *Monuments de Chypre*.
5. Sacred Tree, lotuses and introrse lotus scrolls. (Compare ix. 9 [p. 91].) Winged solar disk, two worshippers. Cypriote seal. CESNOLA, *Cyprus;* KING'S Appendix for Gems.
6. Curium *patera* detail, sketch from original, showing three bars as normal lotus palmettes in outline. New York Museum.
7. Sphinxes and " Phenician palmette " bars, conventional; six normal lotus palmettes spring from this Sacred Tree.
8. " Phenician palmettes," alternate lotuses. Terra-cotta whorl, Sardinia. Same references as No. 2.
9. Phenician metal detail in the Louvre, among Assyrian pieces. Ionic lotus supporting introrse lotus scroll, and two trefoil lotuses. LAJARD, xlvii.; also in LONGPÉRIER, *Musée Napoléon III*.
10. Ibexes, " Phenician palmettes." Curium *patera* detail.
11. Seal ring, " Phenician palmette," Sardinia. PERROT ET CHIPIEZ, *Phénicie*, p. 644.
12. Sphinx, " Phenician palmettes." Syrian stelè (Rouad), Louvre. LONGPÉRIER, *Musée Napoléon III*. xviii.
13. Ibexes rampant. Sacred Tree of "Phenician palmettes" supporting lotus. Sun disk above. LAJARD, xvi. 76.
14. Hawk-headed Sphinxes (Gryphons) rampant; Sacred Tree of " Phenician palmettes;" same detail above. Syrian stelè (Rouad), Louvre. Same reference as No. 12.

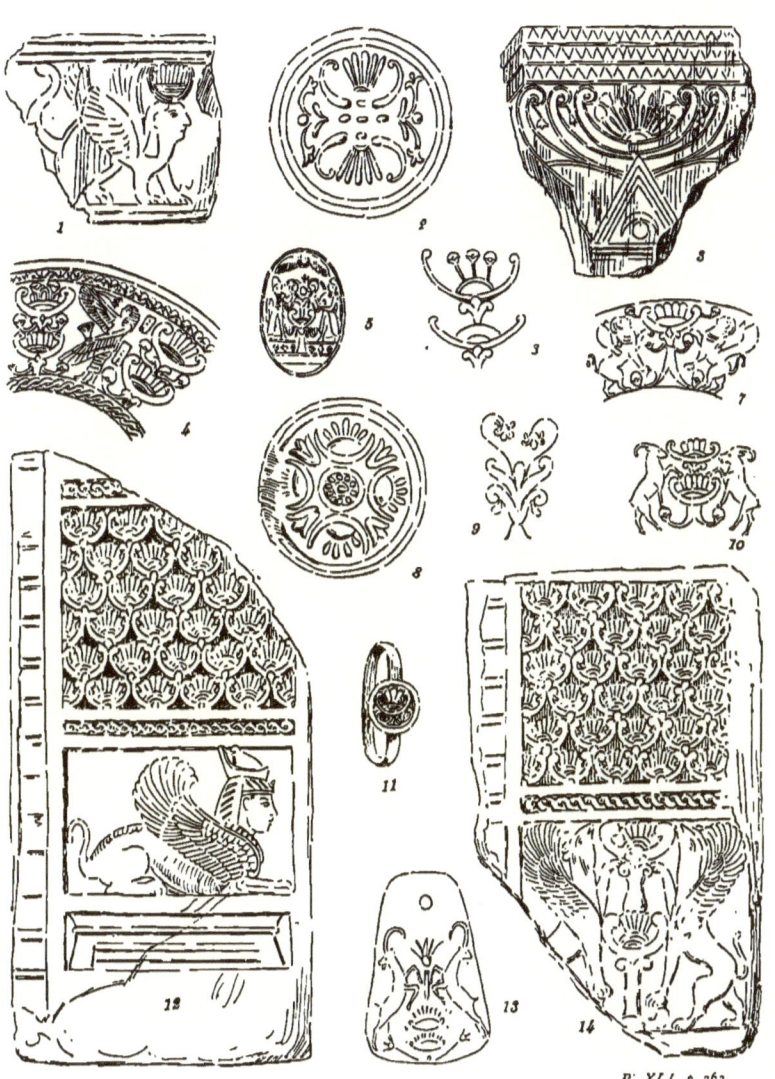

Pl. XLI, p. 263.

THE FISH AND THE LOTUS.

(PLATE XLII, PAGE 267.)

THE fish was known to the Roman period as an emblem of Venus.[1] As an equivalent and emblem of Isis or Hathor it figures, in various species,[2] among Egyptian amulets and on Egyptian utensils and enamels (9, 10), and the Liverpool bronze (7) is a patent indication on this head. The sacred fish-pond of Ascalon was a quoted feature of a Syrian sanctuary,[3] and Phenician tablets of Carthage (3) verify this symbolism as a widespread feature of Phenician cults.

The Fish-god Dagon of Ascalon is referred to the Assyrian and Chaldean Fish-god (5, 8).[4] Egyptian Isis worship can only have supplemented in Phenicia a cult which goes back to the beginning of Babylonian history, and which has left its mark on the modern Zodiac.[5] The Father-god Ea of ancient Chaldea was both the divine antelope and the divine fish. Both fish and ibex are found on the Cypriote cylinder, xxxv. 7 [p. 245]. Traces of fish symbolism are found with the lotus on Greek and "Mycenæ" vases (1, 6). The fish and the lotus can be dated to the XIIth[6] and XVIIIth Dynasties.[7]

144. SEAL. Naukratis.

That the scarab No. 2 (xlii.) points to Isis worship is clear from the cat, as Bast

---

1. KENRICK, *Phenicia*, p. 306. "Fish were consecrated to Venus and forbidden to her worshippers," quoting from Ovid, *Fasti*, 463.

2. BIRCH, *Egyptian Antiquities in the British Museum*. The Oxyrynchus, sacred to Hathor (p. 32). The Silurus, sacred to Isis (p. 59).

3. Quoted by COLONNA-CECCALDI, *Monuments de Chypre*, p. 98, in matter relating to Paphos, whose cult was derived from Ascalon.

4. SAYCE, *Hibbert Lectures*. Ea, "the Culture God of Southern Babylonia, was an amalgamation of two earlier deities, one the divine antelope, and the other the divine fish" (p. 280). Ea as Sea-god and River-god (p. 139). Ea, equivalent of Oannes, the fish (p. 131). For relations of the Dagon of Ascalon to the Assyrian and Chaldean Fish-god, see PIETSCHMANN, *Geschichte der Phönizier*, p. 145.

5. The fish undoubtedly owes its place in the Chaldean Zodiac to its divine associations. Compare ROBERT BROWN, Jun., on the causes which placed various animals in the Zodiac, *Proceedings of Society of Biblical Archæology*, 1890.

6. FLINDERS PETRIE, *Catalogue of Antiquities Discovered 1890*, p. 5, "Various pottery of the XIIth Dynasty, including some curious dishes with incised patterns of fish and lotus plants."

7. In the Louvre a golden bowl with *repoussé* decoration of fish and lotuses, "presented by Thothmes III. to a functionary named Tothi" (XVIIIth Dynasty).

is an equivalent of Isis. The lotus bud and flower of No. 2 explain the lotus triangle of No. 4, and the *Ankh* of No. 4 is an equivalent emblem.

The Oxyrynchus was not confined to Isis, but was also sacred to Thoth[u] (the Moon).

8. According to designations of amulets in the British Museum. It may be significant that the only male god in Egypt specified for the fish is a distinct Moon-god, as its better known relations in Egypt are with a Moon-goddess. The sign of the fish in the Chaldean Zodiac is assigned to the "nocturnal sun" by ROBERT BROWN, Jun., *Proceedings, Society of Biblical Archaeology*, 1890. The Chaldean sign of the goat has a fish tail (same reference). On the same Rhodian vase with the detail xlii. 1 is represented the Chimæra.

PLATE XLII.

THE FISH AND THE LOTUS.

1. Fish and the Lotus. Detail, Rhodian vase in the Louvre. SALZMANN, *Nécropole de Camire*, xlix.
2. Fish; lotus bud and flower in its mouth, sun disk above; cat (Bast = Isis). Egyptian or Syrian scarab. KLAPROTH xxxiii., 1749.
3. Fish, from Phenician votive tablet to sun and moon (Baal Hamman and Tanith), Carthage. DAVIS, *Phenician Inscriptions in the British Museum*, xvi. 47.
4. Fish, *Ankh* in its mouth; fish, lotus in its mouth. Scarab. KLAPROTH, xxxiii., 1749.
5. Assyrian Fish-god. PERROT ET CHIPIEZ, *Assyrie*, p. 65. Compare Fish-gods, lotus, and winged sun, xxiv. 3 [p. 183].
6. Fish, lotus, birds (see xxxv. 7 [p. 245]; xlv. 7, 9 [p. 287]). Vase of Calymna. *Journal of Hellenic Studies*. This vase belongs to the "Mycenæ" style of the Archipelago.
7. Isis and the fish. Bronze, Liverpool. INMAN, *Ancient Symbol Worship*, p. 68 and Frontispiece. A similar bronze in the Gizeh Museum and a similar representation in a tomb-painting at Thebes.
8. Fish-god and lotus. Assyrian Seal. *Revue Archéologique*, 1874, xiv. 5.
9. Fish, lotus leaves and flowers, detail. PRISSE D'AVENNES, *Ustensiles de Toilette*.
10. Fish and lotuses. Blue enamel plate. MASPERO, *Archæology*, tr. by Miss AMELIA B. EDWARDS.

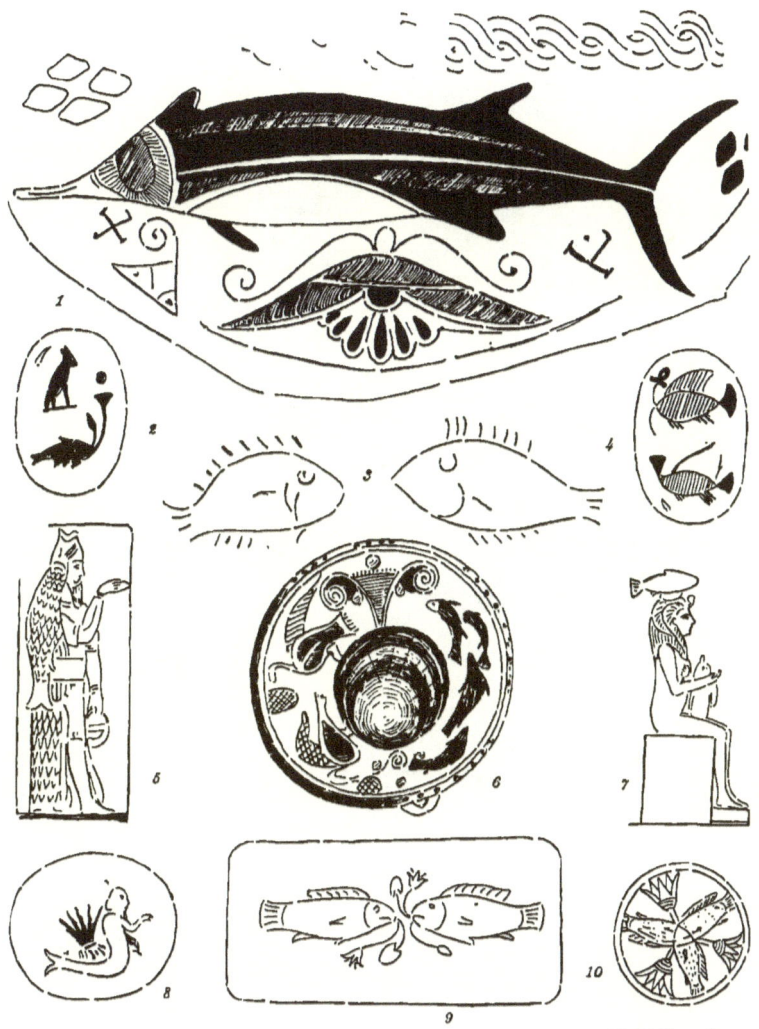

Pl. XLII., p. 267.

THE BIRD AND THE LOTUS.

(PLATES XLIII., XLIV., XLV., XLVI., PAGES 283, 285, 287, 289.)

MURRAY[1] and Birch[2] have both remarked the number of birds on Cypriote vases. The former has suggested symbolism, without going into detail. That the Cypriote bird constantly appears in association with the lotus, confronting it or bearing it attached to head or body, has not been observed in publication; nor has the instance of the Cypriote bird bearing the winged solar disk upon its back been brought to notice (xlv. 8, 11, 13). The term "aquatic" is generally applied to these birds, and there is a suspicion that they may be swans, which supposition is generally correct under curious limitations.

As the number of illustrations is very limited, considering the number and variety of originals involved, I should be glad to have the reader fortify himself by glancing at the illustrated Cypriote vases, aside from Plate xlv. where the Cypriote bird is especially represented.

Our *pièce de résistance* is xxxvii. 5 [p. 249]. A highly characteristic vase is lx. 15 [p. 359]. A Plate indicating, both in large details and in small pictures, the number of objects involved, is xlviii. [p. 305]. Plates xlvii. 14 [p. 303], xlix. 8 [p. 307], l. 9, 12 [p. 309], and lvii. 12 [p. 341], also offer important illustrations of the Cypriote bird. His peculiar style of design is not only largely geometric, but shows a geometry which is based, occasionally at least, on lotuses. His body generally bears the stamp of a lotus bud. His wings, when multiplied indefinitely, sometimes suggest the same motive (lx. 15 [p. 359]).

Were it not that the ultimate outcome of this Cypriote bird with the lotus is a

---

1. A. S. MURRAY, *Pottery Appendix to* CESNOLA's *Cyprus*, p. 406. "The animals generally found on Cypriote pottery are swans, or at any rate aquatic birds. . . . The swan may have had some symbolic signification which determined its use on the vases."

2. BIRCH, *Preface to* A. DI CESNOLA's *Salaminia*, p. xvi. "A great peculiarity of Cypriote pottery is the employment of birds in its earliest development."

swan with the anthemion (xlv. 12), it would be difficult to specify his species, which is, moreover, subject to the curious proviso that the swan is a glorified goose, and that, when he is not glorified, he is a goose pure and simple, or was once. It is difficult to be more exact than the designer, or more accurate than the tradition which controlled him. This tradition, as the Greek "Geometric" style and the prehistoric monuments of Italy and of Northern Europe prove (lvi. lvii., [pp. 339, 341]), is as old as the art of Europe itself, always excepting the drawings on bone or ivory of the Palæolithic epoch. The goose is the faithful companion of the deer and the goat or ibex, but a much more important, because a much more frequent symbol.

The most obvious cases of the goose are on Rhodian vases (Fig. 145; xxxviii. [p. 251], xlvi. 3, 7, 10), and their evidence becomes weighty when their great number is considered; as scattered between Berlin, London, and Paris. The rare cases of the ibis (xlvi. 1, 4), and of the hawk (xlv. 3; xlvi. 6), and the occasional cases of the cock (xlvi. 8, 12) are sufficient, when collected on one Plate, to weigh the Rhodian vases out of sight, as regards the illustrations. But in the argument this lack of balance must be restored. Considering that the bird of prehistoric Northern Europe was frequently reduced to a pot-hook (lvi. 10, 11, 13; lvii. 7 [pp. 339, 341]) and occasionally represented with the mane of a horse (Figs. 180, 181, [pp. 362, 363]), that the Greek "Geometric" style is largely faithful to its title, and that the Cypriote geometric style is wilfully obscure, it follows that the question of the bird hangs on the Rhodian vases, and their more careful pictures, which are very numerous, all point to the goose (Fig. 145).

The domesticated cock and hen were unknown in Greece or in Europe till the fifth or sixth century B.C., and came originally from India.[3] Although the cock is a well-known symbol of Apollo,[4] possibly as the herald of dawn, and the association of the cock with the lotus (xlvi. 8, 12) is undoubtedly symbolic, this one fact of his late arrival in Europe puts him out of the argument. The hawk, also an emblem of Apollo,[5] is rare in Greek art. His association with the lotus (xliii. 3; xlvi. 6) is undoubtedly symbolic, but offers no assistance to the problem of "the bird" in general. The heron (Osiris) and the vulture (Maut) are associated with

---

3. Rev. W. HOUGHTON, *Proceedings, Society of Biblical Archæology*, Dec., 1889, p. 81. O. KELLER, *Thiere, &c.*, p. 288. HEHN, *Wanderungen der Thiere und Pflanzen*, is original authority on this matter.

4. DAREMBERG ET SAGLIO, *Dictionnaire des Antiquités Grecques et Romaines*, under "Apollo."

5. LAJARD, *Culte de Mithra*, p. 532, &c., quotes Homer, Plutarch, Porphyry, and Aelian, to this effect.

the solar lotus in Egyptian art (p. 24), but need not detain us here. The ibis (xlvi. 1, 4) is scarcely worth mentioning in the problem, were it not to show that the bird of Thoth had not lost his lotus in a foreign home, and we fall back once more, restfully, on the goose of the Rhodian vases.

When one takes up the book of Keller[6] expecting to extract materials for a history of the swan, and finds that the bird of Zeus and Apollo and Aphrodite has not even a single page of references, to say nothing of a chapter; and when one finds that the goose has page after page of solid matter in Keller's book, then it becomes necessary to prove that "the bird" is a goose or was one once. It is

145. THE GOOSE AND THE LOTUS. Detail, Rhodian vase. From Salzmann.

impossible to be wiser than Keller—and the Rhodian vases. Stephani has proven the swan of Leda to have been a goose,[7] therefore we are in good company.

The history of the hawk and the eagle is repeated in the case of the goose and the swan. Both the former were solar birds, and the hawk the better of the two. His superior qualities were well known to the early Ancients and they accordingly preferred him, whether in Egypt or in Persia.[8] The hawk is swifter, more intelligent, more sharp-sighted. The eagle is larger, more showy, and more pretentious. He became the bird of the Romans, and his later fortune is already prophesied in Assyrian times. The case of the goose and the swan is similar. Let one examine in a Museum of Natural History, the varieties of goose which are nearest to the swan and the varieties of swan which are nearest to the goose, and it will not be found surprising that the Greeks confused the two, and ultimately, by

---

6. O. KELLER, *Thiere des Classischen Alterthums in Culturhistorischer Beziehung*, has no special chapter for the swan. The very brief references indicate an absolute lack of traditional material.

7. KELLER, p. 288.

8. LAJARD, *Culte de Mithra*, p. 531. The Chaldeans, Persians, and Egyptians, were united in this perception.

their beautifying tendencies, raised the swan to the dignity once assigned the bird of Seb, of Horus, of Isis, and Osiris.

The latest known instance of the superstitious reverence for the goose was in the First Crusade, which was headed by a goose and a goat,[9] (compare lvii. 2 [p. 341] of the "Geometric" style). His earliest distinction appears to have been that he was the first domesticated bird of prehistoric Europe,[10] but this leads us to remember that the wild goose is included in the veneration. The flying birds of Cypriote vases thus become more comprehensible, as do the representations of the flying swans in the later art of Greece. We shall do well to remember also that the Egyptian goose, or "Nile goose," is a beautifully plumaged and elegant variety.[11]

According to current presumptions of Egyptology, the goose is the distinctive bird of Seb, the father of Osiris; but I was advised some years ago by Mr. Charles Edwin Wilbour of a tablet, in the Abbott Collection of the New York Historical Society, to "the good goose of Osiris." This advice is substantiated by Keller,[12] who mentions several ancient references for the goose as the bird both of Horus and Osiris and also of Isis. The most important Egyptian references are, however, unpublished reliefs at Denderah photographed for this work (Figs. 19 [p. 51], 134 [p. 236], 140 [p. 250], 148 [p. 277], 149 [p. 278]). A silver statuette of Harpocrates and the goose is also quoted.[13] The very large number of Cypriote statuettes of a squatting boy with a bird, in the New York Museum, must, I think, be interpreted accordingly.[14]

9. KELLER, p. 298, quoting WACKERNAGEL, ἔπεα πτερόεντα, 21.

10. As apparent in the fact that the word for goose is common to Sanscrit, Greek, Latin, Sclavonic, and Old German, and in the fact that the goose long preceded the domestic fowl in Europe as a tame animal, but Keller adds that there were not many tame geese in the time of Homer.

11. KELLER, p. 286; also reference to mummies of geese found at Thebes.

12. KELLER, p. 286.

13. KELLER, p. 454, Note 6, with reference to *Arch. Zeit.*, xxvi. 71.

14. CESNOLA, *Atlas*, I., cxxx., cxxxi., cxxxii. Since making this suggestion I have found in the Egyptian Collection at Naples a statue of the class in New York, which is labelled as "Harpocrates" (No. 551). The boy is squatting and holds a goose and places a finger on his lip, which gesture specifies Harpocrates. The Cypriote statuettes are similar in all particulars except the gesture. An important class of Cypriote statues not designated by Birch (who wrote the text for the Cesnola Atlas), is thus explained, and I should be sorry to have the brevity of this reference obscure its importance. There are forty-one of these statuettes on three Plates of the Atlas, all of which Plates I personally arranged for the photographer. Most of the statuettes hold a bird, which is specified for No. 951 as a "goose." No. 970 holds a cock. One statuette holds a rabbit (Osiris), and one holds a tortoise (Horus killing the tortoise is a subject in an inner wall chamber at Denderah). Three statuettes of the type, but without birds, are illustrated in CESNOLA'S *Cyprus*, p. 347. These statuettes are all said to come from the site of the temple of Apollo Hylates at Curium.

THE BIRD AND THE LOTUS.   273

The goose belongs to the small number of objects for which a common word is found in Sanscrit, German, Greek, and Latin.[15] In Etruscan art he is the attendant of the goddess who presides over births.[16] He was sacrificed to Venus in Cyprus,[17] was an emblem of love, and in Italy was sacred to Priapus.[18] To the Hindus he was a symbol of eloquence,[19] and to the Greeks he was an attendant of Peitho, the goddess of winning speech.[20] He was sacred to Apollo at Daphne and in Delos,[21] to the Roman Mars,[22] to Dionysus and Hermes, and to Eros.[23] Eros on the goose is the subject of a Tanagra figurine in the British Museum. The geese of Juno at Rome are to be mentioned, of course. On Greek tombs he represented love and watchfulness,[24] and it is expressly stated by tomb inscriptions that he represented the watchfulness of a good housewife.[25] He was a weather prophet.[26] The oath of Socrates and his disciples was "by the goose."[27] In France and Germany prophetic power was ascribed to him.[28] Finally, *pâté de foie gras* was much enjoyed by the Ancients.[29]

When we find that none of these good things are recorded of the swan, it is difficult not to believe that the swan of early Greek art was a goose.

The transformation was undoubtedly accomplished mainly during the fifth and fourth centuries B.C., that is, during a time when representations of the gods by solar animals, outside of Cyprus and Rhodes, had been entirely displaced by pictures of actual divinities and of myths. As the purely conventional style of Cypriote art continued long after this time, and as early dates in Cypriote art are not implied by an archaic style,[30] the character of the Cypriote bird, as between the two alternatives of goose and swan, must be left in debate in most individual cases, not being open to settlement by reference to birds whose bodies are lotus buds or deformed by geometric methods.

A point of great importance, not mentioned by Keller, is that the goose is the sacred bird and "vehicle" of Brahma.[31] The relations of Brahma to the sun are at once evaded and conceded by the Brahmans,[32] and his birth from the lotus flower

---

15. KELLER, p. 303.—16, p. 288.—17, p. 288.—18, p. 288 —19, p. 289.—20, p. 289.—21, p. 290 —22, p. 290.— 23, p. 289.—24, p. 291.—25, p. 291.—26, p. 297.— 27, p. 297.—28, p. 297.—29, p. 249.

30. This fact, noted by CONZE, *Anfänge der Griechischen Kunst*, in 1870, is universally conceded.

31. MOOR, *Hindu Pantheon*, p. 9. "The Sakti or wife of Brahma is Saraswati, the goddess of harmony and the arts. . . . Many deities have, as well as their wives, vehicles or *vahans* allotted to them; that of Brahma and of his *Sakti* is the swan or goose."

32. MOOR, *Hindu Pantheon*. The goose is known to WARING, *Ceramic Art in Remote Ages*, as "sacred to the sun in Egypt, Greece, India, and Britain."

has been mentioned (p. 5). The Hindu word for the bird of Brahma is *hanassa*,[33] also recorded as (old Hindu) *hamsa*; identical, according to the well-known transformations of the same word in different "Aryan" tongues, with the Greek χῆν, the Latin *anser*, the Letto-Slavonic *gansi*, and the German *gans*—with which the English word "gannet," although transferred to another bird, is related.[34]

There is the same confusion in the Hindu art with the swan, the same doubt as to individual cases on the part of Hindu specialists.[35] It is amusing to one who has struggled with the Cypriote bird to find the specification of "goose or swan" recurring in the descriptions of the bird of Brahma. But there is also on the part of Hindu specialists the same abiding conviction that the goose is the original form and the swan an afterthought or beautifying development.

More important still, the goose with the lotus is a typical Buddhist decorative detail[36] open to the observation of anyone ascending the main stairway of the British Museum (Buddhist sculptures from the Amaravati Tope, Southern India; for instance, the first relief on the right in ascending the stairway, No. 66). The same detail of the "swan" and the lotus has been observed by the author of the "Hindu Pantheon" as connected with Brahma, in the rock-carved Hindu temple of Elephanta,[37] and is mentioned by him in his chapter on the worship of Brahma. In Mr. Fergusson's "Cave Temples of India" we find mention for the Avanta Cave of "a frieze of twelve geese bearing lotus buds in their beaks" (p. 75), and on his Plate lxxxiii. 1, geese and the lotus are associated with the Sun-god Surya. I could cite other instances, and the association must have been common in ancient Hindu art.

146. THE BIRD AND THE SPIRAL. Dahomey.

The bird with the lotus (also with wings) can be seen on the Byzantine Portal of San Giovanni Evangelista at Ravenna (Fig. 147), and occurs as bird and

33. Moor, *Hindu Pantheon*, p. 9.
34. Keller, *Thiere*, p. 302.
35. Moor, p. 296. "Swan or goose," many instances; the same hesitation also in Birdwood, *Industrial Arts of India*.
36. In quoting instances of the honeysuckle pattern on "Edict pillars" of Buddhist art, Birdwood says of the pillar at Bettiah in Tirhut: "In this instance, however, the honeysuckle and palmette ornament is replaced by a line of geese going round the top of the capital in single file" (p. 112). This is an instance of the equivalence of the goose and the lotus.
37. "Except in the Elephanta cave I do not remember to have seen Brahma or his *Sakti*, attended by the swan, and there it is in several compartments, seen very well embossed on the calyx of the lotus, on which Brahma is sitting. Three or four of the animals are there portrayed as if swimming after one another" (p. 41).

anthemion on a Byzantine ear-ring in the British Museum. It made its way as the bird and spiral, even to Dahomey [38] (Fig. 146), a fact probably related to the modern survival in Northern Africa of the geometric style of Cyprus (lxiv. [p. 385]) and to the presence of the Swastika in Dahomey mentioned by Schliemann. It figures on a valuable Oriental vase of so rare a type that one of the leading Ceramic experts of the world cannot specify its exact origin,[39] and it is positively connected with the ordinary Oriental textile motive which figures two birds facing a vase.

147. DETAIL OF BIRDS AND WINGED LOTUS TREE.
Portal of San Giovanni Evangelista, Ravenna. From a photograph.

The motive of the birds and the vase can be traced to Etruscan ivories of early date [40] and to Oriental cylinders (xliv. 9). The swan in his turn was displaced by a still more pretentious and still more vainglorious bird, and the peacock became a later form of the motive both in East and West (Byzantine sarcophagi, Ravenna, &c.). The peacock was a Christian symbol of immortality, but the duplicate arrangement of the birds and the intervening ornamental motives in Christian art point to a common origin.

The dove is by no means to be ignored in this question, as a distinctly recognized emblem of Venus, of the equivalent Phenician Astarte [41] and of the Assyrian cults.[42] The dove and the lotus can be specified in pictured Egyptian vases under Syrian influence (xliii. 1). The dove is connected with Venus by Cypriote coins

---

38. T. EDWARD BOWDITCH, *Superstitions, Customs, and Arts common to the Ancient Egyptians, Abyssinians, and Ashantees*, is source for the illustration Fig. 146. Ashantee gold ornaments exhibit also normal lotuses (Brit. Mus.).

39. A vase owned by Mrs. Professor Huggins.

40. Among Etruscan objects of the British Museum, in the room for bronzes, a small ivory comb with relief of two birds bearing lotuses on their backs, and facing a vase holding a lotus. This undoubtedly represents the original type of the birds with the vase.

41. Plutarch relates the fable that Isis was transformed into a dove at Byblus; quoted by Colonna-Ceccaldi, *Monumente de Chypre*, p. 96—a story which shows her assimilation to Astarte in Syria.

42. In Jeremiah it is said, "Their land was made desolate by the face and wrath of the Dove."—*Vulgate.*

(xlv. 6) and appears on Carthaginian Phenician votive tablets to the sun and moon (lxvi. 2, 3 [p. 399]).

The dove may possibly be the bird, with lotus on the head, of the Oriental cylinder xliv. 9; where the vase (a sign of the Zodiac, Aquarius)[43] also appears as an interesting proof of the relation between the motive of the birds with the vase and the bird with the lotus. The dove may also be intended on certain Cypriote vases (xlviii. 12 [p. 305]), but the length of the neck (xlviii. 8 [p. 303]) in most cases, and the generally pretentious dimensions and self-important bearing of the bird (xlvii. 14 [p. 249]), generally forbid this supposition. The association of the swan with the fish on Cilician coins (xlv. 7) points to the goose or swan in the parallel association of the fish and bird (xlii. 6 [p. 267]; xlv. 9) on vases.

The association of the hawk with the lotus is a well-marked feature in Egyptian symbolism (v. 5, 6, 7 [p. 65]; xliii. 3, 9; xliv. 2, 6). An enamel amulet of the Leyden Museum shows the lotus supporting the hawk's head.[44] Various reasons given by the Ancients for associating the hawk with the sun (xliii. 6; xliv. 4, 5, 11) are quoted by modern writers, and the relations of the hawk to Apollo were familiar to Homer.[45] The hawk is the bird of Ra and of Horus (pp. 6, 7, Notes 12, 13, 14, 21) and the wings of the solar winged disk as form of Horus are hence derived (xliii. 6).

It is not certain that the bird-headed deity of Assyrian art (Fig. 121 [p. 180]) has the head of an eagle as generally assumed. The eagle was a solar bird,[46] but the Persians, whose ancient texts specify both eagle and hawk as birds of Mithra (the sun), gave the preference to the hawk, and these texts are later than the Assyrian time. The double-headed "eagle" of the Hittites,[47] which is the earliest known instance of the emblem of various modern States, may easily be a double-headed hawk. The same double-headed bird appears on a Cypriote vase in New York. The cylinder xliv. 1, which has been specified as Hittite by Menant, shows the hawk in an attitude exactly paralleled by Egyptian art (xliii. 6; xliv. 4), which

---

43. ROBERT BROWN, Jun., *Proceedings, Society of Biblical Archæology*, 1890, mentions the Chaldean sign *Aquarius* as "the rain-giving sun."

44. LEEMANS, I., Plate xxiv., 400. "La tête de l'épervier placée sur un calice épanoui de lotus, emblème du dieu Phré" [Ra]. A similar very large porcelain amulet in the Polytechnic at Athens.

45. *Iliad*, xv. 236-238; *Odyssey*, xv. 525-526.

46. LAJARD, *Culte de Mithra*. The eagle was symbol of Ormuzd (the sun) (p. 274), and of Mithra (p. 450). For Mithra as the sun, see *Encyclopædia Britannica*, 9th Edit., "Zoroaster."

47. See PERROT et CHIPIEZ, Vol. iv., Fig. 343.

gave the eagle a place in its hieroglyphics but preferred the hawk as a solar emblem.

The much-debated Cypriote vase xlv. 2, 3 shows an unmistakable hawk.[48] We have then, either a picture of a worshipper or of a god, with solar emblems of the hawk and lotus.

The illustrations of the lotus cult in Assyria, which have been collected on Plates xxiv. [p. 183], xxv. [p. 185], include many examples of the normal lotus hitherto overlooked. Subsequent Plates have added many others (xxxii. [p. 223], xxxvi. [p. 247], xlii. [p. 267]). Aside from many Phenician illustrations in these Plates, I have already called attention to the normal lotus on Carthaginian votive tablets (lxvi., lxvii. [pp. 399, 401]). It must therefore appear that the Cypriote vases are a much neglected and highly important connecting link in Mediterranean history. Matter has been quoted from Perrot as illustration of the prevailing opinion that the subjects of these vases have no significance (p. 230, Note 20).

The prevalence of normal flowers on these vases (xlvii. [p. 303]) makes their evidence direct and unmistakable. This by no means argues a direct or unmixed Egyptian influence, since both Phenicia and Assyria were saturated with a lotus symbolism whose exterior forms are Egyptian. The instance of Hindustan, whither the Egyptian forms also penetrated (pp. 35, 36, and p. 151, Note 6), proves that a distinct national religion may borrow foreign art forms for a native symbol. But the goose with the lotus, which is by far the most prevalent and important association of the bird and the lotus, is Egyptian in origin.

The most obvious, numerous, and interesting associations of the goose and the lotus in Egypt are found at Denderah; but these very beautiful reliefs in small dimensions arranged along the lower walls of the temple-portico have not been published. The goose occurs here constantly on the tops of bouquets held by Hathor (Fig. 19, p. 51)

148. ISIS-HATHOR, THE COW, THE GOOSE, THE GAZELLE, AND THE LOTUS. Detail of a relief panel in the temple-portico at Denderah. Photographed for the Author.

---

48. The references for this vase are given in the description of the Plate.

278   THE BIRD AND THE LOTUS.

and also in the "Lotus bower." It is associated with the gazelle (Figs. 134, 140 [pp. 236, 250]), just as the deer and goose or swan are associated with the lotus on Cypriote vases. In other panels and in similar association with the "Lotus bower" we have the goose, gazelle and cow (Fig. 148), showing that the symbolism which has collected representations of nearly all the Egyptian deities on the column bases of the portico is also in question here. The evidence of this last relief, on which Isis-Hathor also appears (lower portion of the body visible in the cut) would indicate that the gazelle was also an animal of Isis at Denderah.

149. THE GOOSE (SWAN?) AND THE LOTUS.
Detail of a panel in the temple-portico at Denderah. Photographed for the Author.

For the goose and the lotus in Egypt, Plate xliii. offers five examples (2, 4, 5, 8, 11), to which the typical representation of Seb (7) is an important addition. Many other cases can be quoted.[49] The offerings of geese and lotuses to Ra and Horus (5, 8) are supplementary evidence for the quotations of Keller and the generally neglected relations of the goose to Ra, Horus, Isis, and Osiris.

The most important Cypriote illustration is undoubtedly the bird with winged solar disk on its back (xlv. 13) facing the lotus, to which we may add the bird and solar diagram (lvii. 12 [p. 341]). Cases of the flower resting on the bird's back and head are next in importance (xxxvii. 5, [p. 249]; xlv. 8 [p. 287]). The large number of unpublished Cypriote vases showing the bird with the lotus in New York is a still more important consideration. When these are connected with the indications of the

49. The large statue of the Nile-god Hapi, from Thebes, in the British Museum, combines the symbolic geese and lotuses. Several instances in ROSELLINI. A blue glazed dish from Gurob, XVIIIth or XIXth Dynasty, shows the combination (PETRIE excavations, 1890).

THE BIRD AND THE LOTUS. 279

Lawrence-Cesnola Collection [50] and with the scattered vases in other Museums and of various publications, the goose takes first rank, while the deer and ibex stand second, among the links which chain the history of Greece to the older civilizations of Africa and Asia.

On the oldest monuments of Greek art, the "Dipylon" vases (lvi. 1, 8, 10 [p. 339]; lvii. 2 [p. 341]; lviii. 3 [p. 343]); on prehistoric bronzes and pottery of Italy (lvi. 12 [p. 339], lvii. 7, 8, 14 [p. 341]); on the bronzes of Hallstatt (lvii. 4 [p. 341]), of ancient Gaul, and of prehistoric Sweden (lvi. 9, 11 [p. 339]), the goose still tells the story of ancient bronze and of ancient civilization in its journey from the South-eastern Mediterranean to Western and Northern Europe.

When once the association with the lotus has cleared the path, the solar significance of the bird without this association also becomes obvious. The lines of birds (geese) which are so common in early Mediterranean art (Plate lvi.) can be traced directly to Egyptian originals. In the British Museum there is a fresco [51] from Thebes showing a golden vase (holding metal lotuses) on which such a line of geese is depicted. This vase can be connected with an actually existing gold original, with a similar line of geese, found in Italy,[52] of Egypto-Phenician style and found with objects of Egyptian style, including lotus ornaments of ivory. This vase again can be connected with hosts of objects showing the line of birds in Etruscan art. These birds were already reduced to the "pot-hook" stage in Greece (lvi, 10) and Italy, and in this shape can be traced as far as Scandinavia (lvi, 11.)

The overthrow of the theory which placed the centre and original home of the "Aryan" nations in Asia is recent but decisive.[53] The relations which connect the goose and the lotus of Brahma with the goose and the lotus of Apollo (Note 21) might easily be assumed to imply a Hindu origin for this association; therefore it

---

50. The Collection has been dispersed (some pieces are in Munich), but the publication of photographs by ALEXANDER DI CESNOLA, entitled *Cyprus Antiquities*, shows a large number of specimens for the bird and the lotus, grouped in one or two plates of typical Cypriote vases. Others appear in A. DI CESNOLA'S *Salaminia*, and one or two from this publication appear on Plate xlviii. 7, 13, 14 [p. 305]. Others have been published by HAMILTON LANG, and by PERROT, *Cypre*. One Cypriote vase, with the bird and normal lotus, is in the British Museum.

51. Hall of Egyptian statues, No. 923.

52. In the Collegio Romano, Kircher Museum, gold vase from Palestrina, No 23.

53. CANON ISAAC TAYLOR'S *Origin of the Aryans* gives a compendious and comprehensive account of the discoveries in Philology and Anthropology which have proven the European origin of the Aryans. In a recent supplement to the Catalogue of the Boston Public Library, the mere list of works on this new subject fills several closely-printed pages.

THE BIRD AND THE LOTUS.

is well to remember that according to the latest discoveries of Philology and of Anthropology the "Aryan" Hindus came from Europe.

The antiquity of the motive in Europe makes it almost positive that the solar goose travelled to India from Europe with the migrations of the Aryan Hindus. It is not impossible that the goose and lotus associations of India are equally ancient, although the worship of Brahma is much later.

For the ostrich (xliv. 12) as a sacred bird there are many references in the Zend-avesta.[54] These Persian citations may be fairly referred to Semitic traditions, from which they are certainly derived. The Persian cult shows many loans from Chaldæa. The Persians proper were recent converts to the religion of Zoroaster in the fifth century B.C.,[55] and their religion must have been, as their art certainly was, largely influenced by Chaldæa. Hence the ostrich in Assyrian art[56] may fairly be connected with known facts from Persian sources, casting light on Chaldean and Assyrian monuments. The ostrich feather was an Egyptian hieroglyph for "Truth" or "Justice," but the bird itself does not appear in Egyptian art.

150. LOTUS BUDS AND IONIC FORMS OF SWANS' HEADS, SUPPORTING DEMI-ROSETTES.
Repoussé design. Silver plaque from the Caucasus.

The symbolisms (or traditions) attaching to the Ionic form, the lotus, and the swan, are curiously illustrated by the Ionic forms of swans' necks, supporting demi-rosettes and alternating with buds, of Fig. 150.[57]

---

54. LAJARD, *Culte de Mithra*. See especially matter relating to the cry of the ostrich as much mentioned by the authors of the sacred books of Persia.

55. *Encyclopædia Britannica*, 9th Edition; under "Zoroaster."

56. In SAYCE, *Hibbert Lectures*, the references are confined to the "divine storm bird" (p. 294, &c.).

57. Design borrowed from PERROT et CHIPIEZ, III., p. 792. Two Rhodian plaques published by LONGPÉRIER, *Musée Napoléon III.*, may also be quoted. The outer border of one is decorated with swans' heads alternating with solar diagrams. A corresponding piece shows the heads of deer in similar alternation.

RHODIAN VASE. From Salzmann. Repeated from Plate xxxviii.

PLATE XLIII.

THE BIRD AND THE LOTUS.

1. Doves and lotuses. Vase detail from a tomb-painting. PRISSE D'AVENNES, *Vases en or.* XIXth Dynasty.

2. Goose (Seb, Osiris, Isis, and Horus) on the lotus. Detail from MARIETTE, *Dendérah*, II. 85D.

3. Sun-hawk on the lotus. Detail from MARIETTE, *Dendérah*, II. 85A.

4. Geese and the lotus. Egyptian blue enamel plate. Boston Museum, Hay Collection, No. 842. Another blue enamel plate with goose and lotus can be dated to the XVIIIth—XIXth Dynasties. (PETRIE'S excavations, 1890.)

5. Egyptian Sceptre, geese on the lotus. From a picture of Ptolemy Euergetes making offering to Horus. ROSELLINI, M.R. clxv.

6. Sun-hawk and winged sun disk (Horus). Syrian relief sculpture, Amrit. RENAN, *Mission de Phénicie*, ix.

7. God Seb (Father of Osiris) and the goose. RAWLINSON, *History of Ancient Egypt*, I. p. 375.

8. Thothmes III. offering geese and lotuses to the Sun-god Ra. ROSELLINI, M.D.C. ix. 4.

9. Sun-hawk on the lotus. Detail from BIRCH and BONOMI, *Antiquities in the British Museum*, xx.

10. The bird and the lotus. Detail of a woven fabric. PRISSE D'AVENNES, *Tissus et Brodéries.*

11. Lotus capital with geese. PRISSE D'AVENNES, *Le Pharaon Khouenaten servi par la reine,* XIXth Dynasty.

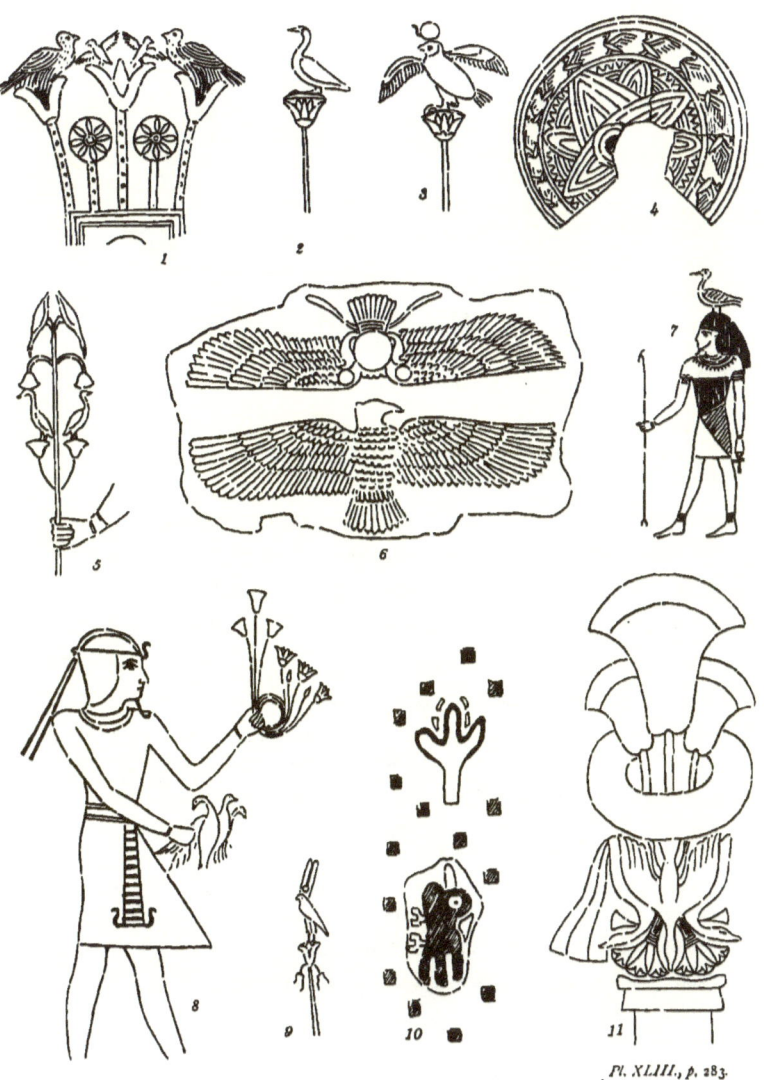

Pl. XLIII., p. 283.

PLATE XLIV.

THE BIRD AND THE LOTUS.

1. Sun-hawk (compare No. 4) and the lotus. The cylinder is pronounced Hittite by MENANT; the cuneiform inscription names the owner (*Cylindres*, II. p. 117). The lotus is mistaken by MENANT for a branch—"*rameau*." From LAJARD, *Culte de Mithra*, xviii. 7.

2. Horus hawks and lotuses. Detail, Cypriote bronze *patera*, New York Museum.

3. Birds with lotus tails, facing three lotuses. Ivory carving, Cære, *Museo Etrusco Vaticano*, I. cvii.

4. Winged sun disk, hawk, beetle, (scarab). *Description de l'Égypte*, A.V. 83, 22.

5. Hawk-headed Sun-god (Ra or Horus) and sun disk. CESNOLA, *Cyprus*, vi. 4.

6. Sun-hawk and lotus. Seal, *Naukratis*, xxvi. 60.

7. Birds (compare xliii. 4 for designation). Cylinder. A. DI CESNOLA, *Salaminia*, xii.

8. Goose or swan, trefoil lotus on the back. For object in front, compare xlii. 4 [p. 267]. For lotus on the back, compare xlv. 8. Scarab. KLAPROTH, xxiv. 1576.

9. Birds with lotuses on the heads. Spiral scrolls below in conventional method. Hematite cylinder at Avignon. For bird with lotus on the head, compare vase xxxvii. 5 [p. 249], and Gryphon cylinder, xxxiv. 5 [p. 227]. LAJARD, *Culte de Mithra*, l. 3.

10. Hawk or eagle, gazelle, fish, dove, trefoil lotus (one-half shown on each side by the cylinder impression). Cylinder. CESNOLA, *Cyprus*; KING'S Appendix for Gems, III. 28.

11. Hawk over winged sun disk; seal. CESNOLA, *Cyprus*, v. 20.

12. Ostriches, lotus bud, lotus palmette with buds, rosettes. LAYARD, *First Series*, xlvii.

Pl. XLIV., p. 285.

PLATE XLV.

THE BIRD AND THE LOTUS.

1. Solar bird and lotus, Adorer, Sacred lotus Tree. Cypriote vase, New York Museum. PERROT et CHIPIEZ, *Cypre*, p. 709.

2, 3. Cypriote vase and detail. Adorer holding lotus, with Sun-hawk; lotus with pendant sepals; lotus with incipient sepal volutes; solar diagram rear of the figure, Swastikas. MAX OHNEFALSCH-RICHTER in *Jahrbuch*, 1886, Plate viii. Subject mistaken by DÜMMLER for a " missverstandene Vogeljagd aus dem alten Reich," i.e. for a misinterpreted copy of a picture of bird hunting of the Old Empire. Figured first by REINACH, *Revue Archéologique*, 1885, II. p. 360. REINACH correctly referred the design to the Assyrian Sacred Tree. Figured also by PERROT et CHIPIEZ, iv. p. 564.

4. Solar bird and lotuses. Cypriote vase, New York Museum, of an extremely numerous type for the bird and lotus. CESNOLA, *Cyprus*, p. 405

5. Cypriote coin. Bull and winged sun disk. Reverse, hawk or dove, lotus leaf. (Compare xxxii. 5 [p. 223] for the leaf.) DE LUYNES, *Num. et In. Cyp.* III. 3.

6. Cypriote coin. Dove, asterism. Reverse, head specified as Venus by De Luynes. DE LUYNES, *Num. et In. Cyp.* v. 5.

7. Cilician coin. Swan, fish, sun diagram. Reverse, winged figure holding a disk. " Ces médailles sont au type d'Astarte portant l'étoile tombé du ciel, qu'elle avait ramassé en Phénicie et consacré à Tyre." DE LUYNES, *Num. et In. Cyp.* vii. 4. His attribution of the coin to Cyprus is reversed (verbal advice of Mr. BARCLAY V. HEAD).

8. Solar bird, lotus on its neck. Compare lotus on the bird's head, xlvi. 2, and cylinder xliv. 9. Detail, Cypriote vase (the vase at xlviii. 4 [p. 305]), New York Museum. CESNOLA, *Cyprus*, xlvi.

9, 10. Solar bird and fish. Cypriote detail and vase, New York Museum. CESNOLA, *Cyprus*; MURRAY'S Pottery Appendix, xlvi.

11. Solar birds and lotus with introrse scrolls and buds; solar diagram. Cypriote vase detail. PERROT et CHIPIEZ, *Cypre*, p. 700.

12. Swans and lotus anthemions. Detail of the Cypriote vase shown at Plate xlviii. 2 [p. 305], New York Museum. CESNOLA, *Cyprus*, in MURRAY'S Appendix, xlvii. 41.

13. Solar bird supporting winged solar disk; facing lotus and buds. Detail of the Cypriote vase, New York Museum, shown at Plate xlviii. 10 [p. 305]. The latter design in CESNOLA, *Cyprus*, p. 405.

The lotus bud is apparently detailed on the bird's body in most instances—Nos. 1, 4, 8, 9, 11, 13. Compare l. 9 [p. 309].

For additional Cypriote vases showing solar bird and lotus, see xlviii. 7, 13, 14 [p. 305]. An especially important vase, as representing a common type, is shown at lx. 15 [p. 359].

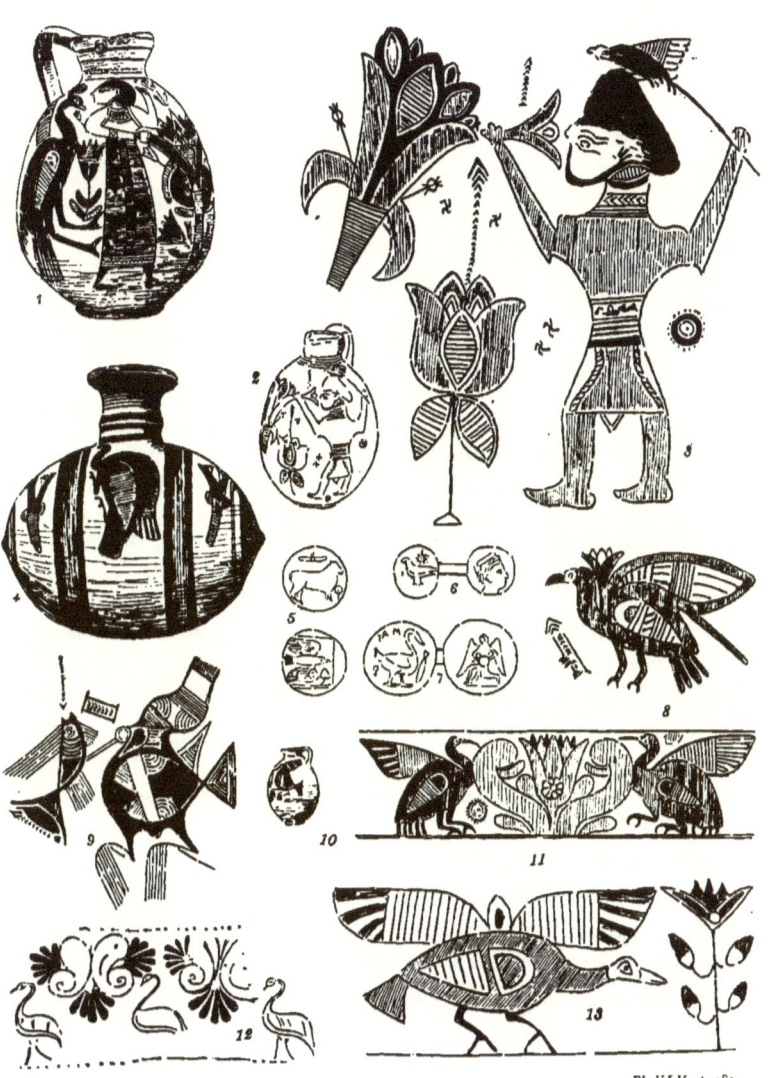

Pl. XLV., p. 287.

PLATE XLVI.

THE BIRD AND THE LOTUS.

1. Ibis and lotus; bouquet of buds; large lotus palmette with introrse scrolls; two lotus palmettes. Detail, early Attic vase. BÖHLAU, *Jahrbuch*, 1886, Taf. 3, 4.

2. Cypriote vase. Sacred Trees of lotus rosettes, Ionic scrolls, and palmettes; solar bird with lotus on the head; a deer rampant. For larger side view of this bird, see Plate xxxvii. 5 [p. 249]. MAX OHNEFALSCH-RICHTER, *Journal of Hellenic Studies*, V. p. 102.

3. Geese and inverted lotus. Detail of a Rhodian vase, British Museum. WARING, *Ceramic Art in Remote Ages*, xxvii. 9.

4. Ibis and three-spiked lotus with tabs on the stem. Compare Plate iv. [p. 63], and related text [p. 50], for the tabs. Early Greek vase. BÖHLAU, *Jahrbuch*, 1887, p. 54.

5. Solar birds, Swastikas, and inverted lotus triangle. Compare No. 3, and xlix. 8 [p. 307]. Detail, Greek "Geometric" vase. WARING, *Ceramic Art in Remote Ages*, xxxiii. 24.

6. Hawk on the lotus anthemion. Greek pottery fragment, Defenneh Kasr. *Tanis*, II. xxv. 1.

7. Goose and the lotus (Compare same detail at xvi. 5 [p. 144]), Swastika and diagrams. Detail of a vase from Thera, Rhodian style. *Monumenti Inediti*, IX. v. 2.

8. Cock and lotus. Detail, BENNDORF, *Vasengemälde*, xxxvi. 7.

9. Geese or swans. Rhodian vase. *Jahrbuch*, 1886, p. 148.

10. Geese and the lotus, Swastikas, and diagrams. Entire vase at Plate xxxviii. [p. 251] for "the Deer and the Lotus." SALZMANN, *Nécropole de Camire*, xliv.

11. Solar birds and rosette. Rhodian vase. *Jahrbuch*, 1886, p. 152.

12. Cocks on the lotus facing doubled lotus flower. Greek vase in the Louvre. *Monumenti Inediti*, V. xv.

13. Swan and anthemion. Early Attic vase. BÖHLAU, *Jahrbuch*, 1887, p. 52.

Pl. XLVI., p. 289.

PART III.
PREHISTORIC DIFFUSION OF THE LOTUS MOTIVE.

GEOMETRIC LOTUSES OF CYPRUS.

(PLATES XLVII., XLVIII., XLIX., L., PAGES 303, 305, 307, 309.)

THE first antiquarian who threw decisive light on the vexed problem of Cypriote vases was Professor F. Dümmler.[1] The causes which had confused their study have been indicated by him, and it is he who cleared the path for all later students. At his side stands Max Ohnefalsch-Richter, who has been unwearied in his efforts to secure exact information as to Cypriote antiquities, and to make this information public.

Professor Dümmler's efforts were entirely directed, however, to the separation of the prehistoric vases of Cyprus (lvii. 11 [p. 341]; lix. 8, 13 [p. 345]) from those of its later culture, and to the proof that the former are directly related to those of prehistoric Troy (Schliemann excavations). The same race and stage of civilization were thus proven to have existed in both territories before the advent of Phenicians and Greeks in Cyprus, and after that advent, for some continued time in the interior.

This race is supposed by Dümmler to have been exterminated in Cyprus by the tenth century B.C. His position regarding the later vases of Cyprus is one obviously indicated by their uniformity of style and character (aside from the "Mycenæ" and "Dipylon" exceptions found in Cyprus), down to a late period of antiquity—viz., that whether Greek or Phenician, they are essentially of one class, undistinguishable in individual examples. The curious conservatism and oriental unprogressiveness of the Cypriote Greeks were supposed to have kept them in the grooves of imitation of Phenician examples, from which the copies could not be distinguished.[2] It remains to be proved even that such originals existed.

---

1. *Mittheilungen, Athen. Abtheil*, 1886.
2. Among the instances of this unprogressive character specified by various authors, are the use of war-chariots in the fifth century, and the fact that Greek Cypriote kings united military, judicial, and priestly functions (as in the times of Homer), down to the period of the Ptolemies.

In later publications Dümmler has tended to question the existence of a Phenician production of Cypriote vases, or to minimize it to the extreme degree. In this tendency he is undoubtedly in the right. Scholars of various tendencies or without tendencies, have asserted the civilization of Cyprus to have been dominantly and essentially Greek, in spite of the Phenician colonies and settlements on the island.[3] It is a curious fact that Phenician ships from the Syrian coast bound west were accustomed to make their first landing at Rhodes, and that their relations with Rhodes were more friendly and intimate than with Cyprus.[4]

Movers has explained the amalgamation and assimilation of Cypriote Phenicians with Cypriote Greeks in the cities which are usually ascribed to Phenician foundation. Dümmler points to the fact that painted vases are a speciality of the Greek race. A more important argument against the Phenician character of Cypriote vases is that none like them are found in Sardinia or at Carthage, and that the rare cases of independent Syrian analogy include only one limited class of no great importance to the general question.[5] The absence of typical Cypriote vases from finds in Sardinia is a conclusive proof of their Greek character when we consider how many objects found in Sardinia are exact counterparts of Cypriote-Phenician pieces.

Our best comprehension of the problem how an island with important Phenician colonies and settlements, from which the Phenicians drew their main supply of copper for the manufacture of bronze, could exhibit an art dominantly Greek, is obtained from a comparison of the ancient Phenicians with the Jews. Both have been merchant races. Both have been tenacious to the last degree in blood and race assertiveness. Both have affiliated with foreign nations to a marvellous extent. The Jew has never had an independent art. His synagogue exhibits the style of the nation in which he has settled, of the period to

---

The survival of the archaic Cypriote syllabary is another indication in the same direction. Vases with concentric rings are quoted for the Roman period by COLONNA-CECCALDI, *Monuments de Chypre*, and they are otherwise unknown later than the sixth century B.C. (for Rhodes), and much earlier dates otherwise. A vase of the primitive traditional lotus style bears a Greek inscription which dates it about 284 B.C. BIRCH, *Preface to Salaminia*, p. xvi. The vase is figured at p. 253 of *Salaminia*.

3. BIRCH, *Preface to Salaminia*, p. xvii. "Dominant civilization, undoubtedly Greek. This is the more remarkable, as there is every evidence that the Phenician population divided the possession of the island with the Greek, and that in some of the chief cities they held an undoubted supremacy."

4. MOVERS, *Geschichte der Phönizier*.

5. Compare PERROT et CHIPIEZ, *Phénicie*, for geometric pottery designs from Jerusalem and Syria. I use the words "independent Syrian analogy" to indicate distinction from the Cypriote pottery found by Mr. Petrie in Syria (1890). This corresponds to the Cypriote pottery found in Egypt, and represents a Cypriote colony or settlement.

which he belongs, but he is not the less a Jew because he is also French, German, English or Portuguese.

This parallel appears to indicate the position of the Phenician race in Cyprus. It is especially important also to remember that all Phenician colonies included large numbers of foreigners, for reasons which Movers has explained. Their armies were entirely composed of mercenaries (especially Carians). Their carriers, sailors, and employees were likewise foreign, and originally mainly Carian. Phenician Tyre is said to have been mainly populated by Carians.[6] It is easy to understand how colonies established by a merchant ruling caste could, under such conditions, diffuse Egyptian patterns by the sale of their wares, influence religious rites and superstitions by the magnificence of their sanctuaries, and by personal contact with their subordinates, and mould a civilization by the mere dead weight of their own wealth and luxury in contrast with provincial barbarism — without being themselves the manufacturers or producers of the national art of Cyprus.

To regard Phenician colonies as composed of solid masses of Phenician blood is, according to Movers, a mistake, and this, with full recognition of their jealousy, exclusiveness, and frequent ill-treatment of their foreign allies and servants. A Phenician colony was a mercantile colony, established from a mercantile point of view; protected by numbers, however obtained, which were the first essential of an ancient state founded in a foreign country. These numbers were recruited from a floating population of mercenaries, adventurers, and starvelings, and were headed by a ruling caste of money-making priests and kings. Under these conditions the Greek settlers of Cyprus, as more numerous in colonies and population, became the dominant race. From this point of view, the Cypriote vases were Greek vases even when made by Phenicians, but they were the vases of Cypriote Greeks, that is to say, of a race saturated with Oriental beliefs, usages, and symbolism.

Whatever doubts may have hitherto existed as to the thoroughly Greek character of Cypriote art in the matter of production must be set at rest by the relations of Cypriote vases to those of Rhodian style in the matter of the bird and deer. Distinct as Cypriote art is from other Greek design, it is still less resemblant in exterior forms to the Egypto-Phenician style with which it was in contact. Its

6. Movers, *Geschichte der Phönizier*.

GEOMETRIC LOTUSES OF CYPRUS.

matter is borrowed, but its forms are independent, and they are, perhaps, the most curious in the history of art.

According to the Pottery Catalogue of the Metropolitan Museum of Art, the most important vases for our present purpose (xlvii. 11, l. 15, &c.), are from the neighbourhood of Ormidia, a Greek colony. Information as to *provenance* is otherwise lacking—a deficiency largely made good by the proofs of Dümmler, that, aside from the "Prehistoric," "Mycenæ," and "Dipylon" styles, the vases of Cyprus belong to one category without reference to time, locality, or race. A still farther exception must be made for the relatively rare cases of the later Greek pottery due to importation, and easily distinguished.

Whatever prior claim to the title of "Geometric," the so-called "Geometric" style of Greek vases ("Dipylon" vases) may assert (lvi. [p. 339]) that style shows a very mild geometry compared with that of Cyprus. The horses, birds, and deer, even of the oldest "Geometric" style, are occasionally fairly well designed, and they are not wilfully misrepresented. The word "geometric," as applied to these vases, relates to the ornament of meanders, chevrons, concentric rings, &c.

In the Cypriote vases the natural forms themselves are so constantly disguised by geometric methods, that it is highly doubtful whether there are any geometric forms which do not conceal a natural object, or portion of a natural object in some remote relation to a natural original. We have had some experience in recent pages of "Geometric" birds, of which the plates now in question furnish additional examples (xlvii.—l. inclusive).

Of geometric lotuses we also have example—xlvii. 2, 3, 4, 7. Of such examples an additional series is offered on Plate xlix.

We have already had occasion to observe the inversion of the lotus in early examples of Greek vases (Rhodian, xxxvii. 4 [p. 249]), an inverted lotus with the deer of the upper frieze; Rhodian, xlvi. 3 [p. 289]; Greek "Geometric," xlvi. 5 [p. 289]).

On Plate xlix. the lotuses are all inverted (No. 7 excepted, not Cypriote). This inversion is a Cypriote method, common to large numbers of vases, and is related to the narrowing of the vase form toward the neck. The inversion of the flower is an accommodation of the shape of the flower to the lines of the vase (1, 2).

The inverted lotuses pass into inverted triangles insensibly, and by gradations which are very numerous. These gradations are happily represented by a vase (1) which shows the geometric triangle and an obvious lotus, separated by an inverted bud (compare the buds xxi. 8, 10 [p. 159]). The triangle is further specified by associations with the solar ibex or gazelle (5) (compare xxxv.-xxxix. [pp. 245-253], and by associations with the solar bird (8) (xliii.-xlvi. [pp. 283-289]). Purely linear triangle lotuses are not unknown to Egyptian and Phenician art v. 4 [p. 65]; xxx. 9 [p. 211]; xxxii. 10 [p. 223]; xlii. 4 [p. 267]; lxvii. 1, 2, 10 [p. 401]).

In some cases the triangles exhibit a "boss" (xlix. 8, 10),[7] which serves as an additional determination. This boss carries us back to Plate xlvii., where it is seen to appear on a number of erect lotuses, and also on two additional cases of the inverted triangle (15, 16). The boss is a geometric treatment of the curling

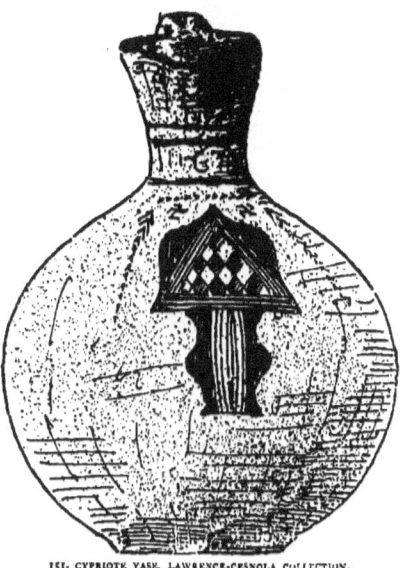

151. CYPRIOTE VASE, LAWRENCE-CESNOLA COLLECTION.
Showing an inverted lotus triangle with "bosses," supported by a panel band with "bosses."

sepals 1, 2, 3, 4, 6, 7, 11 (compare Fig. 4 from nature [p. 27]). No. 3 is an exact sketch, showing one sepal which attaches itself to the side of the flower at both extremities. No. 8 shows an approximate geometric form. If the sepals of No. 2 are filled in with black we obtain the outline of xlix. 10 for the boss.

The transfer of the boss to the upright panel bands of the vases is also a constant appearance. Sometimes the boss is found both on flowers and panel bands (xlvii. 14); sometimes on the panel bands alone, in cases where flowers appear (12); sometimes on the panel band alone (xlviii. 5) where no flowers appear.

---

7. The only mentions of this boss are by A. di Cesnola, *Salaminia*, p. 255, who speaks of "a peculiar tear-like thickening on the middle of a black line;" and by Max Ohnefalsch-Richter, who mentions the boss as borrowed from "Mycenæ" vases. It is, however, the latter which borrowed it.

GEOMETRIC LOTUSES OF CYPRUS.

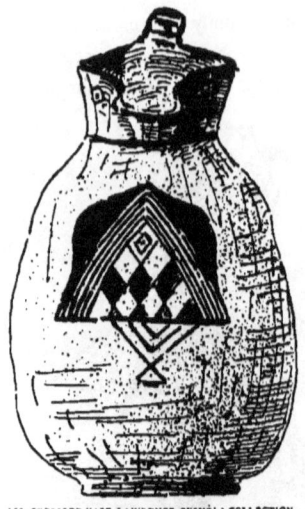

152. CYPRIOTE VASE, LAWRENCE-CESNOLA COLLECTION.
Showing an inverted lotus triangle with "bosses."

In xlviii. 5 the lotus buds are an assistance. They serve to refer the motive to a flower, like xlviii. 1, where the buds also appear. The lower panel of xlviii. 3 illustrates a class of vases where two buds remain on the panel band. These carry us to 15, where the buds have a conventional treatment related to that of No. 11. In No. 17 we find a decisive case for the buds in both aspects from one vase (compare xxxvii. 10 [p. 249]). Hence an explanation of the curious diagram No. 8, which consists of several of these buds supported by an inverted lotus triangle.

The designation of these unique lotuses is assisted by the solar birds (6, 8, 12). No. 8 has been published by Murray in Cesnola's "Cyprus." No. 6 has been published by Perrot. Fig. 153 shows the panel band with bosses, "geometric" buds attached to the bosses, and three buds at the base of the band.

Another curious diagram attests the symbolism of the boss. No. 9 shows concentric rings (or a solar disk) with four projecting buds, which support a panel band with bosses. The entire vase is figured at lvii. 3 [p 341]. The solar diagram supported by an inverted lotus triangle on a staff is shown at xlix. 11 [p. 307] (compare Figs. 151, 152). Assyriologists are familiar with a similar design on cylinders.[8]

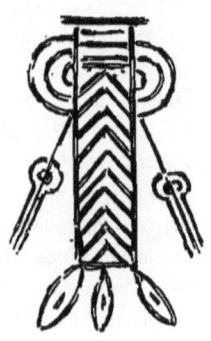

153. DETAIL OF A CYPRIOTE VASE, NEW YORK.
Panel band with bosses and pendant geometric buds. Three geometric buds at the base of the band.

The reaction of the boss to lotuses which continue to show the curling sepals is another point to be noticed (xv. 7, 13 [p. 139]). The pendant tendrils of these later examples prove that a lotus may also be represented by a pendant line; for

---

[8] LAJARD, Culte de Mithra, x. 12; xl. 5; where the moon crescent takes the place of the sun. LAJARD, xxx. 3; xliv. 2; where the winged disk takes the place of the solar diagram. Compare Phenician seal, lxvii. 3 [p. 401], of this Work.

they are explained as rudimentary survival of the small pendant flowers at xlvii. 1. This example also shows the boss as reacting on a flower with curling sepals.

The most curious case of transfer, parallel to that which carried the geometric sepal boss to the panel bands of Cypriote vases, is found in the prehistoric Celtic bronzes of Hallstatt which occasionally exhibit a highly conventional form of "the bird" with a horse's mane. I have found among the original colour designs from Hallstatt in the Museum of St. Germain a bronze on which both horses with the mane and birds with the mane are represented, thus demonstrating the source of transfer (Figs. 180, 181 [pp. 362, 363]). It is within the range of possibility that the panel band itself is an outcome of triangles like xlvii. 16. Compare xlix. 3 and l. 15.

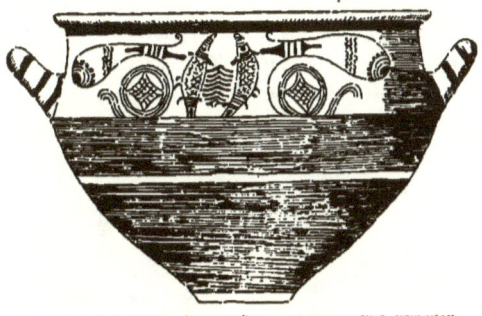

154. VASE FROM CYPRUS. "MYCENÆ" OR ARCHIPELAGO STYLE, NEW YORK. Showing an outline ornament derived from the elongated Cypriote boss. Compare Fig. 156.

The Cypriote boss made its way into the "Mycenæ" pottery and explains motives which have hitherto been interpreted as "mussels," "bent sticks,"[9] &c. (liii. 1, 2, 3, 4, 5, 7, 8 [p. 323]). It also occurs in curious shapes on vases of the Archipelago (liii. 3 [p. 323] and Fig. 154). Fig. 155 shows an elongated Cypriote boss, and Fig. 156 illustrates the development of the boss to the pattern of liii. 3, liii. 4 [p. 323], and Fig. 154.

The elongated boss first occurs in Cyprus, and it occurs there in relation to the narrow limits of

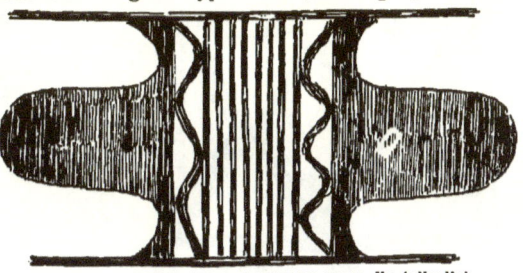

155. CYPRIOTE POTTERY MOTIVE OF ELONGATED BOSSES. Vase in New York.

---

9. FURTWÄNGLER AND LOESCHKE, *Mykenische Vasen*. See my reference at p. 49, Notes 24, 25.

certain panel borders (xlvii. 15, 16). The Cypriote inverted lotus triangle is also found in "Mycenæ" pottery (liii. 9, 10, 11, 12, 13 [p. 323]). The examples

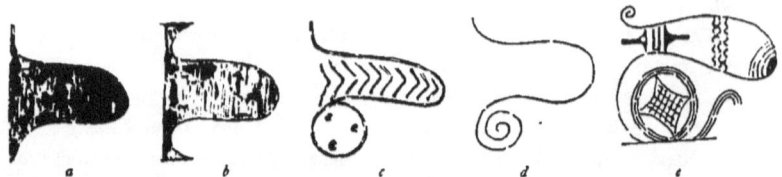

1·6. EVOLUTION OF THE CYPRIOTE "BOSS" IN VASES OF THE ARCHIPELAGO AND "MYCENÆ" STYLE
(*a*, *b*, from Cypriote vases; *c*, *d*, from "Mycenæ" vases (Plate liii.); *e*, from Archipelago "Mycenæ" vase at Fig. 154.)

9, 10 are "Mycenæ" pieces of a transition type, from Cyprus in the New York Museum

It is probable that the transfers of motives from Cypriote pottery to the "Mycenæ" vases were originally made in Cyprus. The population of the "Mycenæ" culture (supposed to be Carian) had settlements in Cyprus, as proven by "masses of fragments"[10] of their peculiar pottery-ware. Settlements of the Carians in Cyprus have been independently demonstrated by Movers long before the Carian hypothesis of "Mycenæ" culture had been originated.

Aside from several important vases of the "Mycenæ" type from Cyprus already published, there are quite a number in the New York Collection. On the other hand, Cypriote vases

157. TYPICAL NECKING ORNAMENT OF CYPRIOTE AMPHORAS.
Origin explained by the diagram, Fig. 159.

158. CYPRIOTE VASE, NEW YORK.
Showing the typical neck border of Cypriote amphoras.

10. FURTWÄNGLER and LOESCHKE, *Mykenische Vasen*, p. 26, text.

GEOMETRIC LOTUSES OF CYPRUS.

have only been found in Egypt outside Cyprus (a few have been recently found in Syria by Mr. Petrie). The transfers of Cypriote motives to the "Mycenæ" style do not imply a Cypriote origin for this style, which is undoubtedly distinct.

We have still to consider in Cypriote geometric lotuses the phenomenon of the lotus quadrangle (Plate 1.).

My study of the quadrangle was made necessary by the existence of a neck border pattern which is entirely confined to Cypriote vases and which, among these vases, is entirely confined to amphoras. Fig. 157 shows a specimen detail. Fig. 158 shows a typical amphora with the neck border. On Plate 1. there is an additional example of this amphora type with the peculiar neck border (No. 15). There are also three more details of the heck ornaments from similar vases (Nos. 7, 13, 14). I was perplexed for some time by these cases of the boss within a lotus triangle, as it belongs logically to the exterior sides (Figs. 151, 152). The explanation is as shown by the diagram Fig. 159. On Plate 1. we have several examples of a quadrangle composed of four lotus triangles, as specified by the boss (Nos. 1, 5, 8, 9, 10, 11). The interior boss is explained here also by considering that if four triangles with exterior bosses are combined, there will result four triangles, having both exterior and interior bosses.

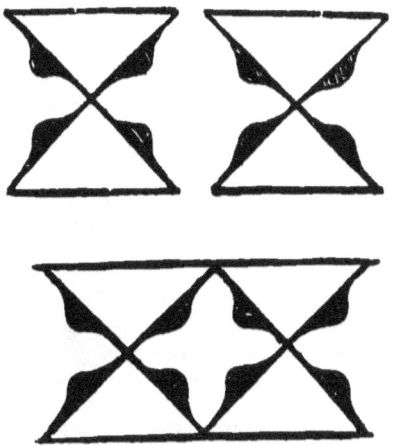

159 DIAGRAM SHOWING THE ORIGIN OF THE NECKING ORNAMENT. Fig. 157

PLATE XLVII.

GEOMETRIC LOTUSES OF CYPRUS.
THE CURLING SEPAL AND THE GEOMETRIC DERIVATIVE BOSS.

1. Detail from neck of the vase l. 15. The small pendant lotuses explain the pendant filaments of xv. 7, 13 [p. 139]. The volutes represent curling sepals. Compare Fig. 4 [p. 27] from nature.
2. From a large amphora. Geometric lotus with variants of the curling sepal, Swastikas and crosses (Swastika variants).
3. From the same vase. Geometric lotus with variants of the curling sepals, carefully sketched. On one side is a knob or "boss," on the other side the sepal is distinct.
4. From another large amphora. Geometric lotus with variants of the curling sepals.
5. Lotus with geometric bosses derived from the curling sepals; from another vase.
6. Variants of the curling sepals with concentric rings.
7. Variants of the curling sepals. From the same vase as Nos. 2 and 3.
8. An early stage of the geometric bosses, derived from curling sepals. Compare right sepal of No. 3.
9, 10. Lotuses from distinct vases, showing the geometric boss derived from curling sepals.
11. Large amphora, with lotuses (curling sepals) and concentric rings. (From this vase is the detail xvi. 3 [p. 144]). Published in colour by LENORMANT in *Gazette Archéologique*, 1883, p. 97—"Vases d'Ormidhia." The details of these colour illustrations are grotesquely distorted (designs forwarded from New York), and absolutely unreliable. Lenormant did not recognize the flowers, which he mentions simply as "fleurons d'un style tout Asiatique."
12. Border from another vase, showing the boss derived from curling sepals AS TRANSFERRED TO THE BANDS OF THE PANEL. Lotuses with pendant sepals roughly represented.
13. Sacred lotus tree of the vase xlv. 1 [p. 287], showing the geometric boss. Conventional association of flowers and buds. In nature each bud grows on a separate stem from the root of the plant.
14. Border from another vase with bosses derived from curling sepals, on the flowers, AND ALSO AS TRANSFERRED TO THE BANDS OF THE PANELS; buds in the corners of the outside panels; geometric bird.
15. Inverted geometric lotus with bosses elongated to suit the narrowness of the panel. From another vase. Such exaggerated bosses are found in the narrow upright panels of the vases like xlv. 4 [p. 287], which does not, however, happen to exhibit them.
16. Inverted geometric lotus with bosses. From the vase l. 15.
17. Panel band with elongated bosses derived from curling sepals. Elongation as explained at No. 15.

All the above details are from vases in the New York Museum.
The boss on "Mycenæ" vases has not been previously recognized as a Cypriote pattern. It is shown by liii. 2, 3, 4, 5, 7, 8 [p. 323].
MAX OHNEFALSCH-RICHTER has erroneously supposed the Cypriote boss to be derived from the "Mycenæ" pattern.

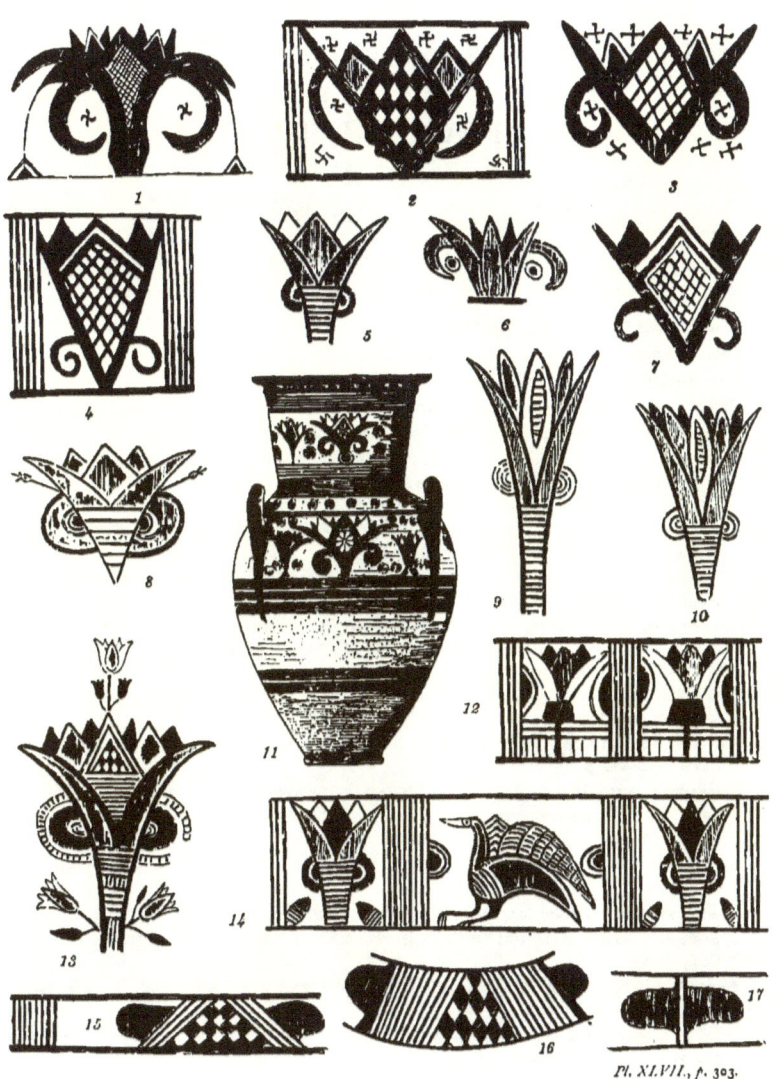

Pl. XLVII, p. 303.

PLATE XLVIII.

GEOMETRIC LOTUSES OF CYPRUS.

THE GEOMETRIC BOSS AND GEOMETRIC BUD

THE details of this Plate are selected to show that Nos. 8, 9, and 12 are lotus symbols.

1. Lotus with geometric bosses and four attached buds.
2. Vase showing solar bird (swan) and lotus anthemions. Detail at xlv. 12 [p. 287].
3. Vase showing an upright panel band with lotus bosses and two buds.
4. Vase with solar bird bearing a lotus on its neck. Detail at xlv. 8 [p. 287].
5. Detail, with four buds, similar to that of No. 3. From A. DI CESNOLA, *Cyprus Antiquities*, a volume of photographs of the "Lawrence-Cesnola Collection," for some time in or near London and now dispersed; some of the vases are in Munich.
6. Cypriote vase, New York Museum, whose detail is shown at No. 12. PERROT et CHIPIEZ, *Cypre*, p. 702.
7. Cypriote vase with solar birds, lotus Ionic form with projecting details like those of the right lotus of No. 17 (buds). A. DI CESNOLA, *Salaminia*, xix.
8. Solar birds (swans) confronting a symbol composed of objects like the projecting details of the right lotus of No. 17; said objects resting on an inverted triangle; two solar diagrams. CESNOLA, *Cyprus*, xlv. 35. Demonstration follows through Nos. 11 and 17.
9. Detail of the vase lvii. 3 [p. 341]. Concentric rings supporting a panel band with geometric bosses; four lotus buds projecting.
10. Vase with solar bird supporting the winged sun disk and confronting a lotus. Detail at xlv. 13 [p. 287]. CESNOLA, *Cyprus*, p. 405.
11. Lotus with geometric bosses and conventional buds projecting from them.
12. Detail of No. 6. Solar birds confronting a lotus symbol consisting of a panel band with geometric bosses. CESNOLA, *Cyprus*, xliv. 34. Compare xlvii. 12, 14.
13. Cypriote vase with solar bird, inverted lotus, and unrecognized object. A. DI CESNOLA, *Salaminia*, xix. 30.
14. Cypriote vase with solar bird confronting lotus; Maltese cross. A. DI CESNOLA, *Salaminia*, p. 257.
15. Cypriote vase, showing the upright band with geometric bosses and two geometric lotus buds attached. Compare No. 17.
16. Border showing upright panel band with lotus bosses spread to full extent of the band. Exterior bosses, each with two lotus buds.
17. Detail of the vase xxxvii. 10 [p. 249]. Ibex and lotuses, one lotus with bosses and buds, one with bosses and buds like those of Nos. 7, 8, 15.

All the above details are from vases in the New York Museum, when not otherwise specified.

Pl. XLVIII., p. 305.

PLATE XLIX.

GEOMETRIC LOTUSES OF CYPRUS.

THE LOTUS TRIANGLE.

ALL below-mentioned vases and details represent vases in the New York Museum, excepting No. 7, detail of a vase in the Louvre from Rhodes, and No. 5, Cypriote vase in the Boston Museum. The inversion of the lotus on these vases is very common in Cypriote pottery, and results from the wish to have the ornamental lines converge towards the neck of the vase and narrow with it.

1. Vase showing a normal lotus inverted, a lotus bud, and a lotus triangle inverted.

2. Vase showing a normal lotus inverted.

3. Vase showing a lotus triangle inverted and concentric rings.

4. Vase showing two lotus triangles inverted, and a neck border explaining the position of corresponding patterns 13 and 14 on the next Plate. This neck border is typical for a very large class of Cypriote vases. It shows triangles with interior bosses, as explained by text [p. 301] and diagrams (Fig. 159).

5. Ibex or gazelle, having three lotus buds (on stems with tabs) hanging from his mouth, and a lotus triangle inverted, on his back. Compare Plates and text for the "Deer, Gazelle, Ibex, and Lotus" [pp. 229-254] For the lotus stems with buds hanging from the mouth, compare xxxix. 4, 6, 7 [p. 253]. Cypriote vase in the Boston Museum.

6. Vase with neck border of spirals and a border of inverted lotuses tending towards the conventional triangle.

7. The "bird and the lotus." Detail illustrating the chevrons on Greek "Geometric" vases. Compare xlvi. 5 [p. 289] and lviii. 3 [p. 343]. From a vase in the Louvre. *Gazette Archéologique*, 1888, xxv.

8. Inverted lotus triangle, supporting the panel band with bosses; solar geometric birds. Compare Plates and text for the "Bird and the Lotus" [pp. 269-289]. A similar vase was in the Lawrence-Cesnola Collection. See photograph publication, *Cyprus Antiquities*, A. DI CESNOLA.

9. Inverted geometric lotus triangle with bosses.

10. Inverted geometric lotus triangle with bosses and two normal flowers.

11. Vase showing an inverted geometric lotus triangle supporting the solar diagram.

Pl. XLIX., p. 307.

PLATE L.

GEOMETRIC LOTUSES OF CYPRUS.

THE LOTUS QUADRANGLE.

ALL vases and details belong to the New York Museum, excepting No. 6.

1. Vase showing the lotus quadrangle as composed of four lotus triangles with bosses. Compare No. 2. Four triangular sections result, each with interior bosses. CESNOLA, *Cyprus*, p. 101.
2. To assist above explanations.
3. Detail of a Greek "Geometric" vase. Compare the similar motive in the panels of No. 6, and the similar pattern in lvi. 2 [p. 339]. The motive No. 3 belongs to the regular patterns of the Greek "Geometric" style, and is derived from the Cypriote lotus quadrangle. The same motive on "Mycenæ" vases is borrowed from the Cypriote liii. 1 [p. 323]. The vase from which this detail is taken is a regular "Dipylon" vase from Cyprus, in the New York Museum.
4. Vase (CESNOLA, *Cyprus*, p. 404) showing an abbreviated form of the lotus quadrangle, simplified from the pattern of No. 1, by way of 8, 10, 5, and 9. This motive is found on Melian vases. See lx. 8 [p. 359]. On the Mycenæ vase liii. 6 [p. 323] is a variant derived from liii. 1, which recurs to the Cypriote lotus quadrangle proper.
5. Variant of No. 1, by way of 10 and 9.
6. Detail of a Greek "Geometric" vase in Copenhagen. *Archæologische Zeitung*, 1888, viii. Showing solar birds, sun diagrams, the solar deer (a doe), and geometric quadrangle pattern derived from the Cypriote.
7. Variant of 13, 14. Compare 15 for the position of such a motive, which is confined to the necks of amphoras.
8. Variant of No. 1.
9. Detail of No. 12.
10. Variant of No. 1, showing the boss in its originally more restricted expansion. Compare No. 2.
11. Variant of No. 5.
12. Illustration for the bird and the lotus quadrangle.
13, 14. Variants of the neck border of 15.
15. Vase showing the habitual combination of normal lotuses (as at the sides of the neck and in the border below), with the highly conventional derivatives.

Pl. L., p. 309.

LOTUS MOTIVES OF THE "MYCENÆ CULTURE."

(PLATES LI., LII., LIII., LIV., LV., PAGES 319, 321, 323, 325, 327.)

THE indications of Egyptian influence in the art work of Orchomenos, Mycenæ, and Tiryns have been abundantly recognized by students. To these indications we may add the Bull fresco of the IVth Dynasty (li. 8), as related to the Bull fresco of Tiryns (li. 1) and the various lotus derivatives pointed out by the following analysis of Mycenæ pottery ornament (pp. 320-326). The supposition that the history of Greek naturalistic art begins with the pottery of the Mycenæ style[1] is probably reversed by this analysis. The Mycenæ art is positively distinct from the Greek, and also had very slight, if any, influence upon it.

It is rather doubtful if there is any realistic art in the Mycenæ culture. The Mycenæ squid, which might be considered an example of such art, is not included in the illustrations, and is the only important motive not considered. There is nothing to antagonize the suggestion of a Squid fetich as long as the scorpion, frog, crocodile, and fish were admitted to the ancient Pantheon. Whoever has seen the preparation of this dainty on the strand of Syra, or knows its importance as an article of food in the Levant, will scarcely deny that familiar contact with this marine animal may have raised it to the dignity of symbolism, or that its picture may have been the ideograph of a god. There is no doubt that the original Hydra was a devil-fish, for the relief of Hercules and the Hydra in the Vatican Etruscan Museum accurately represents the squid.

At least two interesting examples of Mycenæ vases with the squid have been found in Egypt,[2] and this animal appears in the reliefs of Dehr-el-Bahri,

---

1. CURTIUS, *Satzungsberichte, Jahrbuch*, II., 1889. "Ein Volk das die Wellen, welche seine Bespülten, die Fische, Muscheln, Schnecken, Polypen, Pflanzen, seines heimatlichen Meeres auf den Thon malte." The cuttle-fish and rare cases of the snail must be conceded, but instances of naturalistic art of "Mycenæ" style which have not a symbolic derivation are rare, if they appear at all.

2. One in the Abbott Collection, New York Historical Society, published by Professor A. S. MURRAY, *American Journal of Archæology*, 1891 [this designation of "Nautilus" appears to me doubtful]; another in the British Museum. That others have been found in Egypt is implied by a passage in PETRIE's *Kahun, Gurob, and Hawara*, 1890 (see p. 162, Note 1, of this Work).

but it is undoubtedly a distinctive motive of the Archipelago in the days of Carian greatness.

An originally direct contact of Carian or Mycenæ civilization with Egypt is not to be argued absolutely from the directly Egyptian examples of the lotus spiral on the tomb ceilings of Orchomenos and Tiryns (Fig. 56 [p. 95], and li. 9), or even from the curious relation of the Bull fresco of Tiryns (li. 1) to a tomb-painting of the IVth Dynasty (li. 8). The people who made the Mycenæ pottery appear, however, to have had settlements in Egypt as early as the XIIth Dynasty, and Movers' matter for the Carians in Egypt would indicate the same fact. It is easy to imagine the importation of Egyptian artists by great princes for the decoration of their tombs, or the employment of artists of specially Egyptian education from among the Mycenæ population of Egypt in such a case. The Mycenæ inlaid swords are not less likely to be of foreign Egyptian manufacture.[3]

The character of the Mycenæ or Carian culture is better argued from its pottery, as scattered throughout the Levant, and especially as found in Egypt, than from these more palpable cases of Egyptian art. The pieces found in Egypt, which are in Leyden,[4] in the Louvre, in the British Museum, in Florence, in the Abbott Collection of New York, above all those found by Mr. Petrie,[5] are no more directly Egyptian in quality than those found exterior to the country. This fact probably argues against a direct diffusion of the style from the foreign population in Egypt, in which case the Mycenæ motives of Egypt would have the more perceptibly Egyptian quality. As my analysis of the vases shows, all those which are illustrated have lotus patterns, but they are more remote from direct Egyptian resemblance than even those of Cyprus. Many of those not borrowed from Cypriote motives, like the boss, the quadrangle, the inverted triangle (liii.) and the "ivy leaf" which was probably obtained there [p. 162], are based on the imitation of motives in metal (liv. 13, 17, &c.). If these metals had been first copied in Egypt we should find other lotuses of the ordinary Egyptian character copied from designs in other materials.

3. The sword of Aahmes in the Gizeh Museum (XVIIIth Dynasty) is a similar work, as observed by SCHUCHARDT, *Schliemann's Ausgrabungen im Lichte der heutigen Wissenschaft* (p. 357).

4. LEEMANS, *Monumens Égyptiens du Musée d'Antiquités des Pays-Bas a Leide*.

5. Especially valued because dated. *Gurob, Kahun and Hawara*, Plate xxviii., text, p. 42; a piece with motive of liv. 17, dated to the XIXth Dynasty. The running Mycenæ leaf motive (type of lii. 9, and vase shape of xxii. 1, 3 [p. 165]) is dated to the XIXth or early XXth Dynasty by finds of 1890. PETRIE, *Catalogue*, &c., 1890, p. 8.

LOTUS MOTIVES OF THE "MYCENÆ CULTURE."

Other motives are barbaric lotuses (liv. 1) originally founded on pottery examples foreign to Egypt, like Fig. 49 [p. 76] from Cyprus.

The leaves (so-called "ivy leaves" in cases like xxii. 1, 3 [p. 165]) are also frequently remote derivatives (lii. 1, 2, 3, 5, 7).

All these facts show what the vases show themselves by locality of find, when taken in mass—that the Mycenæ pottery style is the style of the Greek Archipelago in the days of Carian ascendancy,[6] for which reason we shall adopt the word "Carian" without further apology, as already suggested by students of much greater learning. The presence of Carians in Egypt and Syria (p. 295, Note 6), of Carian settlers in Cyprus. (p. 300, Note 10), and of Carians in alliance with Phenicians, wherever Phenicians were found,[7] as their carriers, sailors, and mercenaries, would explain the peculiar character of their art, especially considering a certain barbaric character (allied to that of the Celtic prehistoric art of Hallstatt,[8] &c., to the Frank Merovingian adaptation of Roman forms, or the "Scythian" adaptations of Greek) as explaining many cases of direct mistranslation of the foreign Egyptian and Phenician motives.

160. RHODIAN VASE.
Showing lotuses with pendant sepals.

As to the question whether the Carians knew their ornaments to be lotus motives, my impression would be decidedly to the contrary; and in this sense their art must be sharply distinguished from the Cypriote Greek, from which they made several loans. In the wildest eccentricities of the Cypriote geometric lotuses there is a logical connection of development and a continued companionship of the solar deer and bird, which shows that the sense of

---

6. That the Carians of the Greek Archipelago are the people of the "Mycenæ culture" was suggested by KÖHLER in 1875. The view has found wide acceptance. The recent work of SCHUCHARDT accepts it, with proviso that the "Mycenæ" culture was that of the early population of the Archipelago in general. As the Carians were the dominant race of the Archipelago in prehistoric times, this comes to the same thing.

7. MOVERS, Geschichte der Phönizier.

8. The most significant fact in the whole matter of Schliemann's Greek excavations is the attribution of his finds to deposits of Northern barbarians of the third century A.D. This attribution by the great St. Petersburg archæologist, Stephani, has found following down to recent date in the case of Penrose and Stillman. The fact is that the style of the prehistoric North lasted down to the third century A.D. and far beyond that date, and that this style had its origin in the beginnings of the "bronze culture," which came from the South, under conditions which the "Mycenæ" culture has first revealed to us.

symbolism was continuous, and the presence of normal lotuses on the vases with highly geometric forms (l. 15 [p. 309]) proves the same thing.

It is another question whether these Carian motives had a symbolic meaning and traditional relation to sun-worship. On this point I decline to express an opinion. The Carian art was probably Celtic, and lotus symbolism can be proven for the Celtic art of Italy, because the solar animals with lotuses pendant from the mouth are original with them.

The Carian art shows the quality of an adventurous, warlike, and semi-barbarian race, employed in the military service of very highly refined and civilized peoples. The Varangians of Constantinople are the closest comparison, although of so much later date. The Batavian cavalry of Cæsar or the Visigoths in Roman pay are also parallels. That the Carians were thus employed by Phenicians and Egyptians we know well. They are quoted as the first people of the Mediterranean who followed the trade of the mercenary soldier. It would be advisable to test the undeciphered Carian inscriptions of later times, as being probably in a Celtic language. Although Maspero has mentioned the Carians as "Cushites," the "Mycenæ" art has not one indication of such a quality.

161. Detail of Fig. 160.

162. CYPRIOTE LOTUS. Pendant sepals. New York.

There is only one motive common to Mycenæ vases and Greek pottery, the wave line of lotus stems and leaves (lii. 9; xxii. 1, 3 [p. 165]). Even this one correspondence of motive does not argue any close relation between early Greek culture and the Carian, for the wave line leaf motive does not occur on Greek vases before the fifth century B.C. apparently. The presumption is therefore that both Greeks and Carians borrowed it from a common source, but at different times.[9]

It has not yet been observed that one problem of the wave line "ivy" pattern of Carian art centres in the Museum of Bologna (Figs. 103 [p. 161], 104 [p. 163], 128 [p. 206], 129 [p. 214], and Plate li. 7). It is only here that

---

9. This common source was possibly Cyprus, where both Greeks and Carians (p. 300, Note 10) were settled in large numbers. The motive appears on Mycenæ vases found in Cyprus (New York Museum), and although it is unknown to Cypriote pottery, it is distinctly known to Cypriote art; for instance, on the large stone vase "found at the entrance to the temple of Golgoi," CESNOLA, *Cyprus*, p. 145, and on a terra-cotta coffin, CESNOLA, *Cyprus*, p. 190. The lotus leaf is common on Syrian sarcophagi; RENAN, *Mission de Phénicie*.

we find it on stone reliefs and in some reliefs which are clearly of late date (fourth or third century B.C.). The presence in Italy of a Celtic and also of a "Carian" population must be conceded. If this population was one and the same, the problem of the "ivy leaf" at Bologna is solved.

There is only one other decorative running motive in Carian pottery, the spiral scroll (lii. 6, 9). This is a direct loan from the Egyptian spiral scroll (x. [p. 97]). I am well aware that the Mycenæ spiral scroll is supposed at present to be a pattern derived from the handiwork of the jeweller, and from the coiling-up of a strand of jeweller's wire. There are certainly many works of Mycenæ jewellery where the pattern is obviously produced by the coiling-up of gold wire. When the point is once proven that the entire Mycenæ art is borrowed, which has not yet been sufficiently appreciated, the question is thrown back to the Egyptian originals, and it becomes necessary to prove that the Egyptian spiral was derived from the coiling of jeweller's wire. This proof will be found difficult, because Egyptian jewellery shows throughout a dependence on other Egyptian ornament rather than an influence on it.

Contrary to possible presumptions the continuous spiral scroll (the "Mycenæ spiral") is not a typical pattern in Greek pottery or in Greek art, which prefers the related guilloche (neck of xxxviii. [p. 251]) and borrowed that from another source. The Greek guilloche first appears on Cypriote and Rhodian pottery. On the other hand, the Egyptian meander (x. [p. 97]) is not familiar in Mycenæ art, and is the dominant motive of early Greek Geometric pottery (Dipylon style, lvi. [p. 339]). These points of divergence relate to the fact that Mycenæ pottery and Greek Geometric pottery are not found in the same tombs,[10] although they are found in the same localities throughout the Levant. No Greek Geometric pottery (Dipylon style) has yet been found in Egypt.

The relations between Carians and Greeks in early times would thus appear to have been either those of hostility or of successive and non-contemporaneous presence in the same localities. That Carians from Caria and Ionic Greeks were both employed as Egyptian mercenaries in the seventh century B.C. has nothing to do with this point, as the Carians had then long since disappeared from the Greek Archipelago. As confined to Caria in historic times the Carians have nothing to do with the Mycenæ period.

10. *Jahrbuch*, 1886, p. 134.

316   LOTUS MOTIVES OF THE "MYCENÆ CULTURE."

The hieroglyphs of the bull fresco (li. 8) as found in Lepsius' *Denkmäler*, have been submitted to competent authority, but there appears to have been an incorrectness of transcription in the publication of Lepsius, which makes them illegible. The interpretation of the bull fresco of Tiryns as a Greek River-god[11] is probably supplanted by this reference. There does not appear to be any Greek art or any Greek quality in the art of the Mycenæ culture.

163. BYZANTINE OR SARACENIC MOTIVE.
Algeria. From Ravoisié.

Figs. 160 and 161 show a Rhodian vase and an enlarged detail, as instances of the pendant lotus sepals—to explain the Mycenæ motives, liv. 1, 2, 3, 4, 15, 24. Fig. 162 is a parallel detail from a Cypriote vase in New York. The Rhodian motive has been mistaken by Professor Furtwängler for an "obvious palm-tree."[12]

Fig. 163 shows an Algerian, Byzantine, or Saracenic survival of a motive as old as the Mycenæ period (lii. 9; lv. 3, 6).

The Gryphon is found in Mycenæ art.[13] The "deer and the lotus" are familiar to it (xxxvii. 11, 12 [p. 249]). The lion pursuing a deer is also found with the lotus,[14] and is a variant or misinterpretation of the lion devouring a deer (p. 256). Instances of the bird and the lotus can be cited (lv. 18). We have seen that the bird without lotus association must also be considered solar (p. 279). The Mycenæ bird (lii. 4) shows very little of the goose, but resembles in this point many of the Italian Celtic art (lvii. 8 [p. 341])

11. MARX. *Jahrbuch*, 1889, II. "Der Stier von Tiryns"—"altursprünglich, allgemein Griechisch."

12. *Jahrbuch*, 1886, p. 135. "Offenbar das Bild des Palmenbaums. . . . Ich kenne nur noch ein Gefäss mit demselben Ornament, aus Kameirus im Louvre. . . . Interressant dieses bedeutsame vegetabilisches Motive in der sonst geometrischen Decoration zu finden." Various utterances of German archæologists like the last sentence indicate a belief in a geometric pottery style antedating any forms of ornament taken from life. There is no evidence that the geometric vases with birds, deer, and horses are not as old as any. The detail 161 is enlarged from the illustration in the *Jahrbuch*, and the central spike may be more definite in the original. The recently discovered gold vases of Vaphio, in the Polytechnic at Athens, certainly give colour to the thought that liv. 1., &c., are palms. The only way out of the difficulty is to suppose that the artist mistook the form for a tree, and copied it as such. This would be thoroughly consonant with the general character of Mycenæ and of Celtic art—witness the case of the bird with horse's mane (Figs. 180, 181, pp. 362, 363).

13. Gold ornaments; SCHLIEMANN'S *Mycenæ*.
14. Ibid.

which are originally geese. The reduction of this prehistoric bird to a pot-hook (lvi. 10, 13 [p. 339]) shows that close resemblance to the original goose is not to be always expected.

The Swastika is known to Mycenæ art, but does not appear frequently.

164. "MYCENÆ" GOLD AMULET.
Cats (?) (Goddess Bast) on the lotus.

Concentric rings with and without tangents, and chevrons (lii. 8), are a current decoration. In these ornaments the style unites with those to be considered in the next two chapters, and the matter there presented must be considered as including these Mycenæ patterns.

165. "MYCENÆ" LEAF MOTIVE IN WOOD CARVING. Lake-Dwellers of Scotland.
From Robert Munro. To be compared with lii. 1, 2.

PLATE LI.

MYCENÆ LOTUS DERIVATIVES, AND CORROBORATIVE MONUMENTS.

TOMBSTONES AND FRESCOES.

1. The Bull fresco of Tiryns. SCHLIEMANN, *Tiryns*, xxiii.

2. Terra-cotta whorl with spiral scrolls. SCHLIEMANN, *Troy*, xxxi.

3. Terra-cotta whorl with triangles. SCHLIEMANN, *Troy*, xliii. Compare lxvii. [p. 399].

4. Spiral scroll, wood carving. SCHLIEMANN, *Mycenæ*, p. 150.

5. Early Italian tombstone. ZANNONI, *Scavi nella Certosa di Bologna*, lxix. 34.

6. Tombstone, "Third Grave," SCHLIEMANN, *Mycenæ*, Fig. 145.

7. Early Italian tombstone. Relief figure holding stems of lotus leaves. ZANNONI, *Scavi*, lxix. 35.

8. Egyptian painting, IVth Dynasty; from a tomb near the Pyramids. *Description de l'Égypte*, A. v. 13; also in LEPSIUS, *Denkmäler*, Ab. II., Bl. 14 b.

9. Lotuses in spiral scrolls. Compare Fig. 56 [p. 95] for the Orchomenos ceiling pattern. SCHLIEMANN, *Tiryns*, v.

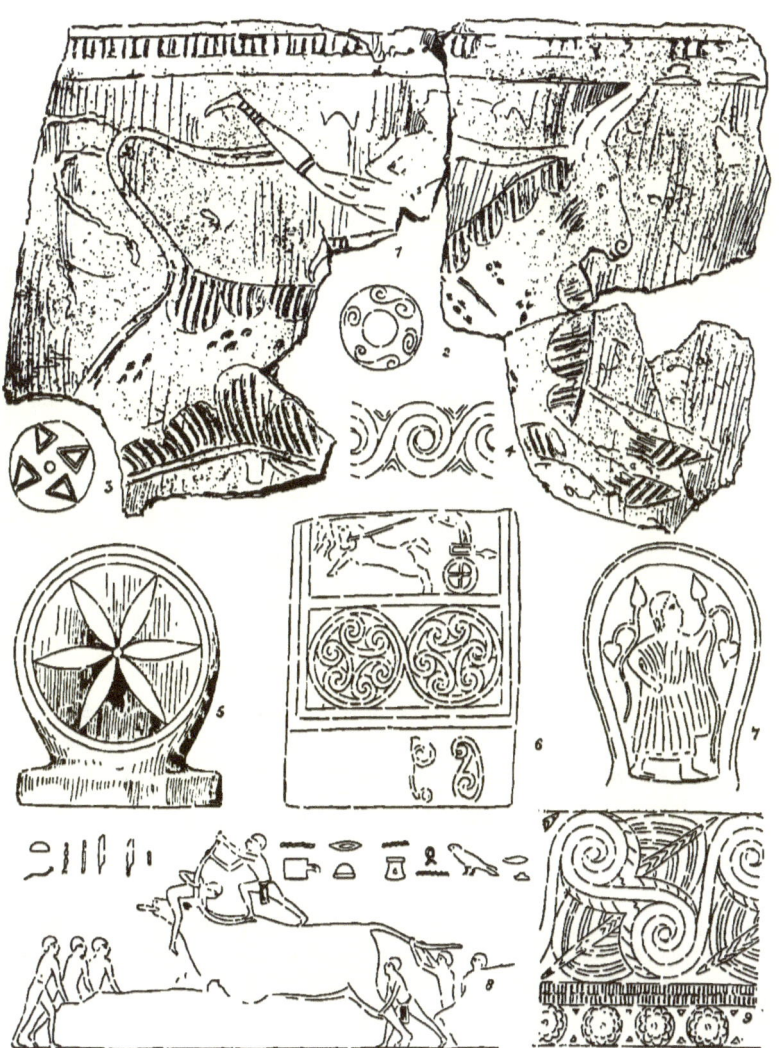

Pl. LI., p. 319.

PLATE LII.

MYCENÆ POTTERY MOTIVES.

1, 2. Pottery motives based on the lotus leaf (Plate xxii. 1, 3 [p. 165]). FURTWÄNGLER and LOESCHKE, *Mykenische Vasen*, 189 c, b (No. 2). SCHLIEMANN, *Mycenæ*, p. 55. Compare Fig. 165 [p. 317].

Considering the presence of a "Mycenæ" population in Cyprus [p. 300, Note 10] and the number of patterns obviously borrowed from Cypriote, it is probable that the "ivy" pattern was also borrowed there or in Syria, as it is attested for both these countries [p. 162].

3. Lotus leaf derivative, Ialysus. FURTWÄNGLER and LOESCHKE, *Mykenische Vasen*, I. 1.

4. Vase from the "Sixth Tomb," Mycenæ. SCHUCHARDT, *Schliemann's Ausgrabungen im Lichte der heutigen Wissenschaft*, Fig. 278.

5. Vase from the "First Tomb," Mycenæ. Lotus leaf motive. SCHUCHARDT, Fig. 261.

6. Vase from the "First Tomb," Mycenæ. Spiral scrolls in "Herzblatt" combination. Compare x. 1 [p. 96]. SCHUCHARDT, Fig. 166.

7. Vase from the "First Tomb," Mycenæ. Lotus leaf derivatives. SCHUCHARDT, Fig. 263.

8. Vase from the "Second Tomb,' Mycenæ. Chevrons. SCHUCHARDT, Fig. 209.

9. Vase from the "Sixth Tomb," Mycenæ. Lotus leaves, spiral scroll, and motive related to iv. 1, 2, 3. SCHUCHARDT, Fig. 277.

10. Bulls and the lotus; for patterns on the right, compare liv. 23, &c. Mistaken by FURTWÄNGLER and LOESCHKE for "Ochsen auf der Weide" (oxen in the pasture). Compare Plate xxvi. [p. 193] and text. FURTWÄNGLER and LOESCHKE, *Mykenische Vasen*, xli.

Pl. LII., p. 321.

PLATE LIII.

MYCENÆ POTTERY MOTIVES.

IT is understood that the word "Mycenæ," as applied to pottery, indicates a style, not a locality. Fragments from Mycenæ are generally mentioned specifically. All illustrations, not otherwise mentioned, are from FURTWANGLER and LOESCHKE, *Mykenische Vasen*.

1. Lotus quadrangle and boss, Mycenæ. Cypriote derivative. Compare Plate l. [p. 309]. FURTWANGLER and LOESCHKE, xxxiii. 321.

2. Cypriote derivative, from Mycenæ. Compare Plate xlviii. [p. 305]. FURTWANGLER and LOESCHKE, xxxiii. 327.

3. From the Archipelago (British Museum). Cypriote elongated boss. Compare Plate xlvii. [p. 303], and especially Fig. 156, p. 300. *Journal of Hellenic Studies*, 1887, lxxxiii.

4. Cypriote elongated boss from Mycenæ. Compare Fig. 156. FURTWANGLER and LOESCHKE, xxvii. 223.

5. Cypriote motive from Tiryns. SCHLIEMANN, *Tiryns*, p. 130.

6. Derivative of No. 1, therefore Cypriote. From Mycenæ. FURTWANGLER and LOESCHKE, xxxiii. 320.

7. Cypriote derivative. From Mycenæ. FURTWANGLER and LOESCHKE, xxxiii. 315.

8. Bosses, Cypriote derivative; the central line of conventional lotuses is a distinct "Mycenæ" motive. FURTWANGLER and LOESCHKE, xxxiii. 322.

9, 10. "Mycenæ" vases from Cyprus (New York Museum). The ware indicates Cypriote manufacture. Cypriote motive of inverted lotus triangles. Compare Plate xlix. [p. 307].

11. Inverted lotus triangle under half-circle. Compare Cypriote xlix. 6 [p. 307]. FURTWANGLER and LOESCHKE.

12. Inverted lotus triangle. Compare Cypriote xlix. [p. 307]. FURTWANGLER and LOESCHKE.

13. Inverted lotus triangle. Cypriote motive. FURTWANGLER and LOESCHKE.

14. "Mycenæ" pottery detail from Cyprus. Inverted lotuses. FURTWANGLER and LOESCHKE, Text, p. 58.

15. Part of a "Mycenæ" vase from Cyprus (New York Museum). Lotus stelès. Compare liv. 14.

Pl. LIII., p. 323.

PLATE LIV.

"MYCENÆ" POTTERY MOTIVES.

Nos. 7 and 11 of this Plate are Egypto-Phenician motives in bronze, to show the origin of certain pottery motives. They are taken from Plate xii. Nos. 8 and 12 [p. 113]. Compare Fig. 166, gold ornament from Spata.

All following illustrations, not otherwise specified, are from *Mykenische Vasen*.

1. From FURTWÄNGLER and LOESCHKE, *Mykenische Vasen*, Text, p. 81. Bending stem, with three-spiked lotus and pendant sepals. Compare pendant sepals (not curling) at xxxix. 5 [p. 253]; xlv. 3 [p. 287]; and Figs. 160, 161, 162 [p. 313, 314]. This "Mycenæ" lotus is probably borrowed from the Cypriote, being too remote for an actual copy of nature. In any case it represents a parallel fact. Of the variants on this Plate (2, 3, 4, 15, and 24), the one at 15 is the most obviously related to a normal decorative lotus. The plant has been mistaken for "palm-tree" by FURTWÄNGLER and LOESCHKE. From a schematic or logical point of view the three-spiked form represents all the sepals visible in profile and the addition of pendant sepals is unnatural, but we have abundant illustration for such representation in Cypriote lotuses (xlvii. [p. 303]).

2. From Nauplia, *Mykenische Vasen*, Text, p. 46. 3. Analogous motive, with addition of lotus-Ionic spirals below and on the sides, in fashion of the Persian Ionic (xxvi. 10 [p. 193]).—4. Similar motive, replacing the lower spirals by repetition of the upper form.

5. Pottery pattern based on the Egyptian palmette. Compare No. 7, an Egypto-Phenician lotus palmette in metal, and Plate xii. [p. 113], where other variants will explain more exactly the double-hooked loop. Nos. 6, 8, 9, 13, 14 are variants (13 from Ialysus; 14 from Haliki, Attica, *Mykenische Vasen*, Text, p. 39).

10. Outline lotus with spiral volutes differing from the Cypriote, which adhere more closely to nature in the point that the sepals generally curl from the base or near it and never from the extreme top of the flower (xv. [p. 139]; xlvii. [p. 303]). The form is a valuable reference for the Egyptian lotus-Ionic, which has the same trait; not only in Capitals but also in surface design (vii. 8, 9 [p. 79]; viii. 5, 7, 11, 12, 15 [p. 87]). In published examples of Mycenæ or Archipelago pottery, the form is rare, but it is illustrated by another example on this Plate, No. 19, from Calymna (entire vase, xlii. 6 [p. 267]). No. 12 is a variant.

166. GOLD ORNAMENT OF A SERIES FROM A TOMB AT SPATA, in Athens. From Author's sketch.

11. Egypto-Phenician palmette in bronze, from the shield of Amathus (repeated from xii. 12 [p. 113]). It exhibits the lotus palmette without volutes, the alternate form of No. 7. [Since making up my Plates and writing the Text of this Work, I have found the exact original on metal within the limits of Mycenæ Art, Fig. 166 represents one of a series of gold ornaments from Spata in the Polytechnic, Athens.]

Pottery variants of No. 11 are 16, 17, 18, 20, 21, 22, 23. To judge from the number of examples in *Mykenische Vasen* this motive was very common.

Pl. LIV., p. 325.

PLATE LV.

MYCENÆ POTTERY MOTIVES.

No. 10 is the Egyptian outline lotus. Compare Plates iv. v. [pp. 63, 65]. The only exact repetition of this Egyptian pattern which has been published is on a vase from Thera (*Mykenische Vasen*, xii. 78); and in other cases (various publications) the closest correspondents to Egyptian design are from Thera.

Nos. 1, 2, 3, 4 (compare Fig. 163), 8, 9, 12, 14, are motives related to No. 10. No. 15 adds the pendant sepals, as borrowed from some remote example like liv. 1.

6. Remote variant of No. 3. Compare vase from the "Sixth Tomb," lii. 9.

7. Variant of the Egg-and-Dart moulding pattern (Plate xxi. [p. 159]); probably an independent development with parallel result.

11. Design borrowed from a running pattern of lotuses in spiral scrolls, and used separately. No examples of an isolated lotus with one spiral volute are independent of such an influence.

13. Ionic spirals related to motives herewith in Text-cuts (repeated from Plate xv. [p. 139]).

Rhodian Detail.

Melian Detail.

The rudimentary central spike above the left-hand volutes has been thrown aside in the right-hand example by the introduction of a third spiral, and still appears, kicked out of place by it, so to speak. This vase is the most valuable example published, of the manner in which detached spirals were evolved from the double volute. Detached single spirals are not found in Egyptian art.

16, 19, 20. Variants of the lotus-Ionic volutes. .No. 16 shows also panels containing inverted lotus forms, a pattern common to Cretan specimens and others.

17. Inverted lotus corresponding to motive herewith in Text-cut (repeated from xlii. 1 [p. 267]).

Rhodian Detail. 18. Rosette and bird with triangles, showing an influence of Greek Geometric pottery. Compare xlix. 7 [p. 307]; lviii. 3 [p. 343].

Pl. LV., p. 327.

THE GREEK GEOMETRIC STYLE AND PREHISTORIC EUROPEAN ORNAMENT.

(PLATES LVI., LVII., LVIII., LIX., PAGES 339, 341, 343 345.)

IT was the happy tact of Professor Conze which singled out both the Melian and the Geometric vases for publications which rank as the first efforts to give these monuments their proper recognition and importance.[1] The designation of Geometric Style, as first applied to the Dipylon vases, is now extended to many connecting links with the later pottery of Greece, but in my use it designates the oldest and distinctive monuments of the style.

The title of Dipylon vases, as derived from the Dipylon Gate at Athens, near which the first important vases of this character were found, tends to obscure their wide diffusion. They represent the earliest art of Greece in general, as known to us.

Their distinctive geometric ornaments are the meander (lvi. 2, 3, 6, 8); the Swastika (lvi. 4; lx. 13 [p. 359]; lxi. 4 [p. 365]); chevrons (xlix. 7 [p. 307]; lvi. 3; lviii. 3); concentric rings joined by tangents (lvi. 7); and a quadrangle panel composed of four triangles (lvi. 2; variant at lvi. 3), which is derived from the Cypriote quadrangle (l. [p. 309]). At l. 3 is one of these quadrangular panel motives, taken from a Geometric vase of Cyprus in the New York Museum. The detail l. 6, from a Copenhagen vase, shows the same motive, which is also developed into an eight-rayed rosette by vases of this style, as on the Dipylon vase of Curium in New York.

Certain vases with irregularly distributed concentric rings without tangents are also assigned to the Geometric style by Professor Conze (lvii. 6). Such

---

1. The first publication regarding Geometric vases, as pointed out by CONZE, was, however, that of BURGON, *Transactions of the Royal Society of Literature*, 2nd Series, Vol. II., 1847. Contributions to this subject have been made by HELBIG, *Annali*, 1875, p. 221; 1878, pp. 311, 312; and by HIRSCHFELD, *Annali*, 1872.

vases are a numerous class in Cyprus (lvii. 1, 10). Concentric rings with tangents are more common (lvi. 3, 7), and are unknown to pure Cypriote vases.

The decoration of these Greek Geometric vases also includes the solar birds (lvi. 1; lvii. 2), but these are frequently arranged in rows (lvi. 7, 8, 10), which arrangement is never found in Cypriote vases. The solar deer and ibex, or wild goat, are also typical (lvi. 2, 6; lvii. 2), and the solar horse (lvi. 1; lxi. 4 [p. 365]) has still to be considered.

The solar bird, deer, and ibex, or wild goat, have never previously been specified as solar for works of Greek art; nor has it been observed that these solar animals are common to the art of Rhodes, Cyprus, and the East, and to that of prehistoric Northern Europe. They occur there in decorative associations which point decisively to Mediterranean influence.

The overthrow of the theory which placed the home of the Aryan race in Asia,[2] is so recent, that the older theories of an "Aryan art," independent of Mediterranean influence, have scarcely had time to sink out of sight. It is very clear, however, that a revision of the history of prehistoric art in Northern Europe will follow close on the heels of the late discoveries in Aryan Ethnology. It is already settled that the home of the Aryan race (if there ever was any such race) is in Europe, that Ethnology has nothing to do with the history of languages, and that the ancestors of the races of modern Europe have been settled in some approximate relation to their present European habitats as far back as the times of Neolithic man.

Scandinavian and other archæologists have long since pointed to the Phenicians as the authors of the "Bronze Culture" of the North, but this view has also been warmly antagonized. The time has now been reached when a spread of the "Bronze Culture" from the South-east Mediterranean countries as a centre must soon be accepted as a common-place of history. Canon Isaac Taylor's recent work on the "Origin of the Aryans" furnishes abundant philological and antiquarian evidence for the fact that the "Stone Age" of Northern Europe grew into a "Bronze Age" by way of metals imported from the South of Europe,[3] and by arts of metallurgy also thence derived. All his

---

2. Isaac Taylor, *The Origin of the Aryans* (p. 17). "No more curious chapter in the whole history of scientific delusion."

3. "We gather also that the knowledge of metals came from the South, and not from the East (p. 127). . . . The theory that bronze weapons were introduced into Europe

indications point to the Phenicians as fathers of the arts of metal in Southern Europe.

With the decisive overthrow of the theory that civilized man came into Europe from Asia with the arts of metal already in possession, or otherwise, the supposition also disappears that the art of metal came into Europe from Asia by Northern roads – and the Brahman Hindus must now be considered as the vanguard of a European emigration into Asia, instead of the rear-guard of an Asiatic migration into Europe.⁴

These new conclusions have been reached by Anthropologists and by Philologists as far as the history of races and of language is concerned, but they are supported by the history of ornament under conditions which oblige us to unite the entire civilization of prehistoric Europe with influences which spread originally from the valley of the Nile.

The Phenicians have been so far regarded as the connecting link between two independent civilizations. To consider them as the fathers of the " Bronze Culture " for Europe, does not settle the question as to the home of the " Bronze

---

by a conquering people coming from the East has been overthrown by the evidence afforded by the Swiss Lake Dwellings, which establish the fact that bronze implements were gradually introduced among a Neolithic population by the peaceful processes of barter (p. 126)." ISAAC TAYLOR, quoting Ferdinand Keller on the Swiss Lake Dwellings, . . . " We conclude that the knowledge of metals penetrated gradually to the North from the Mediterranean lands, which were visited by Phenician ships (p. 142). . . . μέταλλον (metal) is regarded by Renan and Oppert as a Semitic loan-word from the Phenician (p. 133). . . . χρυσός (gold), a Semitic loan-word from the Phenician (p. 135). . . . The Greeks obtained gold from the Phenicians. The Celts, Illyrians, and Lithuanians obtained it from the people of Italy (p. 137). . . . The Slaves borrowed the word for gold from the Teutons (p. 137). [and were settled East of them]. . . . 'Silver' (Gothic, *silubr*), a word common to Lithuanians, Slaves, and Teutons, is believed to be a loan-word from the Semitic—an indication that the Baltic people first obtained it by the trade route of the Dnieper from the region of the Euxine (p. 143). . . . κασσίτερος (tin), borrowed from Semitic Assyrian, which borrowed the word from Accadian (p. 138). . . . Homeric word for sword,

ξίφος, a Semitic loan-word (p. 151). . . . Teutons obtained knowledge of iron from the Celts (p. 146). . . . Close relations of the Celts to the Latins (p. 169). . . . *Ferrum* (iron), believed to be a loan-word from the Semitic (p. 145). . . . *Mina* and *μνᾶ*, Semitic loan-words (p. 195). . . . Weights and measures brought to Europe by the Phenicians (p. 195). . . . The mason's art and the use of mortar are believed to have been introduced into Europe by the Phenicians (p. 177). . . . Celts, Albanians, Slaves, and Teutons, have all borrowed the Latin *Murus*, 'showing that the arts of masonry were borrowed from Italy' (p. 195). . . . ' Cheese,' a loan-word from *Caseus*, spread from Teutonic to Slavonic languages (p. 168). . . . The Italic and Hellenic races must, at the time when agriculture began, have been dwelling in peaceful proximity in some more northern regions, probably in Danubian lands, in contact with Slaves and Teutons " (p. 166).

4. The tendency of recent studies is to minimize the amount of Aryan blood in India, and to show that a borrowed language does not imply a proportionate or parallel infusion of borrowed blood. " Very little Aryan blood in India. . . . The Brahmans of Benares represent the early Aryans."—TAYLOR (p. 201).

Culture" which, as far as they are concerned, might have originally centred in the Tigris-Euphrates valley. I consider it, therefore, of great importance to show that the history of prehistoric European patterns is also the history of metals, and that the history of patterns points to Egypt as the home of the "Bronze Culture."

There is no trace of pattern ornament in prehistoric Northern Europe prior to the introduction of bronze weapons and utensils from the South. Even the pottery on which such ornament could, as a matter of possibility, be found does not appear before the age of polished stone implements, which grew into that of bronze, and was partly contemporaneous with it.[5] The Palæolithic cave-dwellers drew the mammoth, the horse, and the wild goat, with great dexterity, but they had no pattern ornaments which are related to those of the "Bronze Age."[6] The earliest European harpoons, and other implements of bone of the Palæolithic Age, have distinct resemblance to those of the modern Arctic Esquimaux[7] and these Esquimaux implements are still mainly without pattern ornament, although the modern Esquimaux have borrowed at some remote period the pattern of concentric rings.

The prehistoric pottery decoration of Scandinavia, Germany, and Hungary, of England, France, Switzerland, and Northern Italy, makes its appearance with the use of bronze, and its ornaments are borrowed from the ornament of metal (gold and silver included). These ornaments are the meander, generally of degraded character, the triangle or chevron, and concentric rings (lvii.-lviii.). On the early bronzes of the prehistoric North, and in all countries mentioned, we find these same ornaments, with addition occasionally of the spiral scroll, the Swastika, and the bird, or a pot-hook derived from it (lvi., lviii.). The more complicated spiral ornaments, so-called Irish or Celtic, which are no less Scandinavian, are all much later developments, also under influence of the spirals of the South, or from starting-points furnished by them.

---

5. "No well-recorded case of pottery with Palæolithic implements."—BOYD DAWKINS, quoted by ISAAC TAYLOR, p. 181. . . . "Pottery extremely rare in the kitchen middens of Denmark and Sweden" (p. 239).

6. SALAMON REINACH, Description Raisonnée du Musée de St. Germain en Laye, I., p. 172. "La croix, le triangle, et le cercle a point central font défaut" (Époque des Cavernes). The drawings are on bone or ivory. Pottery and metals were unknown. The races and culture of this period are quite distinct from those of the Age of Polished Stone, which gradually passed into the Age of Bronze. For this "hiatus" between the Palæolithic and the Neolithic Age, see REINACH, Description Raisonnée.

7. Professor BOYD DAWKINS seems to have been foremost in recognizing the Europeans of the Glacial Epoch as Esquimaux. REINACH, Description Raisonnée.

GREEK GEOMETRIC & PREHISTORIC EUROPEAN ORNAMENT. 333

The most widely diffused pottery ornament of early Europe is the chevron in rows (lviii., lix.), which is frequently mistaken for a "zigzag." In the original combination, the zigzag is a series of united chevrons.[8] We can trace this chevron, as it appears in Denmark (lviii., 14), in Britain (lviii. 10), in Germany (lix. 5), or in France (lviii. 7), by way of the Swiss Lake-dwellers, or the tombs of Hallstatt, to the prehistoric pottery and bronzes of North Italy (lviii. 1, 6, 12, 13); to the Geometric style of Greece (lvi. 3; lviii. 3), and to the prehistoric pottery of Cyprus (lix. 8, 13).

In the last example, which shows a lotus expanded "in plan," the chevron is an Egyptian lotus petal or sepal, as the case may be. One connection of the apparent zigzag with the lotus is gathered from this piece and from the Egyptian vase lix. 9, which shows the inverted lotus on the body of the vase, and the derivative petals inverted on the neck. The chevron triangle, as it appears in Egypt, frequently has this petal and sepal derivation, as the four ornamented columns at the corners of the plate are intended to indicate. In Greek vases, the chevron frequently has the same origin (Plates xlvi. 13; lxi. 3 [pp. 289, 365]).

In general, however, the chevron ornament of prehistoric Europe belongs to an Egyptian type, which is most easily explained by reference to the method of the Egg-and-Dart moulding, as illustrated on Plate lxvi., Nos. 11, 13 [p. 399]. It is obvious that we have here two variants of one arrangement, in which

8. The Egyptian indication for water is a zigzag, and there is an Egyptian zigzag ornament which is probably hence derived. The distinction between this zigzag and the apparent zigzag of united chevrons is easily drawn. In one case (water) the zigzag lines are indefinitely numerous, and the angles are obtuse. In the zigzag of united chevrons (lotuses) the angles are more pointed and the pattern does not consist of superimposed lines, but of really independent, although united, triangles (which are often filled in with cross lines). The Egyptian zigzag (water) does not occur on mummy-cases, on metal, or on pottery. It appears at Denderah on the ceiling portico, in indications for water which are so extensive that they may come under the designation of pattern ornament. I have also observed the superimposed zigzags on the helt of the colossal statue of Ramses II. at Mitrahenny (Memphis). Superimposed zigzags in European prehistoric ornament occur in prehistoric Cypriote pottery, but the indications of my illustrative Plates show the dominant chevron pattern. There are cases in the British Museum of the single zigzag with obtuse angles on prehistoric bone implements of the Palæolithic cave-dwellers. This obtuse zigzag is independent of the prehistoric chevron of Northern Europe, which has no very high antiquity, as compared with the Palæolithic Age. In the Museum of St. Germain, where the number of examples makes comparison on such points easy, the chevron on pottery, or otherwise, belongs to the "Bronze Culture" immediately preceding the classic influence, and continues long after that influence began. On the pottery of the Age of Polished Stone, ornament is rare, and does not occur before the indications of the "Bronze Culture," which began in that period and very gradually displaced it. The races of the Age of Polished Stone did not develop in Europe from the races of the Palæolithic Age, but displaced them, and there is a "hiatus" between the two periods (Note 6).

the lotuses placed side by side, and inverted, have in one instance (viz. 11) straight outlines. The chevron, pure and simple, was reached from No. 11 by dropping the central sepal spike. The same Plate shows a case of the Egg-and-Dart moulding (No. 14), which has dropped the "Dart" or central sepal spike—a parallel case.

Figs. 167, 167A are illustrations from the necklaces represented on mummy-cases, where this ornament is frequently employed. There are many of these chevrons on similar necklace ornaments where the sepal spike has entirely disappeared, and many others in which it appears in a still more rudimentary or hasty indication than in these Figures. In the case of the chevron, pure and simple, on such mummy cases, the continued association with lotus buds, lotus rosettes, and lotus leaves, shows the identity of the motive.

167. CHEVRON ORNAMENT. LOTUSES INVERTED.
Detail of a mummy-case in the Turin Museum. Case O, No. 1145.
From Author's sketch.

There is no doubt that the Egyptian chevron lix. 7, 11 has this derivation in general. It is the distinctive Egyptian counterpart of the Egg-and-Dart moulding (xxi. [p. 159]). The chevron, pure and simple, was already a typical and frequent ornament under the XIth Dynasty, which precedes by many centuries any dated cases of the ornament exterior to Egypt.[9] It can be dated as a ceiling pattern to the XIIIth Dynasty (Tomb of Meri-ka-ra at Siout).

The Egyptian vase lix. 14, in Florence, shows the chevron with buds and lotuses. The vases on Plate lix. from Cyprus (4), from Rhodes (3), from prehistoric tombs of Italy (2), and from Germany (5), are types of derivate chevron ornament. To these we may add the Etruscan find, lviii. 5, as related to Rhodian enamelled vases of Egyptian origin or technique.[10]

167A. CHEVRON ORNAMENT. LOTUSES INVERTED; ROSETTES;
LOTUS BUDS.
Detail of a mummy-case (No. 5604) in the Gizeh Museum. From Author's sketch.

9. Mummy-case of King An-Antef (XIth Dynasty) in the British Museum, No. 6652. Mummy-cases in the Hall of the XIth Dynasty, Gizeh Museum.

10. In the Louvre; Salzmann excavations.

GREEK GEOMETRIC & PREHISTORIC EUROPEAN ORNAMENT.

The triangles of the Cypriote vase lviii. 2 are connected with the inverted lotus triangles of Plate xlix. [p. 307]. This will also hold good of the Mycenæ triangles liii. 9, 10, 11, 12, 13 [p. 323]. The Mycenæ vase lii. 8 [p. 321] from the " Second Tomb " shows a case of the chevron analogous to the Egg-and-Dart moulding.

The gradual diffusion of this chevron ornament over Europe is by no means exclusively attributable to bronze, although the bronze originals (lviii. 1, 13) which assisted this diffusion are found in the prehistoric Celtic tombs of North Italy and Hallstatt, side by side with the pottery copies. The influence of primitive pottery decoration itself, spreading gradually from Northern Greece and Northern Italy to the Danube countries, Switzerland, Germany, and France, must have had full share of influence.

The chevron style of the prehistoric Cypriote pottery lix. 8, 13 is the nearest to the original motive, which is now accessible in large masses. I was not aware when making up my Plates, of the small amount of this prehistoric Cypriote pottery in the Museums of Europe. Professor Dümmler has offered no matter or illustrations for the decoration of this pottery.[11] In default of a larger number of Plate illustrations, I can refer to the modern Kabyle survivals of this chevron style (lxiv. [p. 385]) as intermixed with lotus triangles, like those of Plate xlix [p. 307], belonging to the later Cypriote Geometric style. Plate lxiv. also supplies examples of the later Cypriote chevrons.

The Kabyle pottery shows many other survivals of lotus motives, including the Egg-and-Dart lotus borders proper.[12]

Mr. Petrie's discovery in Egypt (1890) of black pottery, with incised chevrons, of Italian prehistoric style, is mentioned at p. 346. This pottery is dated to the XIIth Dynasty, and none is known in Egypt later than the XIIIth Dynasty. Admitting the probability that Italian foreigners were the makers, as Mr. Petrie supposes, and the probability that the style had been already developed in Italy from imported chevron patterns in metal and then carried back to Egypt by these foreign settlers, it is still important to know that a race of prehistoric Europe was in direct contact with Egyptian patterns as early as 3000 B.C.

11. In his paper, quoted at p. 293, Note 1.
12. As shown to me by General Loring in the Boston Museum of Fine Arts, on a vase which he purchased at the Philadelphia Centennial Exhibition.

336 GREEK GEOMETRIC & PREHISTORIC EUROPEAN ORNAMENT.

Everything which demonstrates direct contact of the prehistoric races of Europe with Egypt assists the imagination in matters of indirect influence, which were probably of far more importance actually. It is also interesting to observe that the link has been supplied whose absence has led one expert in prehistoric North-European pottery to expressly deny an Egyptian influence as appearing in it, viz. the supposed fact that such pottery was not found in Egypt (p. 346).

The mixed influences carrying Mediterranean ornament into Northern Europe, partly by way of gradual diffusion of a pottery style which was especially spread by the Celts of North Italy, France, and South Germany, and partly by way of bronze utensils and implements of Carian, Phenician, Etruscan, and Greek manufacture, are again apparent in the motive of concentric rings.

RHODIAN POTTERY DIAGRAM.

Concentric rings, with or without tangents, were a favoured method of indicating spirals in metals. This method can be demonstrated in Egypt for scarabs (viii. 21-25 [p. 87]), and in existing bronzes of an early Greek[13] and Italian period (lvii. 8, 14, 16). The original motive in bronze was possibly the concentric rings and tangents, which latter were easily omitted, as already illustrated for scarabs.

As concentric rings without tangents (derived from concentric rings with tangents) were already a hieratic symbol in Egypt (viii. [p. 87]), it is not necessary to assume positively that they were not directly transferred to metal. Concentric rings in Egypt are not confined to scarabs; they are also found on ivories and on wood,[14] two materials which, like the hard material of a scarab, were ill-adapted to the working of a spiral scroll.

With the assistance of pottery examples, which were probably themselves copies of bronzes (there are many indications of this derivation both for forms and motives of the Greek Geometric pottery), we can pass without difficulty from concentric rings with tangents to the concentric rings without tangents, in the prehistoric art of Europe. From the solar birds at lvi. 7, with concentric

13. Bronze plaque in the Louvre, from Dodona; ornament of concentric rings joined by tangents. Similar bronze plaque in the Polytechnic at Athens; concentric rings joined by tangents (representing spirals) are common on ivories from Rhodes (British Museum), and from Spata "Mycenæ Culture," both found with objects of Egyptian styles.

14. Egyptian ivories with concentric rings are not uncommon. They are found also on large wooden Egyptian implements for carding and spinning in the British Museum. They were a favourite decoration on combs all over prehistoric Europe, and can be traced to Egyptian wooden combs in the British Museum and in Florence (p. 84, Note 10).

GREEK GEOMETRIC & PREHISTORIC EUROPEAN ORNAMENT. 337

rings and tangents, we pass to the solar birds and concentric rings lvii. 8, or again to the birds with concentric rings, lvii. 14 (both bronzes).

The same transition is illustrated, with assistance of pottery examples, for the solar deer or ibex and wild goat. From the ibex or wild goat with concentric rings and tangents (lvii. 2) we move to the deer and concentric rings (lvii. 16).

The motive of the solar bird is found on prehistoric bronze in Sweden (lvi. 9), and is common all over prehistoric Europe. The bronzes of Hallstatt (Celtic, fourth century B.C. or earlier) show many examples (lvii. 4), as also of the solar deer and horse.

The bird had already reached the pot-hook stage at Tiryns, lvi. 10 (but such pieces are not found with the "Mycenæ" pottery of Tiryns). We find it in this shape at Bologna (lvii. 7), at Villanova (lvi. 13; lviii. 9), in France, Germany, and Sweden (lvi. 11). The concentric rings of Northern Europe, as in England (lviii. 11), are no less clearly of Mediterranean origin in the cases when the bird or deer are wanting.

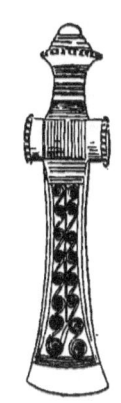

168. SWEDISH BRONZE AXE, WITH SPIRAL SCROLLS. From Montelius.

Among the more isolated examples of Mediterranean influence in Northern Europe, one of the most curious is the appearance of the leaf in treatment peculiar to "Mycenæ" style on a wood carving from the Lake Dwellings of Scotland. Fig. 165 [p. 317].[15] Compare lii. 1 [p. 321].

The path of the meander is not less obvious. As we find it in Northern France (lviii. 7, rudimentary survival) or among the Lake-dwellers of Switzerland (lviii. 8), it is the same meander as in the prehistoric art of Italy (lviii. 12), and as derived from the bronzes (lviii. 13), which still survive to tell the tale of its origin, or as found in the Geometric vases of Greece (lvi.); themselves once founded on a style in bronze.

The decisive demonstration for this unity in the history of the meander lies in the Swastika, which is treated in my next chapter.

15. From a Crannog at Lochlee; a small piece of oak, five inches square with "curious diagrams carved on both sides," ROBERT MONRO, *Ancient Scottish Lake Dwellings*, p. 135. The coincidence of "Mycenæ" culture with the Carian, and the companionship of Carians with Phenicians (p. 313), offer a ready explanation for such transfers of ornamental motives, but indications that the "Mycenæ" (Carian) race was Celtic are so strong that we may also preferably consider this piece as a relic of a land diffusion of "Mycenæ" patterns, explained by community of race.

PLATE LVI.

GREEK GEOMETRIC AND PREHISTORIC EUROPEAN ORNAMENT.

THE SOLAR GOOSE.

1. Greek Geometric pottery, a barrel-shaped stand for support of a metal vase or large amphora. Solar geese and horse, solar diagram. For the horse, compare Plates lvii. 5 and lxi. [p. 365].
2. Greek Geometric pottery, a barrel-shaped stand, meander pattern, Cypriote "quadrangle" (see Plate I. [p. 309]. Solar geese and deer, solar diagram. For the deer, compare Trojan stags, lx. 1 [p. 359] (many similar); lvii. 2 (ibex); and lvii. 16.
3. Greek Geometric vase. On the neck, concentric rings joined by tangents and representing spirals, meander, chevrons, solar goose, solar diagram.
4. Greek Geometric vase, solar geese, large Swastika.
5. Greek Geometric vase, solar geese.
6. Greek Geometric vase, meander, solar geese, solar deer, concentric rings joined by tangents and representing spirals.
7. Greek Geometric vase, solar geese, solar diagrams, concentric rings joined by tangents and representing spirals.
8. Greek Geometric pottery fragment, solar geese, meander. SCHLIEMANN, *Mycenæ*, p. 103.
9. Detail in bronze *repoussé*, Sweden. Solar geese, concentric rings. MONTELIUS, *The Civilization of Sweden in Heathen Times*.
10. Greek Geometric pottery fragment, solar geese, resembling pot-hooks. SCHLIEMANN, *Tiryns*, p. 96.
11. Pot-hooks derived from solar geese. Bronze *repoussé* detail. Sweden. Compare Nos. 10, 13, lvii. 7, lviii. 9. MONTELIUS, *The Civilization of Sweden in Heathen Times*.
12. Geometric pottery detail, vase found at Corneto. *Monumenti Inediti*, X. xd. Solar geese, rudiments of concentric rings, chevrons.
13. Geometric pottery fragment, from Villanova, Italy, prehistoric tombs. WARING, *Ceramic Art in Remote Ages*, iv. 55. Pot-hooks derived from solar geese and concentric rings. Compare adjacent examples, Plate lvii. Nos. 4, 7, 8, 14. and especially lviii. 9, also from Villanova.

The illustrations from Sweden and Italy represent a very large number of prehistoric examples in publication and a much larger number of examples in Museums.

Nos. 1—7, inclusive, are from CONZE, *Anfänge der Griechischen Kunst* (Vienna, 1870). Scarce reprint from *Sitzungsberichte der Philos. Hist. Cl. der Kais. Akademie der Wissenschaften*, lxiv. p. 505, Februarheft, 1870. Additional vases of the Greek Geometric style from the same publication, are lvii. 2, 6; lviii. 3; lx. 13 [p. 359]; lxi. 1, 4 [p. 365]. The following indication of present location and derivation includes all above numbers. The most important collections for "Geometric" (so-called "Dipylon") vases are the British Museum, Louvre, *Cabinet des Médailles* (Paris), Museums of Sèvres, Leyden, Copenhagen, and Athens. There are several examples from Cyprus in New York besides the large "Dipylon vase of Curium." (CESNOLA, *Cyprus*, xxix.)

lvi. 1. From the Piræus, in Würzburg.—2. In British Museum, three similar at Sèvres from Thera, "under the lava." The specification found "under the lava" is supposed to indicate an antiquity earlier than 1600 B.C.—3. In Leyden, from Smyrna; most of the Leyden vases are "from Smyrna," an indication which argues Asia Minor as probable place of discovery, but does not argue more; one Leyden vase is from Tripolis.—4. In British Museum (some of the finest Geometric vases in London are from Athens, from the original "Dipylon" finds, near the Dipylon Gate).—5. In Leyden, from Smyrna.—6. In the *Cabinet des Médailles*, from Thera, "under the lava."—7. At Sèvres, from Thera, "under the lava."—lvii. 2. In the Louvre.—lvii. 7. In Leyden, from Smyrna.—lviii. 3. In British Museum, from Camirus.—lx. 13. In British Museum.—lxi. 1, 4. In Leyden, from Smyrna (?)

Pl. LVI., p. 339.

PLATE LVII.

GREEK GEOMETRIC AND PREHISTORIC EUROPEAN ORNAMENT.
CONCENTRIC RINGS.

ALL pieces are types representing large numbers of examples in each style indicated, except No. 6. It is not clear that pottery vases with decoration confined to concentric rings were very common in the Greek Geometric style.

Concentric rings are occasionally represented in prehistoric Northern Europe by concentric squares, if this term may be allowed, and especially at Hallstatt.

1. Cypriote vase, New York Museum. PERROT et CHIPIEZ, *Cypre*, Fig. 497. Representing the well-known and numerous type of Cypriote vases, with concentric rings; another example at No. 10. Compare concentric rings on Cypriote vases, xlvii. 11 [p. 303]; xlix. 3 [p. 307]; l. 12 [p. 309]; and CESNOLA, *Cyprus*, Plate ii.
2. Greek Geometric detail from a barrel-shaped stand in the Louvre. CONZE, *Anfänge*, &c., viii. Ibexes or wild goats (compare Plates xxxvi.—xxxix. inclusive [pp. 247-253]); diagram containing concentric rings joined by tangents (compare the Egyptian scarab viii. 22 [p. 87]); bird and asterism (compare Plates xliii.-xlvi., inclusive [pp. 283-289]).
3. Cypriote vase, New York Museum; concentric rings with four lotus buds, supporting a panel band with bosses derived from lotus sepals. Detail at xlviii. 9 [p. 305], with demonstration for the boss, and the panel band.
4. Bronze *repoussé* detail, from the prehistoric Celtic tombs of Hallstatt (near Salzburg). Birds and concentric rings. WARING, *Ceramic Art*, &c., xxviii. 18. Compare VON SACKEN, *Das Grabfeld von Hallstadt*. Much more numerous and complete colour illustrations (original sketches of the director of the excavations) in the Museum of St. Germain en Laye.
5. Bronze *repoussé* detail; horses and concentric rings. *Museo Etrusco Vaticano*, v. 5. Compare Plate lxi. [p. 365] for the horse. The Hallstatt examples of the horse and concentric rings are very numerous.
6. Greek Geometric vase with concentric rings. CONZE, *Anfänge*, I. 2. The type of Geometric vases confined to this ornament is rare. Connection with the Cypriote type is positive.
7. Prehistoric vase from Bologna. WARING, *Ceramic Art*, pot-hook, III. 48. Geese of the pot-hook variety, concentric rings. Compare lvi. 10, 11, 13, for the pot-hook.
8. Detail of a bronze *repoussé*, prehistoric, Italian vase. Geese and concentric rings. ZANNONI, *Scavi nella Certosa di Bologna*.
9. Rhodian vase of the type with concentric rings. *Jahrbuch*, 1886, p. 137. Compare No. 15. The type is less numerous than the Cypriote, connection positive.
10. Cypriote vase, New York Museum, of the type with concentric rings, CESNOLA, *Cyprus*, Plate ii.
11. Cypriote vase, New York Museum, of the "Prehistoric" type, with incised patterns. Compare lix. 8, 13. The race which produced these vases is supposed to have been exterminated as early as the tenth century B.C., but Professor Dümmler's presumption of a sharp separation in type between these vases and the Cypriote Greek is not demonstrated. There are many illustrations of fusion and transition in the New York Collection. See p. 381.
12. Cypriote Greek vase, New York Museum. Bird and solar diagrams (not concentric rings). The bird with concentric rings is not found on Cypriote vases, or must be extremely rare.
13. Detail of No. 14. Prehistoric bronze vase from an Italian *Tomba a pozzo*. Birds and concentric rings. *Monumenti Inediti*, XI., lix.
15. Rhodian vase of the type with concentric rings. *Jahrbuch*, 1886, p. 184.
16. Prehistoric bronze vase found with prehistoric pottery. (From the same tomb, the horse with lotus bud in mouth lxi. 9 [p. 365].) ZANNONI, *Scavi*, xxxv. Solar deer, and concentric rings; type also common at Hallstatt, according to illustrations in the Museum of St. Germain en Laye. Compare ibexes at No. 2, and stags on Trojan whorls, lx. 1 [p. 359]. Compare the prehistoric and Hallstatt bronzes with deer, ibexes, and antelopes, Plate xxxix. [p. 253].

Pl. LVII., p. 341.

PLATE LVIII.

GREEK GEOMETRIC AND PREHISTORIC EUROPEAN ORNAMENT.
THE CHEVRON.

ALL pieces represent types having large numbers of examples.

1. Italy. Bronze vase from a prehistoric *Tomba a Pozzo*. Chevrons on the rim. *Monumenti Inediti*, XI. lx.

2. Cyprus. Vase in the New York Museum, belonging to a numerous type, illustrating the chevron as derived from an entire inverted lotus (see Plate xlix. [p. 307]).

3. Rhodes. Greek Geometric vase from Camirus, British Museum. Goose and chevrons. (For a more obvious illustration of the chevron in the Greek Geometric style, see neck of the vase, lvi. 3) The goose faces a rudely indicated section of meander, of the type seen at No. 12. Compare the geese and the Swastika lvi. 4.

4. Italy. Prehistoric vase from Bologna, chevrons on the neck, rude indication of concentric rings. WARING, *Ceramic Art in Remote Ages*, ii. 36.

5. Italy. Enamelled vase from an Etruscan tomb, of the Egyptian style found at Rhodes by Salzmann, decoration of chevrons. *Museo Etrusco Vaticano*, II. cv.

6. Italy. Prehistoric vases from Bologna; chevrons. WARING, ii. 36.

7. France. Celtic vase, Museum of St. Germain, from Department of the Marne; chevrons and section of meander (very numerous type); compare meander No. 12. *Revue Archéologique*, 1863, Plate iii.

8. Switzerland. Lake-Dwellers' vase; meander and concentric rings. WARING, iii. 47.

9. Italy. Pottery fragment, Villanova. Compare lvi. 13. Geese resembling the pot-hook variety; concentric rings, circle and cross (compare xxiii. 3 [p. 173], human figures (?)). WARING, iv. 54.

10. England. Celtic or Saxon pottery, Nottinghamshire. Chevrons, solar diagrams, and an uncommon pattern. WARING, xi. 147.

11. England. Celtic or Saxon pottery, Lincolnshire. Concentric rings. WARING, xi. 141.

12. Italy. Prehistoric pottery, San Marino. Chevrons, meander variant. WARING, iv. 61.

13. Italy. Prehistoric bronze vase from a *Tomba a Pozzo*. Chevrons, meanders. *Monumenti Inediti*, XI. lx.

14. Denmark. Prehistoric pottery. Chevrons. WARING, vii. 96.

Pl. LVIII., p. 343.

PLATE LIX.

GREEK GEOMETRIC AND PREHISTORIC EUROPEAN ORNAMENT.

THE CHEVRON (*continued*).

ALL pieces represent types with large numbers of examples for each style illustrated.
1. Egyptian column, lower section, from a tomb-painting. Lotus petals and sepals. PRISSE D'AVENNES, *Colonnettes en bois.*
2. Italy. Prehistoric pottery. Chevrons, concentric rings, pot-hooks (birds).
3. Rhodes. Greek pottery. Chevrons. *Jahrbuch*, 1888, Fig. 32.
4. Cyprus. Serpentine vase. Chevrons. CESNOLA, *Cyprus*, p. 24.
5. Germany. Prehistoric pottery. Chevrons. WARING, ii. 28.
6. Egyptian column, lower section, from a tomb-painting. Lotus sepals. PRISSE D'AVENNES, *Colonnettes en bois.*
7. Egyptian vase from a tomb-painting. Chevrons. PRISSE D'AVENNES.
8. Cyprus. Prehistoric incised pottery; compare lvii. 11. Chevrons. CESNOLA, *Cyprus*, p. 408.
9. Egyptian vase from a tomb-painting. Chevrons on the neck; inverted lotus sepals and petals on the body. PRISSE D'AVENNES, *Vases des Tributaires Asiatiques.*
10. Caria. Greek pottery. Chevrons. WINTER, in *Mittheilungen aus Athen,* "*Vasen aus Karien,*" design copied by PERROT et CHIPIEZ, v. p. 327.
11. Egyptian vase from a tomb-painting. Chevrons. PRISSE D'AVENNES, *Vases du Tombeau de Ramses III.*
12. Lower portion of an Egyptian column. Lotus sepals. PRISSE D'AVENNES.
13. Cyprus. Prehistoric incised pottery. Chevrons representing an expanded lotus. CESNOLA, *Cyprus*, vii.
14. Egyptian vase in Florence. Lotuses, chevrons. ROSELLINI, liv. 61.
15. Lower section of an Egyptian column from a tomb-painting. Lotus petals and sepals. PRISSE D'AVENNES, *Colonnettes en bois.*

Compare the Mycenæ vase lii. 8 [p. 321], the early Attic vase xlvi. 13 [p. 289], the Greek vase xxx. 4 [p. 211], and an especially distinct example of the petal chevron at the base of the Greek vase lxi. 3 [p. 365].

Black pottery with incised chevrons has been found in Egypt by Mr. PETRIE'S excavations of 1890, and also by Mr. NAVILLE'S excavations. Mr. Petrie's specimens are dated to the XIIth Dynasty, and Mr. Naville's are not later than the XIIIth Dynasty. Mr. Petrie believes this pottery to be the manufacture of Italian foreigners settled in Egypt. PETRIE, *Kahun, Gurob, and Hawara,* Plate xxvii. p. 202; Text, p. 42.

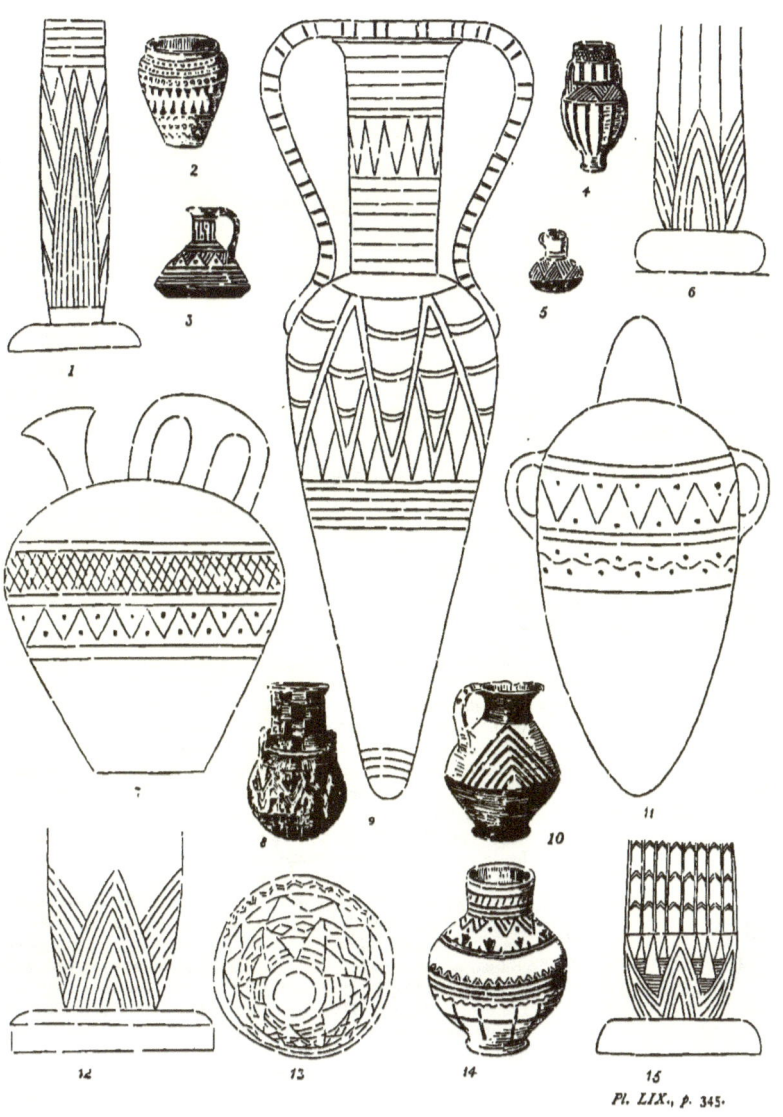

Pl. LIX., p. 345.

APPENDIX.

ADDITIONAL CITATIONS.

Denmark. Chevrons on swords, and bronze axes. Concentric rings on bronze, gold, and ivory. Swastikas (meander) on bronze (Museum of St. Germain en Laye).

Hungary. Chevrons on bronze axes (St. Germain).

Germany. Bronze pilgrim bottle (Rodenbach). Concentric rings, deer, chevron, meander. Concentric rings on gold, several cases (St. Germain). Hallstatt metals; horses and concentric rings, birds and concentric rings, deer, meanders, chevrons. (Copies at St. Germain and VON SACKEN, *Das Grabfeld von Hallstatt.*)

For the Swiss Lake-Dwellers' ornament compare FERDINAND KELLER.

France and Italy, innumerable repetitions of the above details. (St. Germain; Rome, Kircher Museum, Etruscan Museum of the Vatican; Florence; Bologna.)

England. Celtic and Saxon metal details, British Museum.

Metals from the Valley of the Koban and from the Caucasus. No birds observed; many deer, horses, spirals, chevrons, Swastikas. No concentric rings observed. (St. Germain.)

All illustrated publications for the prehistoric monuments of Northern Europe exhibit the same ornamental patterns. A fine series of very numerous comparative examples for prehistoric pottery and for all ancient nations of the North and South, in WARING, *Ceramic Art in Remote Ages.* WARING observes (p. 1) that there is "no evidence of influence from Phenician art upon such remains of British, Keltic, or Teutonic art, as have come down to us" (!!!). WARING considers the influence Greek and Italian ("Alban"), but does not concede the influence of Egypt, for the reason that similar pottery is not found there. This difficulty has been removed by Mr. PETRIE's excavations of 1890, but Mr. PETRIE is doubtless correct in assuming this black pottery with chevron ornaments to be of foreign Italian style. It is not necessary to assume that the foreign chevron style was copied by foreigners in Egypt, but it was based on Egyptian chevron patterns. WARING'S objection that pottery like the prehistoric Northern is not found in Egypt (which is now surmounted) does not apply in any case. If the Egyptians had been in a similar stage of civilization, and therefore producing an absolutely similar style of pottery, they could not have influenced so powerfully the nations of the North by a superior civilization. There is not the slightest reason for demanding that the chevron ornament should be found on Egyptian pottery, because the chevron ornament came from Egypt. As a matter of fact, however, it does occur, even on modern Egyptian pottery (Fig. 169), and can be traced on Egyptian pottery back to the XIIth Dynasty without break of continuity. PETRIE, *Kahun, Gurob, and Hawara.*

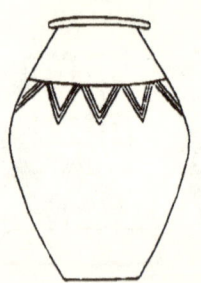

169. MODERN EGYPTIAN WATER JAR. From Author's sketch. Many examples.

THE SWASTIKA.

(PLATE LX., PAGE 359.)

IT is not long since that the Swastika was an "Aryan emblem," but the Aryans have disappeared,[1] and with them must disappear the "Aryan" Swastika, and the theory of its Asiatic origin, which is still generally accepted.[2] All theories founded on Buddhist symbolism have a weak basis as regards the matter of antiquity,[3] as there is no known Buddhist art before the third century B.C. Since the Greek element in Buddhist art has been recognized, theories based on Buddhist art have no weight whatever for early Hindu antiquity. Above all, since the Aryan Hindus are proven to have come from the West, the supposed Indian home of the Swastika is no more. The supposition that the Aryan Hindus carried the Swastika with them to India is, however, perfectly tenable, since it belongs to early prehistoric art of Europe, whence they came (pp. 330, 331, Notes 2, 3, 4).

The theory of the crossed fire-sticks as the origin of the "Aryan Swastika" also disappears with the Aryans themselves. The Malays and Burmese make fire with crossed sticks,[4] but our present knowledge of prehistoric Europe would

---

1. In the sense which has specified the "Indo-European" races as being of originally common blood because they spoke cognate languages. Canon Isaac Taylor has pointed out that the same argument would prove the negroes of the United States to be English, and the Indians of Mexico to be Spaniards, and that it would also prove the Spaniards and French to be Romans. ISAAC TAYLOR, *Origin of the Aryans*.

2. SCHUCHARDT, *Schliemann's Ausgrabungen im Lichte der heutigen Wissenschaft*, 1890. "Das Hakenkreuz ... stammt aus Asien und scheint das symbol einer uralten Gottheit zu sein."

3. BIRDWOOD, *Industrial Arts of India* (South Kensington Series). "The earliest illustrations of the Buddhistic architecture of India are the edict pillars (*lats*) of Asoka [third century B.C.]. ... There is no known Hindu temple, Mr. Fergusson says, older than the sixth or fifth century of the Christian era (p. 99). ... Apart from the Buddhist monuments and inscriptions, it is only in the sacred books of the Hindus that we are able to trace the vague and broken outlines of the history of ancient India (p. 99). ... No Hindu temple has been brought to light in Southern India earlier than the eighth century A.D. ... Architecture thus appears to have arisen in Southern India a thousand years later than in Northern India" [where it began third century B.C.] (p. 110).

4. WALTER HOUGH, *American Anthropologist*, October, 1890. "Aboriginal Fire-making" (p. 360). A method also practised by the Dyaks, Javanese, and in Australia, and New Guinea.

lead us to suppose that the early Aryans of Europe made fire like the Esquimaux, i.e., with the drill and bow.[5] It is a similar method which is used by the modern Brahmans in producing their sacred fire for the temple.[6] As the traditional Hindu method of making fire does not use the crossed sticks, the association of the crossed-stick theory with the Hindu-Aryan theory of Swastika origin is unfortunate.[7] Mr. Walter Hough, of the Smithsonian Institute and National Museum at Washington, can make fire with wooden sticks in every known method, and by some methods within five or ten seconds of taking his implements in hand, and I have seen him practise the Malay method with crossed sticks, but he is not a believer in the fire-stick origin of the Swastika—a theory, moreover, which might apply to the Greek cross, but which does not apply to the Swastika form.

The true home of the Swastika is the Greek Geometric Style, as will be immediately obvious to every expert who examines the question through the study of that style.

In seeking the home of a symbol we should consider where it appears in the largest dimension, and where it appears in the most formal and prominent way. The Greek Geometric vases are the only monuments on which the Swastika systematically appears in panels exclusively assigned to it (lx. 13; lvi. 4 [p. 339]). There are no other monuments on which the Swastika can be found in a dimension taking up one-half the height of the entire object (lvi. 4).

5. "The Eskimo compound drill is of two varieties—one worked with a thong and hand-rest by two persons, and the other worked by one man with the aid of a bow and mouthpiece. The apparatus consists of four parts; the lower piece or hearth, which may have fire-cups on the sides with a canal opening upon a flat step, or the holes may be bored on a central groove; the spindle; the mouthpiece or hand-rest with a stone bearing; and the cord which may be stretched on an ivory bow, or fitted with two handles as the cord on the ancient Hindu fire-drill." Ibid, p. 364.

6. MOOR, *Hindu Pantheon*, p. 214. "On the pin and socket mode of making fire—"The fire used by Brahmans for cooking and for religious purposes is produced by the friction of two pieces of hard wood, one about five inches in diameter with a small conical hole or socket in the upper part, into which the other, shaped like a pin, is introduced and worked about, backward and forward, by a bow." I have seen the implements used by the modern Brahmans, in possession of Mr. Hough; see his account of the ancient Hindu method (Note 5). The drill and bow were also used by the ancient Egyptians. Mr. PETRIE has found the "hearth" sticks with the burnt holes, and refers to the use of the bow. *Kahun, Gurob, and Hawara*, Plate ix., Note 6.

7. Mr. HOUGH's matter indicates his belief that some *savants*, who have discussed the problem of making fire by the friction of wooden sticks, lack the practical experience of the art in their own persons. "The writer can make fire in ten seconds with the twirling sticks, and in five seconds with the bow-drill." The ease with which fire can be made with wooden sticks by experts is quoted as antagonizing the view of Sir John Lubbock that the *culte de feu* is based on the difficulty of making it, and the necessity for jealously preserving it.

The ordinary size of a Swastika, in very primitive times, is under a third of an inch in diameter. They are found in Greek Geometric pottery two or three inches in diameter, but they also appear in the informal scattering way (lxi. 4 [p. 365]), which characterizes the Swastika in other styles.

As the Swastika came into prominence through Dr. Schliemann's excavations, and its appearance on Trojan whorls (lx. 1), and through the attention he was wise enough to give this symbol, it is natural that it should have been studied from a Trojan—i.e., to say from the supposed "primitive Aryan"—standpoint.[8] As far, however, as the "primitive" character of the symbol is concerned, it does not appear in the "First City" of Troy,[9] and it does not appear on the "prehistoric" pottery of Cyprus (by which I understand the Cypriote pottery of the prehistoric race of Cyprus). It would make not the slightest difference with the argument if it did however so appear, for it is a highly "primitive" symbol.

The Swastika dates from the earliest diffusion of the Egyptian meander in the basin of the Mediterranean, and it is a profound remark of De Morgan[10] that the area of the Swastika appears to be co-extensive with the area of bronze. In Northern Prehistoric Europe, where the Swastika has attracted considerable attention, it is distinctly connected with the "Bronze Culture" derived from the South. When found on the prehistoric pottery of the North, the Southern home of its beginnings is equally clear.

In seeking the home of a symbol we should consider not only the nature of its appearance, but also where it is found in the largest amount, for this shows the centre of vogue and of power, that is to say, the centre of diffusion. The vogue of the Swastika at Troy is not as great as its vogue in Cypriote Greek pottery (lx. 15), and in Rhodian pottery (lx. 2). (See the list of Plates on which the Swastika appears [p. 357].) For the given number of known examples it is well known to Melian vases (lx. 8), and to archaic Greek vases

---

8. As, for instance, by MICHAEL V. ZMIGRODKY, *Archiv für Anthropologie*, June, 1890. "Zur Geschichte der Suastika."

9. SCHLIEMANN, *Ilios*, p. 346. It belongs to the "third city," never to the first or second.

10. J. DE MORGAN, *Mission Scientifique au Caucase*. But this author believes China to be the original home of bronze. Since the recent discoveries regarding the derivation of Chinese culture from Chaldea, this is not likely. For these discoveries see recent publications of Rev. C. J. BALL, in *Proceedings, Society of Biblical Archæology*, and of Professor TERRIEN DELACOUPÉRIE, in the *Oriental and Babylonian Record*.

(lxi. 12 [p. 365]), but its greatest prominence is on the pottery of the Greek Geometric style (lx. 13; lvi. 4 [p. 339]; lxi. 1, 4 [p. 365]; and Figs. 173, 174 (pp. 353, 354).

In Carian or "Mycenæ" art the Swastika is relatively rare, but it occasionally appears. The natural conclusion would be that the bronzes of the North which show the Swastika date from early Greek influences spreading from Marseilles, from the mountains of Northern Greece, and from the Northern shores of the Black Sea. There was intercourse with the North before the Doric Migration, for the amber of the "Mycenæ Culture" was drawn from the Baltic.[11]

Aside from the Greek Geometric style our earliest reference for the Swastika, and very possibly an earlier reference than the first, is its appearance on the burial "Hut-urns" of Italy. On such it appears rather as a fragment of the more complicated meander patterns, from which it is derived. My precise view is that the earliest and consequently imperfect forms of the Swastika are on the "Hut-urns" of Italy, but that, as an independent and definitely shaped pattern, it first belongs to the Greek Geometric style. I do not assert that the Swastika is very common on "Hut-urns," which are often undecorated.

The high antiquity of the Greek Geometric style has been especially dwelt upon by Professor Conze, although examples are also found as late as the "Corinthian" style of Greek pottery.[12] There is no proof that the Swastika found its way to China and Japan before the time of the Hindu Buddhists, or that it was a Brahman emblem before the Buddhist time. The well-known Greek influences on Buddhist art would thus explain the Hindu symbol, but it is more likely that the Swastika travelled Eastward with the Hindus themselves.

Our present intermediate link with India for the Swastika lies in the Caucasus and in the adjacent territory of the Koban. This last ancient centre

---

[11] Schuchardt, *Schliemann's Ausgrabungen*, p. 223.

[12] The designation "found under the lava at Thera" is supposed to indicate a higher antiquity than 1600 B.C. It is not thought that the volcanic eruption, which changed the configuration of the island, can have occurred later. As Professor Conze has pointed out, the antiquity of the Geometric style is proven by its fixed and clearly traditional character. It is at least as old as the oldest Greek tombs which have been opened in Greece. On the other hand it lasted as late as the sixth or seventh century B.C., according to the evidence of a tomb in Corfu, which has supplied a vase of the distinctive ancient Geometric style with another of the "Corinthian" fashion. (British Museum).

of the arts in metal has lately attracted attention through the publication of Virchow.[13] In the original Koban bronzes of the prehistoric Museum of St. Germain there is also abundant matter for study.

The presumption that the bronze manufactures of the Caucasus and of the Koban represent an independent centre,[14] or a half-way station of a movement from East to West must be abandoned. The Gryphon is found on them, the solar deer are very largely represented, and the traditional bronze motives of the spiral, chevron, and swastikas are abundant. The style of the patterns is strictly limited to those of the "Bronze Culture" of Europe under consideration.

The character of the Koban ornament implies rather an Eastward spread of the "Bronze Culture" of Northern Europe than an influence penetrating through the Caucasus from the South. This would have had a "Mesopotamian" flavour which is lacking, and in this sense the remarks of Reinach are just (Note 14). Both direct Egyptian, and primitive Greek influences (Colchis) are quoted for the Eastern Pontus.[15] The Swastika in territories of the Caucasus has first received attention from De Morgan.

It is clear then that the Hindu Swastika must share the fate of the Hindus themselves in the recent catastrophe which has befallen the primitive Asiatic

---

13. RUDOLF VIRCHOW, *Das Gräberfeld von Koban.*

14. SALAMON REINACH, *Musée de St. Germain en Laye, Catalogue*, p. 102. "Le Caucase est un des centres primitifs de la Métallurgie, en même temps que la seule route de terre entre l'Asie centrale et l'Europe. Les bronzes découvertes à Koban n'offrent aucune trace d'influence Assyrienne, Égyptienne, ou Phénicienne; en revanche, on y trouve certains caractères communs à l'art celtique et a l'art du bronze Scandinave. Le courant civilisateur qui a porté le bronze dans l'Europe du Nord, a donc, suivant toute vraisemblance passé par Koban" (p. 102). The relations to Celtic and Scandinavian metal ornament, which are here specified, are undoubtedly present, but these relations indicate an original Phenician origin. The influences very possibly represent a North-European migration toward the East after the Northern "Age of Bronze" had begun, and related to the now known facts for the European "Aryans" in India. At p. 183, Reinach has related the Merovingian ornaments to the style of Hallstatt, and both to the Koban bronzes and to movements of civilization from the East. The fact is that the bronze ornament of prehistoric Europe moved from the South and East Mediterranean to the West, North-West, and North. When it reached the North it turned to the East, according to the movement of civilization, which in our own time leaves Russia inferior to Germany and subject to a civilizing movement from the West. This fact is represented by the history of words for metal, quoted from ISAAC TAYLOR, p. 330, Note 3. These quotations from the Catalogue of the St. Germain Museum are important, as showing that the relations of the Hallstatt style lvii. 4 [p. 341] to Italy and Southern Europe have not yet been sufficiently recognized, for we must presume REINACH'S *Catalogue* to be fully on a level with present science. The history of the deer and the lotus (Hallstatt, xxxix. 4 [p. 253]), of the bird, and of the horse (in style of lvii. 5 [p. 341], common at Hallstatt), is thus seen to be important as fixing the source of ornaments which travelled with them. The birds and deer of Hallstatt are well represented by the Tyrol piece xxxix. 8 [p. 253], and the Italian pieces lvii. 8, 13, 16 [p. 341].

15. J. DE MORGAN, *Mission Scientifique au Caucase.*

Aryans, and that a similar migration from the West must be ascribed to it. As to the Swastikas of Troy, they are far less numerous than those of Cyprus, of Rhodes, or of Greek Geometric vases, and must be subordinated to them in a general explanation.

The Swastika plays no rôle in Africa. Its presence in Dahomey[16] must be classed with the problems of the solar bird and lotus spiral in the same quarter (Fig. 146 [p. 274]), and of the Kabyle pottery (lxiv. [p. 385]).[17]

The Swastika in Yucatan (lxiii. 14 [p. 379]) on pottery of the Zunis,[18] and otherwise in ancient American art, must be considered the lightest feather in the load which has been so inconsiderately laid on the shoulders of American archæology by the Ninth Edition of the *Encyclopedia Britannica*, in its treatise on the Zodiac.[19]

Having posed the centre from which the Swastika must be studied, it remains to point out its origin.

There is no proposition in archæology which can be so easily demonstrated as the assertion that the Swastika is originally a fragment of the Egyptian meander, provided Greek Geometric vases are called in evidence. The connection between the meander and the Swastika has been long since suggested by Professor A. S. Murray.[20] On the side of Hindu specialists it has been even suggested that the Swastika produced the meander.[21]

A recent publication on the Swastika has not only reproposed this derivation of the meander, but has even connected the Mycenæ spirals with this supposed development,[22] and has proposed to change the name of the spiral ornament accordingly. The actual fact is as supposed by Murray.

---

16. SCHLIEMANN's *Ilios*, which also mentions the Swastika on a vase from Yucatan, in the Berlin Museum.

17. The beautiful Ashantee jewellery of the British Museum comprises several very obvious lotus patterns, and also shows the entire flower in gold.

18. On Zuni pottery in the Peabody Museum at Cambridge, Mass. I believe that I am the first to announce it in publication. The culture of the Zunis is a survival from ancient times, and probably Toltic.

19. The Aztec Zodiac is the exact counterpart of the Hindu, the three animals which are not found in Mexico being replaced by others which correspond to them in character. Moreover "the Aztec Calendar includes Nak-shatra titles borrowed, not only through the medium of the Tartar Zodiac, but likewise straight from the Indian scheme, without any known intervention."

20. In Pottery Appendix to CESNOLA's *Cyprus*, p. 410. "The crosses which Dr. Schliemann calls suastikas, but which, in fact, appear to be only the simplest form or element of the meander pattern."

21. BIRDWOOD, *Industrial Arts of India*, p. 107. "I believe the *swastika* to be the origin of the key-pattern ornament of Greek and Chinese decorative art."

22. "Wir sehen also, das dass sogenannte Spiral-ornament der Prähistorischen Epoche ebenfalls auf der Suastika-ornament basirt. . . . Desshalb ist die Benennung Spiral-

THE SWASTIKA. 353

The equivalence of the Swastika with the meander pattern is suggested, in the first instance, by its appearance in the shape of the meander on Rhodian (xxviii. 7 [p. 203]), Melian (lx. 8), archaic Greek (lx. 9; lxi. 12 [p. 365]), and Greek Geometric vases (lvi. [p. 339]). The appearance in shape of the meander may be verified in the British Museum on one Geometric vase of the oldest type, and it also occurs in the Louvre.

Instances of the simultaneous appearance of the Swastika in both forms on the same piece (lx. 8) and of transitions from one form to the other on the same piece are easily illustrated (lx. 9; lxi. 12 [p. 365]).

The most interesting evidence lies in the correspondence between the Swastika panels of Greek Geometric vases (lx. 13; lvi. 4 [p. 339]) and corresponding panels of other vases in which other sections of the meander pattern are given

170. MEANDER DETAIL WITH SOLAR GEESE. GREEK "GEOMETRIC" VASE in the Louvre.

171. MEANDER DETAIL WITH SOLAR GEESE. GREEK "GEOMETRIC" VASE in the Cabinet des Médailles.

172. MEANDER DETAIL WITH SOLAR GEESE. GREEK "GEOMETRIC" VASE in the British Museum.

173. SWASTIKA WITH SOLAR GEESE. GREEK "GEOMETRIC" VASE in the British Museum.

the same distinction (lviii. 3 [p. 343], and Figs. 170, 171, 172, 173). The evidence of a vase in the Polytechnic at Athens, one of whose details is shown by Fig. 174, may be considered decisive.

We may add that there is no style which presents so many meander variants. Compare lxi. 2 [p. 365] (a later vase, but showing a meander pattern of the old style) with various patterns of lvi. [p. 339]. Finally the evidence of the solar geese (p. 270) comes into play. When we find them facing on one occasion a

---

ornament eine unvollständige, weil sie bloss die form Suastika-ornament zu ersetzen?" *Zur Geschichte der* berücksichtigt. Wäre es nicht möglich, dieselbe mit *Suastika* (p. 179). See Note 8.

Z Z

354 THE SWASTIKA.

Swastika (Fig. 173) and on another occasion some other sectional variant of the meander (Figs. 170, 171, 172), the conclusion is obvious that the same symbolism is at stake in either case.

The solar significance of the Swastika is proven by Hindu coins of the Jains.[23] Its generative significance is proven by a leaden statuette from Troy.[24]

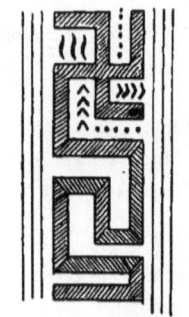

174. MEANDER WITH SWASTIKA.
Detail of the vase No. 2843 in the Polytechnic, Athens. From Author's sketch.

It is an equivalent of the lotus (xlvii. 1, 2, 3 [p. 303]); of the solar diagram (lvii. 12 [p. 341]; lx. 8); of the rosette (xx. 8 [p. 153]) centre of the rosette; of concentric rings (xlvii. 11 [p. 303]); of the spiral scroll (xxxiv. 8 [p. 227]; xxxix. 2 [p. 253]); of the geometric "boss" (xlviii. 12 [p. 305]); of the "triangle" (xlvi. 5 [p. 289]); and of the anthemion (xxviii. 7 [p. 203]; xxx. 4 [p. 211]). It appears with the solar deer (lx. 1, 2 [p. 359]); with the solar antelope (xxxvii. 9 [p. 249]); with the symbolic fish (xlii. 1 [p. 267]); with the solar ibex (xxxvii. 4 [p. 249]); with the solar Sphinx (xxxiv. 8 [p. 227]); with the solar lion (xxx. 4 [p. 211]); the solar ram (xxviii. 7 [p. 203]; and the solar horse (lxi. 1, 4, 5, 12 [p. 365]). Its most emphatic and constant association is with the solar bird (lx. 15; Fig. 173).

The appearance of the meander pattern on two Egyptian scarabs has been noticed (p. 94). It is also found on an "Eye" amulet of the British Museum.[25] The equivalence of the Egyptian spiral scroll with the Egyptian meander has been specified (p. 93), and the relations of the spiral scroll to the Egyptian lotus spirals (x. [p. 97]), and to Egyptian concentric rings, have been observed (viii. [p. 87]). Since the evidence for the original symbolism of the Ionic form has been presented, we may recur with greater emphasis to the Cypriote Ionic capital in form of concentric rings (viii. 14).

Much learning has been devoted to the symbolism of the cross in ante-Christian times. It is apparent from pottery examples (lx. 9; lxi. 12 [p. 365], that the ante-Christian cross is a Swastika and meander variant. The adoption of the Swastika by Christian symbolism, and its symbolic

---

23. SCHLIEMANN, *Ilios*, p. 346. The matter being furnished by Mr. EDWARD THOMAS, the Oriental Numismatist.

24. Quoted to that effect by SCHLIEMANN. See lx. 4.

25. British Museum, Third Egyptian Room, No. 17,943.

THE SWASTIKA. 355

juxtaposition with the Christian cross on early Christian monuments are well-known facts.

An intermediate form of abbreviation for the meander is the cross with spots in the angles (lx. 6). The equivalence of this form with the Trojan Swastika has been recognized,[26] (compare lx. 11; lx. 12). By actual count of Trojan whorls from Schliemann excavations this form is nearly as common at Troy as the Swastika proper. On Cypriote and Rhodian vases this variant is nearly as common as the ordinary Swastika.

Another common Rhodian Swastika variant moves from the Swastika with

175. SWASTIKA DIAGRAMS.

spiral arms to a form which joins the arms with the central cross, preserving the dots (Fig. 175). Compare the two forms at lx. 2; and at xlvi. 7 [p. 289].

A similar variant was obtained from the rectangular Swastika (Fig. 176). Compare xxxiv. 7 [p. 227].

Another variant was obtained by drawing the Swastika in two strokes and inclining the arms of the cross (Fig. 177).

176. SWASTIKA DIAGRAMS.

The demonstration for this form of the Swastika is obtained from the Dipylon vase of Curium, in New York, where the stroke may be observed in both forms. This form of the Swastika stroke, with arms nearly joined in form of a diamond, is also found on a Geometric vase at Athens.

177. SWASTIKA DIAGRAMS.

The above variants are mainly confined to pottery, excepting the simple cross, and for obvious reasons. It is only on pottery that such variants would naturally develop, because here the pattern was so frequently repeated, and because an off-hand execution was employed.

The Rhodian pottery is the distinctive home of these and other solar diagrams (xxviii. 7 [p. 203]), and was as expert and as metaphysical in their manufacture as the Cypriote pottery in the manufacture of geometric lotuses. The only Swastika variants of the Cypriote pottery are the cross and the cross with dots. The cross is not found in the early Greek Geometric style, and of all other meander variants the Swastika was destined, by the case with which

---

26. By MICHAEL V. ZMIGRODZKI, p. 174, as above (Note 6). By actual count from the Schliemann Atlas, it shows thirty-five Swastikas of the cross form with dots in the angles, as against fifty-five normal Swastikas. The proportion of cross forms must be fully as large on Cypriote vases.

it was designed, and the peculiarity of its appearance to survive the longest and to travel farthest.

The Greek cross is no rarity, however, in ante-Christian symbolism. Its large dimensions on the Cypriote vase lx. 10 are especially interesting. The ordinary solar diagrams also appear here. The projecting lotus buds are specified

178. COPTIC LOTUS CROSSES.
Relief at Medinet Habou. Specially photographed for the Author.

179. CROSS OF LOTUSES.
Turin Senrab, No. 1009.
From Author's sketch.

by the demonstration for xlviii. 17 [p. 305]. The Maltese cross is not rare, and is composed of four lotus triangles (lx. 3, 14; compare xlix. 11 [p. 307]). The Christian Coptic cross is a lotus cross (Fig. 178), and I do not remember ever to have seen it without the trefoil indication. The Latin cross appears in ante-Christian times, on a Cypriote cylinder,[27] and is otherwise known.

These forms were avoided by native Egyptian art, but the cross is worn as neck amulet by a captive in an Egyptian picture.[28] The amulets lx. 5, 6, 7 are Egyptian in locality of find and in material, but are probably of foreign character. The presence of these diagrams on amulets is, however, significant.

The earliest dated Swastikas are of the third millenium B.C., and occur on the foreign Cypriote and Carian (?) pottery fragments of the time of the XIIth Dynasty, discovered by Mr. Petrie in 1889.[29] They appear on the "Hut-urns" of prehistoric Italy in shapes which are clearly sections of meanders.[30] The evidence of Fig. 174 is decisive as regards the question of origin.

27. CESNOLA, *Cyprus*, KING'S Gem Appendix, vii. 14.
28. CHAMPOLLION, I. lxvii. From Beit-Ouali. For Greek crosses on cylinders see MENANT, *Cylindres*, ii. p. 141. A small gold Greek cross in Athens was found in one of the Mycenæ tombs.
29. PETRIE, *Kahun, Gurob, and Hawara*, Plate xxvii., Nos. 162, 173.
30. In the Kircher Museum at Rome.

APPENDIX.

LIST OF PLATES SHOWING THE SWASTIKA.—xxviii. [p. 203], Rhodian, meander and ram.—xxx. 2, 4, 10 [p. 211], Naukratic, early Greek, normal Swastikas and lions.—xxxiv. 2 [p. 227], Trojan, cross and Sphinx.—xxxiv. 8 [p. 227], Melian, meander and Sphinx.—xxxvii. 9 [p. 249], early Attic, normal Swastika and antelope.—xxxviii. [p. 251], Rhodian, variants, including cross, ibexes, and lotuses.—xxxix. 2 [p. 253], Melian, meander and ibex.—xlii. [p. 267], Rhodian, cross and fish.—xlv. 3 [p. 287], Cypriote, with lotuses.—xlvi. [p. 289], Greek and Rhodian. No. 4, bird, lotus, crosses. Nos. 5, 7, 10, with birds and lotuses.—xlvii. 1, 2, 3 [p. 303], Cypriote, with lotuses, good examples of cross variants.—xlviii. 3, 6, 15 [p. 305], Cypriote, with geometric lotuses.—l. 11 [p. 309], Cypriote, with quadrangle.—lvi. 4 [p. 339], Greek Geometric vase with birds—the most important of all examples, as showing the distinct Swastika type of Geometric vases.—lxi. 1, 4 [p. 365], Greek Geometric, with horse.—lxi. 5 [p. 365], Corinthian coin, with Pegasus.—lxi. 12 [p. 365], early Greek, with horse.—lxiii. 14 [p. 379], Yucatan stone relief.—lxiv. 4, 7 [p. 385], Cypriote geometric.

PLATE LX.

THE SWASTIKA.

1. Troy Pottery whorl. Swastikas and deer (many similar). SCHLIEMANN, *Troy*.
2. Rhodian pottery detail. Deer and Swastika, diagrams. *Monumenti Inediti*, ix., v. 2.
3. Cypriote vase, New York Museum. Maltese cross of four geometric lotuses (compare Plate xlix. [p. 307]).
4. Trojan idol of lead, Swastika. SCHLIEMANN, *Ilios*, p. 337.
5. Egyptian (intrusive ?) seal with cross. KLAPROTH, v. 228.
6. Egyptian (intrusive ?) seal with Swastika variant. KLAPROTH, v. 228.
7. Egyptian (intrusive ?) seal, related to No. 6. *Description de l'Égypte*, A., v. 88, 46.
8. Detail, Melian vase; deer (held by Artemis); four solar diagrams; a motive derived from pattern l. 4 [p. 309]; diagram of four similar objects, and three Swastikas, one of them a section of meander. (Compare Plate x. 9 [p. 97].) CONZE, *Melische Thongefässe*.
9. Detail, archaic Bœotian vase. Two serpents and Swastikas, showing meander patterns approaching the simplified Swastika, and variant Swastika crosses. Plate lxi. 12 [p. 365] shows the Meander Swastika, Swastika, and Swastika cross on one detail.
10. Cypriote vase, New York Museum. Cross with four motives derived from lotus buds (Pl. xlviii. 17 [p. 305]); two solar diagrams.
11. Bird-headed vase; Swastika. SCHLIEMANN, *Troy*, p. 191.
12. Bird-headed vase; Swastika variant No. 6. SCHLIEMANN, *Ilios*, p. 521. (For bird-headed female idols, see CESNOLA, *Cyprus*, p. 164.)
13. Greek Geometric vase, London; similar ones at Sèvres. CONZE, *Anfänge*, &c., v. 4. Only Geometric vases show Swastikas in large dimension and in symmetrical relation to entire panels, which, in related examples, contain other sections of meander patterns; but other Geometric vases show Swastikas of intermediate dimension and also the usual small ones, without symmetrical relation to a panel.
14. Cypriote vase, New York Museum. Maltese cross (compare No. 3), various examples; also Rhodian.
15. Cypriote vase, New York Museum. Typical example of many pieces for the bird and lotus with Swastikas. Other examples show only the bird and Swastika, but never in the large dimension of the Geometric style. Many vases of form l. 4 [p. 309] show the small Swastika in centre of a panel, corresponding to others of same form in which the solar diagram replaces the Swastika. The deer and Swastika, horse and Swastika, are also found on Cypriote vases in New York.

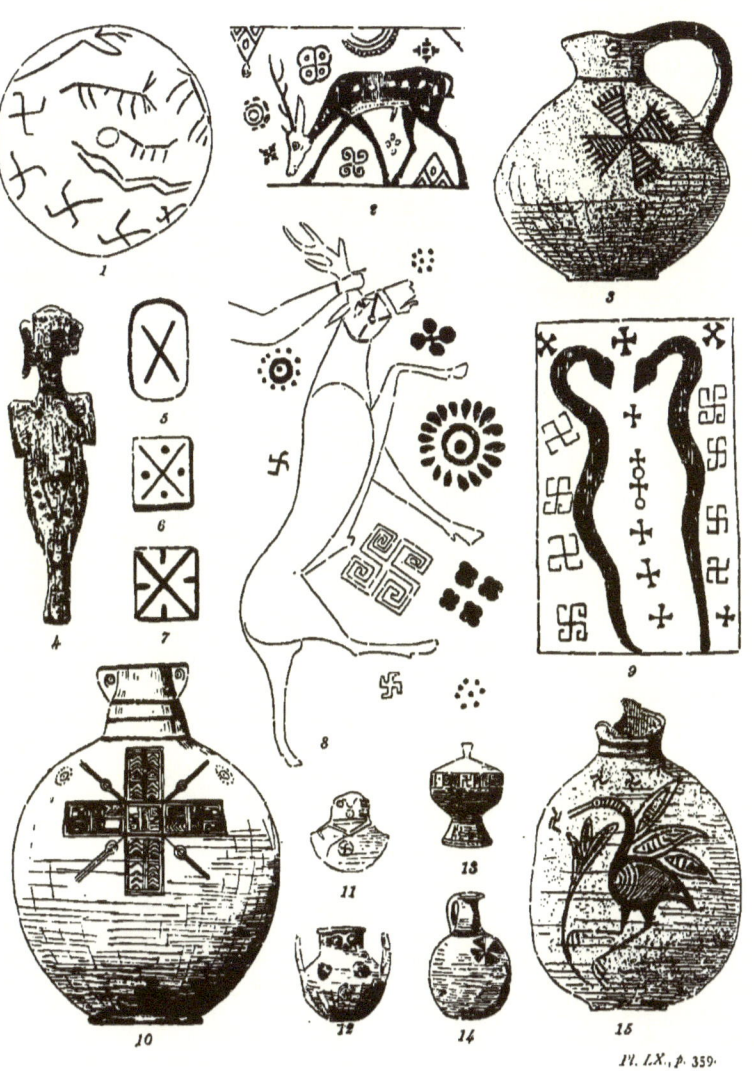

THE HORSE AND THE LOTUS.

(PLATE LXI., PAGE 365.)

THE horse was known to Herodotus[1] as a solar animal among the "Scythians" (who have been identified with the European Aryans),[2] but he did not know that it had been a solar animal of the Greeks. Under the form of Pegasus, whose solar associations are recognized,[3] the horse had been idealized, and his own bodily symbolism was generally unknown to the Greeks of the fifth century B.C.

It was, however, a Rhodian custom to sacrifice annually four horses to the sun,[4] and the sacrifice of a horse to the sun was also made at Taygetus.[5] With the Celts,[6] Germans,[7] Persians,[8] and Hindus,[9] the horse was a well-known sun symbol, and he is also quoted for Chaldean,[10] Syrian,[11] and Carthaginian[12] worship, aside from the evidence furnished by the winged horse of Assyrian reliefs,[13] with Sacred Tree of buds.

---

1. See also Note 9 for Indo-Scythian coins.

2. According to a note in the *Academy*, July 6, 1889; the Scyths and Thracians were Germanic peoples.

3. BAUMEISTER, *Antike Denkmäler*, under "Pegasus."

4. ROBERTSON SMITH, *Religion of the Semites*, p. 275. Four horses were cast in the sea at the annual feast of the sun.

5. *Ibid.*, quoting from PAUSANIAS, iii. 20.

6, 7. WARING, *Ceramic Art in Remote Ages*, p. 59. "The horse, which was a national emblem with the Kelts as with the Teutons, has always been an animal sacred to the sun."

8. LAJARD, *Culte de Mithra*, p. 8.

9. BIRDWOOD. Matter relating to sacrifice of the horse in the Ramayana (p. 66). "The twelve adventures of the horse which Yudhisthira loosed are twelve legends connected with the countries over which the sun is supposed to shine in his annual course (p. 19). . . . The *Arushas* ('red') of the Rig-Veda, and Rohitas ('red') of the Atharva-Veda, are the red horses of the rising sun; and the *Haritas* ('green'), or green horses, are typical of the radiant beams of the rising and setting sun. The winged horse, *Tarkshya*, is a very ancient mythological personification of the sun (p. 52)." See also paper in *Babylonian Record*, 1887, No. 10, by Dr. MARK AUREL STEIN, on Zoroastrian deities on Indo-Scythian coins. "A bearded god beside a horse with an epithet meaning swift-horsed— the common epithet of the sun and the god Apâm napât, an old Aryan personification of the fire and lightning."

10. SAYCE, *Hibbert Lectures*, p. 279. "Eagle, horse, lion; totem gods of Accad."

11. ROBERTSON SMITH, quoting 2 *Kings* xxiii. 11, for the horse which the kings of Judah had consecrated to the Sun god.

12. ROBERTSON SMITH, p. 276. "Winged horse, Pegasus, a sacred symbol to the Carthaginians."

13. LAYARD's *Plates*.

Pegasus without wings is supposed to be a rarity in Greek art,[14] but Greek Geometric vases would lead to a contrary supposition, as at least indicating the solar origins of a possibly later myth. To the winged Pegasus with Swastika (lxi. 5), and with lotus spirals (lxi. 13), we may add mention of a vase in the British Museum, which shows him with a "Tree" of lotus leaves.[15]

The horse with the normal lotus can be quoted in several instances.[16] There is an Egyptian tomb-picture of a vase with this association,[17] undoubtedly of Syrian style or importation. The presence of the horse in Egypt is generally dated from the XVIIIth Dynasty, but he must have been well known under Hyksos (Mongolian) rule.[18] According to a reference by Dr. Birch to the horse—"Traces of worship are supposed to be found."[19]

180. BIRDS WITH A HORSE'S MANE.
From the coloured designs of Hallstatt bronzes in the Museum of St. Germain. Photographed for the Author.

In Plate lxi. 8 the distinctly Egyptian lotus (for the pendant tabs see vii. [p. 79]; ix. [p. 91]) with rampant horses is Phenician art, or possibly Greek or Etruscan, under that influence. The vase from Thera (2, 3) shows the horse with spiral scroll on the haunch and inverted lotus triangles. The latest typical appearance of the solar horse without wings on Greek vases would date from the style of such examples, or from the Melian, lxi. 7. The tomb-sculpture of Asia Minor (6) is interesting for the sepulchral association with all solar symbolism carried with it.

The solar horse appears occasionally on Cypriote vases with the lotus (11), more frequently with the Swastika, but he is confined as a frequent type to the Greek Geometric style (lxi. 4; lvi. 1 [p. 339]), to Celtic Italian art (lxi. 9; lvii. 5 [p. 341]), and to Hallstatt. With concentric rings, as in the last example, he is very common at Hallstatt. An

---

14. BAUMEISTER, *Antike Denkmäler*, mentions a case of Pegasus without wings, "merkwürdiger Weise."

15. Second Vase Room, Case 29-30, B. 148.

16. *Monumenti Inediti*, IX. xliv. Silver *patera*, Egypto-Phenician style, horse in the lotus "grove" or bower. Similar gold *patera* from Cyprus in the New York Museum; bull and horses in the lotus "grove." Miss AMELIA B. EDWARDS has been good enough to send me a photograph

of a terra-cotta fragment from Egypt, representing a horse's head resting on the flower.

17. PRISSE D'AVENNES, *Vases en or émaillé*.

18. As noted by Canon ISAAC TAYLOR, *Origin of the Aryans*, p. 159.

19. BIRCH, in WILKINSON'S *Ancient Egyptians*, III., 3rd Edit., p. 299, in a foot-note to Wilkinson's statement that "the horse did not enjoy sacred honours."

exactly corresponding treatment of the mane connects the Hallstatt art directly with the Italian. This treatment of the mane (Fig. 181) will be found to correspond with the projections occasionally appearing on the head of the Hallstatt "bird" as at Fig. 180. Such instances show the habits of a barbaric art, copying, without comprehension, patterns which have been handed over to it along with a technique in metals, also borrowed. The bird with horse's mane represents the same general fact as the bird in shape of a pot-hook. Both are proofs that the patterns which attend them—concentric rings, chevrons, meanders, and spirals, are also borrowed.

181. HORSES AND BIRDS WITH A HORSE'S MANE.
From the coloured designs of Hallstatt bronzes in the Museum of St. Germain.
Photographed for the Author.

PLATE LXI.

THE HORSE AND THE LOTUS.

1. Greek Geometric vase, in Leyden, from Smyrna (?), detail at No. 4; Swastikas and solar diagram. A similar vase in the New York Museum from Cyprus, with the double axe (an indication of Carian origin).* CONZE, *Anfänge*, iv. a.

2. Detail of No. 3. Vase from Thera, British Museum. Horse, spiral scroll on the haunch, and lotus triangles. Compare xlvi. 3, 5 [p. 289], and Plate xlix. [p. 307]. The form of meander pattern here found is a common abbreviation on the earliest Geometric vases, but the guilloche of this vase is not found in the pure Geometric style. On the vase, indications of concentric rings, lotus triangles inverted but terminating in Ionic volutes and palmette ; chevrons at the base. Compare lix. [p. 345] for the base. On reverse, lion attacking a deer (Fig. 141 [p. 256]). *Monumenti Inediti*, viii. 6.

5. Corinthian coin. Pegasus and solar diagram like xxviii. 5 [p. 203], uncompleted or obscured. Reverse, the Swastika. J. DE MORGAN, *Mission Scientifique au Caucase*, i. p. 161.

6. Rock carving over tomb, Yapyl Dak, Asia Minor ; from CANINA, *Etruria Maritima*, cxxvii.

7. Horses and lotus, Melian pottery detail, repeated from Plate xviii. [p. 146]; entire vase, xix. 1 [p. 147]. Compare xvii. [p. 145.]

8. Horses rampant, two lotus forms. Bronze detail. *Monumenti Inediti*, xii. 2.

9. Prehistoric bronze vase, Southern Tyrol. *Repoussé* detail. Inverted trefoil lotus, rudimentary rosette, lotus bud in the horse's mouth. From the same vase as detail xxxix. 8 [p. 253] of antelopes, and deer with lotus spirals in the mouth, and lotus bud border. On the same Plate, Hallstatt and other prehistoric details of normal lotuses springing from mouths of animals. See also xxxiv. 3 [p. 227] ; xxvii. 3 [p. 197]. All quoted are prehistoric "Umbrian" or Celtic. *Monumenti Inediti*, x. 6. An antelope with lotus stems and buds hanging from the mouth on a Cypriote vase, xlix. 5 [p. 307].

10. Horses and solar diagrams. Archaic Greek vase, Copenhagen. *Archæologische Zeitung*, 1885, Taf. 8.

11. Cypriote vase, New York Museum. Horse, lotus, and solar diagram.

12. Early Bœotian vase detail ; horse, solar diagram, Artemis with geese,† Swastikas. This detail shows three Swastika variants—meander, normal, and cross.

13. Pegasus and lotus spirals. Greek vase, Athens. BENNDORF, *Vasengemälde*, V. lii.

---

* The double axe is an emblem of the Carian Zeus. It occurs on Carian coins. SCHUCHARDT, *Schliemann's Ausgrabungen*, p. 285.

† Such pictures have been mistaken for a goddess strangling geese, but the geese are simply held as symbols. This is the natural view, and is supported by O. KELLER, *Thiere*, &c. (p. 292).

THE LOTUS IN ANCIENT AMERICA.

(PLATES LXII., LXIII., PAGES 377, 379.)

It is beyond my purpose and my strength to carry the history of ornament outside of Europe, and in admitting the Plates for ancient American ornament, limited as they must be, I have but one end—to point out that the burden of proof rests with those who claim that the meander, spiral scroll, concentric rings, and chevron, have developed in ancient America without European or Asiatic contact.[1] It is for such to prove that ancient America had no contact with Europe or with Asia.

In making this proof they will be obliged to explain the following facts:— that there is an Egyptian winged disk at Ococingo, in Yucatan (lxii. 2); that the winged disk of Assyrian style is found in Yucatan (lxii. 8); that there is a statue holding an Egyptian hieroglyph at Palenque (lxii. 7)[2]; that the "Semitic Venus" is a familiar type of ancient Mexican art (lxii. 1); that the "Bird and  the Lotus" occur in ancient Mexico (lxiii. 16), and on Zuni pottery (Figs. 182, 183); that the Swastika is found in ancient America (lxiii. 14) with its variants

182. THE BIRD AND THE LOTUS.
From a Zuni Vase in the National Museum at Washington. From Author's sketch. Compare Plates xliii.-xlvi. [pp. 283-289].

183. THE BIRD AND THE LOTUS TRIANGLE (?).
From a Zuni Vase, owned by a lady in Chicago. Compare Plate xlvi. 5 [p. 289] and Plate xlix. 8 [p. 307].

1. As long as these patterns are supposed to be independent of one another in various Mediterranean countries, it would be unnatural to suppose that they were not also independent in America; but, on the instant that their unity becomes apparent for the Mediterranean world, their independence in America becomes problematic.

2. The hieroglyph is *Men*.

(lxiii. 3); that the "Deer and the Lotus" occur on Zuni pottery (Fig. 184); and that the ordinary Egyptian trefoil or three-spiked lotus is a familiar feature of ancient American ornament (lxiii. 1, 4, 6, 7, 10, 11, 12, 13, 21, and details on page herewith).[3]

184. THE DEER (ELK) AND THE LOTUS. From a Zuni Vase in the National Museum at Washington. From Author's sketch. Compare Plates xxxv.-xxxviii. (pp. 245-251).

It will be also necessary for those who appeal to the American meanders, scrolls, and spirals, as proof that such ornaments develop spontaneously and independently in all quarters of the globe, to explain the Hindu character of the Aztec Zodiac as specified by the "Encyclopædia Britannica," and to show that there was no Buddhist art in ancient America.[4]

The ancient accounts of early voyages to America are very numerous,[5] and very specific. The most interesting summary of

3. These details are from KINGSBOROUGH, according to following references, beginning at the top: (1) Vol. II., 66; (2) Vol. II., 31; (3) Vol. III., 37; (4) no reference; (5) Vol. II., 82; (6) Vol. II., 1; (7) Vol. II., 65. The details are from pictures of religious subjects in ancient Mexican MSS., and represent a very large number of others. Kingsborough's second volume is full of them.

4. CHARLES G. LELAND, *Fusang, or the discovery of America by Chinese Buddhist priests in the fifth century,; containing the narrative of Hoei-Shin, with comments by . . . C. F. Neumann; a letter from Colonel B. Kennon, on the Navigation of the North Pacific Ocean, &c.*, London, 1875.

5. A. L. FROTHINGHAM, Jun., Professor of Archæology in Princeton College, has recently published a mention of the existence of America as occurring in a Syrian author of the seventh century A.D., *American Journal of Archæology*, 1888. The following passage is quoted in BALDWIN'S *Ancient America*, from DIODORUS: "Over against Africa lies a very great continent in the vast ocean, many days' sail from Libya westward. . . . The Phenicians (Tyrians), having found out the coasts beyond the pillars of Hercules, sailed along by the coast of Africa. One of their ships, on a sudden, was driven by a furious storm far off into the main ocean. After they had lain under this tempest many days, they at length arrived at this island." The description omitted mentions, among other ordinary characteristics of large continents, the fact that it contained many navigable streams. The experience above narrated befell a small barque bound from Lancerota to Teneriffe in 1731. It was picked up by an English cruiser within two days' sail of Caraccas, with the crew still living.—GLASS, in his History of the Canary Islands, quoted by A. P. DUNLOP in *New York Saturday Review*, August 9, 1890. Chinese junks have reached Hawaii and the coast of North America with living sailors under similar conditions (*Encyclopædia Britannica*, 9th Edition, "Polynesia").

ancient records on this head is furnished by the "Antiquités Mexicaines," published about 1832, as result of the three expeditions of Captain Dupaix. A

185. SUN-DISK SURROUNDED BY LOTUSES AND LOTUS BUDS.
Detail of a Pompeian fresco from the temple of Isis, No. 9189, Naples Museum. From Author's sketch. To be compared with Mexican detail lxiii. 4 [p. 379].

similar summary is offered by the first chapter of the recently published "Critical History of America," edited by Mr. Justin Winsor, the librarian of Harvard University. The attitude of this latter publication is entirely agnostic and sceptical, which does not lessen the interest or value of the quotations.

The voyages of the Phenicians around Africa under Necho, about 600 B.C., and of the Greek Pytheas, of Marseilles to Iceland in the third century, B.C., are matters of current information. It is also known that the Phenicians were acquainted with the Canaries and with the Sarragossa Sea.[6] The probability of Phenician voyages to America has been favourably considered by various writers of conservative tendencies. The destruction of Phenician records in the great temple at Carthage by the Romans, and the Phenician jealousy of foreign competition with their trading connections, as explaining reticence about them, are well-known facts. Movers has furnished the most interesting information regarding the seaworthy quality of Phenician vessels, and the distinction between their galleys and their heavier sailing vessels.[7]

One of the greatest modern Anthropologists has related the skulls of the Guaranas of Brazil to those of the Guanches of the Canary Islands.[8] The un-American characteristics of the Caribs have been pointed out by other writers.[9] At least three inscriptions in alphabets related to those of ancient Europe have been found intact in American tombs under convincing circumstances, attested by unimpeachable testimony.[10] An inscription in characters corresponding

6. PAUL GAFFAREL in *Congrès des Américanistes*, 1875.
7. *Geschichte de Phönizier*.
8. RETZIUS; as quoted in JUSTIN WINSOR'S *Critical History of America*; First Chapter.
9. A. P. DUNLOP, in *New York Saturday Review*, August 9th, 1890.

10. Rev. J. GASS in *Proceedings of the Davenport (Iowa) Academy of Natural Sciences*, Vol. II. "An account of the discovery of inscribed tablets, with a description by Dr. R. J. Farquaharson," 1877. The characters indicate a much-degraded or very primitive Mediterranean alphabet. A copy of another inscription lately discovered in Ohio has

to those of the Carian alphabet was found at Grave Creek in Western Virginia, in 1838, in an intact tumulus; seven years at least before Lepsius saw the Carian incriptions at Ipsamboul, which were the first ones ever recognized, and thirty-four years before Professor A. H. Sayce published the first collation of a Carian alphabet.[11] This inscription contains letters which are not found in the Celtiberian alphabet, published by Grotefend, in 1836, which mainly corresponds with the Carian alphabet (Fig. 186).[12]

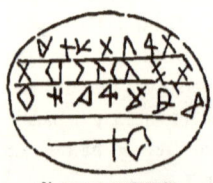

186. CARIAN INSCRIPTION.
From Grave Creek, West Virginia. Discovered in 1838. Announced as Carian (Celtic) 1890, by the Author.

It may be difficult to prove that the Phenicians were in ancient America, but it appears necessary for those who assert the independent origin of the American spiral (lxii. 6), chevron (lxii. 9), "Mycenæ" leaf (lxii. 10), meander (lxii. 11), Ionic form (lxiii. 15), and anthemion (lxiii. 17), to prove that they were not there, which

been forwarded me by the courtesy of the Smithsonian Institution. As this Institution has been extremely conservative and circumspect in the matter of American inscriptions, their action may be considered to guarantee the authenticity of the one which has been sent to me.

11. PROFESSOR A. H. SAYCE, in *Transactions of the Royal Society of Literature*, 1873, and *Transactions of the Society of Biblical Archæology*, 1887.

12. The facts regarding the discovery of the Grave Creek Tablet have been published by SCHOOLCRAFT in his *Indian Tribes*, Vol. I., and were also published by SCHOOLCRAFT in the *Proceedings of the New York Ethnological Society*, 1847. The tablet has been published in Europe by RAFN, *Mémoires des Antiquaires du Nord*, 1844, who found a majority of the characters to be Celtiberian; by JOMARD, President and founder of the Geographical Society of France, who announced them, in 1843, to be related to the alphabet of the Touaregs of the Sahara; by MOÏSE SCHWAB, who announced them as Punic in the *Revue Archéologique*, 1867; by OPPERT, who offered another translation of the inscription as being Punic in the paper prepared by Schwab; and by LEVY BING, in *Congrès des Américanistes*, 1875, who also considered the alphabet Semitic. I called attention to the Carian equivalents of the characters of the Grave Creek Tablet in the *New York Herald*, July 27th, 1890. There is no other alphabet which has an equivalent for every character. The copies of the tablet published in European journals have all been slightly defective as compared with the copy taken by Schoolcraft. The stone is described by Schoolcraft as of dark-coloured sandstone, showing ancient natural cleavage, and having an oval form, 2¾ inches by 2¼ inches, and 7/10 of an inch in thickness. It was found in an intact tumulus 70 feet high, in which there were two tombs—one at the base of the mound, and one near its centre. Other objects found in the tombs did not show decorative features. Three bodies had been buried in the mound. The skeletons were in advanced decay, and the skulls were broken. The various objects, discovered by a systematic excavation in 1838, were at first kept together at Grave Creek, but were subsequently dispersed. There is no mention of the tablet since about 1850, when it was supposed to be owned in Richmond, Virginia. There were found with the tablet many hundreds (1700) of small beads, supposed by the finders to be ivory, but noted by Schoolcraft as of sea-shell; five copper bracelets, and 150 small pieces of mica, each piece having perforations. A small sandstone tablet, decorated with concentric rings, was found in a "Mound-builder's" tomb, of the same neighbourhood. There are Indian traditions regarding a white race as having been settled in this part of America, which were brought to the notice of the Royal Geographical Society in 1842. Professor F. W. Putnam, of the Peabody Museum, at Cambridge, Mass., has recently mentioned statuettes found in "Mound-builder" tombs of the Ohio Valley as having Egyptian head-dress, but does not specify the whereabouts of these figures.

THE LOTUS IN ANCIENT AMERICA.

may also be difficult. The existence of three hundred Phenician cities on the West Coast of Africa, settlements of Carians and "Mycenæans" [Carians] among them, is not to be overlooked.[13]

187. MEXICAN TERRA-COTTA SPHINX.
New York Museum.

An absolutely conclusive proof of the influence of foreign civilizations on the ancient American lies in the correspondence between the Aztec and the Hindu Zodiac.[14] As the Hindu Zodiac came to Hindustan from the West, it is perhaps not necessary to assume that its transmission to America was by way of the Pacific American Coast, or that this transmission was made from Hindustan, but influences from Asia are otherwise certainly demonstrated (Note 4). It is apparently certain that ancient American civilization experienced foreign influences, both from East and West. It is therefore necessary to turn to a brief review of the ornament of Polynesia as related to that of the Malays and of the Indian Archipelago.

The indications for scroll and spiral ornament in Polynesia are generally very slight, according to the evidence of the best Ethnological Collections. The Collection of the New York Museum of Natural History is very valuable. To these we may add the evidence of the Trocadero Museum in Paris, the National Museum at Washington, the British Museum Ethnological Collections, and the Museo Kircheriano at Rome.[15]

Examination of the British Museum Collection will show that the scroll, spiral, and Ionic forms of ornament in Pacific and South Asiatic waters have moved from a Malay centre, that they are most prevalent, specific, and well-defined in the Malay Peninsula and contiguous strongholds of Malay blood, and that they become barbaric, weak, and fragmentary, in exact ratio to the distance from this Malay influence. The New York Collection, which is strongest for Pacific Islands remote from the Malay centre, offers valuable negative evidence.

---

13. MOVERS, *Geschichte der Phönizier*, ii, p. 525. These cities were all ruined and deserted before the beginning of the Christian Era.

14. *Encyclopædia Britannica*, 9th Edition, "Zodiac."

15. I have not seen the Collections of Leyden, nor those of Berlin in recent years.

THE LOTUS IN ANCIENT AMERICA.

It is matter of common information that all the islands of the Pacific have been settled by their present populations within the historic period and since the Christian era,[16] and that they have been settled by populations infused with Malay blood, and subject to Malay influences. The history of the spiral in Asiatic waters is the history of Malay influence. If we turn to the original centre of this influence and contiguous points, we shall find that the ornament of the Dyaks of Borneo, or of the inhabitants of the Island of Timor, or of Perak (Malay Peninsula), is not only closely within the ordinary problems of the lotus motive, but that it offers some of the most astounding indications of dependence on the one original source of ornamental patterns (Fig. 188).

188. DYAK LOTUS SPIRAL, BORNEO. Carving on wooden scabbard, British Museum, Ethnographic Gallery, Case 204, marked "Dyak sword from Malay."

The alphabet of the Malays is Phenician[17] by way of Pali. The whole civilization of the Malay Peninsula and the Archipelago, South and South-East of India, has been coloured and created by Indian, Buddhist, or other Hindu influences. Therefore, we should find nothing surprising in the evidences of Dyak ornament, or in that of the aboriginal populations of Perak or Timor, as influenced by the Malays. But the relation to Egyptian character is even more striking than these Hindu relations would imply. A Dyak sword in the British Museum shows the lotus spiral (x. 6) in a more distinctly Egyptian detail of the lotus than is even to be found in the ordinary ancient Phenician copies. This is one instance of a generally close correspondence in the Malay Dyak ornamental details to those which have been in question through this Work—concentric rings, meanders, and chevrons included.

The most pronounced cases of survival of purely ancient forms of ornament are to be found in semi-barbaric peoples which have remained at a given stage of development, after experiencing a certain amount of civilizing influence. The Kabyles of modern Algeria offer most important evidence on this head (Plate lxiv.). The evidence of Zuni pottery is not less striking (lxii. 10; lxiii. 24, Figs. 182, 183, 184). Beside these may be placed the instance of Dyak ornament and that of the primitive tribes of Perak and of Timor.

The Malays are the Phenicians of the East, and it cannot be supposed that they had no share in that active intercourse by sea between India and Egypt

16. *Encyclopædia Britannica*, 9th Edition, "Polynesia."   17. ISAAC TAYLOR, *The Alphabet*.

which is dated at least from the seventh century B.C. The Malay influences, like the Malay blood, have penetrated as far West as Madagascar,[18] and are well attested for the Maoris of New Zealand.

The cases of meander and spiral ornament in China are within the limits of Buddhist influence, and of Mongolian contact with the West, since the days of the Hyksos in Egypt. The obvious lotus patterns of China are very interesting and numerous. They are mainly, but not all, obviously derivative. There is, for instance, a representation in Chinese art of the curling lotus sepals as seen in the "bird's-eye view," a thing unknown to lotus ornament in its supposed original home.[19]

The study of Ethnological Collections for Africa, in which the Museo Kircheriano is especially strong, does not militate against my conclusions. The indications for pattern ornament in purely barbaric Africa are related to the points of exterior contact, or influences of the Northern portion of the continent.

Icelandic ornament of the eighteenth century shows some very primitive and obvious lotus patterns.[20] The Esquimaux of Arctic America have only reached the stage of concentric rings on ivories,[21] and otherwise have no traditional ornament. This motive has probably reached them from Siberia. There are also indications that the ornament of the Ainos of Japan would, if better known, bring one near to the aboriginal characteristics of pattern ornament,[22] which are in question.

It is by no means assumed that the naturalism which invaded ancient ornamental art as early as the fourth century B.C. has not had also an influence of wide-spread character. Nor is it assumed that a Dyak, for example, does not, from his own motion, supplement the patterns which have been in question, by others drawn from naturalistic instinct or his own peculiar

---

18. *Encyclopædia Britannica*, 9th Edition, "Malays."

19. I am indebted, for valuable examples of the lotus motive in Dyak and Chinese ornament, to the studies of Mrs. MARGARET LINDSAY HUGGINS, wife and scientific assistant of the great astronomer. Her interest in the lotus is connected with her study of Sun-worship.

20. South Kensington Museum; wood carvings.

21. British Museum; Ethnological Collections.

22. The Ainos are supposed to be an intrusive population of originally European habitat, ISAAC TAYLOR, *Origin of the Aryans*, p. 109; quoting from DE QUATREFAGES. The beards and profiles of the Ainos and Todas are of European character, unlike the Japanese, or Dravidians, according to this authority. I have similar advice regarding the European traits of the Ainos from an English military officer.

374   *THE LOTUS IN ANCIENT AMERICA.*

symbolisms. The position taken is simply that the civilization which first perfected pattern ornament had so high a degree of development in very early times as compared with any other, that it has insensibly affected all, first by its civilization, second, by the patterns which went with it. It is a matter of historic fact which is in question, a matter of fact to which the history of the alphabet offers surprising analogies, and which the history of the alphabet largely explains.[23]

23. See Canon Isaac Taylor's *History of the Alphabet*.

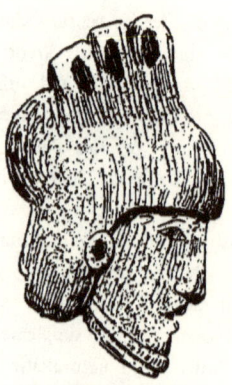

189. HELMETED HEAD. ANCIENT MEXICAN RELIEF.
From Dupaix, *Antiq. Mex.*

PLATE LXII.

THE LOTUS IN ANCIENT AMERICA.
CORROBORATIVE MONUMENTS.

1. Type of the "Semitic" and Chaldæan "Venus." DUPAIX, *Antiq. Mex.*, 2nd *Exped*, lx. Several instances in Dupaix. Very common in terra-cotta statuettes.

2. Portion of an Egyptian winged solar disk, in stucco, over a doorway near the village of Ococingo, Yucatan. The original is upside down, from an Egyptian standpoint. The Egyptian character has been noted by Waldeck and by Stephens. WALDECK, *Monumens Anciens*, &c., Plate 54 ; STEPHENS, *Yucatan*, i., p. 259. Each traveller made his own independent drawing for publication. When Stephens' design was made (here repeated) a portion of the disk had fallen away, since the time of Waldeck's copy, which shows about half the disk.

3. Winged sun-disk in shape of a human face ; stone carving, Nueva Segovia, Nicaragua. BANCROFT, *Native Races of the Pacific States*, iv. 62.

4. Terra-cotta Mexican Sphinx, about three inches high, relief style for front view only. One of several in the Lamborn Collection, New York Museum.

5. Couchant animals, a common Cypriote type (xxx. 7 [p. 211]). Stone carving, Uxmal. STEPHENS, *Yucatan*, i., 183. I am not familiar with any publication showing the lions so attached in Egyptian art, but I have observed the combination in no small number of unpublished Egyptian instances.

6. Ancient American Pottery type (many examples) ; fine black and white ware, from the Pueblos, Province of Tusayan, valley of the Little Colorado, New Mexico. To illustrate the spiral scrolls of ancient American art. National Museum, Washington, Ream Collection. *Reports of the Bureau of Ethnology*, iv., Fig. 349.

7. Stone statue, holding the hieroglyph *Men ;* Palenque, Yucatan. STEPHENS, *Central America and Yucatan*, p. 349.

8. Stone relief carving, winged sun-disk, one side broken away, of a type common in Assyrian cylinders. DUPAIX, *Antiq. Mex.*, 2nd *Exped.*, iii.

9. Ancient "Chiriqui" vase, Panama. To illustrate the chevron decoration of ancient American pottery. National Museum, Washington. *Reports, Bur. of Eth.*, 1884-5, Fig. 160.

10. Zuni vase, to illustrate the "Mycenæ" leaf (lii. 1 [p. 321] in Zuni pottery. Numerous examples (compare lxiii. 24). National Museum. *Reports*, &c., ii., Fig. 406.

11. Ancient American pottery type (many examples), fine black and white ware. To illustrate the meander in ancient American ornament. Pueblos, Province of Tusayan, New Mexico. *Reports*, &c., iv., Fig. 347.

Pl. LXII., p. 377.
3 c

PLATE LXIII.

ANCIENT AMERICAN LOTUS MOTIVES AND FOREIGN SYMBOLS.

1. Stone relief detail, lotus and curling sepals in meander treatment. At Huahuapan, Province of Oajaca, Mexico. DUPAIX, *Antiq. Mex.*, *2nd Exped.*, xix 5.
2. Mexican stone relief. DUPAIX, *2nd Exped.*, iv. 7.
3. Pottery motive. Museum, Mexico. Compare lx. 6 [p. 359]. WALDECK, *Mon.* 55.
4. Mexican stone relief. Four lotuses grouped about a solar face (compare lxii. 3). DUPAIX, *2nd Exped.*, viii. 20. Compare Fig. 185 [p. 369] from a Pompeian fresco.
5. Mexican stone relief. "Herzblatts." DUPAIX, *2nd Exped.*, iv. 7.
6. Inverted trefoil lotus with spiral scrolls. Detail from stone relief of goddess holding a child. DUPAIX, *3rd Exped.*, xxxi.
7. Stone relief fragment. Spiral and inverted trefoil lotus. Tula, Mexico. CHARNAY, *Ancient Cities of the New World*, Fig. 105.
8. Meander from an ancient Mexican stone vase. DUPAIX, *Planches Supplémentaires*, vii. 11.
9. Mexican stone relief, palmettes (?), and buds. DUPAIX, *2nd Exped.*, iv.
10. Lotus staff and streamers; type common in the ancient Mexican MS.; held by deities, priests, and devotees. HUMBOLDT, *Voyage*, &c., Plate 14.
11. Mexican stone relief detail. Three-spiked lotus; ordinary type in ancient American art. DUPAIX, *3rd Exped.*, xxxvi.
12. Ancient Peruvian pottery detail. Three-spiked lotus; vase at Cuzco. *Exped. de* F. DE CASTELNAU, *3me partie, Antiq. des Incas*, Plate 52.
13. Mexican stone relief detail; trefoil lotus with spirals. DUPAIX, *3rd Exped.*, xxvi.
14. Swastika, and solar diagram (?). From stone relief slab, Mayapan. Swastika mistaken for a hieroglyphic by LE PLONGEON, *Proc. Am. Oriental Soc., April*, 1881. Schliemann mentions the Swastika as on a vase from Yucatan in Berlin. It is found on Zuni pottery and elsewhere, in ancient American art. The cross variant within a circle is very common on North American shell disks, &c., as it is in Mycenæ and ancient Celtic ornament. (Irish and British gold ornaments in the British Museum).
15. Ionic form, stone relief. STEPHENS, *Yucatan*, i., p. 134.
16. "The Bird and the Lotus." Stone relief carving. DUPAIX, *1st Exped.*, i.
17. Stone anthemion; Labnah, Yucatan. STEPHENS, ii., p. 57 (compare lxvii. 2 [p. 401]).
18. Stone relief rosette of buds. STEPHENS, *Yucatan*, i., p. 134.
19. Ancient "Chiriqui" vase; lotus motive. *Reports, Bur. Eth.*, 1884-5, p. 134.
20. Stone relief meander. STEPHENS, *Yucatan*, i., p. 134.
21. Spiral scroll with lotus at each end. Terra cotta stamp holding paints for tattooing, or similar bodily decoration. Museum, Mexico. This explanation of such Mexican stamps is given by labels in the Trocadéro Ethnographical Museum at Paris. WALDECK, *Mon.*, Plate 34.
22. Stone relief; Mexican rosette. DUPAIX, *2nd Exped.*, xiii.
23. Mexican stone relief; rosette of buds. DUPAIX, *2nd Exped.*, xvi.
24. Zuni pottery lotus, typical for an extremely numerous class of vases. Vase in Boston Museum.
25. Mexican stone relief rosette (similar Egyptian enamels). DUPAIX, *2nd Exped.*, iv.

MODERN KABYLE AND ANCIENT CYPRIOTE POTTERY.

(PLATE LXIV., PAGE 385.)

THE problem offered by the modern Kabyle pottery is herewith laid before the Ethnologist and the Historian. One type offers an exact survival of the Cypriote Geometric Style; as first observed in Boston and subsequently verified in Washington, London, and Paris. The patterns are related to the prehistoric Cypriote, which are represented on the same plate—exhibiting a mixture of the Cypriote chevron style like lix. 13 [p. 345], with later Cypriote Greek geometric motives.

I have been of opinion that the Cypriote Greek Geometric style developed from the Cypriote prehistoric chevron style and then reacted on it; on this head differing with Dümmler as to the extinction of the prehistoric race. His views are based on the excavation of certain cemeteries which he supervised, and on the lack of vases of both classes (i.e. prehistoric and ordinary Cypriote) from the same tombs. The extinction of the race is argued from the absolute deficiency of their pottery in certain excavated cemeteries, and from the absolute deficiency of the ordinary Cypriote pottery in the prehistoric cemeteries. But it is dangerous to argue that what is not found in one place may not be found elsewhere. The Museum of New York has the largest collection of Cypriote vases in the world, and in this collection I do not see where the line can be drawn between prehistoric pottery and the conventional Cypriote style. Each seems to have reacted on the other.

I do not say that "prehistoric" pottery has been found in tombs with Greek, but I do say that the styles appear to have reacted on one another, in a way which can be only explained by such peaceable intermixture and friendly relations as would make a subsequent extermination unlikely, and perhaps impossible. Professor Dümmler's point is the identity of the prehistoric Cypriote race with the prehistoric race of Troy. This point he has proven, and has proven through forms of vases. His illustrations do not argue any acquaintance with the varieties of coloured ornament offered by the prehistoric pottery (and the Museums of Europe appear to be deficient in such examples, so largely represented in New York). This point was not essential to Professor Dümmler's argument. The survival of the prehistoric race does not invalidate his contribution to science, and we are also perfectly at one as to the unreliability of certain statements which he holds open to suspicion.

In the plate for Kabyle pottery, lxiv., the quadrangle in diamond position with two triangles attached (1, 2) is a Cypriote Greek motive (3, 4), which does not appear in Cypriote prehistoric pottery. The Kabyle motive 5 would not be found in the Cypriote prehistoric chevron style. The Kabyle motive 8 (triangle supporting a panel band) also belongs to the Cypriote Greek geometry (xlix. 4 [p. 307]), but the style of the vases 6, 9, 11, as a whole, belongs absolutely to the "prehistoric" Cypriote chevron style, by which I understand the style of a race in Cyprus, which experienced reacting influences from the Cypriote Greek.

According to ethnological facts supplied by Canon Isaac Taylor's "Origin of the Aryans" it is probable that the original Iberian race[1] of Spain, which was subsequently conquered by Celts and mixed with them, was the same race with the Guanches,[2] Berbers,[3] Kabyles,[4] Libyans, Egyptians,[5] Gallas, and Somalis. This race is also supposed to have been a prehistoric race of Southern Italy[6] and of Syria. Its presence in Cyprus is probably indicated by the passage of Herodotus relating to the "Ethiopians" as there settled, and according to this view the earliest Trojan population must have been of the same type.

The correspondence of the modern Kabyle pottery with the prehistoric Cypriote would be thus explained, and it is desirable that Anthropologists should make examination of the skulls of the prehistoric race of Cyprus to examine this possible relation. Considering that the Gallas and Somalis may be fairly called "Ethiopians," it would appear that the designation of Herodotus is sufficiently exact, and that we are brought a step nearer to some knowledge of the much-quoted "Cushites." It is desirable that this name should be supplanted by one

1, p. 206.—2, p. 221.—3, p. 219.—4, p. 219.—5, p. 219.—6, pp. 40, 87.

indicating the stock in a more specific way and conceding the Egyptians to be its most important representative.

The Kabyle pottery type, represented on Plate lxiv. by pieces from Boston, must be of an extremely well-defined and numerous class. It could not otherwise be explained how the distinct collections of Sèvres, of the Trocadéro in Paris, of the Museum of St. Germain, of the British and South Kensington Museums, and of the Washington National Museum, each consisting of only a few pieces, should have almost exclusively the same character. It is clear, however, from the Boston Collection that there are other types of Kabyle pottery which exhibit normal lotus patterns. There is one modern piece in Boston, purchased by General Loring at the Philadelphia Centennial Exhibition, which would be directly classed with certain "Mycenæ" types belonging to ancient Cyprus, if it had been found in an ancient tomb. This piece has a lotus border of the Egg-and-Dart moulding type.

PLATE LXIV.

MODERN KABYLE AND ANCIENT CYPRIOTE POTTERY.

1, 2. Modern Kabyle vase and detail, Boston Museum of Fine Arts. Moorish form; ancient Cypriote geometric ornament. Compare Cypriote details, Nos. 3, 4, 7, and 10.

3, 4. Cypriote geometric ornament on necks of vases. The position of this particular combination in Cypriote vases is explained by l. 13, 14 [p. 309], as compared with the necks of l. 15 and xlix. 4. Such geometric variants of the neck motives mentioned, are typical forms for a large class of vases, and in this particular combination are placed horizontally in Cypriote art. In this sense the Kabyle use (1, 2) is distinct, although the motives are parallel on the Plate.

5, 6. Kabyle vase and detail, Boston Museum.

7. Cypriote pottery plaque, New York Museum. CESNOLA, *Cyprus*, xlvii. 40.

8, 9. Kabyle vase and detail, Boston Museum (detail from reverse of No. 9); to be compared with Cypriote No. 10, which is a detail of the vase xlix. 4 [p. 307].

11 Kabyle vase, Boston Museum of Fine Arts.

There are similar Kabyle (Algerian) vases in the National Museum, Washington; South Kensington Museum; British Museum; Trocadéro Museum, Paris; Museum of Sèvres; Museum of St. Germain; and Museum of Bologna.

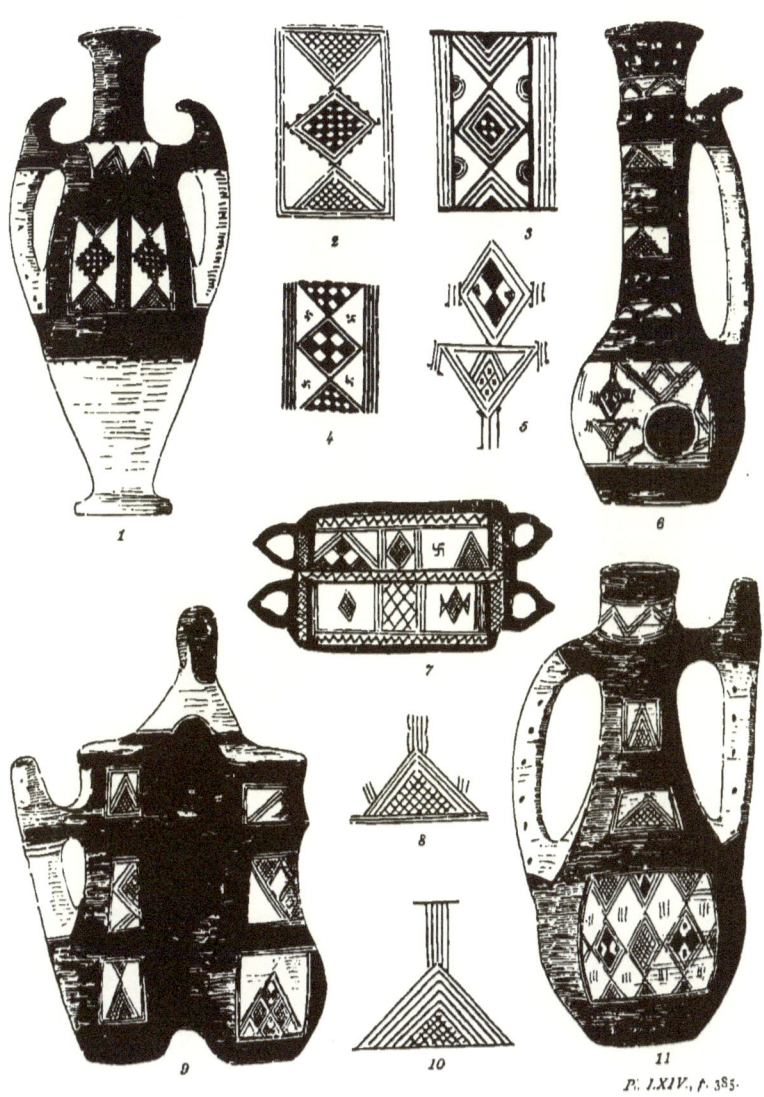

Pl. LXIV, p. 385.

PART IV.

MISCELLANIES.

THE ANKH AND THE LOTUS.

(PLATE LXV., PAGE 393.)

I AM familiar with the usually accepted explanation of the *Ankh*;[1] but the illustrations of Plate lxv. seem to show that the amulet known as the "Buckle of Isis"[2] is an inverted lotus with ring for suspension (6, 12), and also that the "Buckle of Isis" is a less conventional form of the *Ankh*. The *Ankh* is possibly an

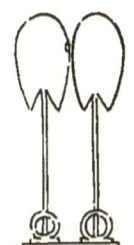   

190. From Prisse d'Avennes. Monuments.   191. From Rosellini.   192. From Champollion.   193. From a mummy-case in the British Museum.

inverted lotus amulet with a handle. Forms of the *Ankh* can be specified without the hilt (7, 9) and with pendant streamers like those of the "Buckle of Isis" (7, 8, 9). It has been observed by other writers that carefully executed carvings of the *Ankh* show a spread at the base (16). This seems to be a survival, by way of forms like 7, 10, of an original 6, 8. The Hittite *Ankh* (15) favours the view that the upper portion of the Egyptian form is a ring for suspension, and otherwise a handle (compare No. 2). As regards the cross portion of the *Ankh*, it is found detailed in normal lotus forms on a vase in

1. As given by WESTROPP, *Ancient Symbol Worship;* INMAN, *Ancient Pagan and Modern Christian Symbolism,* and many others.   2. The "Buckle of Isis" is an "emblem of life," according to British Museum amulet designations.

THE ANKH AND THE LOTUS.

the Egyptian Collection of the British Museum. This treatment of the cross is illustrated in 5.

It is at least interesting to observe that the "symbol for life" is an exact counterpart of the lotus as regards the solar association (14), as regards direct juxtaposition (1), and as regards equivalence of use (2, 5, 3, 4).

The ibexes with Bes (10) are reminders of the Typhonic cult considered in an earlier chapter (p. 235).

I have placed on p. 389 some text-cuts of Egyptian hieroglyphics based on the lotus leaf (compare Plate iii. [p. 41]), which are not generally recognized. The most important specification on the head of the leaf relates, however, to the symbol sometimes found with the God Khem (i. 10 [p. 21]).

The origin of the Tat ("emblem of Osiris and stability"—British Museum designations) is probably shown by cuts herewith: Figs. 194, 195.

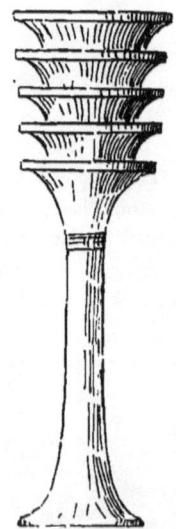

194. SUPERIMPOSED LOTUSES. Detail of a typical motive from a votive stele in Florence (XIXth Dynasty). From Author's sketch. To compare with Fig. 195.

195. BLUE ENAMEL TAT in the Louvre, of a class fairly numerous, which is detailed like Fig. 194. From Author's sketch.

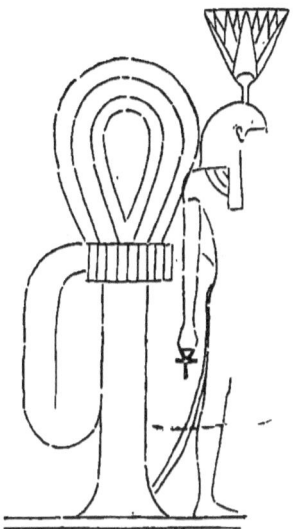

196. NEFER-TOUM WITH ANKH.
From a Royal Tomb, Thebes.

PLATE LXV.

THE ANKH AND THE LOTUS.

1. Upper portion of a lotus "bouquet," from an Egyptian tomb-painting, showing the *Ankh* in lotus association. From PRISSE D'AVENNES.
2. Solar bull, *Ankh* pendant from the collar. CHAMPOLLION, I. xci. Philae, Temple of Isis. Compare No. 5.
3. Gryphon and *Ankh*. CESNOLA, *Cyprus, Gems*, vii. 15. Compare No. 4.
4. Gryphon and lotus (for the tabs of stem, see Plate iv. [p. 63] and Text [p. 50]. CESNOLA, *Cyprus, Gems*, vii. 17.
5. Bull; lotus amulet pendant from the collar. Beni Hasan tomb detail. LEPSIUS, *Deukmäler*, iv. 11, 152; many similar in ROSELLINI.
6. Blue enamel amulet, called the "Buckle of Isis" (lotus inverted). Barringer Collection, New York Museum.
7. A form of the *Ankh*; conventional outline of No. 6, alternated, as usual, with Tats; detail from PRISSE D'AVENNES, *Chapiteau a Caulicoles*.
8. Lotus inverted with amulet handle, cross hilt (compare No. 5), and streamers, with buds on stems (compare No. 6). Painting from the side of a sarcophagus. The entire side is covered with large repetitions, alternated with Tats. New York Museum, Maspero Collection.
9. *Ankh* without cross hilt and with pendant streamers. Detail in *Revue Archéologique*, 1846, ii. Plate 41.
10. Ceremonial *Ankh* in metal, from a tomb-painting. Ibexes and God Bes (Set). Compare Text for Set and the gazelle [p. 235, Note 53]. This object shows an expansion of the lower part of the *Ankh*, corresponding to Nos. 6, 7, 8. PRISSE D'AVENNES, *Offrandes de Seti I. et de Ramses II.*
11. *Ankh* from a tomb-painting, having the cleft termination of the inverted lotus No. 6. CHAMPOLLION, III., ccxxxv. Biban-el-Molook, Thebes.
12. The "Buckle of Isis;" inverted lotus amulet with handle and streamers. Of the ordinary type in blue enamel. PERROT et CHIPIEZ, *Égypte*, p. 162.
13. "Buckles of Isis;" one having the *Ankh* cross hilt, showing the identity of these amulets. As photographed by MARIETTE, *Album du Musée de Boulaq*, xvii.
14. *Ankh* supporting the solar disk. From a Papyrus painting in LEEMANS' *Pap. Leyden*.
15. The Hittite *Ankh*; corroborating the view that the upper portion of the *Ankh* may be a suspensory ring and handle, and non-symbolic appendix. C. R. CONDER, *Archæological Review*, 1889, p. 110.
16. Normal form of the *Ankh*, which has, in carefully sculptured examples, a slight expansion towards the end of the staff. This peculiarity has been noticed by other publications. PRISSE D'AVENNES, *Animaux, Races Félines*.
17. "Belt buckle of Isis," without the cleft, showing the identity of this amulet with the *Ankh*. Red carnelian, Louvre. From tomb of Apis IX., on a gold chain with ordinary lotus amulet attached. MARIETTE, *Serapeum de Memphis*.

Pl. LXV., p. 393.
3 E

THE PHENICIAN "SACRED TRIANGLE."

(PLATES LXVI., LXVII., PAGES 399, 401.)

As result of various demonstrations in foregoing pages relating to solar animals in Greek art, and the symbolism of lotus derivatives connected with them, the question may be put as to how, and when, the original symbolism became a mere tradition, as regards continuance of the forms, without reference to continued symbolic interpretation. It is therefore interesting to observe in the Phenician votive tablets herewith that the anthemions lxvi. 5, 10 are of late date, and that the "Egg-and-Dart" mouldings, rosette, and bud are obviously related in meaning to the normal lotus forms which also appear. At Carthage, at least, it is clear that remote derivatives of the lotus retained a symbolic meaning until near the time of the Christian era.

We should presume that tradition may have supplanted definite symbolism with the Greeks at an earlier time. It must be observed, however, that a traditional symbolism by no means argues a consciousness of the origin of the symbol. The Buddhist "Trisula" is an illustration (p. 151).

Aside from the value of Plates lxvi., lxvii. in this sense, they are intended to open the question regarding the Phenician "Sacred Triangle," which is frequently found in independent use (li. 3 [p. 319]), and also—as here in several cases—supporting the "sun bark," or representation of the "horizon" or "mount" with solar disk (lxvi. 11, lxvii. 5). Representations of a staff or pillar supporting the sun disk and moon crescent will also be noted (lxvi. 4, 7 : lxvii. 5, 9). From the conventional lotus triangles of lxvii. 10 we pass easily enough to lxvii. 11, an inverted lotus with stem serving as staff and transfixing the sun and moon emblem. From this piece the argument moves to 1, 2, with the query, whether the erect lotuses are supporting inverted triangles which have the same lotiform origin. These inverted triangles support the sun in its "bark" or "horizon." Compare xlix. 11, 5, 8, 10, &c. [p. 307], Figs. 151, 152 [pp. 297, 298].

THE PHENICIAN "SACRED TRIANGLE."

The birds of lxvi. 2, 3, lxvii. 7 are obviously doves. It is difficult not to connect the Cypriote triangle and birds of Plate xlix. [p. 307] with these monuments, although the birds in that case are probably geese.

The usual explanation of the "Sacred Triangle" connects it with the cone of Phenician sanctuaries,[1] which has consequently been represented at lxvii. 8. The triangle is a Buddhist symbol, and has clearly travelled to India with the Swastika and the lotus motive.

197. CADUCEUS ON AN ITALIAN WEIGHT.
From the Monumenti Inediti. Compare Plate lxvii. for combination of the sun and moon crescent.

It does not appear that the true interpretation of the *Caduceus* as a staff supporting sun and moon crescent has previously been offered. Compare Fig. 197, from an Italian weight, with various illustrations of Plates in question.

198. BŒOTIAN VASE. DOUBLED LOTUS.
From Böhlau.

None of the various forms of doubled lotus in Greek art (erect and inverted forms joined) have yet been recognized in publication (xvi. 2 [p. 144]; xxxiii. 6 [p. 225]; xlvi. 12 [p. 289]). A porcelain amulet proves that this was an Egyptian combination.[2] The simplified form on Greek vases (Figs. 198, 199)[3] seems to explain the "three-forked thunderbolt" and "winged thunderbolt" of conventional archæology. Fig.

199. GREEK POTTERY DETAIL. DOUBLED LOTUS.
From the *Archæologische Zeitung*.

200 is undoubtedly a winged sun disk with attached lotuses. Fig. 202 is the same.

---

1. The "triangle" is said to be the cone of Tanit in *Revue Archéologique*, September, October, 1888, p. 247. According to Dr. E. B. TYLOR in *Academy*, December 10, 1887, the triangle corresponds to the Assyrian *din*, meaning "life." Dr. Tylor has made various contributions to the *Academy* (August 13, November 12, December 10, 1887), and one to the *Babylonian Record* (August, 1887) on this subject. See also ERNEST BABELON, *Manuel d'Archéologie Orientale*, p. 283 (*Bibliothèque de l'Enseignement des Beaux Arts*).

2. Among the "Miscellaneous Objects," Third Egyptian Gallery, British Museum.

3. Fig. 198, vase published by BÖHLAU in the *Jahrbuch*, 1888, p. 33. Lotuses not recognized. Fig. 199 is the detail from a vase in the *Archæologische Zeitung*, 1881, Plate iii. The human-headed birds must be referred to matter for the Bird and the Lotus. On Assyrian cylinders the human-headed bird is an ostrich, see the cylinder in LAJARD, *Culte de Mithra*, xlix. 2; two human-headed birds facing an altar which supports the "triangle," winged sun disk above. These figures have been mistaken for human scorpions, "l'homme scorpion," by MENANT, *Cylindres*.

200. GEM. WINGED SUN DISK WITH ATTACHED LOTUSES. From the *Jahrbuch*, 1887, p. 175. Compare Fig. 202.

201. SUPPOSED THUNDERBOLT. Compare Figs. 198, 199. From a vase in the *Monumenti Inediti*, I. xliv.

202. SUPPOSED THUNDERBOLT. Compare Fig. 200. From Schliemann's *Ilios*, p. 618.

PLATE LXVI.

THE PHENICIAN "SACRED TRIANGLE."

1. Inverted lotus spirals (an inverted variant of xv. 5 [p. 139]); stone relief fragment, Phenician votive tablet, Malta. PERROT et CHIPIEZ, *Phénicie*, p. 303.

2. Phenician stone relief detail, votive tablet. Doves, and sun disk, supported by Sacred Triangle, Carthage. *Gazette Archéologique*, 1880, Plate 3. Compare birds and the lotus triangle, xlvi. 5 [p. 289]; xlix. 8 [p. 307].

3. Phenician stone relief detail, votive tablet to Baal (the sun)—according to the translation of Gesenius— "*Domino Baali Solari*" Numidia, time of Jugurtha. Doves, sun and moon crescent. GESENIUS, *Monumenti*, Tab. 22.

4. Sun and moon crescent on staff, lotus. Detail of a Phenician stone tablet to Baal Hamman and Tanith (sun and moon), British Museum, from Carthage. DAVIS, *Phenician Inscriptions in the British Museum*, xxii.

5. Lotus anthemion (Plate xiii. 12 [p. 121]) and inverted lotus border (Egg-and-Dart Moulding, Plate xxi. [p. 159]). Detail of a Phenician votive tablet to Baal Hamman and Tanith, from Carthage, British Museum. DAVIS, xix.

6. Lotus and buds. Relief fragment of a Phenician votive tablet. PERROT et CHIPIEZ, *Judée*, &c., p. 326.

7. Pillar, supporting sun and moon crescent, with streamers (for the streamers compare No. 4 and lxvi. 5 [p. 401]). Detail of a Phenician tablet to Baal Hamman and Tanith, British Museum. DAVIS, xx.

8. Rosette, detail of similar tablet. DAVIS.

9. Lotus bud, detail of similar tablet, DAVIS, xxiv.

10. Portion of similar tablet. Anthemion, solar diagram, open hand, sun disk and moon crescent. DAVIS, xxvi.

11. Portion of similar tablet. Sacred triangle, supporting sun disk. Inverted lotus border, showing the chevron variant of the Egg-and-Dart moulding. DAVIS, lxxvi.

12. Portion of similar tablet. Lotus and two open hands. DAVIS, lxxv.

13. Portion of similar tablet. Inverted lotus border, "Egg-and-Dart" moulding (xxi. [p. 159]). DAVIS, liii.

14. Portion of similar tablet. Inverted lotus border. "Egg" moulding, derived from type of No. 13. DAVIS, lxvii. Although the term moulding has been applied to motives 11, 13, 14, they are simply surface incised patterns, but they explain mouldings otherwise found in Phenician use.

All the details quoted from Davis are from separate tablets; all are in the British Museum; all are from Carthage; all are specified as bearing votive inscriptions to Baal Hamman and Tanith. Same remark for plate following.

Pl. LXVI., p. 399.

PLATE LXVII.

THE PHENICIAN "SACRED TRIANGLE."

1. Portion of a Carthaginian votive tablet to Baal Hamman and Tanith, British Museum, showing two conventional lotuses supporting the Phenician "Sacred Triangle" and solar disk. DAVIS, xxxvii.

2. Portion of a Carthaginian votive tablet to Baal Hamman and Tanith. Conventional voluted lotus, from which two conventional outline lotuses branch out. These support the Phenician "Sacred Triangle" and sun disk. GESENIUS, *Monumenti*, xvi.

3. "Sacred Triangle" and winged disk. Phenician seal. MENANT, *Cylindres*, ii. p. 222.

4. Inverted lotus, to illustrate the frequent inversion of the lotus on Phenician votive tablets (compare No. 11). Fragment of a votive tablet from Carthage. PERROT et CHIPIEZ, *Phénicie*, p. 460.

5. Two pillars, with streamers, supporting sun disk and moon crescent; Phenician "Sacred Triangle" supporting sun disk. Detail from DAVIS, ii., with usual inscription.

6. Trefoil lotus, upper fragment of a moon crescent. Detail from DAVIS, xix., usual inscription.

7. Bird on the triangle. Compare xlvi. 5 [p. 289]; xlix. 8 [p. 307] with lxvi. 2, 3 [p. 399]. Hittite, with sun and moon symbol like No. 9. From Ramsay, in PERROT et CHIPIEZ, iv. p. 722.

8. Sacred cone, supposed origin of the "Sacred Triangle." Cone with asps supporting solar bark, winged disk above; hawk-headed Gods. Cypriote seal. CESNOLA, *Cyprus*, KING'S Appendix for *Gems*, vii. 10.

9. Staff supporting sun and moon crescent (origin of Mercury's staff), with inverted lotus triangle wanting stem. Compare No. 11. Detail from DAVIS, lxxxviii.

10. Three-spiked lotus; two conventional lotuses. Detail from DAVIS, xxi.

11. Inverted lotus with stem, sun and moon crescent. Detail from DAVIS, lii.

Pl. LXVII., p. 401.

INDEX.

Ægis, explained, 232.
ALTARS crowned with the lotus, 12 and Pls. I. 4 [p. 21], II. 11 [p. 23].
AMARAVATI Tope: Egyptian lotus patterns, 36.
AMENTI, see Genii of.
AMERICA, Ancient: lotus patterns and corroborative monuments, 367-379 (Pls. LXII., LXIII.).
AMON: as the sun, 6; worshipped by offerings of the lotus, 6, and Pl. I. 6 [p. 21]; identified with Khnoum, 9; identified with Osiris, 12; identified with the ram, 9, 200.
ANIMAL worship of the Egyptians reconciled with monotheistic conceptions, 13.
ANKH: symbol of "life" and equivalent of the lotus, 12, 389-390; with solar hieroglyphics, Fig. 54 [p. 83]; frequently found on Assyrian cylinders, 238; possibly derived from the lotus, 389-391 (Pl. LXV).
ANTELOPE: as divine and solar animal, with the lotus, see in general 12, 229-254, and Pls. XXXV.-XXXIX. [pp. 245-253]; an equivalent of the goat and deer, 257; with lotus spiral on Celtic bronzes, 239, and Swiss Lake Dwellers' iron, 239 (Note 64); on a Cypriote vase bearing the lotus triangle, Pl. XLIX. 5 [p. 307]; for verbal distinctions regarding words 'gazelle,' 'oryx,' 244.
ANTHEMION: see in general 109-133 and Pls. XII. [p. 113], XIII. [p. 121], XIV. [p. 133], XVI., XVII., XVIII., XIX. [pp. 144-147].
Anthemion: identified with the Egyptian lotus palmette, 116; announced as a lotus by DIEULAFOY, 116; announced as a lotus by PETRIE, 116; identified with Ionic forms by CLARKE, 116; identified with Assyrian palmette, 117; earliest Greek examples, 117; supposed palm origin disproven, 117, 118; observed as a lotus by NEWBERRY, 116; announced as Egyptian by PENNETHORNE, 119.
Anthemions: on Greek pottery, 123-133; originally borrowed from Egyptian patterns in hard material, 123; remote variants of Greek art in general, 123, 124; relation of style to date, 124.
Anthemion: symbolism as a lotus form illustrated by association with the winged solar disk, Pl. XXIV. 9 [p. 183]; by association with the solar bull, Pl. XXVI. 11 [p. 193]; by association with the solar ram, Pl. XXVIII. 7 [p. 203]; by association with the solar lion, Pl. XXX. 1, 3, 4, 8 [p. 211]; by association with the solar Sphinx, Pl. XXXII. 2, 8, 14 [p. 225], Pl. XXXIII. 3, 4, 11 [p. 225], Pl. XXXIV. 1 [p. 227]; by association with the solar deer, Pl. XXXVI. 10 [p. 247], Pl. XXXVII. 5 [p. 249]; by association with the solar goat or ibex, Pl. XXXVI. 1 [p. 247]; by association with the lion attacking a bull, Pl. XL. 4 [p. 259]; by association with the solar swan, Pl. XLV. [p. 287], Pl. XLVI. 13 [p. 289]; by association with the ibis, Pl. XLVI. 1 [p. 289]; by association with the solar hawk, Pl. XLVI. 6 [p. 289]; by association with the solar horse, Pl. LXI. 7 [p. 365]; by association with sun and moon on Carthaginian tablets, Pl. LXVI. 5, 10 [p. 399].
ANUBIS with the lotus, 24.
APHRODITE, see Venus.
APIS bull and lotus, 8, and Pl. XXVI. 1 [p. 193]; Apis symbolism, 8, 190 (Note 5), 195. See also under Bull.
APOLLO: as lion, 206; as gryphon, 217; as deer, 229, 230; as cock and hawk, 270; as swan, 271; as goose, 273.
AQUARIUS, 276.

ARAB patterns of the scroll and trefoil, in India and elsewhere, borrowed, 36, 126, and Fig. 78 [p. 127].
ARIES, see Ram and p. 200
ARTEMIS and the Deer, 230; with the goose, 364 (No. 12).
ARYAN race, not derived from Asia, 279, 280, 330, 331, 347.
ASHERAH: Tree of Life with lotus symbols, 180.
ASP and lotus, 8, Pls. II. 2 [p. 23], V. 2, 3 [p. 65], and Fig. 33 [p. 57].
ASSYRIAN ORNAMENT, borrowed from Phenician and Egyptian, 99-104, 110, 187-191.
ASSYRIAN STYLE, so called, Greco-Egyptian or Phenician, 205, 206.
ASTARTE: as Moon-goddess, 170; connected with the palm, 180; with the bull, 190; with the ram, 200; with the stag, 231; with the goat, 233; with the dove, 275.
ATHENE: as Moon-goddess, the deer her emblem, 230; with the Ægis, 233.
AUER, HANS, on the Egyptian Ionic Capital, 72.

BAAL: connected with the solar bull, 190; with Merodach, 190; with Ea and Mul-lil, 231; with the antelope, 131; with the solar goat, 233; with the gazelle, 233; with the sun, 233 (see also Baal Hamman); with Vishnu and Siva, 234; with Bes, Set, and Typhon, 235; with the lotus, 240.
BAAL HAMMAN, worshipped with lotus symbols at Carthage, 189, 395-401 (Pls. LXVI., LXVII.).
BAST (or P'akht), as cat with the lotus, 24, and in Mycenæ art, Fig. 164 [p. 317]; an equivalent of Isis, 265, 266; on a scarab with fish (Isis) and lotus, Pl. XLII. 2 [p. 267]. See also Sekhet.
BEETLE: as Ptah, 12; with the lotus, 12.
BES: identified with Set and Typhon, 12, 235; with the winged solar disk, 12; on the lotus, 12, 235; connected with Siva, 234; with the gazelle, 235; with the Ankh and ibex, Pl. LXV. 10 [p. 393].
BHARHUT STUPA: Hindu lotus patterns derived from Egypt, 19, 151.
BIRDS: solar, with lotus symbols, see in general 269-289 (Pls. XLIII.-XLVI.). See also Pls. I. [p. 21], III. [p. 41], V. [p. 65], XXX. [p. 211], XXXVII. [p. 249], XLII. [p. 267], XLVIII.-L. [pp. 305-307], LII. [p. 321], LV. [p. 327], LVI. LVIII. [pp. 339-343], LX. [p. 359], LXIII. [p. 379], LXVI.-LXVII. [pp. 399, 401]. See also Figs. 134 [p. 236], 140 [p. 250], 145 [p. 271], 146 [p. 274], 147 [p. 275], 148 [p. 277], 149 [p. 278], 150 [p. 280], 170-173 [p. 353], 180 [p. 364], 181 [p. 363], 182, 183 [p. 367]. Bird and lotus in Egyptian art, 6, 7, 24, 269-283; in Assyrian art, see cylinder XLIV. 9 [p. 285]; in Cypriote art, 269-283; in Greek art, 269-283; in Hindu art, 273, 274; in Dahomey, 274, 275; in Etruscan art, 275; in Byzantine art, 274, 275; in Oriental art, 275; in "Mycenæ" art, 316; on Dipylon vases, 331, 337; in Prehistoric and Scandinavian art, 279, 337; in Hallstatt art, 279, 337, and Figs. 180, 181 [pp. 362, 363] (birds with a horse's mane); on Zuni pottery, 367; in Yucatan, 367. See also under Eagle, Goose, Swan, Hawk, Cock, Dove, Ibis, Vulture, Heron, Peacock.
BOOK OF THE DEAD: doctrine of Transmigration and the lotus, 19; the gazelle as a divine animal, 260.
BOSS: on Cypriote vases, derived from lotus sepals; on "Mycenæ" vases, derived from Cypriote ornament, 297-301.
BRAHMA and the lotus, 5, 14; with the goose and lotus, 273, 274.

3 F 2

INDEX.

BRAHMAN explanations of lotus symbolism, 14-16.
BRONZE AGE: Egyptian origins of its pattern ornament, 329-359. See also Metal.
BUCKLE OF ISIS: an equivalent of the Ankh and lotus, 389-393.
BUDDHA and the lotus, 11.
BUDDHIST lotus patterns, derived from Egyptian, 35, 36; Trisula explained, 150-151.
BULB (seed-pod) of the lotus, Fig. 7 [p. 28]: in pattern ornament, 181, Fig. 60 [p. 110], Figs. 123, 124, 125, 126 [p. 181].
BULL: as solar symbol with the lotus, 8, 187-193 (Pl. XXVI.), see also Pls. II. [p. 23], LXV. [p. 393]; on "Mycenæ" pottery, Pl. LII. [p. 321]; bull fresco of Tiryns, 311, 312, 316, Pl. LI. [p. 319]; bull unicorn explained, 192; bull an incarnation of Osiris and offspring of Ptah, see Apis; a form of Merodach, Baal, Astarte, and Europa, 190; placed in the Zodiac, 190.
BYZANTINE patterns, derived from Roman, Greek and Neo-Persian, 126.

CADUCEUS, origin explained, 396.
CALF: as Horus, 13 (Note 62); with cow in lotus bower, 13, 43. Compare Pl. XXVII. [p. 197].
CAMPANIFORM Capital: Perrot's view, 43; Mariette's view, 51; derived from the lotus, 51, 53-61; Figs. 20, 23, 24, 28, 29 and Pl. VI. [p. 69].
CANARY ISLANDS: Guanche skulls related to Brazilian, 361; Guanches related to Berbers, &c., 382.
CANOPUS, Decree of: compares the Sceptre of the goddesses to papyrus, 61.
CAPRICORN: and the Goat-god, 234; represented by the oryx and gazelle, 234; connected with designs of lion attacking a deer, 257; connected with the Chimæra, 257; see in general the Goat and the Lotus, 229-254.
CARIAN Art: of Cyprus, 300; of Mycenæ, 311-327; of Italy, 315; probably Celtic, 314; inscription of Grave Creek, West Virginia, 369, 370 (Fig. 186).
CAT (Goddess Bast) on the lotus, 24; on a scarab with fish and lotus, Pl. XLII. [p. 267]; in Mycenæ art, 316 (Fig. 164).
CEDAR: a sacred tree in Assyria, 178.
CELTIC ornament: related to Carian, 314, 315; originally identical with Scandinavian, 332; both derived from Southern Europe, 332-337. See also Hallstatt, and Umbrian Art.
CERNUNNAS (Gallic deity) connected with the solar deer, 238, 239 (Fig. 136).
CHAMPOLLION: quoted for the so-called papyrus as a lotus, 57 (Note 47).
CHANDRA and the antelope, 241.
CHEVRON ornament: see in general 329-346 (Pls. LVI.-LIX.); from lotus petals, 67; connected with the meander and concentric rings, 77; in Egyptian and prehistoric ornament, as derived from triangle lotuses and connected with the Egg-and-Dart motive, 333-334 (Figs. 165, 166); in Mycenæ art, Pl. LII. [p. 321]; on ancient American pottery, Pl. LXII. [p. 377]; on Kabyle pottery, Pl. LXIV. [p. 385].
CHIMÆRA, explained, 255-257.
CHINA, Rose Lotus a food plant, 35; lotus patterns, probably derived from the Buddhists, 18; or Mongol contact with the West, 373.
CLARKE, Joseph Thacher: identification of the Anthemion with the Ionic Capital, 116, 135.
COCK, as Apollo and with the lotus, 270.
COLONNA-CECCALDI, Georges: announcement of the Ionic Capital as a lotus, 71, 72, 75; revision of his explanation, 75, 135, 261; announces the Guilloche as hieratic symbol, 127.
COMBS, Egyptian and ancient European; decorated with concentric rings, 84.
CONCENTRIC RINGS: derived from lotus spirals, 81-87

(Pl. VIII.); in Prehistoric and Greek "Geometric" ornament, 331-343 (Pl. LVII.); in Mound-Builders' ornament, 370; on Esquimaux ivories, 373. Symbolism as a derivative from lotus spiral scrolls (when represented by concentric rings with tangents) illustrated by use on Egyptian scarabs, Pl. VIII. [p. 87]: illustrated by association with the solar goose, deer, goat and horse, Pls. LVI. 9 [p. 339]; LVII. 2, 4, 5, 8, 14, 16; LVIII. 9 [p. 343]: illustrated by association with pot-hooks derived from solar birds, Pl. LVI. 13 [p. 339].
CONE, see Sacred Cone.
CONZE, Professor: publication on Melian vases, 141-147, on "Geometric" vases, 329.
COPTIC use of the lotus, 10; Coptic lotus cross, 350 (Fig. 178).
COW, with the lotus; as form of Isis and Hathor, 13, 195-197 (Pl. XXVII.). See also Pl. IV. 1 [p. 63].
CRESCENT Moon and lotus, 7, Pls. XXIII. [p. 173], XXIV. [p. 183], LXVI. [p. 339], LXVII. [p. 401]. Crescent with the gazelle, 241; an attribute of Siva, 241.
CROCODILE (god Sebak), on the lotus, 24; crocodile-headed god Sebak holding papyrus and facing altar with the lotus, 60 (Fig. 35).
CROSS, ancient-Christian, 354-359 (Pl. LX.); Coptic, of lotuses, 356 (Fig. 178).
CYLINDERS, Assyrian: with lotus and winged sun disk or moon crescent, 7; unrecognized by experts, 175, 176.
CYNOCEPHALUS (Thoth), on the lotus, 24.
CYPERUS PAPYRUS, 46-61. See also Papyrus.
CYPRIOTE VASES: showing the Ionic lotus, 74 (Figs. 46-48), 141-144 (Pl. XVI.); with symbolic deer and ibexes, 229-253 (Pls. XXXVII., XXXIX.); with solar birds, 269-289 (Pls. XLV., XLVI.); with geometric lotuses, 293-309 (Pls. XLVII.-L.); with concentric rings, Pl. LVII. [p. 341]; with Swastika and Cross, Pl. LX. [p. 359]; with the horse and lotus, Pl. LXI. [p. 365]; compared with Kabyle pottery, Pl. LXIV. [p. 385].

DAGON, 265. For Fish-god and lotus see Pls. XXIV. 3 [p. 183], XLII. 8 [p. 267].
DEER: solar, and with lotus symbols, 229-254 (Pls. XXXVI.-XXXIX.); in Assyrian art, Pl. XXXVI. [p. 247]; on Cypriote and Rhodian vases, Pl. XXXVII. [p. 249]; at Hallstatt, 239; in Celtic art, Pl. XXXIX. [p. 253]; in Hindu art, 254; in Mycenæ art, 316 and Pl. XXXVII. 11, 12 [p. 249]; in the Greek "Geometric" style, 239, 330, 337, Pl. LVI. [p. 339], Pl. LVII. [p. 341]; on Kobun bronzes, 351; with the Swastika, Pl. IX. [p. 359]; on Trojan whorls, Pls. XXXVII. [p. 249], IX. [p. 359]; on Zuni pottery (the elk), Fig. 184 [p. 368]. Deer attacked by lion, a sign of the Zodiac, 255-257 (Fig. 141); in Mycenæ art, 316.
DENDERAH: hieroglyphic text for the sun and the lotus, 6; unpublished reliefs of lotus stems with buds, explaining tabs, Fig. 19 [p. 51], of the gazelle and lotus, Fig. 134 [p. 226], Fig. 140 [p. 250]; unpublished reliefs of the goose and lotus, Fig. 19 [p. 51], Fig. 140 [p. 250], Fig. 148 [p. 277], Fig. 149 [p. 278].
DIAGRAM, the solar, 149; list of illustrated instances, 162 (Note 4).
DIANA and the deer, 241. See also Artemis.
DIEU CORNU, 238 (Fig. 136).
DIEULAFOY, Marcel: announcement of the Ionic Capital as a lotus, 72, 135; revision of his theory, 73, 136; supposed derivation of the Assyrian palmette from the *flabellum*, 116 (Note 1); observation on the lotiform character of the Anthemion, 116; matter on the Persian Ionic Capital, 137.
DIPYLON VASES, see "Geometric" Style.
DOVE and lotus, 275, 276.
DÜMMLER, Professor F.: publication on Cypriote vases, 294, 381, 382.

DYAK lotus spirals, 372 (Fig. 188); theory of Dyak ornament, 373, 374.

EA, as gazelle or antelope, 233; as fish, 266.
EAGLE, as solar bird compared with the hawk, 271; double-headed, in Hittite art, 276; supposed eagle-headed deity of Assyria, 276.
EDWARDS, Miss Amelia B., presents the Author a photograph from an Egyptian terra-cotta, of the horse and lotus, 362 (Note 16).
EGG moulding, 156.
EGG-AND-DART moulding: lotiform origin, 155-159 Pl. XXI.); compared with the Egyptian and prehistoric chevron, 333, 334; symbolism suggested by association, Pl. LXVI. [p. 399].
ESQUIMAUX: implements related to those of the Palæolithic Epoch, 332; concentric rings on ivories, 373 (compare p. 84).
EUROPA and the bull, 190.

FARMAN COLLECTION of scarabs, 81.
FECUNDITY indicated by the lotus, 4.
FIR-CONE, not the Sacred Cone; see under this heading.
FISH: as form of Isis, with the lotus, 13 (Pl. I. [p. 21]); as form of Seb, Dagon, Ea, and Thoth, 265-267 (Pl. XLII.); Assyrian Fish-god with lotus, Pl. XXIV. 3 [p. 183]; on Mycenæ vases, 299 (Fig. 154) and p. 266.
FLEUR-DE-LYS, see Trefoil.
FRET, Greek; see Meander.
FROG (Hyk and Khnoum) on the lotus, 14.
FROTHINGHAM, Professor A. L., Jr.: publication regarding mention of America in a Syrian author of the 7th century A.D., 368 (Note 5).
FUNERALS, Egyptian; the lotus given to guests, 4, 10.

GAZELLE, see Deer and lotus.
GENERATIVE symbolism of the lotus, 9.
GENII OF AMENTI on the lotus, 10, Pls. II. [p. 23], V. [p. 65].
GEOMETRIC LOTUSES of Cyprus, 293-309 (Pls. XLVII.-L.).
GEOMETRIC STYLE of Greek vases (Dipylon vases): see in general 329-346 (Pls. LVI.-LVIII.); with solar deer and goats, 239; with solar birds, 279; found in Cyprus, 293, 329; not found in Egypt, 315; distinct from Mycenæ art, 315; quadrangle motive borrowed from Cypriote art, 329.
GOAT, wild, as solar animal with lotus symbols: see in general the Deer and the Lotus, 229-254 (Pls. XXXV.-XXXIX.); an equivalent of the ibex, 233, of the gazelle, 234; in Celtic art, Pl. XXXIX., at Halstatt, Pl. XXXIX.; on Greek "Geometric" pottery, Pl. LVII. 2 [p. 341]. See also Ægis and Chimæra.
GOOSE: as solar bird with lotus symbols, and original form of the swan in Greek art, 269-289 (Pls. XLIII.-XLVI.); as form of Seb, Osiris, Isis, and Horus, 7, 272; on reliefs at Denderah with lotus, see Denderah; in Hindu art, 273, 274; on Dipylon vases, 279, 330, 336, 337; in Celtic, Scandinavian, and Prehistoric art as "pot-hook" and otherwise, Pls. LVI.-LVIII. [pp. 339-343]. For entire list of Plates on which the goose appears examine list for Bird and lotus.
GRAMMAR OF ORNAMENT by Owen Jones: prejudice regarding the papyrus, 3; influence on modern decorators, 127; revision of its view of the Egg-and-Dart moulding, 155-157; its view of Assyrian art as debased Egyptian, 177.
GROVE, see Asherah.
GRYPHON as solar form and with the lotus: see in general the Sphinx and lotus, 213-227; a form of Horus, 9; with lotus in Phenician and Mesopotamian art, 189; dated with lotus to XIIth Dynasty, 207; connected with Apollo, 217; symbolism in general, 216, 217; in Mycenæ art, 316; on Koban bronzes, 351.
GUILLOCHE: evolution from the spiral scroll, 127 (Fig. 79); announced as a hieratic symbol by Colonna-Ceccaldi, p. 127; symbolism illustrated, Pl. XXXVI. 7 [p. 247], Pl. XLIV. 9 [p. 285].

HALLSTATT or Hallstadt: summary of information, 239 (Note 63); designs of the Sphinx, 214, solar deer and ibex, 239, solar bird, 279, 362, 363, Figs. 180, 181; chevron ornament, 333, 335, 346; concentric rings, meanders, 346; "concentric squares," 340; solar horse, 346, 362.
HARPOCRATES, as goose, 7; explained as god of silence, 169; with goose in Cypriote sculpture, 272.
HATHOR: for identity or assimilation with Isis, 13 (Note 61); character and attributes, 13; with the lotus, 13; Hathor cow and Horus calf mistaken for "rustic scene" by Perrot, 43; Hathor with lotus sceptre, 52; as cow, 195-197 (Pl. XXVII.).
HAWK: as solar bird with the lotus, and form of Horus, Ra, Osiris, Apollo, Mithra, Ormuzd, 6, 7, 270. See otherwise Bird and lotus and Pls. I. (p. 21), V. [p. 65], XLIII.-XLVI. [pp. 283-289].
HERCULES, as Sun-god and with deer on Cypriote coins, 239.
HERON (Osiris) with the lotus, 24, 270.
HERZBLATT pattern: in Egypt, 89-94; as derived from the Anthemion, 126, 127; on Melian vases, 142; related to the Mycenæ leaf, 207; symbolism as a lotus derivative illustrated by association with the solar lion, Pl. XXIX. 9 [p. 209], with the solar deer or doe, Pl. XXXIX. 3 [p. 253].
HINDU: lotus symbolism, 4 19; patterns derived from Egypt, 19, 35-37, 150, 151; by Assyrian transmission, 191; Sindh pottery details, 128 (Figs. 84, 85); deer and lotus in India, 254; goose and swan, with lotus, in India, 273, 274, 279; Hindu Swastika, 347, 348, 351, 352, 354. See also Buddha, Buddhist, Brahma, Brahman, Chandra, Kamala, Krishna, Lakshmi, Padma, Puranas, Siva, Surya, Vishnu, Zodiac, Amaravati, Bharhut, Trefoil, Rosette, and Linga-Yoni worship.
HIPPOPOTAMUS (Thoueris and Hathor) with the lotus, 12.
HITTITE Art: Ionic solar symbolism at Boghaz Keui, 171; solar ram, 201; double-headed eagle, 276; Ankh, 389.
HONEYSUCKLE pattern, so-called: derived from the lotus, 115-133. See otherwise Anthemion and Palmette.
HOM, see Soma-tree.
HORSE: as solar animal and with the lotus, 12; with Anthemions, Pls. XVII., XVIII., XIX. [pp. 145-147]; on Greek "Geometric" pottery, Pl. LVI. [p. 339]; with concentric rings (Celtic art), Pl. LVII. [p. 341]; with the Swastika, lotus triangle, spiral scroll, anthemion, lotus bud, rosette, and trefoil lotus, Pl. LXI. [p. 365]; on Cypriote pottery with lotus, Pl. LXI. See also Text, 361-363.
HORUS: various forms of the god in Egyptian art, 6; connected with the lotus by Egyptian texts, 6; represented as a child rising from the flower, 6; this subject paralleled in myth of Brahma, 15, and explained by Plutarch, 16. Horus as winged solar disk, 6; as goose, 7, 272; as Sphinx, 8, 213; as Gryphon, 9, 213; as hawk on the lotus, see Hawk; worshipped by Phenicians, 214.
HYK (Hek or Heka) as frog on the lotus, 14.

IAMBLICHUS quoted for lotus symbolism, 18.
IBEX: an animal of Set, with the lotus, 12, 235. See in general the Deer and lotus, 229-253 (Pls. XXXV.-XXXIX.), for the Ibex and lotus in Assyrian art, on Cypriote and Rhodian vases, &c. See also Keshep.
IBIS (Thoth) with lotus, 12, 24, 271.
ICHNEUMON (Toum) on the lotus, 24.

INDEX.

INDIA, see Hindu.
INTRORSE SCROLLS: in Egypt, 89-91 (Pl. IX.); Phenician, 261-263 (Pl. XLI.); symbolism as a lotus derivative illustrated by association with the solar Sphinx, Pl. XXXIII. 12 [p. 225], Pl. XLI. 1, 7 [p. 263]; by association with the solar gryphon, Fig. 143 [p. 261], Pl. XLI. 14 [p. 263]; by association with the solar ibex, Pl. XLI. 10 [p. 263]; by association with the solar deer, Pl. XXXVII. 5, 7 [p. 249]; by association with the solar bird, Pl. XLVI. 1 [p. 289].
IONIC CAPITAL: lotiform character in Egypt, 71-79 (Pl. VII.); Ionic forms connected with spirals and concentric rings, 81-87 (Pl. VIII.), with introrse scrolls, 89-91 (Pl. IX.). Greek Ionic Capitals and forms as identified with the lotus anthemion or palmette, 116-121 (Pl. XIII.); as related to the lotus by the central sepal spike, 135-139 (Pl. XV.); as related to the spirals of Greek pottery through the Anthemion, Pl. XIV. [p. 133], and through Cypriote vases, Pls. XVI-XIX. [pp. 144-147.] Assyrian Ionic, 136; Syrian, 137; Persian, 137; Mycenæ Ionic forms, 137. Ionic Capitals and Ionic forms illustrated as lotuses, by association with the solar bull, Pl. XXVI. 10 [p. 193]; by association with the solar Sphinx, Pl. XXXIII. 5, 7 [p. 225]; by association with the solar deer and solar ibex, Pls. XXXVI. 2, 7, 8 [p. 247]. Ionic lotus forms illustrated as hieratic symbols by their use on Egyptian scarabs, Pl. VIII. and Fig. 179 [p. 350].
ISIS: character and attributes, 13; as fish and with the lotus, 265-267 (Pl. XLII.); with the goose and lotus, Fig. 19 [p. 51]; on the rosette, 152; with the gazelle, goose, and lotus, Fig. 140 [p. 250]; with cow, goose, gazelle, and lotus, Fig. 148 [p. 277]; authority for the goose as Isis, 272. See otherwise Hathor.
IVORIES, a material favoured for concentric rings, 84.
IVY: supposed origin of the Herzblatt, 89. See also Ivy-leaf.
IVY-LEAF, so-called; roven a lotus pattern, 161-165 (Pl. XXII.); on Rhodian vases, 161; in Mycenæ and Celtic art, 161-163, 312, 314; by symbolic association with the lion, 206 (Fig. 128), with the Sphinx, 214 (Fig. 129) and XXXII. 5 [p. 223], with the solar bird, Pl. XLV. [p. 287].

JAPAN: festival connecting the sun with the lotus, 18; lotus ornament probably derived from the Buddhists, 18.
JONES, Owen; see Grammar of Ornament.
JONES, Sir William; allusions to Hindu lotus symbolism, 4, 5; to an Egyptian colony in India, 16.
JUNO: identified with the Cow-goddess, 195.

KABYLE patterns related to prehistoric Cypriote, 335, 381-385 (Pl. LXIV.).
KADESH, her lotus bouquet mistaken for papyrus by Pierret, 43.
KAMALA (the lotus), a title of Lakshmi, 11.
KEY PATTERN, see Meander.
KHEM, ithyphallic; with lotus, 10, 63.
KHNOUM, an equivalent of Amon and Osiris, 9; of Noun, 16; represented by the ram, 9, 200; by the frog, 14, 15.
KHONS: a form of Horus, 12; of the Moon, 14.
KNOP and flower pattern, 129.
KOBAN bronzes, 346, 350, 351.
KRISHNA and the lotus, 11; a Trisula (lotus symbol) worshipped as his image, 151.

LAJARD: account of his *Culte de Mithra*, 175.
LEAF of the lotus, botanic forms, 25-31; with ithyphallic Khem, Pl. I. [p. 21]; as supposed ivy pattern of Greek art, see Ivy-leaf; in Mycenæ patterns, 314, 320, 337.
LEEMANS: his classification of concentric rings, 81.
LILY of the Virgin and lotus of Isis, 4, 13.
LINGA-YONI worship, 10.
LION: as solar animal, and with lotus symbols, 7, 8, 205-211 (Pls. XXIX.-XXX.), 216. See also the following heads.

LION ATTACKING THE BULL; a solar emblem, 255-259 (Pl. XL.).
LION ATTACKING THE DEER; a solar emblem, 255-257 (Fig. 141); in Mycenæ art, 316.
LOTUS: see in general the Table of Contents and Index; botanical forms, 25-41; erroneous designations summarized, 49.

MADAGASCAR: Malay influence as accounting for diffusion of patterns, 373.
MAHADEVA. See Siva.
MALAY ornament, 371-373; in Polynesia, 371-373.
MARIETTE: theory of the Campaniform Capital, 51; excavated tombs sanded up, 66; theory of spirals on scarabs, 81.
MAUT: as form of Isis, 12; as vulture, with lotus, 24.
MEANDER: a conventional form of the spiral scroll as derived from lotus scrolls, 77, 93-97 (Pl X.; symbolic use on scarabs and amulets, 94; associated with lotus rosettes, 95; not found in Mycenæ art, 315; in the Greek "Geometric" style, and prehistoric ornament, 331-343 (Pls. LVI.-LVIII.); original form of the Swastika, 94, 347-359 (Pl. LX.); in ancient America, 367-379 (Pls. LXII., LXIII.); in China, 373. Symbolism illustrated by use on Egyptian scarabs, p. 354; by association of sections of the pattern with the solar ram, Pl. XXVIII. 7 [p. 203], solar Sphinx, Pl. XXXIV. 8 [p. 227], solar ibex, Pl. XXXIX. 2 [p. 253], solar goose, Figs. 170-173 [p. 353], and deer, Pl. LX. [p. 359]. For Meander symbolism, see also Swastika.
MERODACH: as bull, 190; as Sun-god, 231.
MELIAN vases, 141-147 (Pls. XVI.-XIX.).
MERCURY'S staff, see Caduceus.
METAL, arts of; history traced by the history of patterns to Egypt, 85, 279, 324, 332; and in general 329-346.
MITHRA, as Sun-god, 6; Lajard's Work on, 175.
MOHAMMEDAN patterns, see Arab patterns.
MONGOL bull symbolism, 191.
MOON and lotus, 7, 14. See also Crescent moon and lotus, Isis. Thoth, Astarte, Siva, Vishnu.
MORTUARY significance of the lotus, 3-23. Anthemion on tombstones, 124, 171, 216-217.
MURRAY, Professor A. S.: view of the Ægis, 233; publication on Cypriote vases, 269; on a Mycenæ vase, 311; identifies the Swastika with the Meander, 352.
MUSSELS, not found on Mycenæ vases, 49, 299.
MYCENÆ Art, 311-327 (Pls. LII.-LV.): Mycenæ swords with so-called papyrus, 43, 312; vases showing the Ionic lotus, 74; and lotus with pendant sepals, 74; pottery patterns from Egyptian palmettes, 117; rosette patterns, 149; lotus leaf pattern (so-called ivy), 161-165 (Pl. XXII.); Hathor cow-head and rosette, 195; Mycenæ vases of the Archipelago, with fish, 266; in Cyprus, 293, 299. (Fig. 154), 300; in Egypt, 311, 312. Bull fresco of Tiryns, see Bull. See also in general Carian Art.

NARAYANA: equivalent of Vishnu, with the lotus, 14.
NATURALISM, in classic ornament, 128.
NEFER-TOUM crowned with the lotus, 6, 20, 391 (Fig. 196).
NELUMBIUM Luteum, 35.
NELUMBIUM Speciosum (Rose Lotus), 25-41, Fig. 10 [p. 30].
NEWBERRY, Percy E.; independent discovery of the Ionic form as derived from curling lotus sepals, 76; observation for the rosette as representing the lotus ovary stigma, 104; observation for the Anthemion, or "honeysuckle," as a lotus, 119; observation for the lotiform origin of the Egg-and-Dart moulding, 156.
NOUN: personification of the watery element, 16, 17.
NYMPHÆAS, 25-41; Nymphæa Zanzibarensis, 38; Nymphæa Rubra, 38.

OHNEFALSCH-RICHTER, Max; publications on Cypriote anti-

quities, 293 ; misapprehension regarding the Cypriote boss, 297.
ORCHOMENOS lotus pattern, 33 95 (Fig. 56).
ORNAMENT : magical character in Egypt, 84.
ORYX : an animal of Set and with the lotus, 12, 229-254; verbal distinctions regarding words "gazelle," "oryx," &c., 244. See also Reshep.
OSIRIS : with the lotus, 6 ; as goose, 7, 272 ; various characters and forms, 9 ; his reproductive character represented by the lotus according to hieroglyphic texts, 10 ; as mummy with the lotus, 9, 19 (Fig. 1) ; as heron, with the lotus, 24.
OSTRICH : symbolism, 280 ; with lotus palmette in Assyrian art, 284.
OXYRYNCHUS: as Isis, 13, 265 ; as Thoth, 266.

PADMA, or Pedma (the lotus) ; a title of Lakshmi, 11.
PAKHT, see Bast and Sekhet.
PALMETTE : Egyptian, 109-113 (Pl. XII.); combination of an Ionic lotus with a lotus rosette, 109 ; compared with the *flabellum*, 109 ; tomb symbolism proven, 110 ; original of the Assyrian palmette, 110 ; original of Mycenæ pottery patterns, 111, 324 ; original of the Greek Anthemion, 111, 115 ; in Greek art, 115, 133 ; a motive of the Assyrian Sacred Tree, 180 (Fig. 121). For symbolism of the palmette in Greek art, see Anthemion symbolism.
PALM TREE: brazen, at Delphi, 17 ; rare in Egyptian tomb-paintings, 47 ; erroneously supposed to be the original of the palmette ornament, 117, 118, 129, 179 ; a sacred tree in Assyria, 177 ; sacred to Astarte, 180 ; erroneously supposed to occur on a Rhodian vase, 316 ; erroneously supposed to occur on Mycenæ vases, 324.
PAPYRUS, Fig. 13 [p. 44]: not found in Egyptian ornament, 4, 43-66 ; realistic Egyptian pictures hitherto unrecognized, 60.
PARLATORE : researches on the Papyrus, 58-61.
PEACOCK symbolism, 275.
PEDESTALS, lotus, of Hindu gods, 37.
PENNETHORNE, John ; observation on the Anthemion as Egyptian, 119.
PERROT, view of Cypriote vases controverted, 230.
PERSEA tree, sacred to Hathor, 44.
PERSIAN ornament and architectural details, see Pls. XII., XX., XXI., XXVI. Persian ornament as significant for Babylonian and Assyrian, 118. Influence of Persian ornament on Byzantine, 126 ; Persian Ionic Capital, 137 ; Persian Bull symbolism, 191 ; Persian symbolism influenced by Chaldæa, 280.
PETRIE, W. M. Flinders : dated examples of lotus spirals on scarabs (Vth and XIth Dyns.), 86 ; dated examples of the Egyptian rosette (XIIth Dyn.), 102 ; dated examples of the Egyptian lotus palmette (XIIth Dyn.), 109 ; observation on the "honeysuckle" pattern as a lotus, 116, 119 ; dated examples of fish and the lotus on pottery (XIIth Dyn.), 265 ; Cypriote pottery found in Syria, 301 ; dated examples of Mycenæ vases in Egypt, 312 ; dated examples of the chevron on foreign pottery found in Egypt (XIIth Dyn.), 335, 346.'
PHALLIC symbolism of the lotus, 9, 10.
PHŒNICIAN ornament: influence on Assyria, 177, 187-191, 207. See also Sacred Triangle.
PHENICIAN PALMETTE, 261-263 (Pl. XLI). See also Introrse Scrolls.
PHŒNICIANS : supposed authors of the "Bronze culture," 330-332 ; in Ancient America, 367 374.
POMEGRANATE ornament, so-called ; a lotus bulb, so recognized by Mr. Percy E. Newberry, 110 ; Assyrian examples traced to Egyptian originals, 181 (Figs. 123-126).
POT-HOOKS, in prehistoric ornament derived from solar birds, 279, 337, 338, 340.
PREHISTORIC ornament : 329-359 ; drawings on bone and ivory, 45, 332 ; pottery patterns derived from metals, 332.
PROCLUS, authority for the lotus as a sun symbol, 4.

PTAH : identified with the sun, 8 ; father of Apis, 8 ; as beetle and with the lotus, 12.
PTAH-SOKAR-OSIRIS and the oryx, 231, 235.
PUCHSTEIN, Otto : Essay on the Ionic Capital, 71.
PURANAS : their knowledge of Egypt, 15 ; connect Vishnu with Egypt, 254.

QUADRANGLE panel patterns on Cypriote vases ; from lotus triangles, 301, 308 ; borrowed by Mycenæ pottery, 322 ; borrowed by Greek "Geometric" pottery, 308, 329, 338.

RA and the lotus, 6, 20.
RAM, as solar animal and with the lotus: a form of Amon and Khnoum, 9, 200 ; symbolism in general, 199-203 (Pl. XXVIII.) ; rams facing lotus on a Turin stelè, 201 (Note 7) ; Hittite, 201.
REBER : on the floral origin of the Ionic Capital, 137.
RESHEP, as Ibex-god and Oryx-god, 237-240.
RESURRECTION, symbolized by the lotus, 4, 9, 19, 22, 216, 217.
RHODIAN vases: specimens of lotus forms derived from Cypriote, 141-144 ; with the ram and anthemion, 202 ; with the lotus, deer, and ibex, 230, 248, 250 ; with the goose and lotus, 270, 271, 281, 288 ; typical solar diagrams explained, 355 ; with the Swastika, 355, 357.
ROSE LOTUS, see Nelumbium Speciosum.
ROSELLINI ; quoted for deficiency of pictures especially devoted to the papyrus, 45.
ROSETTE : as related to the lotus ovary stigma, 25, 27, 28, 29 (Figs. 5, 6, 8) ; in Egyptian ornament with lotus associations, 99-107 (Pl. XI.) ; in ancient ornament, 149-153 (Pl. XX.) ; Assyrian derivation disproven, 101, 149, 150 ; earliest dated examples, 101-102 ; on Nefert's head-band, 101 ; on vases of the Kefa, 101 ; various lotiform aspects, 103 ; on Greek vases, 149 ; in Mycenæ ornament, 149 ; distinguished from the solar diagram, 149 ; a clue to Mediterranean history, 150 ; in Hindu ornament, 36, 151, 152. Symbolism as a lotus form illustrated by association with Assyrian deities, Pl. XXIV. 4 [p. 183] ; by association with the solar bull, Pl. XXVI. 9 [p. 193] ; by association with the cow, Pl. XXVII. 5, 7, 9 ; by association with the solar lion, Pl. XXIX. 4, 5 [p. 209], Pl. XXX. 2, 10 [p. 211] ; by association with the solar Sphinx, Pl. XXXI. 2, 3, 4 [p. 221], Pl. XXXII. 3 [p. 223] ; by association with solar deer, ibex, or goat, Pl. XXXVI. 9, 10 [p. 247], Pl. XXXVII. 7, 12 [p. 249], Pl. XXXIX. 1 [p. 253] ; by association with the lion attacking a bull, Pl. XL. 3 [p. 259] ; by association with the Chimæra, Pl. XL. 5, 6 [p. 259] ; by association with solar birds, Pl. XLVI. 2, 11, 12 [p. 289], Pl. LV, 18 [p. 327] ; by association with the solar horse, Pl. LXI. 12 [p. 365] ; by use on Carthaginian votive tablets to sun and moon, Pl. LXVI. 8 [p. 399].
ROPE pattern, see Guilloche.

SACRED BARK : ornamental head a lotus, 53 (Fig. 25) ; or oryx, 231, 235.
SACRED CONE, Assyrian ; a lotus-bud, 176-178, 184.
SACRED EYE : with the lotus, 24 ; with meander, 94, 354.
SACRED TREE, Assyrian : various lotiform aspects, 175-185 (Pls. XXIV., XXV.) ; of palmettes, 110, 117-118, 179-180 ; of rosettes, 176, 248, 288 ; of buds, 176 ; of normal lotuses, 176, 246 ; associated with the Sphinx, 224 ; of "Phenician palmettes," 261-263 (Pl. XLI.) ; on Cypriote vases, 176, 286, 302.
SACRED TRIANGLE, 395-401 (Pls. LXVI., LXVII.).
ST. GERMAIN EN LAYE, Prehistoric Museum : Hallstatt bronzes, 239 ; prehistoric ornament, 346 ; Koban bronzes, 346, 351 ; Kabyle ornament, 383.
SAM : with so-called papyrus forms or "water-plants" shown to be lotuses, 57.
SAYCE, Professor A. H. : view of the Mycenæ rosette, as

implying Babylonian influence, controverted, 195; quoted for the stag, antelope, gazelle, and goat in Chaldean mythology, 231-234

SCEPTRE of Egyptian gods and goddesses: so-called papyrus sceptre a lotus sceptre, 51, 52 (Fig. 21); the *Tam* sceptre specified as bearing a gazelle head, 242-243 (Figs. 138, 139, 139A).

SCHLIEMANN; see Mycenæ.

SCORPION (Selk) on the lotus, 24.

SEB: as the goose, 7, 22, 272, 282.

SEBAK: as crocodile on the lotus, 24; holding the true papyrus, 61.

SEKHET: with lotus sceptre, 52; with rosette, 152; as the lion, 205. See also Bast (Pakht).

SELK: as scorpion, with the lotus, 24.

SERPENT as solar animal and with the lotus, 9, 22; with the Swastika, Pl. LX. [p. 359].

SET (Bes, Typhon): as ibex, antelope, oryx, gazelle, and with the lotus, 12, 235, 236.

SIVA (Mahadeva): and the lotus, 11; related to Bes, 234; connected with the antelope, 241; with the moon, 241.

SOLAR symbolism of the lotus, 3-24 (Pls. I., II.); specified by authorities and hieroglyphic texts, 4, 5, 6, 9, 16-18; three-fold character, 9, 10, 216.

SOLAR DISK and lotus: in Egypt, 7, 20, 24; in Oriental art, 172; at Pompeii, 369 (Fig. 185); in ancient America, 378 (No. 4). Winged solar disk and lotus, 7; in Oriental art, 171, 172, 176, 182, and conceded to be Egyptian, 7; with the bull, 192; with the lion, 210; with the Sphinx, 222; with the ibex or oryx and deer, 246 (No. 5); with the Sacred Tree, 262 (No. 5); with the hawk, 282; on the Cypriote bird's back, with lotus, 286 (No. 13); in ancient America, 376.

SOMA-tree (*Hom*): supposed relation to the "honeysuckle" pattern and Sacred Tree, 117 (Note 6); lotus bud mistaken for fruit of the *Hom* by BIRDWOOD, 129; supposed relation of the Soma-tree to the Sacred Tree disproven, 179.

SPHINX: as solar emblem and with the lotus, 8, 9, 189, 213-227 (Pls. XXXI.-XXXIV.); 262; in ancient American art, 371 (Fig. 187), 376. See also Lion, and Gryphon.

SPIRALS and Spiral Scrolls: in Egyptian and Greek art; derived from the lotus spiral, 71-79 (Pl. VII.), 81-87 (Pl. VIII.), 89-91 (Pl. IX.), 93-97 (Pl. X.); as derivatives from the Palmette or Anthemion, 115-121 (Pl. XIII.), 123-133 (Pl. XIV.); as derivatives from the Ionic form, 135-139 (Pl. XV.); lotiform origin illustrated by Cypriote, Rhodian, and Melian vases, 141-147 (Pl. XVI.-XIX). Solar symbolism of spiral scrolls and spirals; illustrated by association with the sun-disk, 169-173 (Pl. XXIII.); by association with the solar ram, Pl. XXVIII. 1 [p. 203]; by association with the solar Sphinx, Pl. XXXIII. 8 [p. 225], Pl. XXXIV. 8 [p. 227]; by association with the solar ibex, Pl. XXXIX. 2 [p. 253]; by association with solar birds, Fig. 146 [p. 274], Pl. XLVI. 8 [p. 289]; by association with the solar horse, Pl. LXI. 7, 13 [p. 365]. Spiral scroll in Mycenæ patterns, 315, 318, 320, 324; connected with the Swastika by Von Zmigrodky, 352; in ancient American ornament, 368, 376, 378; in Malay ornament, 371-372; in Polynesian ornament, 371; in China, 373; represented by concentric rings with tangents and by concentric rings with tangents omitted, see Concentric Rings; represented by the meander, see Meander and Swastika.

SQUID, on Mycenæ vases, 311, 312.

SUN-DISK and lotus, see Solar Disk.

SURYA (Hindu Sun-god) and the lotus, 4, 11 (Note 47).

SUTEKH: Hittite equivalent of Set and Baal, 236.

SWAN: of Greek art originally a goose 270-273. See also Goose and Bird.

SWASTIKA: see especially 347-359 (Pl. LX.) and the list of Plate references for the Swastika at p. 351. See also, as

demonstrating Symbolism of the Mæander, 77; with solar deer at Troy, 239; in Mycenæ art, 316; in the Greek "Geometric" style, 337; in ancient America, 367, 378; on Zuni pottery, 367.

SYCAMORE, sacred to Nout, 44.

TABS: on lotus stems, derived from imitations of lotus buds and leaves artificially attached to amulet staves, hence proving the so-called papyrus form to be a lotus, 50, 51, 55, 56, 57. Tabs pendant from the volutes of the Ionic lotus and palmette, possible explanation, 90; an indication of Egyptian *provenance* as found in Phenician art, 111.

TAM sceptre: proven to bear the head of a solar gazelle, 242, 243 (Figs. 138, 139, 139A).

TAMARISK, sacred to Osiris, 44.

TANITH (the Moon): worshipped with lotus symbols at Carthage, 189.

TAT: origin explained, 390 (Figs. 194, 195).

TAURUS, as sign of the Zodiac, 190 (Note 3). See, in general, the Bull.

THEOSOPHIST lotus symbolism, 10.

THOTH, as ibis, cynocephalus, or oxyrynchus, and with the lotus, 24, 266, 271.

THUNDERBOLT, supposed, of Greek mythologic art, 395, 396 (Figs. 200, 201, 202).

TIRYNS; bull fresco, see Bull; lotus pattern, 33, 318.

TOUM, see Nefer-Toum.

TREE OF LIFE, with lotus symbols, 180.

TREFOIL pattern and Fleur-de-Lys; derived from the three-spiked form of the Egyptian lotus patterns, 36, 39; lotuses mistaken for "Fleur-de-Lys," 49; trefoil in Byzantine, Arab, and Medieval art, 126-127 (Fig. 78); in Greek Art, 132 (No. 3).

TRIANGLE: a geometric lotus form in Egyptian art, 64 (No. 4), 334 (Figs. 165, 165A); on Greek pottery, 288 (No. 5, compare No. 3), 364 (No. 2); on Cypriote pottery, 296-298 (Figs. 151, 152), 306; on Mycenæ pottery, copies from Cypriote motives, 322, in Phenician art, 400. See also Sacred Triangle and Chevron ornament.

TRISULA (Buddhist): explained, 151, 152.

TYPHON: see Set, Bes, Baal, Sutekh.

UMBRIAN Art: the word "Umbrian" defined as meaning Italian Celtic, 171; representation of solar animals holding their symbolic lotus in the mouth, 196 (No. 3), 226 (No. 3), 142, 252 (Nos. 6, 7, 8), 314, 364 (No. 9).

VAPHIO: gold vases, 316 (Note 12).

VASE; as sign of Aquarius, 276.

VENUS symbols: bull, 191; ram, 200; fish, 265; swan, 271; goose, 273; dove, 275; "Phenician Venus" in ancient America, 374-376.

VISHNU and the lotus: 5, 14; connected with Egypt by the Puranas, 234; identified with the Moon, 234, with Set, 234.

WARING: value of his work on *Ceramic Art* for study of prehistoric ornament; opinions regarding the chevron in Egypt controverted, 346.

WILKINSON, Sir J. Gardner: announcement of the Ionic Capital as an Egyptian "water-plant," 72.

WINGED Solar Disk, see Solar Disk.

ZEUS, Cretan, and the Ægis, 233.

ZIGZAG ornament, 333, 334.

ZODIAC: Hindu, related to Greek and Egyptian, 234; of the Aztecs identified with the Hindu, 368. See also Taurus, Bull, Ram, Lion, Fish, Chimæra, Lion attacking the Bull, Lion attacking the Deer, Deer, Gazelle, Goat, Vase, Aquarius.

ZUNI Indians: magical use of ornament, 84; foreign pottery symbols, 367.

www.ingramcontent.com/pod-product-compliance
Lightning Source LLC
Chambersburg PA
CBHW030545300426
44111CB00009B/866